LITERATURE AND CHEMISTRY

LITERATURE AND CHEMISTRY

Elective Affinities

Edited by
Margareth Hagen and Margery Vibe Skagen

AARHUS UNIVERSITY PRESS |

Literature and Chemistry: Elective Affinities
© The authors and Aarhus University Press 2013
Cover by Jørgen Sparre
Typeset by Anette Ryevad, Ryevad Grafisk
Printed by Narayana Press, Denmark 2013

ISSN 0065-1354 (Acta Jutlandica)
ISSN 0901-0556 (Humanities Series/14)
ISBN 978 87 7124 174 7

Aarhus University Press
Langelandsgade 177
DK – 8200 Aarhus N
www.unipress.dk

INTERNATIONAL DISTRIBUTORS:
Gazelle Book Services Ltd.
White Cross Mills
Hightown, Lancaster, LA1 4XS
United Kingdom
www.gazellebookservices.co.uk

ISD
70 Enterprise Drive
Bristol, CT 06010
USA
www.isdistribution.com

Published with the financial support of:
Bergen University Fund and Department of Foreign Languages,
University of Bergen

CONTENTS

POETICS OF CHEMISTRY AND ALCHEMY

INTRODUCTION

LITERATURE AND CHEMISTRY: ARTS AND CRAFTS OF TRANSFORMATION

Scientia sine conscientia ruina animae[1]

The present volume represents the continuation of a dialogue between literary scholars, historians of culture and science, and chemists that started two years ago. On the occasion of the UNESCO International Year of Chemistry 2011, the interdisciplinary conference "Literature and Chemistry: Elective Affinities" was organised by the research group "Literature and Science" at the Department of Foreign Languages of the University of Bergen (Norway) on 27-8 October. The sixteen essays that came out of this event, all excursions into the mostly uncultivated field of "chemical humanities", are here addressed to scholars and students of literature as well as to all readers interested in the historical and cultural affinities between the natural sciences and the arts. Covering a wide range of topics, epochs, and approaches, the essays are loosely organised into six different sections. In the following, they will be introduced progressively as pertaining to the branch of literary studies known as "Literature and Science".

The first section below presents our general approach to the subdiscipline of literature and science, while the second summarises the recent development of the sub-subdiscipline of literature and chemistry. The five following sections contextualise the descriptions of the volume's essays within their respective subject areas, while the final parts add up the numerous affinities between the literary and chemical crafts, arguing for the relevance of literature and chemistry in the study of the past, present, and future of human culture.

---

1   "Science without conscience ruins the soul": a scholastic axiom quoted by Rabelais (p. 109).

LITERATURE AND SCIENCE: RECIPROCITY AND RESPECT FOR DIFFERENCES

Explorations of the interfaces of literature and science over recent decades have consolidated this subdiscipline's academic status as a necessary and rewarding area of research. In the 1978 manifesto "Literature and Science: The State of the Field", cultural historian George Rousseau relates its evolution up to that date through the works of literary and intellectual historians attentive to the documentation of scientific influence on creative literature; further, he states the urgent need of cultivating reciprocity and facing that vastly demanding question of "how literature has shaped or can shape scientific development" (Rousseau, p. 587). Since then, the enriching and clarifying consequences of literature and science studies for each of "the two cultures" have become increasingly evident. Authors, readers, and literary scholars find in the different branches of "hard" science, motives, models, and metaphoric instruments for grasping, describing, and plotting seen, unseen, and unforeseen realities. On the other hand, literary rhetoric, philosophy, aesthetics, and histories of science are acknowledged not only as intrinsic tools for scientific communication, but as fundamental methods and theories for understanding the human nature of all science, and the importance of a conscious human engagement with scientific realities.

In spite of acknowledged interdependency, encounters in literature and science are seldom motivated by ongoing disciplinary harmonisation. The differences between the two cultures are not merely obstacles to mutual understanding, they challenge and energize disciplinary identities and provoke innovation. The insertion of scientific discourse in a literary text may be a simple way of creating an impression of rupture, strangeness, or incongruity, introducing that slight but productive alienation which takes nothing for granted, and gives the reader an urge to rediscover and redefine the world. "Scientific discovery can thrive on lack of familiarity",[2] states the chemist and science writer Pierre Laszlo, encouraging "the spirit of intellectual nomadism": an ideal of interdisciplinary border-crossing, modelled on the ventures of nomadic tribes, people and nations, and the cultural and scientific fertilisation they have occasioned throughout history. According to Laszlo, whose writing on chemistry makes use of a variety of approaches and genres from cultural history to essays on aesthetics, and scientific pa-

---

2   The following quotes are from Pierre Laszlo, "The nomadic state" on the author's website: www.pierrelaszlo.com.

pers, there is not just a border but a chasm separating natural scientists and academics in the humanities:

> These are different tribes! [...] That they misunderstand one another occasionally is to be expected. The main obstacle is a dissymmetry. It has to do with linguistic competence. It runs deep. Humanists in general lack the technical language, hence the understanding of science, whether astronomy or chemistry. Scientists are not trained to value opinions or viewpoints. For them, any working hypothesis is only as good as its conformity with the data. At a deeper level, scientists are unaware of the dominion from language on the mind.

Notwithstanding the persistent gap between the two cultures, literature and science studies are constant reminders of the once thinkable ideal of universal knowledge, and of the polymathic striving characteristic of many literary and scientific writers of the past. Among the authors discussed in this anthology there are several literary and scientific writers of great, specialised, and varied learning: Mikhail Lomonosov, Johann Wolfgang Goethe, Humphry Davy, August Strindberg, Ludwig Boltzmann, Raymond Queneau, Primo Levi, Oliver Sacks. If some have regarded literature and science as different means in a common pursuit, one may ask to what degree they believed in the possibility of infusing – without significant distortion – their scientific knowledge into literary writing. But as Gillian Beer has emphasised, science in literature is not so much translation of stable meanings as transformation:

> Scientific material does not have clear boundaries once it has entered literature. Once scientific arguments and ideas are read outside the genre of the scientific paper and the institution of the scientific journal, change has already begun. (Beer, p. 90)

In sharp contrast to technical writers' striving for univocality, everyday language is vague, allowing the play of a vast range of shadow significations alongside each word's functional meaning. The often deliberate openness of literary language is an obvious indicator of how science changes, becoming inaccurate and plurivocal in new settings. Closer analysis of how specific texts reformulate, transform, or twist scientific material for their own purposes can make us more aware of "the apparent ease with which, in language, we inhabit multiple, often contradictory, epistemologies at the same time, all the time" (Beer, p. 82).

The valorisation of reading and writing literary texts generally implies that there is some knowledge to be gained from sharing the phenomenality of subjective experience. Literature is modelled on inter-subjective communication between subjective writers and readers, encompassing their biographical, social, or most private selves and their imaginary self-projections. Variations between personal and impersonal points of view, engaged and detached gazes, create tensions vital to much modern literature. As with all dichotomies, subject-object dualism has been under fire also in literature and science scholarship. An awareness of the questionable status of the objectivity of natural sciences has been underscored recently by Bruno Latour, who asks "Which language shall we speak with Gaia?"[3] and proposes a new empathic scientific language capable of animating the objects of scientific scrutiny:

> [T]he Earth is no longer "objective", it cannot be put at a distance and emptied of all Its humans. Human action is visible everywhere – in the construction of knowledge *as well as* in the production of the phenomena those sciences are called to register. (Latour, p. 7)[4]

We will not dispute the necessity of levelling humankind and nature in a future inter-subjective scientific discourse; we will, however, look to the debate between philosopher Paul Ricoeur and neuroscientist and founder of "neuroesthetics" Jean-Pierre Changeux as a reminder of the necessity of maintaining some clear distinctions when it comes to literary and philosophical discourses on subjective experience. Responding critically to Changeux's attempt to define aesthetics with the tools and technologies of

---

3   This was the title of Bruno Latour's lecture for the Holberg Prize Symposium held in Bergen June 4th 2013.

4   "As the whole history of science – and Serres himself for a large part in his earlier work – has often shown, it is difficult to follow the emergence of any scientific concept without taking into account the vast cultural background that allows scientists to first *animate* them, and then, but only later, to *de-animate* them. Although the official philosophy of science takes the last movement as the only important and rational one, just the opposite is true: animation is the essential phenomenon; de-animation a superficial, ancillary, polemical and more often than not a vindicatory one. One of the main puzzles of Western history is not that "there are people who still believe in animism", but the rather naive belief that many still have in a de-animated world of mere stuff; and this, just at the moment when they themselves multiply the agencies with which they are more deeply entangled every day. The more we move in geostory, the more this belief seems difficult to understand" (Latour, p. 9).

neuroscience, and art as productions of the physical-chemical machinery of the brain, Ricoeur simply reminds us of the semantic distinction between the brain as an object of science – its neurons, synapses, neurotransmitters, etc. – and "my brain" as it is inhabited by my subjective thinking. The lived body cannot be reduced to the body of scientific study.[5] It is crucial both to avoid confusing the two different discursive orders and to develop a third order which respects, distinguishes, and articulates the differences between the electro-chemical processes on one level and consciousness on another. "The brain thinks" is a typical example of semantic confusion between scientific and phenomenological discourses: "The brain does not think", replies Ricoeur, "I think".

In contexts of interdisciplinary rivalry, scientific generalisation and objectivisation are automatically associated with reductionism. But in the same way as scientists have been told that they need to be more conscious of their dependency on language, culture, and society, scientists have often accused literature and science scholars of dilettantism. Some see them as high-flying theoretical misreaders of scientists' hard-earned laboratory knowledge. Accusations of reductionism are also heard within the humanities against the literary scholar forgetful of disciplinary essentials in his or her search for a common ground with the hard sciences.

This anthology's main focus is on the presence of chemistry *in* literature; it presents various examples of how alchemical and chemical doctrines and concrete chemical phenomena are transferred and metamorphosed into narrative, poetic, cinematic, aesthetical, ethical, and metaphysical processes and representations. A truly reciprocal investigation, not only of chemistry in literature, but also of literature in chemistry, lies beyond the framework and ambition of its authors, the majority of which are primarily literary scholars, not trained chemists. In the chapters of this book, specialists in literature, cultural history, history of science, and chemistry interpret verbal and visual media belonging to different languages and ages from different theoretical viewpoints, but they all share a basic understanding of literature and science as a sub-discipline of *literary* studies. Their principle concern is the literary text, analysed and contextualised by an informed reader interacting with the object of his or her investigation.

Different metaphors have been used to evoke the dynamic and fertilising relationships between literature and science: dialogue, encounter, nomad-

---

5   "[L]e mental vécu implique le corporel, mais en un sens du mot corps irréductible au corps objectif tel qu'il est connu des sciences de la nature" (Ricoeur, p. 11-12).

ism, border-crossing, sharing of tools, transfer, and transformation, among many others. Inspired by Michel de Montaigne's open-ended work of self-inquiry, his ever accumulating multi-topical essays, and the conviction he demonstrates that you best learn to know yourself (and your right measure) by addressing otherness, we will propose a most basic and traditional apparatus of chemistry to illustrate our approach to the field emblematically.

Literature and chemistry are different disciplines, but they can be tried against each other, they can be compared. Our practice in this particular interdisciplinary zone may be considered a pragmatic essaying of lesser known intellectual and imaginary combinations, preferably in the undogmatic and dialogical spirit of Montaigne. In his *Essais*, the humanist scholar examines himself, assesses and tries out his literary and philosophical heritage by addressing close and distant, practical and theoretical topics that often pertain to contradictory discourses and doctrines. Ceaselessly confronting truths, alternating discursive registers, bringing together knowledge of all sorts, he remains respectful of differences and wary of absolute conclusions. Montaigne's famous medallion inscribed with the phrase "What do I know?" bears on its reverse side the image of scales, alluding to skepticism and skeptical aphorisms the essayist had inscribed in the beams of his library.[6] Applicable to our literature and chemistry studies, the scales or "assay balance"[7] represents the experimental craft of measuring, testing, and comparing the composition, taste, and touch of all possible substances, as well as their worth, weight, and usefulness, and also the loss and gain of a specimen's transport from one context to another. The scales can remind us of the huge task that is yet to be done, the unfinished, precarious state of the art. It symbolises the search for accuracy but also an awareness of indeterminacy. The balance evokes the trial of strength the Montaignean essayist and knowledge-seeker undergoes in confrontation with unfamiliar thoughts, theories, and truths. In motion, it may represent the fluctuating, overlapping, and unstable power balance of literature and science in history, the evolutions and oscillations in literary and scientific theory, and indeed

---

6   The most relevant quotation in this context is: "I hold back – I examine – I do not understand – I remain poised in the balance – I take for my guide the ways of the world and the experiences of the senses" (Sextus Empiricus).

7   From the French "balance d'essai", which was originally a sensitive set of scales used by chemists for weighing substances, especially precious metals. It seems worth recalling that in 1623 Galileo entitled his famous polemic book against the Aristotelian theories *The Assayer* (*Il saggiatore*).

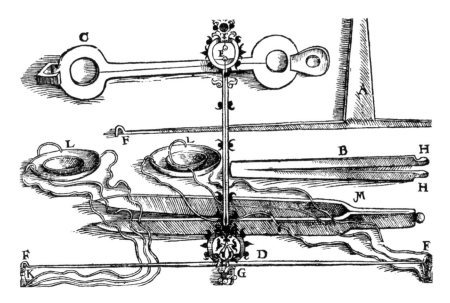

An assayer's balance. The illustration is from Lazarus Ercker's "Assaying book" *Aula Subterranea* (1574).

the swing and movement of all things. To scale is to ponder; it is not to equalise but to estimate carefully the analogous and incongruous aspects of different matters, of measurable and immeasurable truths, in the hope of acquiring – as in the art of chemistry – new insights of separation and combination.

LITERATURE AND CHEMISTRY: THE STATE OF THE FIELD

In recent encyclopedias and manuals on literature and science, chemistry is not accorded much space. Pamela Gossin's *Encyclopedia of Literature and Science* portrays chemistry as a science of marvellous and uncanny transformations, thus charged with metaphorical potential. Goethe's *Faust* and *Elective Affinities* are remembered, and so is the romantic perception of chemistry: the active, organic Nature of Humphry Davy, and his friends Coleridge and Wordsworth.

Stephen J. Weininger, author of the article on chemistry in the aforementioned *Encyclopedia*, comments on the fact that even though chemistry became increasingly indispensable to daily life in the industrialised world, its concepts and practitioners have not inspired much imaginative literature. He eventually points to the novels of Thomas Pynchon as one of the most prominent exceptions, before remembering the contributions of the chemist

Carl Djerassi and the Nobel Prize laureate Roald Hoffman, and finally, the literary work of Primo Levi.

In *The Routledge Companion to Literature and Science* (2011) Jay Labinger's chapter distinguishes between the historic development of chemistry in literature in the nineteenth and the twentieth centuries, since the status of chemistry within science changed around 1900, affecting the relationship between science and literature. In the earlier century, chemistry is included in literary portrayals of contemporary and experimental science, while in the twentieth century chemistry has been less visible, mainly due to its falling between the disciplines of biology and physics. Among the authors mentioned by Labinger are Davy, Coleridge, Wordsworth, Goethe, Balzac, Dickens, Zola, Christie, Hoffmann, Laszlo, Djerassi, DeLillo, and Levi. Labinger's article points to the role of chemistry in detective and science fiction.[8] But chemistry does not play a dominant role in science fiction either; physics and biology, and more recently neurology, typically occupy centre stage in this genre.

The volume *Chemistry and Science Fiction*, edited by Jack H. Stocker, highlights the contributions of Isaac Asimov (who held a Ph.D. in chemistry), H. C. Wells, and Thomas Pynchon, among others, but again makes it clear that chemistry is not the scientific discipline preferred by science fiction authors.

Chemistry's fairly minor role in last century's fiction should not lead us to conclude that this discipline has been neglected in literature. The fact is rather, as Labinger also states, that it has always been there, since the first Greek authors speculated about a world constructed of elements and atoms. Following chemistry's role in literature is thus a journey through the history of ideas, in natural philosophy and in the historical development of the symbolism and nomenclature of the elements.

CHEMISTRY AND LIFE-WRITING

The professional chemist and internationally acclaimed novelist and essayist Primo Levi wrote extensively on chemistry, and remains the twentieth century's most persuasive example both of combined literary and scientific craftsmanship and of literature and chemistry as a relevant field of literary studies:

---

8   The chemist and highly successful science writer John Emsley has published two volumes on chemistry and crime fiction: *Elements of Murder* and *Molecules of Murder: Criminal Molecules and Classic Murders*.

Chemistry is the art of separating, weighing, and distinguishing: these are three useful exercises also for the person who sets out to describe events or give body to his own imagination. Moreover, there is an immense treasure of metaphors that the writer can take from the chemistry of today and yesterday, which those who have not frequented the laboratory and factory know only approximately. [...] Even a layman knows what to filter, crystallize, and distil means, but he knows it only at second hand: he does not know "the passion infused by them", he does not know the emotions that are tied to these gestures, has not perceived the symbolic shadow they cast. (Levi, p. 175)

The present volume's first section, *Literature and Chemical Sensitivity: Primo Levi*, is dedicated to the author of *The Periodic Table* (1975). In "Primo Levi's Chemical Sensorium", Robert S. C. Gordon expands the general view that Levi's distinctive writing style and his achievements as a witness to the Holocaust is rooted in the rational, analytical clarity of the scientist and of the experimental chemist in particular. Gordon demonstrates how Levi's *Periodic Table*, a series of essays and science-fiction narratives, are built as much on the sensory complexity and responsiveness of the chemist's contact with matter as it is on cool detachment. It is made clear that Levi develops key dimensions of his ethical worldview out of this chemical dimension of sensory contact.

Margareth Hagen's chapter, "Autobiography and Chemistry: Primo Levi and Oliver Sacks", addresses the use of chemistry in the aforementioned semi-autobiographical work *Il sistema periodico*. She explores the analogy Levi develops between practical chemistry and creative writing and demonstrates how his tales about chemistry represent the qualities of this science, characterised as knowing by making, highly dependent on narrativisation, and constantly involved in problems of identifying, classifying, and naming matter. Levi's rhetoric, narrativisation, and ethics of chemistry are compared with its representation in the more recent autobiography of Oliver Sacks, *Uncle Tungsten: Memories of a Chemical Boyhood* (2001).

Section two, *From the Literary Lives of Two Epochal Scientists: Humphry Davy ans Ludwig Boltzmann*, begins with Sharon Ruston's chapter "From 'The Life of the Spinosist' to 'Life': Humphry Davy, Chemist and Poet". Few people know that Humphry Davy (1778-1829), the foremost chemist in Britain in the nineteenth century, who found fame for his invention of the miner's safety lamp and who isolated more chemical elements than any other individual in history, also wrote more than a hundred poems over the course of his life. He revised one poem at least four times, extending and developing it with each revision, and finally printing it anonymously twice within his lifetime. Sharon Ruston's close reading of this poem tracks the changes it undergoes and reveals developments in Davy's character, as the poem evolves from a youthful materialism to a more orthodox Christianity.

The following chapter by George Rousseau is entitled "An Unlikely Candidate for Literature and Science: The Nostalgic Ludwig Boltzmann in Eldorado". The Austrian Ludwig Boltzmann (1844-1906) was one of the foremost theoretical physicists of the late nineteenth century and a pioneering theorist of chemical gases, remembered for his founding contributions to the fields of statistical mechanics and statistical thermodynamics. He was one of the most important advocates for atomic theory at a time when it was still highly controversial. Based on Boltzmann's end-of-life confessional narrative, *Journey to Eldorado*, which is presented as a kind of modernist life-writing, blending autobiography, memoir, travelogue, and scientific commentary, this chapter retells the story leading up to the famous scientist's suicide in 1906. George Rousseau recreates the specific stress that caused Boltzmann's death, contextualises it biographically and historically, and asks what difference its identification makes to future interpretations of his biography.

Unsurprisingly, these four first chapters – dealing with authors who were or are primarily professional scientists and/or chemists – are all centred on life-writing: the biographical intertwining of scientific practice and theorisation with subjective perception, emotional and psychological development, self-understanding, and understanding of the world. Whether it is the correlation between Primo Levi's practical experience as a chemist and the sensitivity and ethics of his writing; the chemical childhood of Oliver Sacks; the evolving philosophical and religious orientation of Humphry Davy; or the story of Ludwig Boltzmann, a victim of the ongoing intellectual war between atomists and energeticists and his own depressive nostalgia – they show, as George Rousseau emphasises in his contribution, how the lived lives of literary and scientific figures can play significant roles in evolving literature and science studies.

A SCIENCE WITH AN AMBIGUOUS REPUTATION

From the days of the alchemists up to modern fears about pollution and the creation of hazardous and unnatural substances, chemistry's imaginary has often had negative connotations. Its Faustian ambitions are old and persistent. Alchemists were not only suspected of serving the devil; their attempts to improve baser metals could easily lead to accusations of greed, fraud, and falsification. Throughout recent decades, chemistry has been associated with environmental harm, intoxication, artificiality, and devastating and dishonorable means of warfare. More than fifty years have passed since Rachel Carson's *Silent Spring* aroused animus against the chemical industries' production of highly damaging pesticides. Additives in food also belong to the list of general concerns people have today about chemistry, not to mention the fear of side effects connected to most types of medication, which may seem almost as powerful as the public appreciation of the essential role chemistry plays in modern medicine. The chemists' unfortunate public image is not a recent development, and neither are the efforts to repair this image. Chemistry's reception has always been twofold: "Also in humanist culture chemistry has a very low profile; philosophers in particular keep to their traditional neglect of anything related to chemistry", write Schummer, Bensaude-Vincent, and Van Tiggelen in the introduction to the volume *The Public Image of Chemistry* (p. 1). Besides investigating the shaping of this public image, their book also focuses on the representation of chemistry in fiction and cinema, where the cliché of the mad, or malevolent, laboratory scientist[9] seems to reflect the common popular perception of the field.[10]

The third section of this volume is entitled *Literary and Cinematic Contributions to the Public Image of Chemistry: Between Celebration and Denigration*. Through analyses of literature and film, this section confirms the equivocal conceptions of the science and how it is generally confused with the all-important chemical industry.

---

9   In a private communication, Sharon Ruston informs us that Victor Frankenstein, the most famous literary example of a mad scientist, studies chemistry under the tutelage of Professor Waldeman, a character who exalts alchemy and modern chemistry and whose model is Humphry Davy.

10 In Diderot and d'Alembert's *Encyclopédie*, the article on chemistry describes the typical chemist as a solitary and obsessed figure in terms that are easily associated with the stereotypically solitary and melancholy poet. "The wisest Chemists agree that an interest in Chemistry is really a madman's passion. And that is because the Chemist must know all these practical processes, must be patient through long tedious experiments and observe them with painstaking care, must cover his expenses, must confront the dangers of the experiments and the temptation to lose sight of everything else. Becher calls Chemists *Certum quoddam genus hominum excentricum, heteroclitum, heterogeneum, anomalum*; a man who has a singular obsession, *quo sanitas, pecunia, tempus & vita perduntur*", see http://quod.lib.umich.edu.

Pierre Laszlo introduces the section with his chapter "Raymond Queneau's 'The Song of Styrene'", presenting popularised chemistry's most jubilatory side. This chapter focuses on the novelist, poet, and co-founder of *Oulipo*, Raymond Queneau, and his verse accompaniment to Alain Resnais' commercial film, *Le Chant du styrene* (1957), which celebrates the wonders of the new universal material – plastic. Laszlo analyses the interplay of voice, music, and movie, and situates Queneau's witty scientific poem in its biographical and cultural historical contexts.

Attentive to the science's more defamatory sides, Folkert Degenring's chapter, "The Invisible Science? Chemistry, Science Fiction, and Popular Culture", discusses chemistry's paradoxical omnipresence and low prestige in contemporary culture. Degenring analyses chemistry's various functions and important role in Anglophone science fiction novels; Alastair Reynolds's *Revelation Space* (2000), McAuley's *The Quiet War* (2008), and Greg Egan's *The Clockwork Rocket* (2011) are used as examples.

Muireann Maguire's chapter "In the Zone: The Strugatskii Brothers and the Poetics of Pollution in Russian Science Fiction", deals with one of our culture's most negative automatisms related to chemistry: the fear of environmental catastrophe. She explores the "poetics of pollution" inaugurated by Chekhov and pursued by Russian ecological science fiction, focusing especially on two of the Strugatskii brothers' most important novels: *The Inhabited Island* (1969) and *Roadside Picnic* (1971). The last novel is most familiar to Western audiences via Tarkovskii's cinematic adaptation of it in *Stalker* (1979).

HISTORIES OF ALCHEMY

Chemistry's relationship with literature reaches back to philosophers and classical poets like Epicurus and Lucretius; to alchemy's rich symbolic representations in verbal and visual media; and to natural philosophy, with its abundant references to literary sources as support for scientific observation and interpretation.

Alchemy is probably the most popular chemical topic in the history of literature, and it has been given renewed actuality in today's fantasy genres. Literary approaches to alchemy are recurrent in the remaining parts of this volume, beginning with section four, *Histories of Alchemy*. This section starts with Matteo Pellegrini's historical survey, "Alchemists and Alchemy in Italian Literature from its Origins to Galileo Galilei", which analyses written representations of the alchemist and his "science", ranging from the medieval

Bonagiunta Orbicciani and Cecco d'Ascoli to Dante Alighieri, Lorenzo de' Medici, and Leonardo da Vinci, and from the Renaissance of Ariosto to Galileo and the scientific revolution.

The subsequent chapter by Lillian Jorunn Helle, "On the Role of Alchemy and Chemistry in Russian Literature and Culture from Peter the Great to the Post-Soviet Period", examines the intertwining of the arts and the sciences in Russian cultural and intellectual history, investigating how topics from scientific and proto-scientific spheres are narrated in literary and cultural settings. It draws attention to the portrayal of Peter the Great and Lenin as God-like alchemists, capable of modelling the New Human. Lillian Helle argues that the esoteric and spiritualistic aspects of alchemy, the *alkimia speculativa*, was equally important as the *alkimia operativa*; she emphasises the idea that transmutation was not limited to metallurgical processes, but included ultimately the transmutation of the human from a lower creature to a higher, perhaps even immortal, being.

The historian of science Bernard Joly, in his chapter "The Literary Distortions of Alchemy", presents a more practical and less speculative version of "the arcane art" than that of several other chapters' hermetical readings of alchemical imagery. Bernard Joly claims that the modern literary figure of the alchemist, as seen in Nathaniel Hawthorne's *The Scarlet Letter* (1850), Gustave Meyrink's *The Angel at the Western Window* (1927), and Marguerite Yourcenar's *L'Oeuvre au noir* (1968), are deformations produced by the esoteric movements of the nineteenth century and do not correspond to well documented historical reality. He analyses the causes of these distortions and their consequences for the modern image of alchemy.

CHEMISTRIES OF PERSONAL INTERACTION

Goethe's late novel, *Elective Affinities*, represents a frequently quoted connection between literature and chemistry from the beginning of the nineteenth century, which – as we will see – is an important moment of transition in the history of the discipline.[11] *Die Wahlverwandtschaften* (1809) is the most notable example of a literary application of chemical theory to a novel's psychological plot, suggesting similar laws of attraction and repulsion in human relationships as between certain substances. The fundamental forces of sympathy and polarity at work in Goethe's natural philosophical uni-

---

11   See also Michel Chaouli's *The Laboratory of Poetry*.

verse are perceptible in the text's narrative and rhetorical use of analogical and antithetical constructions. Goethe uses current (though today invalid) chemical theory to raise problems of determinism and freedom of choice that never go out of date. The reader will have noted that the technical expression Goethe imported from chemistry, and which can be read as a metaphor or an oxymoron in the context of the novel, has been adopted as the present volume's title.

In section five, *Demonic, Divine, and Mystical: Chemistries of Personal Interaction*, the first chapter by Frode Helmich Pedersen is entitled "Demonic Affinities: On the Chemical Analogy in Goethe's *Die Wahlverwandtschaften*". It examines how the central chemical analogy of the novel's title affects the reader's understanding of human behaviour in the narrative, and to what extent the same chemical metaphor works as an interpretative key to the entire plot. He also explores the relationship between the chemical theory of elective affinities, the novel's notion of the demonic, and the category of the tragic.

Henrik Johnsson's chapter in the same section, "Strindberg, chemistry, and the devine", sheds light on the Swedish author's chemical and alchemical competences and interests, his monistic world-view, and his metaphorical language that is rooted in chemistry and alchemy. Johnsson further argues that Strindberg's chemical and scientific-poetic texts can lead to a more profound understanding of him both as an author and as a Christian thinker who was deeply invested in the religious debates of his time.

Eivind Tjønneland's chapter, "The Mystical Power of Chemistry – A Blind Spot in Dag Solstad's First Novel, *Irr! Grønt!*", examines the implicit use of the homunculus theme in the prominent Norwegian author Dag Solstad's modernist novel, and demonstrates the persistence, up to the present age, of the prestige of the chemist and of alchemical fantasies of creating and perfecting human beings.

AFFINITIES OF POETRY AND CHEMISTRY

Another example of notable interaction between literature and chemistry in the beginning of the nineteenth century – no less famous than Goethe's novel – is the direct influence the chemist Humphry Davy had on Wordsworth and Coleridge, and the romantic conjunction of chemistry, poetry, and philosophical worldview which Sharon Ruston comments on in her chapter (see supra). In the Preface to the *Lyrical Ballads* (1800/1802), Wordsworth defines poetry – the "image of man and nature" – as the pursuit of truth, and pleasure as the effect of both poetic and scientific truth. The Poet is attentive to the naked manifestations of natural laws, of movements in and outside his mind; he is:

> … a man pleased with his own passions and volitions, and who rejoices more than other men in the spirit of life that is in him; delighting to contemplate similar volitions and passions as manifested in the goings-on of the Universe. (Wordsworth, p. 13)

In analogy (we would say) with the chemist's experimentation with dynamic principles and processes in matter, Wordsworth's poet experiences, contemplates, and communicates powerful "elementary feelings", and pays homage to "the grand elementary principle of pleasure, by which he knows, and feels, and lives, and moves". It is characteristic of the period that Wordsworth's prophetic sentence on the future reconciliation of poetry and science pays a special tribute to chemistry, as well as to the neighbouring disciplines and suppliers of those vegetal and mineral substances the chemist's experiments depend on:

> The remotest discoveries of the Chemist, the Botanist, or Mineralogist, will be as proper objects of the Poet's art as any upon which it can be employed, if the time should ever come when these things shall be familiar to us, and the relations under which they are contemplated by the followers of these respective Sciences shall be manifestly and palpably material to us as enjoying and suffering beings. If the time should ever come when what is now called Science, thus familiarized to men, shall be ready to put on, as it were, a form of flesh and blood, the Poet will lend his divine spirit to aid the transfiguration, and will welcome the Being thus produced, as a dear and genuine inmate of the household of man. (Wordsworth, p. 17)

This possibility of reconciliation presupposes an already suggested analogy, not just between science and poetry as providers of pleasure, but between *chemistry* and poetry as formative processes, active in external nature as well as in the human mind. This romantic conception is reminiscent of the alchemical worldview and the hermetic idea of a correspondence between the micro- and the macro-cosmos, applying to spiritual and practical operations, to animate and inanimate matter, and to processes natural and supernatural. A prescientific consciousness resonates in the anthropomorphism of traditional poetry as well as in the rhetoric of romanticism and symbolism. In alchemy the minerals suffer, marry, and give birth to new life; and likewise, from Ficino and Paracelsus to Jung, the workings of the elements may be recognised within the faculties of the human soul. Modern poets – as the final section of this volume will show – may still exploit a "strange alchemy of thought" (Poe), experience "The alchemy of pain" (Baudelaire), or experiment with "The Alchemy of the Word" (Rimbaud).

The idea of a special affinity between chemistry and poetry is indebted to alchemy, but it seems to have flourished most intensely around 1800, in the period of transition after which chemistry emerges as a modern science. In the entry "Alchymistes" in the French *Encyclopédie* (1751-72), Diderot is quoted to have said that:

> Chemistry imitates and competes with nature; its object is almost as vast as nature itself: this part of Physics is among the others, what Poetry is among the other genres of literature: either it decomposes beings or regenerates them or transforms them & c.[12]

Following the same encyclopedia's classification of human knowledge, the category of "poetry" includes all artistic forms that can be related to the "imagination". The correspondence between chemistry – "Nature's rival and corrector" – and the beaux arts resides in their imitation and enhancement of nature. Coleridge's writing on the transformative, "fusing power" of the imagination – which "dissolves, diffuses, dissipates in order to re-create" – also bares traces of chemical inspiration. And Baudelaire seems to paraphrase and develop the ideas of both of his predecessors as he attributes the qualities Diderot sees in chemistry and poetry to the Imagination, "the Queen of faculties":

> All the other faculties are subordinate to it. It engages in both analysis and synthesis and yet is more than these. (…) It decomposes all creation, and from the materials, accumulated and arranged according to rules whose origin is found only in the depths of the soul, it creates a new world, it produces the sensation of

---

12 Editors' translation "[L]a Chimie est imitatrice & rivale de la nature; son objet est presqu'aussi étendu que celui de la nature même: cette partie de la Physique est entre les autres, ce que la Poësie est entre les autres genres de littérature; ou elle décompose les êtres, ou elle les revivifie, ou elle les transforme, &c. Quoted in the entry "Alchymistes", see http://portail.atilf.fr.

novelty. Since it has created the world, (…) it is only right that it should govern it. (Baudelaire, II p. 622)

Coleridge's proposition – "Imagination is possibly in man a lesser degree of the creative power of God" – strengthens the recurrent association of poet and chemist as demiurge makers. This status is not only reminiscent of alchemy; it reflects the new prestige of chemistry in the hierarchy of the sciences. David Knight makes clear how chemistry – especially through its growing practical and speculative comprehension of oxygen, magnetism and electricity – replaces mechanics as the dominating science, and becomes the fundamental key to understanding nature and life. As "the fundamental science" it is considered capable of answering fundamental questions, and gains special relevance for philosophers like Hegel and Schelling, who asks:

> What then is that secret bond which couples our mind to Nature, or that hidden organ through which Nature speaks to our Mind or our Mind to Nature? (Schelling, p. 41)

For many romantics this organ is the imagination, which in likeness with the new chemistry of vital forces and transformations reaches down into a living reality's primordial ground. This is in accordance with the thinking of the influential sixteenth-century physicist and alchemist Paracelsus – a Faustian figure well known to the romantics – for whom the imagination conveys a supernatural transformative power ("magica imaginatio") akin to the transformative potential of faith (Weeks, p. 140). When Jean Starobinski, in his short history of the imagination, sums up the tradition of medical thought that construed the imagination not only as a mimetic but as a vital and creative source of genius, it is no coincidence that the physicians and philosophers he mentions were all informed by and practised in alchemy and chemistry: "From Paracelsus to Van Helmont, to Fludd and Digby, to Boehme, to Stahl, to Mesmer and to the romantic philosophers (…) ideas were to be transmitted." (Starobinski, p. 186).

Literature and chemistry can merge metaphorically in many ways, as they are both powerful manipulators of the imagination. Diderot and d'Alembert's *Encyclopédie* confirms how the enlightened craft and science of chemistry continued to be associated with secrecy, magic, and illusionism.[13] Illusion-

---

13 "The strangest and most magical branch of natural magic is the one in which chemical agents operate. Different kinds of phosphorus, oils ignited by acids, exploding

making is an overlapping area of chemistry and art; hallucinogenic drugs are only one example of this link. The romantics brought poetic feeling and sensation closer to the natural world, but through Davy's experiments with chemically-induced inspiration, Coleridge and de Quincey's experiences with opium, and Baudelaire's with hash, romantic chemists, essayists, and poets also introduced their readers to *artificial* or "pharmaceutical paradises", comparable in many respects to the paradises of art. In the twentieth century, Aldous Huxley and Henri Michaux carried out similar chemical experiments with mescaline and LSD, the latter in a scientific setting. Reports of chemical-poetical experimentation often include experiences of merging of the outside and inside worlds, in terms of anthropomorphic correspondences, sometimes reminiscent of alchemical hermetism.

Chemistry's dominance over the literary imagination in the romantic age was supplanted by biology, owing to the impact of Darwinism on human self-understanding. Zola's essay "The Experimental Novel" (1880) illustrates the transition, as he aligns himself with the physiologist Claude Bernard to recommend that novel writing should follow the experimental method of chemistry. And while Einsteinian physics inspired much literature in the twentieth century, science fiction included, we are now said to be in the age of neurology, "neuromania" being the new catchword.[14] As future realities are expected to be more and more synthetic, and biochemical engineers steadily increase their capacity to adjust human genetic material, moods, desires, life rhythms, gender, growth, fertility, ageing, and all general body functions, we can expect that chemistry will renew its presence in literature, and that the role of biochemistry in shaping a new medically manipulable humankind will continue to activate the alchemical topos of the homunculus.

This volume's final section, *Poetics of Chemistry and Alchemy*, begins with Margery Vibe Skagen's chapter, which is entitled "'The phosphorescence of putrefaction and the scent of thunderstorms': Approaching a Baudelairean

---

powders, violent effervescences, artificial vulcanoes, the production, destruction and sudden changes in the color of certain liquids, unexpected precipitations and coagulations can astonish and amuse people even in our enlightened times, not to mention such apparent fantasies as the philospher's stone, Parecelsus's homunculus, the miracles of palengenesis and all such marvels", see http://quod.lib.umich.edu.

14 Cf. George S. Rousseau's argument about the importance of neuroscience for the future of literature and science scholarship in *Nervous Acts*. See also Raymond Tallis' recent critique of the claims made for the ability of neuroscience and evolutionary theory to explain human consciousness, behaviour, culture, and society, in *Aping Mankind*.

Metaphor by Way of Literature and Chemistry". It explores the relation between creative imagination and early chemistry as manifested in Baudelaire's aesthetic writing, and more specifically the literary, medical, chemical, and alchemical connotations that nourish the recurring figure of phosphorescence. Through a close reading of a significant extract, which describes the sublime, "phosphorescent" art of Poe and Delacroix, this figure is defined as a structuring metaphor that encompasses essential components of the poet-critic's supernaturalism.

Brita Lotsberg Bryn's chapter, "Pasternak's Wassermann Test", takes as its starting point a polemical article written by the famous Russian author during his brief futurist period, and focuses on the inspiration he drew from recent biochemical discoveries. This fruitful dialogue with chemistry may, as Brita Lotsberg Bryn argues, have influenced Pasternak's "metonymical system". The chapter demonstrates how this system is realised in his third volume of poems, *My Sister Life*, and rendered theoretically in his article "The Wassermann Test".

The conjunction of alchemy and poetry did not cease to be relevant with the decline of romanticism. Michael Grote's chapter, which concludes the present collection, is entitled "'der stein der weisen ist blau': Alchemistic Thought in Konrad Bayer's Literary Work", and it informs us that "linguistic alchemy" is a recurring topic in German and Austrian experimental literature after the Second World War. While assessing the Austrian writer and poet Konrad Bayer's literary debut, "der stein der weisen", Grote clarifies how the link between alchemistic thought and experimental literature becomes apparent as an aspect of text production, or *poiesis*.

EARTH, AIR, FIRE, AND WATER *VERSUS* THE PERIODIC TABLE

As a hybrid science, located between technology and theory, and between observation and experiment, chemistry can be said to share with literature not only fundamental processes of creation but also epistemological problems of representation. More than other sciences, chemistry stands in an analogical relation to literature. This claim can also be made for contemporary, theoretical chemistry with its extreme conceptual objectivity and abstraction, compared to the rich mythological and symbolic connotations conveyed by the verses and narratives of alchemy. A modern chemical symbol or diagram speaks a different language from an alchemical allegory. Still, Primo Levi recalls that when he was a young student, Mendeleev's periodic table seemed poetry "loftier and more solemn than all the poetry we had swallowed down in the *liceo*, and come to think of it, it even rhymed!" (Levi, p. 41).[15] T. S. Eliot also uses the precise vocabulary of modern chemistry – gazes, catalysts, platinum, sulphurous acid ... – to metaphorise processes in the poet's mind, describing it as "a receptacle for seizing and storing up numberless feelings, phrases, images, which remains there until all the particles which can unite to form a new compound are present together"(Eliot, p. 155).[16]

The semiotics of the language of chemistry – with its molecular models, symbols, formulas, its historically and sometimes mythologically rooted terminology, the common names of the substances and elements, and the IUPAC nomenclature[17] – is particularly interesting, being simultaneously *iconic,* in the form of molecular models, and *symbolic.* The history of al-chemical and chemical nomenclature also attracts scholars of conceptual history. In one of her articles on the philosophy of chemistry, Bernadette Bensuade-Vincent stresses how identifying, naming, and classifying are the principal obligations of chemists. An enormous number of new molecules are reported each year, demanding a name and a place in the databases, while the IUPAC is continuously revising the rules of chemical nomenclature (Bensuade-Vincent, p. 172).

The French chemist Marcellin Berthelot (1827-1907) stated that, like litera-ture and art, chemistry creates its object, and that the creative faculty forms an essential distinction between chemistry and the other natural or historical sciences. This specificity of chemistry – the art and craft of substances and

---

15 Levi repeatedly stated the similarities between the work of the chemist and the work of the writer. "To discern and create symmetry, 'put something in its proper place', is a mental adventure common to the poet and the scientist", claimed Levi when the physicist Tullio Regge commented upon his aesthetic idea of the periodic table (Regge and Levi, p. 10).

16 "The analogy was that of the catalyst. When the two gases previously mentioned are mixed in the presence of a filament of platinum, they form sulphurous acid. This combination takes place only if the platinum is present; nevertheless the newly formed acid contains no trace of platinum, and the platinum itself is apparently unaffected; has remained inert, neutral, and unchanged. The mind of the poet is the shred of platinum. It may partly or exclusively operate upon the experience of the man himself; but, the more perfect the artist, the more completely separate in him will be the man who suffers and the mind which creates; the more perfectly will the mind digest and transmute the passions which are its material" (Eliot, p. 156).

17 IUPAC: International Union of Pure and Applied Chemistry.

LITERATURE AND CHEMISTRY

their transformation, the work of hands and mind combined – is concretised by Roald Hoffmann in his article "What Might Philosophy of Science Look like if Chemists Built It?". The chemist, playwright, and essayist discusses why philosophers of science do not emphasise construction, experiment, and invention (Hoffmann, p. 33). Chemistry is different because its observations are not passive: today it relies on creation rather than discovery. Its craft of synthesis does not fit into the Popperian conjecture/refutation process. Many chemical papers do not test theories; the construction of matter, molecules and so on is narrated; and chemical explanations are also often based on narrative.

Considering all these affinities, one may wonder why the enlightened public's and poets' "chemical" approach to reality is so often outdated from a scientific point of view. Why does Tarkovskii's *Nostalgia* – the characters' trials of initiation through fire and water – move us precisely by its lingering celebration of the traditional elements? Literature does not age in the same way as science, and neither do its topics and thought structures. For the philosopher of science Gaston Bachelard (1884-1962), the intersection between the imaginary and the natural world may be understood not through the elements of the periodic table, but through the primal, material symbols of earth, fire, water, and air. Whether we believe in the material imagination's ontological or merely psychological status, urbanised Westerners still confirm their nostalgia for a truly synecdochic relation to the natural world by cultivating vacation rituals of open air, earth, water, and fire, or by regenerating their sense of belonging to elemental reality through imaginative reading. Bachelard explored rêverie and persistent, subjective intuitions about the elements in order to uncover the subconscious of scientific objectivity. Literary scholars can practise a similar "auto-critical irony" and discover some of their assumptions, blind spots, and core beliefs by measuring themselves against science.

LITERATURE, CHEMISTRY, AND THE SUBLIME

Introducing the anthology *Literature and Science*, Sharon Ruston reminds us of yet another important connection between the two cultures, the sense of wonder at the natural world: "The idea that one can find the miraculous or the wonderful in the material and the everyday is something both literature and science have claimed for themselves at different times" (Ruston, p. 6). As several science writers mentioned by Ruston have argued, scientific knowledge of the natural world may serve to reinvest this world with value, meaning, and enchantment.[18]

Chemistry means focusing on what the world is made of, and the eternal, undiscriminating circulation of the elements, atoms, and sub-

"Sublimatio" (Hieronimus Reussner, *Pandora, das ist die edleste Gab Gottes oder der werde und heilsamme Stein der Weisen*. Basel, 1582).

---

18 Among the authors and works mentioned are Stephen Jay Gould, *Wonderful Life*; Richard Dawkins, *Unweaving the Rainbow: Science, Delusion and the Appetite for Wonder*; and George Levine, *Darwin Loves you: Natural Selection and the Re-enchantment of the World*.

stances. Fascination with matter is a recurring theme when literature encounters chemistry, and the chemical etymologies of sublimation and the sublime are not forgotten. Science, however, is not the domain of rapture and fury; the rhetoric of science is not consistent with hyperbole, or with the "inaccurate and vague state of perception" and the broken, obscure language "wild with metaphor" Ruskin associates with true inspiration (Ruskin, p. 209). The rhetorical sublime is of little relevance to the author of a scientific article whose purpose is to communicate emotionally flat, paraphrasable knowledge. Primo Levi typically plays down pathos in his writing, which privileges lucidity and precision; his is a style inspired by practical chemistry. All the more remarkable is how Levi expresses emotions and feelings of wonder and beauty when describing the world of chemistry. According to Roald Hoffmann, the practice of science usually leads away from awe. Speaking on behalf of chemistry in his article "On the Sublime in Science", he claims:

> We do not have the very small of elementary particles or the soaring large of galaxies. Chemistry lacks that easy ladder to the sublime of boundlessness, of the downward or outward freeways to infinity. (Hoffmann, p. 150)

The layman or woman would not always agree. The idea that the same molecular structures that constitute the chemical building blocks of our living brains and bodies are to be found in the remotest nebulae of the cosmos is a source of fright and fascination. Just thinking about the conjunction of the universal and the particular, or the macro- and microscopic avenues underlying vast and small material phenomena, is enough to overwhelm most imaginations. The chemical and alchemical sublime is not absent from the literary examples presented in this volume. And for Hoffmann too, chemistry has its wonders. In his article he points to functional aspects of chemistry that touch upon the sublime, some of which are metaphorically transferable to our context of literary creation and scholarship. As seen in the chemical process of sublimation, in which a solid is transformed into gas and then back to a solid, *change* is "the defining essence of chemistry" (p. 152).[19] The chemical object's *potential* for change is an aspect of the dy-

---

19 "Chemistry was and is the art, craft and business of substances and their transformations. And now that we have learned to look inside the innards of the beast, there has emerged a parallel microscopic perspective – chemistry is the art, craft, business, and science of persistent groupings of atoms called molecules" (Hoffmann, p. 152).

namic sublime (p. 154).[20] Furthermore, Hoffmann recognises a "median sublime" in "the living middle of human beings and molecules in equilibrium", in the captured energy "suspended in a multidimensional space defined by crisscrossing polarities", with its potential for reaction in one direction or the other. In our context of chemical and literary affinities, we note that the precarious state of balance between opposing forces, which some slight but decisive perturbation will release, is also an infinite source of narrative if we follow the basic schema of classical structuralism: when action is sparked off by some initial provocation and the characters are compelled to respond to the consequential trials and choices of the complication until the dilemmas are resolved through processes of separation and reconnection, allowing a new state of equilibrium to emerge, awaiting new narratives of transformation in turn.

Chemical discovery and invention by way of experiment and theory is a continuous cause of the astonishment of novelty, touching upon the sublime of infinite variability. As the emphasis has shifted from analysis – the aim of understanding the mysteries of matter by separation – to synthesis and the creation of millions of new compounds, chemistry's capacity to transform the natural world for better or worse nourishes the public's admiration and concern.

Hoffmann's considerations of chemistry's transformational power is here a reminder of imaginative literature's alleged power to form and transform readers: building or corrupting their characters, edifying them, enlarging, refining, or polluting their minds. Like its ancestor alchemy, chemistry has always had a darker and decidedly troubling side, infected with the guilt of hubris, with artifice and contamination, faults that, since Plato, have also been associated with literature. Chemistry is associated with humankind's apparently boundless powers of destruction and creation, for most of us beyond control or comprehension, with its capacity to produce lasting changes in the world's atmosphere or in the climates of our minds. Whether salubrious or intoxicating, literature and chemistry's potential to build and dissolve, consolidate and transcend material and immaterial life is dependent on the large community of authors and readers transcending temporal and spatial as well as cultural and disciplinary barriers. The present volume is dedicated to this communication.

In this spirit of affinity, the sixteen authors of this anthology break new ground in demonstrating chemistry's particular status as one of the sciences

---

20 Transmutation of matter was also something Humphry Davy found to be sublime. See Ruston, "Humphry Davy and the Sublime".

in which the humanities should interest itself, the overlaps and reciprocities of the two fields, and – perhaps most importantly – chemistry's role in the production of narrative, metaphor, and literary form. This volume makes the silent presence of chemistry everywhere more perceptible, uncovering its historical and present appeal to material sensitivity, imagination, and creativity, as well as its call for philosophical and ethical concern, and for wonder.

Bergen, November 2013
Margareth Hagen and Margery Vibe Skagen

WORKS CITED

Bachelard, Gaston: *La Psychanalyse du feu*. Paris: Gallimard, 1968.

Baudelaire, Charles: *Œuvres complètes I–II*. Claude Pichois (ed.). Paris: Gallimard, 1975.

Beer, Gillian: "Translation or Transformation? The Relations of Literature and Science". *Notes and Records of the Royal Society of London* 44.1 (Jan. 1990): 81-99. Web. 2 May 2013.

Bensaude-Vincent, Bernadette, and Simon, Jonathan. *Chemistry: The Impure* Science. London: Imperial College Press, 2008.

Bensuade-Vincent, Bernadette: "Philosophy of Chemistry". *French Studies in the Philosophy of Science: Contemporary Research in France*. Anastasios Brenner and Jean Gayon (eds.). Springer, 2009.

Carson, Rachel: *Silent Spring*. Boston: Houghton Middlin, 1962.

Chaouli, Michel: *The Laboratory of Poetry: Chemistry and Poetics in the Work of Friedrich Schlegel*. Baltimore: Johns Hopkins UP, 2002

Clarke, Bruce and Rossini, Manuela: *The Routledge Companion to Literature and Science*. New York: Taylor & Francis, 2011.

The Encyclopedia of Diderot and d'Alembert, Collaborative Translation Project, http://quod.lib.umich.edu/d/did/.

Diderot, Denis: *Prospectus de l'Encyclopédie* in *Oeuvre de Denis Diderot*, vol. 2. Berlin, Paris, 1818.

Eliot, T. S: "Tradition and the Individual Talent". *Modernism: An Anthology*. Laurence Rainey (ed.). London: Blackwell, 2005.

Emsley, John: *Elements of Murder*. Oxford: Oxford University Press, 2006.

—: *Molecules of Murder: Criminal Molecules and Classic Murders*. Cambridge: The Royal Society of Chemistry, 2008.

Gossin, Pamela: *Encyclopedia of Literature and Science*. Westport: Greenwood, 2002.

Greenberg, Arthur: *A chemical History Tour: Picturing Chemistry from Alchemy to Modern Molecular Science*. New York: John Wiley, 2000.

Hoffmann, Roald: "On the Sublime in Science". *Beyond the Finite: The Sublime in Art and Science*. Roald Hoffmann and Iain Boyd Whyte (eds.). Oxford: Oxford University Press, 2011.

Hoffmann, Roald: "What Might Philosophy of Science Look Like If Chemists Built It?" *Roald Hoffmann on the Philosophy, Art, and Science of Chemistry.* Jeffrey Kovac and Michael Weisberg (eds.). Oxford: Oxford University Press, 2012, 21-38.

Knight, David: *Ideas in Chemistry: A History of the Science.* New Brunswick NJ: Rutgers University Press, 1992.

Laszlo, Pierre: *Terre & eau air & feu.* Collection Histoires des sciences. Paris: Le Pommier, 2000.

Laszlo, Pierre: "The Nomadic State". Web. 2 May 2013.

Latour, Bruno: "From Economics to Ecology." Paris Lecture prepared for the Holberg Prize Symposium, Bergen, 4 June 2013. Web. 25 Aug 2013.

Levi, Primo: *Other People's Trades.* Trans. Raymond Rosenthal. London: Abacus, 1991.

Levi, Primo and Tullio Regge: *Conversations.* Trans. Raymond Rosenthal. London: I.B. Tauris, 1989.

Rabelais, Francois: *Pantagruel. Oeuvres complètes.* Paris: Gallimard, 1995.

Ricoeur, Paul: *Ce qui nous fait penser. La Nature et la Règle.* With J.P. Changeux. Paris: Odile Jacob, 2000 (1998).

Rousseau, George: "Literature and Science: The State of the Field". *Isis* 69.4 (Dec. 1978): 583-591. Web. 2 May 2013.

Rousseau, George: *Nervous Acts: Essays on Literature, Culture and Sensibility.* Houndmills / Basingstoke: Palgrave 2004.

Ruskin, John: *The Works of John Ruskin*, vol. 5. Cambridge: Cambridge University Press, 2010.

Ruston, Sharon, ed.: *Literature and Science*, vol. 61, Essays and Studies. Cambridge: D. S. Brewer, 2008.

Ruston, Sharon: "Humphry Davy and the Sublime". *Creating Romanticism: Case Studies in the Literature, Science and Medicine of the 1790s.* Palgrave Macmillian, Hampshire 2013. 132-174.

Schelling, F.W.J.: *Ideas for a Philosophy of Nature.* Cambridge: Cambridge University Press, 1988.

Schummer, Joachim, Bensaude-Vincent, Bernadette and Van Tiggelen, Birgitte, eds.: *The Public Image of Chemistry.* London: World Scientific Publishing Company, 2007.

Sleigh, Charlotte: *Literature and Science.* Basingstoke: Palgrave Macmillan, 2010.

Starobinski, Jean: "L'Empire de l'imaginaire." *L'Oeil vivant II: La Relation critique.* Paris: Gallimard, 1970.

Starobinski, Jean: *Montaigne en mouvement.* Paris: Gallimard, 1982.

Stocker, Jack H., ed.: *Chemistry and Science Fiction.* Washington: American Chemical Society, 1998.

Tallis, Raymond: *Aping Mankind: Neuromania, Darwinitis and the Misrepresentation of Humanity.* Durham: Acumen, 2011.

Weeks, Andrew: *Paracelsus: Speculative Theory and the Crisis of the Early Reformation.* SUNY Series in Western Esoteric Traditions. Albany: State University of New York Press, 1997.

Wordsworth,William, Coleridge, Samuel Taylor, Scoifield, Martin: *Lyrical Ballads and Other Poems.* Ware: Wordsworth Editions 2003.

LITERATURE AND CHEMICAL SENSITIVITY: PRIMO LEVI

PRIMO LEVI'S CHEMICAL SENSORIUM

Robert S. C. Gordon, University of Cambridge

THE CHEMIST

Primo Levi graduated from the University of Turin in 1941 with a degree in chemistry, although the director of his theoretical dissertation was from the physics faculty, the only place he could find a professor willing to take him on. His main thesis was on so-called "Walden Inversions", the inversion in certain chemical reactions of the 'chiral' asymmetric centres found in certain molecules.[1]

This was 1941 in Fascist Italy and the war was already raging across Europe. Levi struggled to get his dissertation and his degree accepted because he was Jewish, in a state which in 1938 had implemented a legislative anti-Semitism that was quite the equal of that of its northern ally, Nazi Germany. Among many other restrictions, Jews were banned from universities, unless like Levi they had already begun their course by 1938.[2] As Levi recalled wryly in his autobiography, *The Periodic Table*:

> I had in my drawer an illuminated parchment on which was written in elegant
> characters that on Primo Levi, of the Jewish race, had been conferred a degree
> in Chemistry *summa cum laude*. It was therefore a dubious document, half glory
> and half derision, half absolution and half condemnation. It had remained in that
> drawer since July 1941, and now we were at the end of November. The world was
> racing to catastrophe, and around me nothing was happening. The Germans had
> spread like a flood in Poland, Norway, Holland, France, and Yugoslavia and had
> penetrated the Russian steppes like a knife cutting through butter. The United

---

1   A 'chiral' form is asymmetric in such a way that the form and its mirror image (or enantiomer) are not superimposable. For Levi's degree and for other biographical information mentioned below, see Angier; Thomson. Levi returned to the subject of his thesis and of principles of asymmetry in general, linking them to key themes in his own thought, in an important later lecture, "Asymmetry and Life" in English in Primo Levi: *Black Hole of Auschwitz*, pp. 142-59.

2   For further detail on the Fascist Racial Laws, see Zimmerman.

States did not move to help the English, who remained alone. I could not find work and was wearing myself out looking for any sort of paid occupation; in the room next to mine, my father, prostrated by a tumour, was living his last months. (*The Periodic Table*, pp. 64-5)[3]

Less than three years later, Levi was arrested as an anti-Fascist partisan, identified as a Jew, and deported by train from a holding camp in central Italy to Auschwitz. He survived nearly a year, from February 1944 to January 1945, in Auschwitz-III Monowitz, and his long journey home took the best part of another year; he reached Turin in late 1945.

In 1947, he published the first edition of what is now recognised as one of the greatest historical documents of that war and of all the horrors of the twentieth century, *If This is a Man*.[4] After 1947, for thirty years Levi combined a career as a part-time writer and speaker with that of a full-time chemist and manager in a paint factory near Turin.

THE CHEMIST-WRITER

Both for critics and for Levi himself, there has long been acknowledged a deep and remarkable bond between his chemistry and his work as a Holocaust survivor, writer, and witness. Many have noted Levi's calm, detached, observational and analytical acuity, in *If This is a Man* and elsewhere, of the systematic degradation of the prisoners at Auschwitz, the moral destruction of human dignity designed to facilitate the physical annihilation that was to follow. And many have linked this observational, analytical capacity to the eye of the young chemistry graduate of 1941 – to Levi the laboratory animal.[5]

In *The Periodic Table*, Levi described how he came to write *If This is a Man* in 1946-47 in two distinct phases, and two successive states of mind. First came a phase of trauma, of outpouring, of catharsis, when he wrote "bloody, concise poems" about the camps and button-holed strangers like Coleridge's ancient mariner.

But then, he says, he somehow reached calmer waters:

---

3   The first Italian edition, *Il sistema periodico*, was published in 1975.

4   Primo Levi: *Se questo è un uomo* (1947; 2nd. ed. 1958). The first English edition, *If This is a Man*, was published in 1959. Subsequent US editions have taken the title *Survival in Auschwitz*. Quotations are from the 1979 dual edition, Levi: *If This is a Man/ The Truce*.

5   On Levi's science-writing, see essays in Gordon, pp. 85-116.

My very writing became a different adventure, no longer the dolorous itinerary of a convalescent, no longer a begging for compassion and friendly faces, but a lucid building, which now was no longer solitary: *the work of a chemist who weighs and divides, measures and judges on the basis of assured proofs, and strives to answer questions.* Alongside the liberating relief of the veteran who tells his story, I now felt in the writing a complex, intense and new pleasure, similar to that I felt as a student when penetrating the solemn order of differential calculus. It was exalting to search and find, or create, the right word, that is, commensurate, concise, and strong; to dredge up events from my memory and describe them with the greatest rigor and the least clutter. Paradoxically, my baggage of atrocious memories became a wealth, a seed; it seemed to me that, by writing, I was growing like a plant. (*Periodic Table*, p. 153; emphasis added)

The chemist's vocation is lucid, rational, measured and measuring. Elsewhere, Levi regularly compared his writing to the drafting of a laboratory report.

There are also, however, more troubling bonds between Auschwitz and Levi's science. In a much bolder, riskier formulation, Levi also insisted in *If This is a Man* on a darkly fundamental undertow to the Nazi system at Auschwitz, on its status and validity as *itself* a scientific experiment, whose results need writing up and analysing:

the Lager was pre-eminently a gigantic biological and social experiment.
Thousands of individuals, differing in age, condition, origin, language, culture and customs are enclosed within barbed wire: there they live a regular, controlled life which is identical for all and inadequate to all needs, and which is much more rigorous than any experimenter could have set up to establish what is essential and what adventitious to the conduct of the human animal in the struggle for life. (*If This is a Man/ The Truce*, p. 93; emphasis added)

Indeed, Levi and his doctor friend and fellow-Auschwitz-survivor Leonardo Debenedetti had themselves written a "lab report" in 1945-46, a medical report on the hygienic and sanitary conditions in Monowitz. It was published in Italy's leading medical journal, *Minerva medica*, in 1946, but was only rediscovered in the 1990s.[6]

---

6   Translated as Leonardo De Benedetti and Primo Levi, *Auschwitz Report*.

Scientific writing, the laboratory experiment, and the rational precision and analysis of results, then, all lie at the heart of Levi's writing, work, and vocation as a Holocaust witness.

There is, however, something limiting, even clichéd in this account of both Levi and of science – and perhaps especially chemistry – as all reason and light, all cerebral observation and reflective analysis.

In fact, Levi's science, as several historians and philosophers of science have noted, was closer to late Renaissance or early Enlightenment empiricist practice than to abstract ratiocination, closer to Bacon than Descartes.[7] It was applied, practical, and material rather than abstractly analytical. In *The Periodic Table*, Levi describes his devotion to chemistry in a mock-epic and mock-mystical style, as a grand struggle against the god-like figure of Matter, *Hyle*. And the struggle is a 'contact sport': touching Matter is itself a 'thinking' process for Levi, just as much as formulating ideas and using language are. The chemist, scientist, and problem-solver thinks as much with his hands as with his brain, as he notes in a story called "His Own Blacksmith":

> I've also noticed that, as you do things, other things come to your mind in a chain: I often have the impression that I'm thinking more with my hand than with my brain.[8]

Levi's manual philosophy of mind points us to a key differentiator between the rationalist and the empiricist, in the history of science and in Levi too: the idea of the senses. It is this sensory domain that I wish to recover here.

"THE MNEMAGOGUES"

To explore Levi's sensory chemistry, and from there his empiricist model for thinking through the Holocaust, let's return to 1946 for a moment.

Alongside his bloody, concise poems, his medical report, and his "calm study of the human mind", as he described *If This is a Man* (*If This is a Man/ The Truce*, p. 15), in 1946 Levi also wrote a strange, disturbing, and apparently disconnected short story about chemistry, pharmacology, and the senses, in particular the sense of smell.

---

7   See e.g. Porro: "Scienza".
8   Primo Levi: *The Sixth Day*, p. 201. On Levi as "homo faber", see Antonello.

The story is called "The Mnemagogues" and it was first published in English in the 1990 collection *The Sixth Day* (pp. 11-18).

"The Mnemagogues" tells of an old provincial doctor, Ignazio Montesanto, who is close to retirement and has withdrawn into a secluded, unhappy world, obsessed with a strange chemical-psychological experiment with smell. Montesanto has distilled his memories into chemical compounds, each of which captures and preserves in a flask the smell of a long-past place, a feeling, a person, or something similar. His battle is against time and loss itself: "I by my nature can only think with horror," he says, "of the eventuality that even a single one of my memories should be erased" (*Sixth Day*, p. 14).

But Montesanto's flasks have become an addiction, a drug, a foggy barrier between himself and lived experience out in the world. He has come to exist only through his perfumes: "some might say that they are my very person" (*Sixth Day*, p. 15). The new young doctor Morandi, from whose point of view the story is told, is at first seduced by the game of identifying the different smells, by the chemical miracle of entering into Montesanto's mind and memories through them, but he comes away strangely disturbed, needing fresh air and contact with friends – clean smells and human touch – as though to cleanse himself of some poison.

"The Mnemagogues" amounts to a filtered, fictional meditation on how best to preserve and use the memories burning within Levi in 1946, on the devastating burdens and dangers of both fading memory and excessive memory – like Borges' famous hero Funes the Memorious. But it is also a reflection, through chemical experiment, on the substances of our knowledge of ourselves and of our world, and how they relate to matter and to our senses.

Montesanto's "chemical sensorium" is prodigious but flawed; his memories are preserved perfectly, but somehow also introverted, desensitised to the present and to lived reality. Levi implicitly asks how we can both retain our sensations and turn them into non-solipsistic knowledge.

Morandi and Montesanto – like Levi and Debenedetti, or like Chekhov, we might say – are expert readers and writers of sensory impressions because they are variously medics, pharmacologists, and chemists. In his later work, Levi was keen to argue that the chemist in him gave him a "surplus" in language and specifically in the language of the senses, by which he meant an ability to distinguish and precisely to describe colour, smells, textures, and structures in a way usually unavailable to the traditional humanistic literary intellectual:

I find that I am richer than my fellow writers, because for me terms such as "bright", "dark", "heavy", "light", "blue" have a far wider range of meanings. For me, blue is not only the blue of the sky, I have five or six other blues to choose from … I have held in my hands materials which are not around in the everyday world, which have properties out of the ordinary, which have helped me extend the technical capacities of my language. (Levi and Regge, p. 59)

Levi's chemistry, then, is also, among other things, a language of the senses, of colour and touch here, or of smell in "The Mnemagogues". This is not merely a sensuous or expressionistic language of sensation, although on occasion it is that too; it is rather an analytical language in which the senses are the toolbox and conduit to forms of understanding, in which the end result is as much a heightened ethical sensitivity as some additional material perception, a sort of laboratory ethics. He outlines this lab ethics in an essay entitled "The Mark of a Chemist":

Here [in the laboratory] other virtues were needed: humility, patience, manual dexterity; and also (why not?) good senses of sight and smell, strength of nerve and muscle, resilience in the face of failure. (*Other People's Trades*, pp. 86-91)[9]

THE SENSES

Once you start exploring Levi's work with this thread of sensory attention in mind, a remarkable array of material emerges. Following on from "The Mnemagogues", for example, the sense of smell is a regular resource for Levi's storytelling and reflections on Auschwitz. This is perhaps not surprising in an ambit – that of Holocaust testimony – so intensely weighed down by the dynamics and problematics of memory. In a remarkable short essay called "The Languages of Smells" – not as far I know published in English – Levi reflects on the sensory impact of a rare return visit in the 1980s to Auschwitz:

the smell of Poland, innocuous, unleashed by the carbon fossil used for heating in the homes, struck me like a blow: it reawoke in an instant a whole world of memories, brutal and concrete, that were lying dormant in me, and it took my breath away. ("Il linguaggio degli odori", p. 840; my translation)

---

9   The first Italian edition, *L'altrui mestiere*, was published in 1985.

This sensory hit not only prompts in his memory a link between to the present and Auschwitz, though. In a chain of senses of memories of senses, he also recalls how back then, in Auschwitz in 1944, the smells of home and of outside erupted into his prisoner's memory with unbearable force:

> With the same violence, "down there", occasional smells from the free world troubled us: hot tar, the smell of boats in the sun; the breath of the woods, with the smell of mushrooms and musk, sent our way by the Carpatian wind; the perfume of soap in the wake of a "civilian" woman encountered during our working hours ("Il linguaggio degli odori", p. 840; my translation).

The same dynamic is recognisable in an important passage of *If This is a Man* on the two types of dreams Levi shared with all his fellow prisoners: first, dreams of return, and the terror of being ignored and disbelieved back home; and second, dreams of the smells and the tastes of food, of home, of friends and family, impossibly vivid and agonizingly out of reach.

Indeed, it is not only the second of these dreams that has a sensory dimension: the first too is linked to a sense of sound, to hearing, in its anxiety of literally not being listened to, not being heard.

Sounds also operate on the dual axis of memory, from now back to the camps and from the camps out to a lost world of home and security. Here is Levi in *If This is a Man* on the blaring marching songs that woke him every freezing dawn in Auschwitz. One morning he is in the grim camp hospital and hears those awful songs from his bed:

> we all feel that this music is sent from hell ... The [marches and songs] lie engraven on our minds and will be the last thing in Lager we shall forget: they are the voice of the Lager, the perceptible expression of its geometrical madness, of the resolution by others to annihilate us first as men in order to kill us more slowly afterwards. (*If This is a Man/ The Truce*, p. 57)

As with Montesanto, Levi's sensitivity to sounds, to music, is full of careful distinctions and precision, but also open to the dangers of giving in to the invasiveness of the senses. His task is to listen acutely, but also to transform the perception into "useful" understanding:

> one had to escape from the enchantment, to hear the music from the outside, as happened in Ka-Be [the hospital] and as we think back now, after the liberation and the rebirth, without obeying it, without enduring it, to understand what it

was, for what meditated reason the Germans had created this monstrous rite, and why even today, when we happen to remember some of those innocent songs, our blood freezes in our veins and we become aware that to escape from Auschwitz was no small fortune. (*If This is a Man/ The Truce*, p. 57)

Already, then, within Levi's account of Auschwitz, the sensitivity to, the dynamics of recollection of, and the risks and violence of smell, taste, and sound are central to his efforts to draw ethical light out of this darkest of places.

Moving beyond this founding text, other chemical-ethical turns to the senses are to be found in *The Periodic Table*. We can usefully point to just two instances of many, two striking examples of the resonance that Levi's tales of chemistry and the senses in that book bring with them, for both Levi's experience and understanding of Auschwitz and for the general ethical dimension of his writing. Both have something to do with the sense of taste, explored in the creatively metaphorical manner familiar from *The Periodic Table*'s general reimagining of the chemical elements themselves in its conception and structure as a work of chemical autobiography.

The first is from the chapter "Iron" (pp. 37-49), and Levi's portrait there of his taciturn fellow chemistry student, Sandro, who for Levi embodied the stern, silent, and dignified, adventurous and practical, and quite masculine, virtues of the laboratory struggle. Sandro, though, was most importantly of all Levi's mountain-climbing companion and it was up in the mountains above Turin, getting lost and stuck for freezing nights, fending for themselves, struggling against the elements of the weather as they would against the elements of the "periodic table" in the lab, forging friendship, that Levi sees the deepest lesson and legacy left to him by Sandro. All this baggage of intimacy and legacy is captured for Levi in one vivid phrase, a mountaineer's phrase and a metaphor for the harsh but maturing experience of the mountain, of chemistry, and of the suffering of war and deportation that was to come for both Sandro and Primo. To taste such hard, formative adventure is, for Sandro, to taste "bear meat": though rarely noted in commentaries on this powerful chapter, Sandro's and Primo's "bear meat" is rooted in a metaphor of the senses, of taste.

The boys are stuck in the mountains overnight. Nearly frozen to death, they only make it back at dawn – Levi's dawns are often moments of acute sensory intensity – reaching a small shelter in a bedraggled state, much to the amusement of the old innkeeper:

This was it – the bear meat; and now that many years have passed, I regret that I ate so little of it, for nothing has had, even distantly, the taste of that meat, which is the taste of being strong and free, free also to make mistakes and be master of one's destiny. That is why I am grateful to Sandro for having led me consciously into trouble, on that trip and other undertakings which were only apparently foolish, and I am certain that they helped me later on.

They didn't help Sandro, or not for long. Sandro was Sandro Delmastro, the first to be killed fighting in the Resistance with the Action Party's Piedmontese Military Command. (*Periodic Table*, p. 48)

The second example also evokes the sense of taste and smell, this time through the visceral dynamics of its etymological opposite, the profoundly important universal human impulse of disgust.[10] The chapter is "Nitrogen," and Levi and a friend are busy trying to make some money extracting make-up from excrement:

far from scandalizing me, the idea of extracting a cosmetic from excrement, that is, *aurum de stercore*, amused me and warmed my heart like a return to the origins, when alchemists extracted phosphorus from urine. It an adventure both unprecedented and gay, and noble besides, because it ennobled, restored and reestablished. That is what nature does: it draws the fern's grace from the putrefaction of the forest floor, and pasturage from manure … (*Periodic Table*, p. 81)

There is a playful comedy to the episode, but also a deep lesson. Levi frames it as a lesson both from chemistry and by analogy also from Auschwitz, a lesson in overcoming disgust, in turning it to good use – and, he implies, in not ceding to visceral hatred or exclusions:

The trade of a chemist (fortified in my case by the experience of Auschwitz) teaches you to overcome, indeed to ignore, certain revulsions, that are neither necessary or congenital: matter is matter, neither noble nor vile, infinitely transformable … (*Periodic Table*, p. 180-81)

Thus far, we have been drawing on examples principally linked to smell, hearing, and taste, since these senses are often neglected compared to the others; and it is telling to see Levi paying careful attention to all of them, perhaps a

10 See McGinn.

distinctive feature of the laboratory chemist. There would be a great deal to add also on sight and touch, but in moving towards the final part of this chapter, I want to dwell on just one thread of Levi's deployment of all the senses that links Auschwitz to his science-fiction stories. The thread is the strangely compelling force for Levi of what he called the "deception of the senses".

Levi – and the chemist in him above all – knew that if our senses are useful, indeed essential tools in our engagement with and understanding of the world around us, a surplus of both data and applied intelligence, they are also dangerous and potentially deceptive. The dreams of food and friends in Auschwitz were excruciating because so seemingly real and yet empty, not "nourishing". Perhaps the most devastating page in Levi's entire oeuvre is that which closes his second book *The Truce* (1963); it contains that very phrase "deception of the senses". When, after his epic journey home to Turin, back with those very friends and family he had dreamed of in Auschwitz, he suffers from another, even more terrifying dream, or rather dream-within-a-dream, in which he dreams of suddenly waking up, once more at dawn, back in Auschwitz:

> … and now, I *know* what this thing means, and I also know that I have always known it; I am in the *Lager* once more, and nothing is true outside the *Lager*. All the rest was a brief pause, a deception of the senses, a dream; my family, nature in flower, my home. Now this inner dream, this dream of peace, is over, and in the outer dream, which continues, gelid, a well-known voice resounds: a single word, not imperious, but brief and subdued. It is the dawn command of Auschwitz, a foreign word, feared and expected: "get up, *Wstawać*". (*If This is a Man/ The Truce*, p. 379-80)[11]

The paradoxes and twists and turns of this deception of the senses are picked up on and explored in one of Levi's most remarkable science-fiction stories, entitled "Retirement Fund" (*Sixth Day* p. 107-25). In this story, Levi's hapless inventor-salesman Simpson convinces the narrator of the story – a figure for Levi himself – to try out his latest machine, the so-called TOREC, what we would call a virtual-reality machine that allows the viewer to experience someone else's pre-recorded actions and sensations. Levi might call it a "deception-of-the-senses" machine. The narrator tries out several TOREC tapes: He scores a goal for AC Milan; he is an immigrant beaten up by rac-

---

11   The first Italian edition, *La tregua*, was published in 1963.

ists; he is a female model waiting to have sex with her lover; he is dying of thirst and then drinks desperately; and finally, he is a bird of prey soaring at two thousand metres before swooping down to kill a hare. He also plays one tape – of a parachute jump – backwards, feeling as though he is being sucked up from the ground back through the sky into the mouth of an aeroplane (echoing a famous passage from Kurt Vonnegut's *Slaughterhouse-5*, about the Allied bombing of Germany).

These mini-narratives are intensely sensory; but they do not only offer an anthology of specific sensory experiences and impulses – of touch, vision, impulses of thirst and hunger, sexual desire and violence, flight, and hatred – and allow the narrator to observe himself as he experiences these sensations. They also particularly imagine altered, inverted, or heightened senses: the transexual experience of another sex's desire, the enhanced vision and instinct for violence of a bird of prey, the refined physique, eye, and touch of a professional footballer, the reverse flight of the parachutist. The experience of other people's or other animal's lives is one of other senses, of impossible sensations, of going beyond the limits of the self, even the physical skin of our own bodies.

But the end of the story takes us straight back to Montesanto and his Mnemagogues, to their cautionary tales of the seductive and addictive dangers of mere sensation, of the thirst for more and more experiences of the senses. We learn at the end of the story that Simpson is devoured by a strange addiction to the ersatz TOREC experience of recorded sensation, which, however, has no pay-off in learning, understanding, or memory. Every time a tape plays, the sensation is as it was recorded, as it was the first time, always new. Without reflection, analysis, heuristic elaboration, the senses are useless simulacra, a circus-ground sensorium, and the virtues of the laboratory are nowhere to be found.

OTHER SENSES

The categories of the Five Senses are, of course, a shorthand and a myth. A cursory glance at the literature suggests that there is a lively debate on what precisely constitutes a 'sense' in neurological terms, and indeed on how many senses there might be, human, animal, or vegetal: the answer seems to be anything between the traditional five and twenty-one.[12] One of the most

---

12   See for example Ackerman; Macpherson.

widely acknowledged, and most biologically and evolutionarily essential, of the senses beyond the standard five is known as nociception, the sense of pain. In closing, I would like to suggest that Levi's chemical sensorium is completed and fulfilled in his writing – made sense of, we might say – through his extraordinary attention to nociception, to the physical and moral senses of pain, and in particular to the need to feel the "pain of others", as Susan Sontag phrased it (Sontag).

"Retirement Fund" already staged as one of its mini-narratives and vicarious sensations the experience of an Italian-American immigrant being beaten up American racists: literally feeling the pain of others. But pain comes not only from physical blows in Levi; it is also distinctly linked to some of the sensory processes we have touched on above. Back in *If This is a Man*, when Levi describes his first dream, of not being listened to by his friends and especially by his sister when he tries to tell them about his ordeal, he veers from the intense, physical (sensuous) pleasure of telling them his story, to a sudden and pure form of pain:

> It is an intense pleasure, physical, inexpressible, to be at home, among friendly people, and to have so many things to recount: but I cannot help noticing that my listeners do not follow me. In fact, they are completely indifferent: they speak confusedly of other things amongst themselves, as if I was not there. My sister looks at me, gets up and goes away without saying a word.
>
> A desolating grief is now born in me, like certain barely remembered pains from one's early infancy. *It is is pain in its pure state* ... (*If This is a Man/ The Truce*, p. 66; emphasis added)

This turn from pleasure to pain, of pleasure into pain, gets close to the ethical heart of Levi's world and to the ethical endpoint of his sensory explorations. "Against Pain" is the title of one of his short essays in *Other People's Trades* (pp. 182-4), a sort of Epicurean universal declaration that our only duty in acting in the world is the avoidance of pain, but especially "the pain of others". We are closer here to Jeremy Bentham's famous declaration on the empathy and the suffering of animals: "The question is not, Can they *reason*? nor, Can they *talk*? but, Can they *suffer*?" (Bentham, 17.6).[13] In another science-fiction story, "Versamina" (*Sixth Day* 45-54), Levi imagines a chemical that converts pleasure into pain and vice versa, and the moral havoc that ensues. He ends

---

13   Thanks to Damiano Benvegnù for this connection.

by quoting Western literature's most terrible wreakers of havoc, inversion, and moral chaos, Shakespeare's witches in *Macbeth*: "Fair is foul and foul is fair / hover through the fog and filthy air" (Shakespeare, *Sixth Day*, p. 54).

If Levi began his chemical explorations with Walden inversions, it is perhaps not too fanciful to hear an echo of the chirality and transformations that fascinated him at a molecular level back in the 1940s, in the chemical-ethical perceptions and inversions that he brought together through his heightened attention to the workings of the senses.

WORKS CITED

Ackerman, Diane: *A Natural History of the Senses*. London: Vintage, 1991.

Angier, Carole: *The Double Bond. Primo Levi: A Biography*. London: Viking, 2002.

Antonello, Pierpaolo: "Primo Levi and 'Man as Maker'" in Robert S. C. Gordon (ed.): *Cambridge Companion to Primo Levi*. London: Verso, 2006, pp. 89-103.

Bentham, Jeremy: *An Introduction to the Principles of Morals and Legislation*. Oxford: Clarendon Press, 1823.

De Benedetti, Leonardo and Levi, Primo: *Auschwitz Report*. Robert S. C. Gordon (ed.), trans. Judith Woolf. London: Verso, 2006.

Gordon, Robert S. C. (ed.): *Cambridge Companion to Primo Levi*. Cambridge: Cambridge University Press, 2007.

Levi, Primo: *L'altrui mestiere*. Turin: Einaudi, 1985.

—: *Black Hole of Auschwitz*, trans. Sharon Wood. Cambridge: Polity, 2005.

—: *If This is a Man*, trans. Stuart Woolf. New York: Orion Press, 1959.

—: *If This is a Man / The Truce*, trans. Stuart Woolf. Harmondsworth: Penguin, 1979.

—: "Il linguaggio degli odori" in Marco Belpoliti (ed.): *Opere*, 2 vols. Turin: Einaudi, 1997.

—: *Other People's Trades*, trans. Raymond Rosenthal. London: Michael Joseph, 1989.

—: *The Periodic Table*, trans. Raymond Rosenthal. London: Michael Joseph, 1985.

—: *Se questo è un uomo*. 1st ed. Turin: De Silva, 1947; 2nd ed. Turin: Einaudi, 1958.

—: *Survival in Auschwitz*, trans. Stuart Woolf. New York: Collier, 1961.

—: *The Sixth Day*. London: Michael Joseph, 1990.

—: *La tregua* (Levi, Primo, and Regge, Tullio). Turin: Einaudi, 1963.

—: *Conversations*, trans. Raymond Rosenthal. London: I.B. Tauris, 1989.

Macpherson, Fiona (ed.): *The Senses: Classic and Contemporary Philosophical Perspectives*. Oxford: Oxford University Press, 2011.

McGinn, Colin: *The Meaning of Disgust*. Oxford: Oxford University Press, 2011.

Porro, Mario: "Scienza" in *Primo Levi*, spec. issue of *Riga* 13 (1997), pp. 434-75.

Sontag, Susan: *Regarding the Pain of Others*. London: Hamish Hamilton, 2003.

Thomson, Ian: *Primo Levi. A Life*. London: Hutchinson, 2002.

Vonnegut, Kurt: *Slaughterhouse-5*. London: Cape, 1970.

Zimmerman, Joshua (ed.): *Jews in Italy under Fascist and Nazi Rule, 1922-1945*. Cambridge: Cambridge University Press, 2005.

AUTOBIOGRAPHY AND CHEMISTRY: PRIMO LEVI AND OLIVER SACKS

Margareth Hagen, University of Bergen

INTRODUCTION

For Italian and international readers, Primo Levi's name is principally linked to his testimonial works of witness and description of the Holocaust. In Italy, his other texts were not appreciated by a larger public until the mid-1970s, and the international audience still perceives him primarily as a Holocaust author.[1] After the enormous impact of his two testimonies of the Shoah, *If*

Primo Levi.

---

1   This is not least thanks to Giorgio Agamben's pointing to Levi as the perfect example of witness (Agamben, p. 16).

This is a Man (1947) and *The Truce* (1963), Levi wrote his highly original autobiography *The Periodic Table* (1975). Using chemical elements as metaphors, the book casts new light on his testimony of the Nazi extermination camps and clears the way for a larger and perhaps more diverse readership, increasing his *renommé* as a scientific writer. *Il sistema periodico* is a collection of twenty-one more or less autobiographical short stories dedicated to and inspired by twenty-one chemical elements. With its blend of personal memoir, chemistry, etymology, and ethics, it has been widely acclaimed as a masterpiece by an international and national readership.[2]

Primo Levi's extraordinary prose is the fruit of his three fundamental life experiences or identities: his having witnessed the Holocaust and giving testimony of it; his training and work as a chemist; and his authoring of books dedicated to the awareness of the materiality of our world and the potential for poetry in concrete phenomena. The blending of these three identities results in literary texts where pathos, even when recalling horrendous events, is played down in order to offer room for an intensely lucid and precise description and analysis of what it means to be human, and also of the chemical material from which we are all made. As Robert S. C. Gordon shows in the previous chapter of the present book, the striking objective style of Levi's texts is rooted in his scientific ideal of clarity and in his chemical training and sensorium.[3] Chemistry has a constant presence in Levi's life journey: in his first childhood experiments, in his university studies, in the chemical laboratory of IG Farben in Monowitz (part of Auschwitz III) where he was assigned to work and was thus able to survive, and later, in his professional and intellectual life.

In Primo Levi's prose the interaction between the discourses of science and autobiography challenges conventional divisions between scientific and

---

2   In fact, the American publication of *The Periodic Table* (1984) made his name there among a wide public. In 2006 the Royal Institution of Great Britain reckoned it to be the best scientific book of all time (the other shortlisted authors were Konrad Lorenz, Tom Stoppard, Steven Jay Gould, and Richard Dawkins).

3   Objective and material descriptions and the presence of chemical terms are also characteristic of Levi's very first publication, a collaborative document co-authored with his friend, fellow survivor, and doctor Leonardo de Benedetti, published in 1946 in the Turin-based medical journal *Minerva medica*, under the title "Rapporto sull'organizzazione igenico-sanitaria del campo di concentramento per ebrei di Monowitz (Auschwitz – Alta Silesia)". In his introduction to the English edition of *Auschwitz Report* (2006), Robert Gordon has described this document as the founding moment, the originary document of *If This is a Man*.

LITERATURE AND CHEMISTRY

humanistic fields. In the following pages I focus on the particular amalgam of the autobiographical genre and the exposition of chemistry, as it appears in Levi's *Periodic Table*. After briefly presenting the importance of chemistry for Levi's writing – and here I use some of Levi's own words – I assess how the tools and ethos of chemistry have structured his autobiography. As a way of drawing out the specific characteristics of Levi's work, I will compare his novel with another autobiography both informed by and dedicated to chemistry: Oliver Sacks' *Uncle Tungsten: Memories of a Chemical Boyhood* (2001).

THE CHEMISTRY OF WRITING

Reading Levi's book with expectations about the autobiographical genre, one might be confused and perhaps also astonished by the distance the narrator imposes between himself and his audience. There is always a filter, or a veil, of objectivity, such that the general laws of nature and the profound ethical issues seem to conceal the particular nature of the individual life. "*The Periodic Table* might be the least lyrical autobiography of Italian modern literature", writes the Italian critic Eraldo Affinati. He continues: "Once again the writer keeps himself at a safe distance by screening in science his conceptual inheritance. The objectivity of the narrative is so strong that it risks consuming the underlying sentiments" (*Affinati*, p. 429; my translation).

Levi explained several times how being a chemist helped him to achieve an extraordinary mindfulness of material reality, to explore the potentiality of the senses, and to extract metaphors that could be used as tools for analysing and describing the world. The tools of the literary trade accompany the tools of chemistry, Levi writes in the essay "Ex-Chemist": "I write precisely because I am a chemist: my old trade has been largely transfused into my new one" (*Other People's Trades*, p. 176). Émile Zola, in the preface to *Thérèse Raquin*, also compares his work to that of a scientist. The author, he says, combines temperaments or characters, introducing them to circumstances which work as catalysts for provoking specific reactions.[4] In Levi's case, however, the literary use of chemistry is always

---

4   "I set out to study temperament, not character. That sums up the whole book. (…) I freely admit that the soul is entirely absent, which is as I wanted it. The reader has started, I hope, to understand that my aim has been above all scientific" (Zola, p. 4). Charlotte Sleigh has treated the theme of realism in literature and the laboratory in *Literature & Science*, (2010).

somehow connected to his own life, and he often uses his own experiences as raw material. This is how he describes the relationship between his writing and chemistry:

> [...] writing is a way of "producing", indeed a process of transformation: the writer transforms his experiences into a form that is accessible and attractive to the "customer" who will be the reader. The experiences (in the broad sense: life experiences) are therefore raw material: the writer who lacks them works in a void ... Now, the things I have seen, experienced, and done during my preceding incarnation are today for me as writer a precious source of raw materials, of events to narrate, and not only events. Also of those fundamental emotions which are one's way of measuring oneself against matter ... and thus winning and losing. This last is a painful but salutary experience without which one does not become adult and responsible. (*Other People's Trades*, p. 175)

I would like to draw attention to three statements in this dense paragraph. Firstly, Levi emphasises that the very profession – or trade – of chemistry is a tool for personal formation, almost in the German sense of *Bildung*. Secondly, in comparing the practices of writing and chemistry, he points not only to life *experiences* as the writer's raw material, but also to *emotions*. Coming from an author who seldom includes explicit descriptions of emotions, this seems to be an important, and somewhat surprising, statement.

Thirdly, in this passage he compares the process of writing to synthetic chemistry, the formation or building of complex compounds, the creation of new chemicals. Levi considers himself a synthetic chemist, a *rigger-chemist*: his speciality is paint. "We are divided into two branches", he explains in the novel *The Monkey's Wrench*, "those who rig and those who dismantle or break down" (*The Monkey's Wrench*, p. 142, 145). But the methods of analytical chemistry underlie all chemical construction. In fact, in the short essay "Ex-Chemist", Levi also compares writing to analytical chemistry:

> Chemistry is the art of separating, weighing and distinguishing: these are three useful exercises also for the person who sets out to describe events or give body to his own imagination. Moreover, there is an immense *inherited wealth* of metaphors that the writer can take from the chemistry of today and yesterday, which those who have not frequented the laboratory and factory know only approximately. The laymen knows what to filter, crystallise, and distil mean (...) but

he does not know the emotions that are tied to these gestures, has not perceived the symbolic shadow they cast. ("Ex-Chemist", pp. 175-6; emphasis added)[5]

Again, Levi stresses the chemist's emotional involvement. His description of the ethos and formation of the chemist is based on the daily work and struggle in the laboratory, the testing and failing, and the constant training of the senses, but fundamentally also on the *symbolic shadow of the elements*, which is connected to their ancient and cultural history.[6]

But the chemist's knowledge of the elements of our world is, in Levi's case, in addition transformed into a profound hylozoic *Weltanschauung*, as Cesare Cases defines it, where the animate and inanimate are tightly linked together and the elements have human connotations. "The overflowing hylozoism is the soul of this remarkable autobiography, where the epic struggle with the *Hyle* marks the stages of a life of fighting" (Cases, p. 12). Hylozoism is the philosophical theory that all matter is endowed with life, and Levi goes on to add human qualities and ethos to his elements. I cannot see any reason for objecting to the idea of hylozoism in Levi, but I do believe it is worth questioning if this world view could be described as an intrinsic part of the philosophy, or better, the style of chemistry. In one of her recent essays Bernadette Bensaude-Vincent has described how chemistry deals with materials rather than matter, with relations rather than substances, and that the chemist's style of reasoning about the world is representing nature as a theatre of transformation ("The Chemists' Style of Thinking").

Keeping in mind Levi's poetic use of chemistry, the emotional memories of the chemist's craft, and how the work of the author can be seen as parallel to processes of chemical analysis and chemical synthesis, I now turn my attention to the structure of *The Periodic Table*, Levi's unique autobiography.

THE PERIODIC TABLE – AN ALLOY OF LITERARY GENRES

There is no systematic scientific order to the succession of the elements used as chapter titles in the book, but it should be noted that all the elements

---

5 The English translation reads "immense patrimony" – I have changed it to the more appropriate "immense inherited wealth".

6 In recent years the cultural history of elements and chemical substances has been the basis for bestsellers like Pierre Laszlo's *Salt: Grain of Life* (2001) and Hugh Aldersey-Williams' *Periodic Tales* (2011). Hugh Aldersey-Williams shares Levi's tendency of anthropomorphising elements.

used by Levi as constructing metaphors and themes in his stories belong to the field of inorganic chemistry, with one exception: the last chapter is on carbon, an element that creates a bridge to organic chemistry.[7] In the book Levi's life history is framed by two stories.

The opening story is dedicated to his ancestors who were Piedmontese Jews: noble, rare, and as inert as argon gas: "They are indeed so inert, so satisfied with their conditions, that they do not interfere in any chemical reaction, do not combine with any other element, and for precisely this reason have gone undetected for centuries" (*PT*, p. 3).[8] The closing chapter is about carbon, an element that, on the contrary, opens up potentially infinite combinations in the eternal metamorphosis of existence. It is also worth mentioning that Levi did plan a sequel to *The Periodic Table* which he worked on during the last year of his life: *The Double Bond* was intended to explore the double, more complex and more stable combinations of organic chemistry.[9]

Levi's autobiography is a story about growing up through the craftsmanship and science of chemistry. Through presentations of the properties of the elements, Levi shares memories from his youth, university years, war experiences, and professional life. The extremely dense quality of this book results from the chemical elements being used as mnemonic vehicles and metaphoric tools not only for presenting his own life story, but also for presenting the history of chemistry, the history of Italy in the twentieth century, and the history of the Jews. The historian Carlo Ginzburg has pointed out that Levi introduced the term "microhistory" into Italian; it occurs in the book's last chapter, "Carbon" (Ginzburg, p. 196). Here Levi begins by dwelling on the hybrid literary genre of his novel and lists the different text types involved:

---

7   Lucie Benchouiha has argued that Levi did play with the atomic numbers in the book, thereby again showing the centrality of the Auschwitz experience: "the chapter dedicated to Levi's time in Auschwitz, 'Cerio', is not just central physically and metaphorically, but also mathematically. The sum of the atomic numbers in the first half of Levi's work, from 'Argon' to 'Oro' total three hundred and seventy eight, a total mirrored exactly by the sum of those in the second half, from 'Cerio' to 'Carbonio'" (Benchouiha, p. 67).

8   I use the abbreviation *PT* to indicate Primo Levi's *The Periodic Table*.

9   Levi's biographer, Ian Thomson, writes that Levi discussed the sequel as early as May 1975: "Levi was asked if he planned to write a sequel to *The Periodic Table*. He said he did, but he had no working title. After discussion the diners came up with The Double Bond. Levi loved the title, which he said remained him of J. D. Watson's The Double Helix, about the discovery of the DNA" (Thomson, p. 376).

LITERATURE AND CHEMISTRY

The reader, at this point, will have realised for some time by now that this is not a *chemical treatise*: my presumption does not reach so far – "ma voix est foible, et même un peu profane." Nor it is an *autobiography*, save in the partial and symbolic limits in which every piece of writing is autobiographical, indeed every human work; but it is in some fashion a *history*. It is – or would have liked to be – a *micro-history*, the history of a trade and its defeats, victories, and miseries ... (emphasis added)

Other genres are also involved in Levi's book, including the detective story and the mythological tale. I will not focus on this interesting list of literary genres here, but simply point out that the use of the term *microhistory* is interesting. Ginzburg comments that the reduction of scale suggested by Levi's notion of microhistory fits in with the acknowledgment of a limited existence, and with the description of reality on the individual level.[10] We cannot know for sure what Levi meant by *microhistory*, but it seems plausible that he wished to draw attention to the importance and role of the individual as a small part of the whole, like an atom, or a microscopic chemical substance.

Although most of the short stories are autobiographical, Levi intended the book to be (and described it as) more generic; that is, it is a portrait of the profession of chemistry and a tool for personal development. Here are Levi's own words about the intentions behind his project:

I had made a kind of project for myself, that was, basically, to write an educational book. I wanted ... to make the non-chemist understand the strong and bitter taste of our profession. Not because it is particular, or privileged, but simply because it is a "profession". If I may be allowed to quote myself, it is "*a more strenuous version of the business of living*". (Poli and Calcagno, p. 77; emphasis added)

---

10 Ginzburg then suggests that Levi arrived at the term *microhistory* through reading Italo Calvino's translation of Queneau's *Les Fleurs bleues*. This might be the case, but it seems more probable that at that time Levi was not aware of the sociological and historical use of the term, and that he simply created it himself. I wish to thank Domenico Scarpa for discussing Levi's use of this notion with me. As Scarpa points out, since Levi's library is not accessible, one cannot know for sure whether Levi had read Queneau's *Les fleurs bleues* when he wrote "Carbon" in the years 1968-70, even though it was translated into Italian by his friend Italo Calvino.

The kind of chemistry that is a strenuous version of the business of living is the chemistry done by a solitary individual whose emotions are engaged, and Levi sees it as a struggle with matter.[11] His auto-quotation is taken from the chapter entitled "Silver", where he describes a class reunion commemorating the twenty-fifth anniversary of his graduation from university. At the gathering he discusses the idea for *The Periodic Table* with his former fellow students:

> [...] in this book I would deliberately neglect the grand chemistry, the triumphant chemistry of colossal plants and dizzying output, because this is collective work and therefore anonymous. I was more interested in the stories of the solitary chemistry, unarmed and on foot, at the measure of man, which with few exceptions has been mine: but it has also been the chemistry of the founders, ... who confronted matter without aids, with their brains and hands, reason and imagination. (*PT*, p. 203)

I believe it is fruitful to read Levi's portrait of chemistry as a representation of what Francois Jacob has labelled *night science*, the world of inspiration, intuition, and struggle, of poring over problems before stumbling over an unexpected solution.[12] This brings back the question of how chemistry, as a science and craft, can be said to be an allegory of fundamental stages in the formation of the protagonist in the novel. The answer requires a consideration of the structure of Levi's autobiography from a broader point of view, questioning how the qualities of the specific scientific discipline shape the textual or narrative representation of the self. In examining the role of chemistry in the structure of Levi's book, I will compare it with Oliver Sacks's autobiography *Uncle Tungsten*.

CHEMISTRY AS *BILDUNG*

In reading *Uncle Tungsten*, Oliver Sacks's autobiographical novel about his boyhood, family, and young love affair with chemistry, it is impossible not to notice the many similarities with Levi's book. The cases of Levi and Sacks

---

11 Levi is evoking the title of Cesare Pavese's posthumously published diary, *Il mestiere di vivere* (1952), a work that had a huge influence on Levi and his generation.

12 "Our breakthrough was the result of 'night science': a stumbling, wandering exploration of the natural world that relies on intuition as much as it does on the cold, orderly logic of 'day science'" (Jacob, p. 767).

are of course mutually relevant since they both transfuse and represent their personal and scientific experiences and competencies in their texts. In addition, both authors favour the short story genre because it allows them to narrate different cases in the form of clinical tales or stories of chemical experiments and experiences.[13]

Brought up in a family of profound scientific culture, Sacks recounts how his parents and some of his close relatives transmitted an eagerness for knowledge, stimulating his scientific interests. In his novel's last chapters, the discovery of biology coincides with his puberty, while the largest part of the book, covering his childhood years, is dedicated to his deep and intense fascination with chemistry.[14] While Levi uses the elements also as metaphorical tools, knowing the chemical elements by experience makes the periodic table primarily a mnemonic catalogue for Sacks, who got the idea for his autobiography through the gift of a small piece of tungsten. In the postscript he writes that in 1997 his friend Roald Hoffmann sent him a parcel containing a poster of the periodic table, a chemical catalogue, and a little bar of a very dense greyish metal. On opening the parcel, the piece of metal fell to the floor with a resonant clonk, which he immediately recognised as the sound of sintered tungsten.

Both Levi's and Sacks's novels are indeed educational projects, as they portray basic qualities of chemistry by describing experiments, lab work, and the history of the subject. While Sacks includes short biographies of celebrated chemists, relating the achievements of the likes of Mendeleev, Curie, Dalton, Davy, and Bohr, Levi's chemical history dwells primarily on

---

13 Sacks masterfully blends science with storytelling and has had huge international success with his books, among which are the collections of case stories *The Man who Mistook his Wife for a Hat* (1985) and *An Anthropologist on Mars* (1995). While comparing *Uncle Tungsten* with *The Periodic Table*, it is of course interesting to note that both authors grew up in Jewish families. Sacks was a child in London during the Second World War; his wartime experience was certainly fundamental to his development, just as Levi's was. Another world-famous chemist born in a Jewish family and with extreme war experiences is Roald Hoffman, who was a child in Ukraine during the Second World War.

14 Sacks describes how he first got the idea to write his childhood memoirs: "I had intended, towards the end of 1997, to write a book on aging, but then found myself flying in the opposite direction, thinking of youth, and my own partly war-dominated, partly chemistry-dominated youth, in particular, and the enormous scientific family I had grown up in. No book has caused me more pain, or given me more fun, than writing Uncle T. – or, finally, such a sense of coming-to-terms with life, and reconciliation and catharsis", www.oliversacks.com.

the nature of the elements. Levi's educational project can therefore be said to have a different objective from Sacks's more encyclopaedic and didactic approach. As mentioned above, to Levi, the trade of chemistry – a science that requires both brain and hands – is in its very essence a tool for identity formation and maturation. Is it then correct, or at least possible, to label these novels *Bildungsromane*? According to Dilthey's classic definition, a *Bildungsroman* portrays a young person who engages in the two tasks of self-integration and integration into society, where the first implies the second. The two autobiographical novels are surely not *Bildungsromane* in this traditional sense, since they do not portray protagonists that gradually accept the values of society. In fact, in Levi's case it is quite the opposite, the choice of chemistry having been a conscious act of elimination of the idealist philosophy that neglected science. To the young Levi, chemistry and physics were "the antidote to Fascism…, because they were clear and distinct and verifiable at every step, and not a tissue of lies and emptiness, like the radio and newspapers"; furthermore, "chemistry was our ally precisely because the Spirit, dear to Fascism, was our enemy" (*PT*, p. 42).

These books can also be said, however, to portray the psychological and moral growth of the protagonist, a process that is infused with the apprehension and craftsmanship of chemistry, the art of distinction, patient observation, and experimentation. Since Sacks ends his story when he is about to enter adulthood and leave chemistry in favour of medicine, and then neuropathology, his chemistry remains domestic. Levi's life journey, by contrast, never leaves chemistry. Reading Levi's autobiography as a *Bildungsroman* has recently also been advocated by Enrico Mattioda, who observes that what is at stake in the book's second half is Levi's reconstruction of a life for himself. In the second half of the book he approaches the memories and the enemies from the *Lager*. Levi's *Bildung* has no ending, writes Mattioda, or more precisely, it ends with the abandoning of the individual and the particular in favour of the universal, through the story of the atom that represents us all: carbon, the element of life (Mattioda, p. 114-5). The eleventh and central chapter of *The Periodic Table*, dedicated to cerium, is the autobiography's nucleus. "Cerium" opens with Levi soberly explaining that he has "lived a different season", narrated elsewhere. He introduces us to the concentration camp and a person identified by the number 174517, whom he is not sure he can still recognise or reconstruct. It is of course significant that the central and only story from the concentration camp is located precisely in the middle of the novel. "Cerium" is in fact a story about the dignity of man, represented by man as maker, *homo faber*, even whilst in deepest misery. In the Buna laboratory Levi manages to steal some cylinders of cerium, and he relates how he and Alberto worked night after night to create small pieces of cerium for lighting purposes. They would sell them through the camp's black market, thus managing to *win the bread* that kept them alive until the Russians arrived.[15] Since "Cerium" is the only story from Auschwitz, it makes the second half of the novel a history of reconstruction, of new employment, love, and the continuous enigmas, challenges, and struggles in the lab. "Since one can't live on poetry and stories, I looked feverishly for work", Levi writes in "Chromium", the first post-war chapter. He finds employment in a big lakeshore paint factory where he is tasked to solve the mystery of the livering (thickening) of a huge stock of paint. Levi begins the half-chemistry, half-detective work by searching in the lab's file cards and archives from the war years. He discovers a transcription error, a mistake that had falsified all subsequent analyses on the basis of a fictitious value, and he finally manages to save the paint by introducing the anti-livering agent ammonium chloride. The successful sleuthing-cum-chemistry research is, for him, parallel to "a happy love and a liberating book" (*PT*, p. 159).

Levi's book has a very different approach to chemistry from Sacks' autobiography: it is dedicated primarily to the handicraft, emotion, and imagination of the solitary chemist, whose adversary is "the Button Molder, the *hyle*: stupid matter, slothfully hostile as human stupidity is hostile" (*PT*, p. 154).[16] Nevertheless, the two autobiographical novels share some basic structures due to their common scientific grounding. In the following I will suggest three shared fundamental features, namely the history of chemistry, the double nature of chemistry (its "impure" status), and the rhetoric of ekphrasis.

THE HISTORY OF CHEMISTRY

Both of the autobiographical novels are about slowly mastering the world through science; they both create paradigmatic parallels between the protagonist's coming of age and the history of chemistry.

---

15 It is a significant parallel that the central chapter of *If This is a Man* is also dedicated to the definition and constitution of human dignity – not through the ideal of *homo faber*, but represented by the search for knowledge and the legacy of classical literature, exemplified by Dante's reinterpretation of Ulysses in *The Divine Comedy*.

16 Levi's narrations of the solitary chemist – the heroic figure in the laboratory, struggling with the enigmas of matter – have much in common with Sacks' most successful books, in which the solitary doctor confronts enigmatic patients.

The chemist's attainment of legal majority might be summarised as follows. There is a gradual discovery of and process of mastering the world, which begins with the small boy's questions about the identity of objects. The boy goes on to make use of his senses in order to recognise and define the entities in the world. He then tries to recreate these things by himself and succeeds in creating an order, a system for classifying the world. The final stage is the theoretical threshold at which the very classification system and even basic trust in the human senses are questioned. The history of chemistry, from alchemy to quantum theory, is therefore infused with the growth and maturation of the protagonist's conscience. It is interesting to note that in his novel Sacks quotes the Italian nineteenth-century chemist Stanislao Cannizzaro (1826-1910), who writes that the history of chemistry should be in the mind of students: "It often happens", Cannizzaro concludes, "that the mind of a person who is learning a new science, has to pass through all the phases which the science itself has exhibited in its historical evolution." Cannizarro's words, Sacks recalls, "had a powerful resonance for me, because I too, in a way, was living through, recapitulating the history of chemistry in myself, rediscovering all the phases through which it had passed" (*UT*, p. 155).[17] This seems to be a precise metapoetic description of both novels, although Sacks' book finishes with the story of the end of his "love affair" with chemistry. Chemistry had been a constant instrument and filter for his understanding and perception of the world. Describing his early childhood, he recalls his endless and obsessive questions on the metals. "Why were they shiny? Why smooth? Why hard? Why heavy? Why did they bend, not break? Why did they ring?" (*UT*, p. 7). But, as Laszlo pointed out in his review of Sacks' book, "he was an Aristotelian essentialist, who became disenchanted with chemistry when he realized that it had jettisoned description and the sensory perceptions".

For both young boys, chemistry means explosions and romantic dangers; Sacks writes that one of his earliest memories (he was two) was seeing the Crystal Palace burn, and then the fireworks every November 5th. His primordial love of fire is soon transferred to practices such as mixing iodine and zinc, or iodine and antimony, or iodine and aluminium (*UT*, p. 83). For Levi, the identification of hydrogen, through provoking an explosion, is among his first experiments; Sacks' introduction to hydrogen is also dramatic and includes an explosion. His fascination with chemistry develops from

17 The abbreviation *UT* indicates Oliver Sacks' *Uncle Tungsten: Memories of a Chemical Boyhood.*

the first tales about the element, through the introduction to the different elements, to nature's building blocks and the first explosions. It then turns into an almost religious experience of awe at the discovery of the system, the periodic table that links it all together and reveals an ordered universe in which every element has its place.

In both autobiographies, chemistry as science is thus presented as an almost sacred revelation of order, *of micro- and macro-cosmos*, while the moment of awe is connected to the revelation of "the enchanted garden of Mendeleev" (*UT*, p. 194). When Sacks, at the end of his novel, interrogates himself on the profound reasons behind his abandoning chemistry, he mentions the loss of his youthful enthusiasm, the finding of stability and order, and the loss of the "lyrical, mystical perception of childhood" (*UT*, p. 314). Quantum calculations could not fully substitute the joy of perception. This is the emotional part of Levi's and Sacks's chemistry. Levi, true to himself, never treats the chemistry of tears,[18] but he does describe the emotion of awe experienced while facing the revelation of the order of chemistry and while conducting experiments. To the young Levi, chemistry is an "indefinite cloud of future potentialities … like those which had hidden Mount Sinai. Like Moses, from that cloud I expected my law, the principle of order in me, and in the world" (*PT*, p. 23). Levi describes his astonishment when he experiences the periodic table's revelations thus: "Mendeleev's Periodic Table, which just during those weeks we were laboriously learning to unravel, was poetry, loftier and more solemn than all the poetry we had swallowed down in *liceo*; and come to think of it, it even rhymed" (*PT*, p 41). Sacks also struggles to emphasise the altogether aesthetic and ethical beauty of Mendeleev's table: "The periodic table was incredibly beautiful, the most beautiful thing I had ever seen. I could never adequately analyse what I meant here by beauty – simplicity? coherence? rhythm? inevitability?" (*UT*, p. 203). And then, almost like a growing agnosticism in an adolescent contemplating the doctrines of religion, the young men discover the new quantum mechanics: "I had looked to chemistry, to science to provide order and certainty, and now suddenly this was gone" recalls Sacks (*UT*, p. 312). For Levi chemistry ceases to represent certainty and becomes another mysterious universe. "Having reached the fourth year of Pure Chemistry, I could no longer ignore the fact that chemistry itself, or at least that which we were being administered, did not answer my questions" (*PT*, p. 52). But for both

---

18 *Chemistry of Tears* is the title of Peter Carey's 2012 novel.

young protagonists, there is something much worse than the disturbance of order, namely, the idea of an entirely theoretical practice of chemistry. Sacks quotes the British chemist and physicist William Crookes (1832-1919):

> "Chemistry," wrote Crookes, "will be established upon an entirely new basis … We shall be set free from the need for experiment, knowing a priori what the result of each and every experiment must be. "I was not sure I liked the sound of it. Did this mean that chemists in the future (if they existed) would never actually need to handle a chemical; might never see the colors of vanadium salts, never smell a hydrogen selenide, never admire the form of a crystal; might live in a colorless, scentless, mathematical world? This, for me, seemed an awful prospect, for *I*, at least, needed to smell and touch and feel, to place myself, my senses in the middle of the perceptual world. (*UT*, p. 312)

For both Sacks and Levi, chemistry is a science of *Bildung* because it is rooted in practice, in laboratory experiments, thus depending on human sensorial capacities. A purely theoretical chemistry would make the science less complete as a means for *Bildung* on the individual level.

THE DOUBLE NATURE OF CHEMISTRY

Bernadette Saint-Vincent and Jonathan Simon present central issues in the philosophy of chemistry in their book *Chemistry: The Impure Science* (2008). They assess chemistry as having the peculiar status of an in-between science. Making, poesis, is the chemist's major activity, but chemistry is also an intellectual practice. Among the definitions of chemistry's particular status they quote Marcellin Berthelot's famous statement: "Chemistry creates its object. This creative faculty, akin to that of art, forms an essential distinction between chemistry and the other natural or historical sciences" (Saint-Vincent and Simon, p. 99). Chemists and historians of science throughout the last century have quoted this claim Berthelot made in the 1870s, even though chemistry has undergone profound transformations since then. The creative and sensorial nature of chemistry – half technical, half theoretical – undoubtedly offers a suitable thematic framework for autobiographical representations, particularly coming-of-age novels that include certain key situations such as the decision to become a chemist, the first experiments as rites of initiation, and the isolated work in the laboratory.

Any reader of Levi's texts knows that his definition of the nobility of humankind is tightly connected to the notion of *homo faber*, man the creator.

Levi sees himself reflected in the nature of chemistry – both he and chemistry are *centaurs* – with a double nature: throught and praxis. The theoretical and metaphysical speculations of the astrophysicist Dallaporta, who in 1941 risked his professional career by volunteering to supervise Levi's final thesis, seem to the young Levi like a "gigantic hippogriff" on which he refuses to mount, since he would prefer to stay grounded, as it were (*PT*, p. 57). Through chemistry, he dreams about a direct encounter with Matter: "We would be chemists, Enrico and I. We would dredge the bowels of the mystery with our strength, our talent, we would grab Proteus by the throat, cut short his inconclusive metamorphoses from Plato to Augustine, from Augustine to Thomas, from Hegel to Croce. We would force him to speak" (*PT*, p. 23).[19]

Levi makes this decision almost as a protest against the blurred and idealist culture of the humanities, as they came to expression in Italy's Fascist years, in the Gentile *liceo* where spirit dominates matter. Sacks's introduction to chemistry is more romantic; it is presented through one of his uncle Tungsten's great heroes, Carl Scheele, the solitary Swedish chemist who discovered oxygen and chlorine, and who paved the way for the discovery of other elements:

> I knew: I wanted to be chemist. A chemist like Scheele, an eighteenth-century chemist coming fresh to the field, looking at the whole undiscovered world of natural substances and minerals, … finding the wonder of unknown and new metals. (*UT*, p. 45)

More mythical situations follow in both of the biographies, not least because the first rudimentary labs and early experiments function as rites of initiation. Sacks recalls how he set up a little lab at home in an unused back room originally intended for doing laundry; Levi's first experiments take place when he and his friend Enrico steal into the primitive lab of Enrico's brother, at the rear of a courtyard (*PT*, p. 24). The young Sacks and Levi incorporate different character traits of the scientist: Sacks imagines himself as

---

19 Roald Hoffmann and Pierre Laszlo have interpreted the significance of the mythical figure of Proteus in this quotation. Proteus is a sea divinity with the capacity to foretell the future to those who can seize him, but when caught he transforms into all kinds of creatures. In their article Hoffmann and Laszlo remember the episode from the fourth book of *The Odyssey* in which Proteus wrestles with Menelao, changes into different forms, but is finally forced to be still and to foretell the future (Hoffmann and Laszlo).

a discoverer and collector of elements, while Levi remains a maker engrossed in a constant struggle with Matter, and a hunter: "We are chemists, that is, hunters: ours are, 'the two experiences of adult life' of which Pavese spoke, success and failure, to kill the white whale or wreck the ship" (*PT*, p. 75).

For Levi, chemistry, because of its double nature, is capable of helping him realise his ideal of human life, to be able to create his objects and use his hands. This makes Levi's first experiments true rituals of initiation. He becomes a man as he enters the lab, and he comments on the feelings of Enrico and himself as they, at sixteen years old, are about to cross the lab's threshold: "It seemed to us an *embarras de richesses*, and it was instead a different embarrassment, deeper and more essential, an embarrassment tied to an ancient atrophy of ours, of our family, of our caste. What were we able to do with our hands?" (*PT*, p. 24).

The laboratory is a privileged space of work, concentration, and isolation. It protects against contamination and the threatening madness beyond the door. The laboratory's isolation also reflects the blindness to, or the escape from, unbearable situations and dangers. In Levi's case, the students who are devoted to work and experiments are sheltered from the threatening situation in Europe,[20] whereas Sacks retreats into his laboratory and its isolation during a tragic period for his family, when his brother Michael becomes psychotic.[21] The primitive, isolated, rudimental chemistry that involves struggling with matter represents the opposite of the irrational Fascist propaganda that surrounded Levi, just as it offers shelter from the confusing and destructive psychosis of Sacks' brother.

The many different stages of character development, of growing up with and through the tools of chemistry, cannot be illustrated here, but I believe I have shown that for both Levi and Sacks, the history and the creative and sensorial qualities of chemistry serve as tools for their self-formation and self-presentation. I now turn to the third structural influence on these

---

20 "Night lay beyond the walls of the Chemical Institute, the night of Europe: Chamberlain had returned from Munich duped, Hitler had marched into Prague without firing a shot, ... Fascist Italy, the small-time pirate, had occupied Albania, and the premonition of imminent catastrophe condensed like grurnous dew in the houses and streets, in wary conversations and dozing consciences. But the night did not penetrate those thick walls" (*PT*, p. 37).

21 Sacks writes: "I became terrified of him, for him, of the nightmare which was becoming reality for him ... What would happen to Michael, and would something similar happen to me too? It was at this time that I set up my own lab in the house, and closed the doors, against Michael's madness" (UT, p. 168).

LITERATURE AND CHEMISTRY

autobiographies, which comes from the philosophy of chemistry and from the genre of chemistry writing: the constant shifting between micro- and the macro-levels.[22]

EKPHRASIS

The vivid and illuminating description of elements, materials, colours, smells, and experiments – ekphrasis – is a poetic quality found in both of the biographies. Bernadette Bensaude-Vincent has stated that a principal task of chemists is to identify, name, and classify things in the world. As for the characteristics of chemistry writing, Bensaude-Vincent mentions a particular chemists' expository style that involves shifting between levels; in chemistry books, one finds narratives from the macro-level juxtaposed with narratives from the micro-level, and a constant shifting between the levels such that the writer never settles on a single scale for reflection. Chemists, says Bensaude-Vincent, make up stories:

> They make up plausible narratives to account for the properties observed in individual substances that they use, or to predict and make new substances with desired properties. In so doing, they are constantly shifting from the macro- to the micro-level. … Chemistry textbooks, whether from the 17th century or most recent ones, tend to juxtapose narratives of experiments performed at the macro-level with narratives about relationships between microscopic invisible entities. (Bensaude-Vincent, p. 169)

Chemistry's narrative and rhetorical structures are thus based on a constant shifting between the levels, the shifting of scale, the naming and the classifying of objects, which shapes its texts and results in a particular aesthetic form. Sacks describes various elements and experiments in *Uncle Tungsten*, but he does not share Levi's profoundly metaphorical and emotional use of ekphrasis. Levi's between macro and micro perspectives throughout the novel, together with his use of ekphrasis to illustrate, explicate, and clarify the experiments and chemical compounds, makes his prose an example

22 Also Hoffmann points out that the mixing up of the microscopic and the macroscopic perspectives in doing chemistry is one of its characteristics: "the practicing (and excellent) chemists inextricably mix macroscopic and microscopic viewpoints of substances and molecules in the productive work of their science" (Hoffmann, p. 35).

of the very visibility and training of the imagination that Calvino, in *Six Memos for the Next Millennium*, sees as one of literature's most important missions in our time. This particular rhetorical strategy of creating parallels between different levels is also closely related to the metaphorical use of the elements and the rhetorical proving of connections between a natural order and a moral order. This is where Levi excels as he oscillates between close-ups of atoms and molecular structures on the one hand, and the great philosophical questions and the human ethos on the other.

Examples of different approaches to ekphrasis can be found in the two authors' stories about potassium. Sacks writes about potassium in his chapter on Humprhy Davy. Here we learn about the young Sacks submerging himself in biographies and chemistry books and attempting to repeat the experiments he finds in them. When he reads about Davy's discovery of potassium and how it reacts with water, he decides to have a try for himself. The episode describes his fascination with comparing the reactions of the five members of the alkali metal family – sodium, potassium, rubidium, caesium, and lithium – and the different nature, shape, and colour of the flames they produce (*UT*, p. 123). Levi's descriptions of his experiments are, by comparison, combinations of ekphrasis and sometimes awe, concluding with moral lectures.

Chemistry is the art of separating, weighing, and distinguishing; it is the search for order, to ensure our judgements are rooted in truth. The analysis is prior to the synthesis. It seems to me that Levi, in his autobiography, first and foremost explores the stamina of the researcher, the slow and meticulous analysis, the objective speculation. For instance, as mentioned above, Levi recalls his analysis of the livered paint after the war, and how he discovered what had happened and caused the damage by searching the archives of the factory. The art of distinction is of vital importance for every judgement. So when he was held captive at the Fossoli camp before being deported to Auschwitz, he longed for the chemical trade in its essential and primordial form, "the *Scheidekunst*, precisely, the art of separating metal from gangue" (*PT*, p. 137). Seen in this light, the most beautiful of all chemical operations or arts seems to be distillation, for it is a meditative activity of slowly metamorphosing matter. In the chapter dedicated to potassium, distilling is described as a philosophical occupation, a metamorphosis towards purity. It is beautiful because it repeats a ritual and thus has symbolic value, part of which is to participate in a larger community with deep historical roots:

> Distilling is beautiful. First of all, because it is a slow, philosophic, and silent occupation, which keeps you busy but gives you time to think of other things,

somewhat like riding a bike. Then, because it involves a metamorphosis from liquid to vapour (invisible), and from this once again to liquid; but in this double journey, up and down, purity is attained, an ambiguous and fascinating condition, which starts with chemistry and goes very far. And finally, when you set about distilling, you acquire the consciousness of repeating a ritual consecrated by the centuries, almost a religious act, in which from imperfect material you obtain the essence, the *usia*, the spirit. (*PT*, p. 58)

When Levi writes on potassium, he recalls how he was set to purify benzene in the Institute of Experimental Physics, and how he, for lack of sodium, turned to its twin, potassium. Levi's story about potassium is scattered with religious terms. He handles the tiny piece of potassium like a holy relic. After using it, he goes down into the institute's courtyard, digs a tiny grave and buries its little "bedevilled corpse". Returning to the lab, he fills the seemingly empty flask with water, but since he did not take care to remove all the liquid, a minuscule residual particle of potassium explodes and causes a fire. The lesson Levi draws from this experience contains a general moral every prudent chemist can confirm: "that one must distrust the almost-the-same … the practically identical, the approximate, the or-even, all surrogates, and all patchwork. The differences can be small, but they can lead to radically different consequences, … the chemist's trade consists in good part in being aware of these differences … and not only the chemist's trade" (*PT*, p. 60).

CONCLUDING REMARKS

In the preface to *Other People's Trades* from 1985, Levi looks back on his career and states that he has travelled as a loner, "examining matters of technique with the eye of a literary man, and literature with the eye of a technician" (*Other People's Trades*, vii). Levi's objective prose and his use of metaphors and analogies from the craft of chemistry are undoubtedly among the most appreciated qualities of his texts. Underlying this descriptive and associative prose we find a project of ethical writing, where the techniques of analysis and synthesis and the particular narratives of chemistry used to account for the properties of the substances serve as intellectual tools. This is the point where the differences between the books are clearest, since Sacks' approach to chemistry is more theoretical than Levi's. Sacks is a collector, while Levi is a narrator of encounters and failed encounters with matter. But in spite of the many, and fundamental, life stories in *The Periodic Table* and in Sacks' *Uncle Tungsten* are both seen and represented in the light of the history of chemistry, while the trade and art of chemistry is strongly perceived as a means for representing life in a way that enables the senses, hands, emotions, and cognition to intersect.

WORKS CITED

Agamben, Giorgio: *Remnants of Auschwitz The Witness and the Archive*. New York: Zone Books, 2002.

Affinati, Araldo: "Responsabilità" in *Primo Levi*. Riga / Milano: Marcos y Marcos, 1997, pp. 426-33.

Antonello, Pierpaolo: "Primo Levi and 'man as maker'" in Robert S. C. Gordon (ed.): *Primo Levi. The Cambridge Companion*. Cambridge: Cambridge University Press, 2007, pp. 89-103.

Benchouiha, L.: *Primo Levi: Rewriting the Holocaust*. London: Troubador Publishing, 2006.

Bensaude-Vincent, Bernadette: "Philosophy of Chemistry" in Anastasios Brenner and Jean Gayon (eds.): *French Studies in the Philosophy of Science*. New York: Springer, 2009, pp. 165-86.

Bensaude-Vincent, Bernadette and Simon, Jonathan: *Chemistry: The Impure Science*. London: Imperial College Press, 2008.

Bensaude-Vincent, Bernadette: "Making up Stories While Making Molecules" in A. Brenner and J. Gayon (eds.): *French Studies in the Philosophy of Science: Contemporary Research in France*. Boston: Springer, 2009a.

—: "The Chemists' Style of Thinking" in *Wissenschaftsgeschichte* 32 (2009b), pp. 365-378.

Calvino, Italo: *Six Memos for the Next Millennium*. London: Penguin, 2009.

Carey, Peter: *The Chemistry of Tears*. New York: Knopf, 2012.

Cases, Cesare: "L'ordine delle cose e l'oridne delle parole" in Ernesto Ferrero (ed.): *Primo Levi: Un'antologia della critica*. Torino: Einaudi, 1997, pp. 5-33.

Ginzburg, Carlo: "Microhistory: Two or Three Things That I Know about It" in *Threads and Traces: True False Fictive*. University of California Press, 2012, pp. 193-214.

Gordon, Robert S. C. (ed.): *Primo Levi. The Cambridge Companion*. Cambridge: Cambridge University Press, 2007.

Herman, David: "Narrative, Science, and Narrative Science" in *Narrative Inquiry* 8.2 (1998), pp. 279-90.

Hoffmann, Roald and Laszlo, Pierre: "Protean" in *Angewandte Chemie International* 40.6 (2001), pp. 1033-36.

Hoffmann, Roald: "What Might Philosophy of Science Look Like If Chemists Built It?" in Jeffrey Kovac and Michael Weisberg (eds.): *Roald Hoffmann on the Philosophy, Art, and Science of Chemistry*. Oxford: Oxford University Press, 2012, pp. 21-38.

Jacob, Francois: *On Flies, Mice and Men*. Harvard: Harvard University Press, 2001.

—: "The Birth of the Operon" in *Science* 13, May 2011, p. 767.

Kovac, Jeffrey and Weisberg, Michael (eds.): *Roald Hoffmann on the Philosophy, Art, and Science of Chemistry*. Oxford: Oxford University Press, 2012.

Laszlo, Pierre: "Enthralled by the Elements. Uncle Tungsten: Memories of a Chemical Boyhood" in *American Scientist* 90.2 (March-April, 2002), p. 1. Levi, Primo: *Il sistema periodico*. Torino: Einaudi, 1975.

—: *The Periodic Table*. New York: Schocken Books, 1984.

—: *Other People's Trades*. London: Michael Joseph, 1989.

—: *The Monkey's Wrench*. London: Penguin, 1986. Montgomery, Scott L.: *Science in Translation: Movements of Knowledge through Cultures and Time*. Chicago: University of Chicago Press, 2000.

Poli, G. G. Calcagno: *Echi di una voce perduta. Incontri, interviste e conversazioni con Primo Levi*. Milano: Mursia, 1992.

Sacks, Oliver: *Uncle Tungsten: Memories of a Chemical Boyhood*. New York: Vintage, 2001.

Sacks, Oliver: "Uncle Tungsten", www.oliversacks.com (6 Apr. 2013).

Saint-Vincent, Bernadette and Simon, Jonathan: *Chemistry: The Impure Science*. London/Hackensack: Imperial College Press, 2008

Sleigh, Charlotte: *Literature and Science*. Basingstoke: Palgrave Macmillan, 2010.

Thomson, Ian: *Primo Levi. A Life*. New York: Picador, 2004.

Zola, Émile: *Thérèse Raquin*. London: Penguin, 2005.

FROM THE LITERARY
LIVES OF TWO EPOCHAL
SCIENTISTS: HUMPHRY DAVY
AND LUDWIG BOLTZMANN

FROM "THE LIFE OF THE SPINOSIST" TO "LIFE": HUMPHRY DAVY, CHEMIST AND POET

Sharon Ruston, Lancaster University

Humphry Davy (1778-1829) was the foremost chemist in Britain in the nineteenth century. He is most famous for his invention of the miner's safety lamp, though he also isolated more chemical elements – including chlorine, potassium, and magnesium – than any other individual in history. He became President of the Royal Society in 1820, the highest honour for a natural philosopher of his day. While Davy remains a household name for British people over a certain age who remember him because of his "Davy lamp", few people know that he also wrote poetry. In fact, he wrote more than a hundred poems over the whole course of his life, in notebooks and letters, though only a handful of these were ever published. He revised one poem that he began sometime before 1800 at least four times, extending and developing it with each revision, and finally printing it anonymously

Portrait of Humphry Davy.

twice within his lifetime. It is clear that this was a poem of which he was particularly proud and there is evidence that it was read aloud and circulated in manuscript among friends and acquaintances. In this poem we see Davy exploring the changing states of matter that also concerned him as a chemist. Close attention to this poem reveals developments in Davy's own character, as the poem evolves from a youthful materialism to a more orthodox Christianity. In this essay I track the changes that this poem undergoes and reveal previously unknown evidence for the publication of Davy's poetry during his lifetime.

THE *ANNUAL ANTHOLOGY* AND BRISTOL, 1799-1801

Davy began writing poetry in Penzance as a young boy, but when he met S. T. Coleridge and Robert Southey in Bristol, where he had moved to take up the post of assistant at the Pneumatic Institute, their encouragement spurred him on to publish. While it appeared to "celebrate literary efforts by poets in the Bristol area", the *Annual Anthology* was actually primarily a showcase for Southey's and Coleridge's poetry, much of which had been published previously in *The Morning Post*. In the first volume, for example, sixty-two of the 104 poems were by Southey despite the fact that they had different initials attached to them (J. Wordsworth n.p.). Davy contributed five poems to the first volume of Robert Southey's *Annual Anthology* (1799) and then one to the second volume (1800). These figures put the extent of Davy's contribution in perspective, but it remains the case that these poems constitute (as far as we know) the only poems Davy published within his lifetime with his name attached to them.[1] The radical political affiliations of the anthology are also suggested when Davy refers to the publication as the "poeticojacobinical Anthology" ("Davy Letters" Letter to James [Tobin?], 21 March 1800). It was also at Bristol Davy discovered that nitrous oxide could in fact be safely respired, and the now famous trials of this gas took place there.[2]

Thomas Beddoes, Davy's mentor at the Pneumatic Institute, also contributed three poems to the *Annual Anthology*, including a parody of Erasmus Darwin's "Botanic Garden", which Beddoes had printed but not published

---

1   It is persuasively alleged by Elizabeth Benger that Davy also wrote the prologue for a play written by John Tobin called *The Honey Moon*, which was published anonymously (vii, n.).

2   For more on these trials, see, for example, Holmes and Jay.

in 1792.[3] Beddoes also parodied the style that would become famous with William Wordsworth and S. T. Coleridge's *Lyrical Ballads* in his "Domiciliary Verses", which were included in the *Annual Anthology* (1: 287-88).[4] In turn, it seems that Davy also wrote a parody of Wordsworth's lyrical ballad form, in a poem that survives in one of his notebooks amongst reports of experiments with nitrous gas and oxygen; it is called "As I was walking up the street".[5] As well as the many Wordsworthian images and themes in this poem, the simple language of Wordsworth's ballads is parodied: the word "shove" for example, towards the end of the poem, might not be thought a particularly poetic word, and it also fails to rhyme with "prove" (other than as an eye rhyme) (RI HD 20c: 52). This may be a sign of Davy giving up on the poem, since this stanza is followed by another that is crossed out and the poem does not appear to be finished (RI HD 20c: 52). There are a number of interesting parallels between this poem and the lyrical ballads though, including the poem's form as a personal anecdote, its lament for the fate of a soldier discharged because he had been wounded (Wordsworth's "The Discharged Soldier" was composed in late January 1798), and the fact that its protagonist is from the labouring class. Davy's character, Matthew Brown, exchanges his red coat for a "sky blue" one, which might also remind us of "Simon Lee's" "long blue livery-coat", while his "sparkling eye" might recall the ancient mariner's "glittering eye" (RI HD 20c: 52, 44). Wordsworth is himself named in Davy's poem as the recorder of related lives remembered: "By poet Wordsworths Rymes [*sic*]" (RI HD 20c:46; Wordsworth and Coleridge 99, 21). In July 1800 Wordsworth, on the suggestion of Coleridge, asked Davy to proofread the second volume of the *Lyrical Ballads* (Wordsworth *Letters* 1: 289). After reading Wordsworth's "Preface", Davy asserted in his 1802 *Discourse, Introductory to a Course of Lectures* that chemistry was creative and that the chemist was able to "modify and change the beings

---

3   See Stansfield on the textual history of this poem (Stansfield, p. 65). The poem was apparently passed off as Darwin's own work by Beddoes after he rose to the challenge "that the poetic effusions of Erasmus Darwin were inimitable" (Stansfield, p. 66).

4   See Vickers for a useful summary of critical opinion on this and other of Beddoes's parodies (Vickers, p. 56). There is a copy of the *Lyrical Ballads* held by the British Library that contains Beddoes's "Domiciliary Verses" printed to look like the other ballads, which Wu believes is Beddoes's own copy.

5   Personal Notebook, HD 20c, Royal Institution, 44, 46, 52. This notebook is marked "Clifton 1800 From August to Nov^r" in the front cover. Hereafter the notebooks are abbreviated to RI HD with their number. The Humphry Davy manuscripts are published here by courtesy of the Royal Institution of Great Britain.

surrounding him" (*Works* 2: 318). Davy uses almost identical language to Wordsworth's "Preface" but substitutes chemistry for poetry (see Sharrock).

Davy's biographer June Z. Fullmer warns us not to overestimate Davy and Coleridge's friendship, which was, she writes "pursued more on paper than by personal contact"; she estimates that "at most, during Davy's Clifton years they were together on thirteen days" (Fullmer, p. 136). During this time, Southey is described by Fullmer as Davy's "chief local companion", and Southey himself recalled in 1831: "No one lived in greater habits of intimacy with Davy during the greater part of his residence at Bristol than I did."[6] Davy can be linked to a number of other poets and writers in these early years. The *Annual Anthology* featured work by Charles Lamb and Amelia Opie as well as Mary Robinson. Coleridge told Godwin on 21 May 1800 that Davy was "exceedingly delighted" with Robinson's two poems in the *Anthology* (*Letters* 1: 589). In London, Davy became friends with Godwin and had dinner with him in a group that included the poet Charlotte Smith on 30 January 1802 (Godwin, n.p.). Later in life, he would become the friend or at least acquaintance of other writers, including Walter Scott, William Sotheby, Byron, Thomas Moore, and Joanna Baillie, often through his wife Jane Apreece, a literary socialite, whom he married in 1812.[7] There are suggestions of Jane's snobbery and literary pretensions. Walter Scott describes her in a journal entry in 1826 with: "Her fortune though handsome and easy was not large enough to make way by dint of showy entertainments and so forth so she took the *blue* line and by great tact and management actually established herself as a leader of literary fashion" (Scott, p. 79). An interesting (and critically ignored) confirmation of this is suggested in Thomas Moore's 1811 farce, *M.P., or, the Blue-Stocking*, where the chemist "Lady Bab Blue" is writing the *Loves of Ammonia* and has a servant called Davy (Moore). It is clear that Davy socialised with both chemists and poets. In his 1817 poetry collection *Sibylline Leaves*, Coleridge wrote that Humphry Davy was:

---

6   Robert Southey to Mrs. Fletcher, Keswick 30 March 1831, quoted in Fullmer (p. 128).

7   Jane also wrote some poetry herself; see the letter written to her in 1811 in which Davy comments on part of a poem she has sent: "You want only the habit of connecting pictures from natural imagery with moods of human passion to become a genuine poet" ("Davy Letters"). Maria Edgeworth's letter dated 16 May 1813 to Sophy Ruxton describes the Davys' "dinners and parties": "They see all the world of wit, and much of the world of fashion and rank" (Edgeworth, p. 50). Edgeworth met Byron, Malthus, Baillie, Opie, and Marcet there, among many others.

a man who would have established himself in the first rank of England's living Poets, if the Genius of our country had not decreed that he should rather be the first in the first rank of its Philosophers and scientific Benefactors. (Coleridge, p. 90)

Walter Scott agreed, noting that Coleridge's compliment was "as just as it is handsomely recorded" and that "I have myself heard [Davy] repeat poetry of the highest order of composition" (*Letters* 11: 442). Joseph Cottle, publisher of the *Lyrical Ballads*, described Davy as such: "it was impossible to doubt, that if he had not shone as a philosopher, he would have become conspicuous as a poet" (*Letters* 1: 263). John Gibson Lockhart is also glowing in his praise: "an illustrious philosopher, who was also a true poet – and might have been one of the greatest of poets had he chosen" (*Letters* 2: 275). Lockhart later writes: "Davy was by nature a poet" (*Letters* 6: 244). In 1799, Southey told Davy he thought that one of the poems he published in first volume of the *Annual Anthology* on Mount's Bay had an "elevation" in its blank verse like an "organ swell", which he had also felt "from the rythm [*sic*] of Milton" (*Southey Letters*, 4 May 1799). But privately to William Taylor, Southey declared of "Sons of Genius," another of Davy's poems, that "towards the close ... there are some fine stanzas, but as a whole it is tedious and feeble" (*Southey Letters*, 27 October 1799). In turn, Taylor considered Davy's poem "Song of Pleasure" to be "brilliant ... but he has not breathed the air of Helicon so familiarly as the light of nature, or not so inspiringly"; the play on the idea of inspiration presumably refers to Davy's chemical experiments with gases and his extensive tests on himself with the euphoria-inducing nitrous oxide (qtd. in Fullmer, p. 129). These texts inspired a poem called "On breathing the Nitrous Oxide", written in a notebook (RI HD 13c: 4-6).[8]

In a postscript to a letter to Coleridge, dated 8-9 June 1800, Davy notes that he has moved his furniture out into the garden and is writing under the shade of an apple tree: "thus I begin to claim a relationship with nature", he writes ("Davy Letters"). A month later, in a notebook entry dated 11 July 1800, Davy records what might be described as a characteristically "Romantic" experience:

To day for the first time in my life I have had a distinct sympathy with nature
I was lying on the top of a rock in leeward, the wind was high & everything

---

8   For a discussion of this poem see Ruston.

in motion, the branches of an oak above waving & murmuring to the breeze, yellow clouds deepened by grey at the base were ^{rapidly} floating over the western hills the whole sky was in motion, the yellow stream below was ^{agitated by the breeze} me was likewise flowing is this analogy? – Every seemed alive & myself part of the series of visible impressions I should have felt pain in tearing a leaf from one of the trees – deeply & intimately connected are all our ideas of motion & life – & – this probably, from very early associations how different is the idea of life in a philsiologist [*sic*] & a poet! (RI HD 13d: 9-10)[9]

This passage is suffused with images of movement and harmony. Everything in the image is in motion; there is a reflection between the motion of the sky and the "stream below" and it is clear that this movement is indicative of life. Davy seems to be suggesting here that leaves feel the same pain as humans, and that he is connected to the living world in such a way that he would also feel the pain of the leaf. Both Fullmer and Davy's other recent biographer, David Knight, quote this passage and regard it as evidence of Davy's growing belief in the diverging sentiments of the poet and the chemist. Fullmer writes, for example: "Davy, the poet, and Davy, the physiologist and chemist, were already or were very soon to be at odds" (Fullmer, p. 148). It does seem clear that it was at Bristol that Davy decided definitively to concentrate his efforts on his scientific pursuits. On 20 February 1800, Southey tells William Taylor of Davy: "chemistry, I clearly see, will possess him wholly and too exclusively … in poetry he will do nothing more" (*Southey Letters*). However, in this passage from his private notebook Davy is not necessarily exclaiming at the differences between the ideas of life held by physiologists and poets. He could instead be saying perhaps that as both a physiologist and poet he has a very different idea of life from other people. The misspelling of 'philsiologist' might also carry an association with Coleridge's interest in philology perhaps. Certainly Davy's idea of life is paramount in the poem discussed for the remainder of this essay, "The Life of the Spinosist".

FROM MANUSCRIPT TO PRINTED POEM

We have in one of his letters from 9 October 1800 Coleridge's comments on an early notebook poem by Davy, titled "The Life of the Spinosist". After

---

9   Knight also quotes this passage (Knight, p. 189) as does Fullmer (Fullmer, p. 148). It seems that they took their text from John Davy's *Memoirs* since the original is far less coherent (*Works*, 1: 66-7).

receiving these comments, the poem was revised following Coleridge's advice (Davy RI HD 13c: 7-10; Coleridge *Letters* 1: 630-34).[10] The same poem is published in this revised form by John Ayrton Paris in his 1831 *Life of Sir Humphry Davy* (Paris 84-86), and by John Davy in his 1836 *Memoirs*, under the title "Written After Recovery from a Dangerous Illness" (1: 390-92). It was then reprinted in John Davy's edited *Collected Works* of 1839 (*Works*, 1: 114-16). The poem was also printed within Davy's lifetime and both Paris and John Davy take their text from this version. An imprint of this "original impression" has survived inserted into Michael Faraday's copy of Paris's *Life* in the Royal Institution archive.[11] A much different version of the poem with the title "Life" also appears anonymously in a book edited by Joanna Baillie in 1823 (Baillie 156-62). This was clearly a poem that Davy valued enough to publish later in his life and which he continued to work on throughout that time. I will here compare the manuscript version (c. 1800), the first published version (c. 1807; reprinted in the *Memoirs*), and the last published version (1823).

It seems likely that the manuscript version called "The Life of the Spinosist" is the original version of the poem and that this is the version that Coleridge had seen and commented upon in his letter of 9 October 1800 (see the p. 96-97 for a transcription of this poem). We can tell this because some of the words that Coleridge objects to are still visible in this version of the poem though they have been overwritten by Davy:

In your Poem "impressive" is used for impress*ible* or passive, is it not? – If so, it is not English – life-diffus*ive* likewise is not English – The last Stanza introduces *confusion* into my mind, and despondency – & has besides been so often said by the Materialists &c, that it is not worth repeating –. If the Poem had ended more originally, in short, but for the last Stanza, I will venture to affirm that there were never so many lines which so uninterruptedly combined natural & beautiful words with strict philosophic Truths, i.e. *scientifically* philosophic. – Of the 2,

---

10 Coleridge was writing to Davy at the Royal Institution from Keswick. Around this time Davy went on an excursion "to see Tintern Abbey by moonlight" ("Davy Letters" 20 October [1800]).

11 Faraday's Life of Davy, Royal Institution, F8, facing page 84. The poem has no title. In Faraday's handwriting at the top of the first page is written: "one of the original impressions MF." The imprint is published by "Savage and Easingwood, Printers, Bedford Bury, London". William Savage was Assistant Secretary at the Royal Institution between 1800 and 1843; he also had a printing press and did some printing work for the R. I. (James, p. 399).

3, 4, 5, 6th, & 7th Stanzas I am doubtful which is the most beautiful. – Do not imagine, that I cling to a fond love of future identity – but the thought, which you have expressed in the last Stanza, might be more grandly, & therefore more consolingly, exemplified – I had forgot to say – that "sameness & identity" are words too etymologically the same to be placed so close to each other. (*Letters* 1: 630)[12]

Coleridge is most impressed with the poem's ability to express scientific truth beautifully. This version of the poem contains ten stanzas, discernible despite the crossings out and revisions. They fall into quatrains, loosely of iambic pentameter, with lines rhyming alternately. Spinosists believe that matter and thought are attributes of God and this poem explores this view, showing us an active nature in the eternal process of becoming living forms, constantly transmuting into other, new forms. In Davy's first published scientific "Essay", this is the most sublime idea of all: "No more sublime idea can be formed of the motions of matter, than to conceive that the different species are continually changing into each other" (*Works* 2: 29 n.). The title of the manuscript poem signifies not the life of a Spinosist, but life according to a Spinosist. Lockhart must be referring to this poem when he writes: "for who that has read his sublime quatrains on the doctrine of Spinoza can doubt that he might have united, if he had pleased, in some great didactic poem, the vigorous ratiocination of Dryden and the moral majesty of Wordsworth?" (6: 245). Though referring to two poets, like Coleridge Lockhart

---

12 John Davy wrote: "Coleridge's critical remarks apply to it as it was first written; the words objected to are not to be found in its corrected printed state" (*Fragmentary Remains* 81n.). Wahida Amin, who has completed a doctoral thesis on Davy's poetry, has discovered what seems to be an intervening text between the original manuscript version ("The Life of the Spinosist") and the "original impression" in another notebook (RI HD 26h: 15). It has the revisions that Coleridge suggested and is almost exactly the same as John Davy's version but with a few interesting (and substantive) changes. It is of course entirely possible that this poem went through other stages of development and that other versions of the text were produced. Amin has also found other manuscript versions that largely follow the text of the first impression. Clement Carlyon presents another version of this poem, which he says Davy gave to him (1: 236-39). This poem was read out by Davy "at the request of Coleridge", but the version published by Carlyon still contains words that Coleridge advised against (1: 235). I am indebted to Wahida Amin for this information. In this essay, I compare what appear to be the major stages of the poem's development, from the original manuscript version, to the "original impression" as quoted in *Collected Works*, to the 1823 published edition in Baillie's collection.

here emphasises the combination in Davy's poetry of two distinct aspects that are perhaps akin to truth and beauty.

While the version in the *Memoirs* (almost identical with the first printed version) generally follows the manuscript version with the revision of the words to which Coleridge objected, the tenth stanza of the manuscript poem is entirely missing in the printed version, and this concerns the relation between human thought and the rest of the natural world. In this stanza the word Coleridge objected to, "Impressive", is still visible beneath the new word "Impressible", and the word "deep" has been inserted between "sameness" and "identity", perhaps to offset their similarity:

> Linked to the whole the human mind displays
> No sameness & no ^{deep} identity ~~divine~~
> Changeful as the surface of the seas
> Impressible as is the ~~blue~~ moving sky
> ~~To scattered thoughts some unknown laws are given~~
> ~~By which they join and move in circling life.~~ (RI HD 13c: 7-8)[13]

These sentiments are entirely absent from the *Memoirs* version; here the human mind is constantly changing and is impressed upon by "the whole" as the sea or the clouds are by wind. Here Davy emphasises both the connections between the individual and the universe and also the constant mutation of the human mind. Despite the changefulness of thoughts, which have no deep identity of their own but are instead part of something much larger than themselves, Davy does believe there is something that connects and brings them together. In the crossed-out lines at the bottom of the stanza, he considers in a scientific manner that there might be "some unknown laws" that unify thoughts and maintain them as a part of the "circling life" described throughout the poem. Such statements can be connected to Davy's scientific writings, in which he suggests that the object of chemistry should be the search for such laws.[14] More generally the poem considers the ways in which life mutates: one living form "becomes" another (such as in the

---

13 Coleridge also objected to the phrase "life diffus*ive*" in his letter. In the manuscript version, this is "life diffus*ing*" but it does look as though Davy has altered the word from "diffus*ive*", perhaps following Coleridge's comments (HD RI 13c: 10).

14 For example, in his 1802 *Discourse* Davy writes that chemistry and natural history are intimately related, for while the latter concerns itself with the bodies of the external world "in their permanent and unchanging forms", chemistry instead looks at "the

way that dew "becomes" a flower), forms are "renovated" from "ancient" times, and all aspects of nature (suns, storms, land) are "but engines of that powerful will", which is God (RI HD 13c: 7).

The poem as it was printed in Davy's lifetime and reprinted by John Davy in *Memoirs* is much longer than the manuscript version. It has eighteen stanzas and is far more polished, though it retains many of the original stanzas, largely intact, and the sentiments of the manuscript version. Broadly, seven stanzas of the original ten are retained with varying degrees of revision. The following stanza is present in the manuscript version but does not appear in the published version:

> To feel the social flame to give to man
> Ten thousand signs of ~~kindling~~ burning energy,
> The nothingness of human words to scan
> The nothingness of human things cares to fly. (RI HD 13c: 9)[15]

This nihilism can also be sensed in the longer version of the poem but in the published version there is more extended contact with other people than is described here. There is a whole section beginning "To mingle with its kindred" that contemplates social relationships and duties, which also eventually recognises "how transient is the breath of praise", perhaps in explication of "the nothingness of human words" (*Memoirs* 1: 391, ll. 45, 53). Towards the end of both versions, there is a turning away from human life to "live in forests mingled with the whole / Of natural forms" (*Memoirs* 1: 391, ll. 57-8). In the lines quoted above from the manuscript version, there is perhaps a greater despondency with the pointlessness of the human world, with the inability of our words to be meaningful more generally, and with the futility of our lives. This might be seen as quite different from Davy's other scientific writings, which characteristically feature bombastic visions of the future (see for example *Works* 2: 319). Perhaps in his poetry, Davy could allow himself to indulge in feelings of despondency and negativity that he could not express in his other work.

---

laws of their alterations" and the "active powers" within them (*Collected Works* II, p. 312).

15 As can be seen here, and as is witnessed in other versions of the poem, Davy uses both the terms 'man' and 'human'. I assume that he uses these terms with specific reference and follow his use in my discussion.

The version that John Davy reprinted in the *Memoirs* was published under the title "Written After Recovery from a Dangerous Illness", referring to the typhus (or "gaol fever") which Davy thought he had contracted at Newgate Prison in 1807. For the first few months of 1808 Davy was unable to lecture or do any research at the Royal Institution. Davy had also been ill in the winter of 1799 (a "fairly serious illness" according to Fullmer) and given that the manuscript version of this poem is written in his notebook immediately after his poem "On breathing the Nitrous Oxide", these facts may date the original manuscript poem to early 1800 (Fullmer, p. 131). In the poem's description of the vitality of the natural world we can perhaps see a renewed sense of life, felt as Davy's health returned to him, which was reflected in the joy he experienced in the life around him. Though the printed version is longer than the poem's manuscript version, it is clear that there was much in the original version that Davy liked and kept. For example, the first two stanzas are almost identical, and small changes, such as "sordid dust" becoming "insensate dust", had already suggested themselves to Davy in the crossed-out lines at the beginning of the poem in manuscript (RI HD 13c: 7; *Memoirs* 1: 390, l. 4). Other words were perhaps changed because they were too scientific; for example, we find "limpid" replacing "liquid" in "limpid dew" (RI HD 13c: 7; *Memoirs* 1: 390, l. 3). The exclamatory, stressed syllable that begins the poem's opening line is retained from the original and emphasised with punctuation; it is perhaps reminiscent of a hymn but is certainly not an unusual feature in poetry at this time. Coleridge even used this device himself in a 1792 translation, "A Wish Written in Jesus Wood", in the opening line: "Lo! through the dusky silence of the groves."[16] From the sixth stanza onwards, Davy's published version of his poem uses the same technique as the manuscript one, increasingly proceeding by means of the infinitive form of the verb to express the earth's and humankind's potentiality. By this technique, Davy presents his sentiments as representative of humankind more generally, while there is also the possibility that these lines also contain more personal reflections upon his own life.

The extra stanzas in the *Memoirs* version, as mentioned, concern social life, and may well reflect Davy's confirmed status as man of the moment around 1807-08: "in public life to shine; ... The idol of to-day, the man divine" (*Memoirs* 1: 391, ll. 46, 48). By this time, Davy had moved from Bristol to the Royal Institution of Great Britain; he was a hugely popular lecturer and

---

16 "A Wish Written in Jesus Wood" was a translation of John Jortin's *Votum* (Coleridge: *Poetical Works* 1 (2), p. 64-5).

in 1807 he isolated potassium through the use of electrochemical apparatus. Interestingly, given the fact that many of the changes Coleridge suggested were made to the published version, Davy does not heed Coleridge's advice that he change the final stanza. The original ends with the following:

> To die in agony & in many days
> To give to Nature all her stolen powers
> Etherial fire to feed the solar rays
> Etherial dew to feed the earth in showers (RI HD 13c: 10)

While the published version is perhaps a little more consoling, as Coleridge requested, it is equally susceptible to Coleridge's charge of materialism. The first line is changed, but the final three are largely the same, with the revision of "borrow'd" for "stolen", which is substantive, and the new use of "glad" as a verb in the final line:

> To quit the burdens of its earthly days,
>   To give to Nature all her borrow'd powers, –
> Etherial fire to feed the solar rays,
>   Etherial dew to glad the earth with showers. (Coleridge 392, ll. 69-72)

Coleridge's greatest objection was to the final stanza of the poem: he found it unoriginal and to the detriment of a poem that he otherwise considered a feat of combined scientific knowledge and poetic expression. Davy may have retained it because of its reference to a scientific process we would now call photosynthesis, which had been discovered (though not named as such) by Joseph Priestley in the early 1770s. While removing the reference to dying in agony might be considered consoling, the sentiments in the final stanza of the published version are certainly not more "grandly" expressed as Coleridge desired – in fact they are strikingly similarly expressed. In other respects too the versions are the same, describing how states change, transforming into other forms, and how animation spreads from one form to the next with the coming of spring. The world is in constant motion; the translucent dew turns red and forms long-forgotten rise again, "renovated" by this renewed life. Davy thought that the study of such transformations defined the science of chemistry. In *Elements of Chemical Philosophy* (1812) he writes that "most of the substances belonging to our globe are constantly undergoing alterations in sensible qualities, and one variety of matter becomes as it were transmuted into another". He adds: "the object of Chemical

Philosophy is to ascertain the causes of all phenomena of this kind, and to discover the laws by which they are governed" (*Works* 4:1). This poem, in its manuscript and first printed form, addresses the same issues of the transmutation of matter and the search for a law to explain such transmutation.

Certainly the final stanza of the published version could still be charged with Coleridge's accusation that it expresses a materialist sentiment. After death we give back the "fire" and "dew" that we had only borrowed from nature during our lifetimes, recognising that the matter from which we are made is the same as that of other natural beings. Perhaps Davy's refusal to revise this as Coleridge suggested is due to the idea that "fire" here refers to a part of us that is immortal rather than material. The idea that the source of living powers is eternal would fit other references in Davy's poetry. This may be further evidence for the case that poetry permitted Davy to be more candid in his philosophy and to express ideas that he would not have expressed in his scientific writings.

"LIFE" (1823)

Given the similarity between the manuscript version and the printed version, and the vast difference between these and the 1823 version of the poem published in Joanna Baillie's collection, I suspect that the latter was written later than the two versions considered so far. It is far longer – thirty-four stanzas in total, almost double the length of the "original impression" – and while it uses some of the earlier versions' words, phrases, and occasionally complete stanzas, it has shifted from a poem describing Spinosist thought to one that identifies itself as a poem on "Life". Baillie had known for many years before this that Davy wrote poetry.[17] We have evidence of this in a letter dated 1816, which Baillie writes to Lady Davy regarding her physician brother, Matthew Baillie: "My brother, who does not read much poetry, has been delighted with Sir Humphrey's [*sic*] verses" (*Letters* 1:497).[18] There is a chance that these "verses" are the poem in question

---

17   Judith Slagle notes that Baillie "probably met Lady and Sir Humphry Davy as neighbors or through the scientific community attached to Dr. Baillie"; both Matthew Baillie and the Davys lived in Grosvenor Square as well as being "close professional acquaintances" (Slagle, p. 281).

18   Baillie and Lady Davy corresponded from 1813 to 1850 and became good friends. This correspondence is held in the Mitchell Library, Glasgow, and has been transcribed by Slagle in Baillie's *Letters* 1: 494-527.

given that Baillie continues: "Mrs Baillie says if they were generally known they would do good to all the young men of the kingdom. Most certainly pious sentiments so finely introduced & expressed, and coming from such a quarter, would not be considered as allied to weakness" (*Letters* 1: 497). The verses Baillie praises here may well have been the "Spinosist" poem revised into its new form with far more orthodox Christian sentiment on show. If so, the poem has come a long way from the materialism to which Coleridge originally objected. The suggestion that writing poems might be considered a "weakness" is interesting and perhaps has some bearing on Davy's decision not to publish his poetry. In any case when Baillie put together her collection of poems in 1823, she was aware that Davy had poetry written in manuscript.

The collection was put together to raise money for a friend, Mrs. James Stirling, and in its title declared that the poems included were *Chiefly Manuscript*. Baillie also asked Anna Barbauld, Thomas Campbell, George Crabbe, Anne Grant of Lagan, Felicia Hemans, Anne Home Hunter (wife of the surgeon John Hunter), Anna Maria Porter, Samuel Rogers, Walter Scott, William Sotheby, Southey, Wordsworth, and Charlotte Dacre to contribute unpublished poems (Slagle, p. 165). Davy published his poem anonymously though he did allow his name to be included in the subscription list, which is itself an interesting mix of scientific, medical and literary figures (Baillie: *Poems* viii). Judith Slagle notes that in Baillie's letters concerning this publication she reveals both her "critical perception, and tactful editing", on one occasion returning John Herschel's poem for revision because it was not good enough (Slagle, p. 165). Asking Sir Thomas Lawrence, then President of the Royal Academy, to contribute Baillie tells him: "Sir Humphrey [*sic*] Davy has been kind enough to give me one of his, and to have poems from two distinguished Presidents would be very flattering to my vanity were there no better purpose to serve by it" (*Letters* 1: 490-91). Davy had become President of the Royal Society by this time and perhaps this role also made him feel that he should not publish poetry with his name attached to it.

As has already been suggested, the "Life" poem is very different from the earlier versions here considered. It certainly is not the case that the earlier poem is simply incorporated into the longer one, though consideration of the longer poem further explicates the shorter one, since many ideas are unpacked at greater length in "Life". In the same vein as the earlier versions, this poem imagines an individual life, from infancy to death, of a person who is always referred to by the pronoun "it", perhaps to suggest that the imagined subject could be female as much as male. The "Life" poem is less concerned with matter changing into other forms; much of this material has been left behind. In the first stanza, the "ministering spirits from above" are made more responsible for the new life that is witnessed, where in the earlier published and manuscript versions "bounteous Nature" "gives" the "flames of life", which are merely poured over the earth by "kindling spirits" (*Memoirs* 1: 390, ll. 1-4). The "Life" poem still concerns new life but at the start of the poem perhaps this is less the coming of spring than the beginning of the universe. There is less the sense of a natural cycle of life and more a sense of entirely new life: "Where all was dull and dark, inert and cold, / Now power and motion, light and heat abound" (Baillie: *Poems* 156, ll. 5-6). The words "dark" and "inert" were used in the *Memoirs* poem to describe the way that all "mortal things" would be but for the "power" of the "One Intelligence" (*Memoirs* 1: 390, ll. 10-14). In "Life" the reference to the earth's dynamic forces is new and the "power" exercised is "creative" (Baillie: *Poems* 157, l. 21).

The mortal world before God's intervention is likened in the earlier published version to "an unharmonious band / Silent as are the harp's untuned strings / Without the touches of the poet's hand" (*Memoirs* 1: 390, ll. 14-16). This is a distinctly Romantic image, reminding us of Coleridge's "The Eolian Harp" (1795). In Davy's poem, God brings the world to life as a poet creates music on an otherwise silent instrument. In the "Life" version there is an interesting alteration of this image. The initial lines are identical but it is the "minstrel's" rather than the "poet's" hand that brings the instrument to life (Baillie: *Poems* 157, l. 21). The change fits the new version's association of the minstrel with heroic poetry and nationalism; the "Life" poem reaches out far more widely than the earlier one, dealing with national and political issues as well as philosophical ones. The change may also indicate a shift away from a more Romantic sentiment, concerned with vitalism and nature's mutability, though Platonic feeling can still be perceived. In the "Life" poem, Davy writes "A portion of the one Intelligence, / Th'immortal mind of man its image bears": while "man" is made in God's image, this phrase still sounds distinctly Platonic (Baillie: *Poems* 157, ll. 29-30). It is also the case that in this instance (though not elsewhere in the poem) the change results in a far less orthodox sentiment. In the *Memoirs* version we have "The immortal mind of man His image bears", which need not be construed as necessarily alluding to Platonism and is far more likely an allusion to God. The "Life" poem continues to mix Platonism with Christianity in the following lines referring to the "child of mortality": "Feelings its life amidst the forms of death / To be eternal, not a spark that flies / But a pure portion of th'immortal breath" (Baillie: *Poems* 158, ll. 41-42). Here Davy rejects the metaphor of the "spark" because it is short-lived and instead finds that human life partakes of God's immortality. He does, though, compare this to a "flame" that endures (Baillie: *Poems* 158, l. 41, 45).

The poem then proceeds to imagine humanity as a child being breast-fed by "its" mother (Baillie: *Poems* 158, l. 50). This person is imagined first appreciating nature's beauty and then the beauty of fellow humans, which is a "higher joy" in the "Life" poem but merely a "nobler charm" in the *Memoirs* version. It awakens "sympathy" and compels "love" in both versions (Baillie: *Poems* 159, ll. 58, 60; *Memoirs* 1: 391, ll. 37, 40). In the "Life" poem this seems to lead to marriage ("The heavenly balm of mutual hope") and even to fatherhood, which Davy never experienced personally, with both states described using natural metaphors (Baillie: *Poems* 159, l. 61). There follows a much-extended passage on the "civic ties" of "the man divine" (159, ll. 68, 72). If this section was extended in the first printed version (compared to the earliest manuscript version) because Davy was at the "meridian" of his career in 1807, this far longer section in "Life" perhaps reveals his awareness of the waning of his fortunes (*Memoirs* 1: 391, l. 32; Baillie: *Poems* 159, l. 76). Knight tells us that had Davy died in 1819 his reputation "would have been glittering" (*DNB*). The year 1823 held a number of disappointments for Davy, including his protégé Michael Faraday's election to the Royal Society (which Davy opposed) and his less than successful research into the copper bottoms of the navy's warships. There are some interesting applications of scientific knowledge in both versions of the poem, such as the use of gravitation as a metaphor in the description of the "strong" influence that "man" uses to "govern others" (*Memoirs* 1: 391, l. 49; Baillie: *Poems* 159, l. 73). Just as gravitation (that "high law") causes waves to occur when the moon is at its highest point (its "meridian"), so "man" can influence others when he is at the height of his power. However, the "Life" poem deals at far greater length with the temporary nature of this "meridian" and notes rather despondently that the "strong arm of power" is "quickly palsied" (*Poems* 159, l. 77). Again we can see that this poem causes Davy to reflect upon his career and achievements, but here the reflection is rather more subdued.

The "Life" poem then moves outwards to consider "the mighty victims of the lust / Of domination fall'n" in a lengthy section that does not appear in earlier versions, which seems to owe much to the death of Napoleon in 1821 (Baillie: *Poems* 160, ll. 81-82). Napoleon could be alluded to as one of "those whose triumphs kept the world in awe", "Who played with sceptres and dispos'd of thrones", and who died in "inglorious exile" on

Saint Helena (Baillie: *Poems* 160, ll. 85, 86, 88). The minstrel is evoked again here as Davy describes how once "millions sung" of these "great achievements" but now "not a tongue / Daring, except in whisp'rings low to speak / Of their high deeds" (Baillie: *Poems*, 160, ll. 86, 88-90). Despite Davy's intense patriotism, his admiration of Napoleon may be witnessed here; such admiration can also be seen in Byron's poems. There is a sense that Davy too sees "glory's light" rising "from arms and empire", or from losing one's freedom, or for those who die "for their country and their laws" (Baillie: *Poems* 160, ll. 90-92). It seems the fate of man to rise in this way only to "wake from low ambition's splendid dream" and recognise the reality of "Its gauds, its playthings, its toys" (Baillie: *Poems* 160, l. 97). The word "gaud" has a number of meanings that are pertinent; it can be a plaything or toy, a sport or trick, and an ornamental bead (*Oxford English Dictionary*). The metaphors drawn from the natural world to explicate this make the allusion clear; these "gauds" are "Like glitt'ring foam upon the turbid stream, / Or Iris' tints upon the falling rain" (Baillie: *Poems* 160, ll. 99-100). These are things that glitter and seem to be precious when in fact they are not. Iris is a Greek goddess and messenger whose sign was the rainbow. The glinting foam in the murky water and the tints of colour in the rain sparkle but have no substance. At this point the individual held to represent humankind evinces characteristics even more strikingly similar to Davy himself. The decision is taken at this point:

> To dwell upon utility alone,
>> As the true source of honour, to aspire
> To something which posterity may own,
>> A guiding lamp, not a consuming fire [.] (Baillie: *Poems* 160, ll. 101-104)

This surely is a reference to the miner's safety lamp, or Davy lamp, which he did not patent and so it is owned by posterity in more senses than simply that it will live on beyond his lifetime. He claims here that he has moved from a destructive ambition to considering only what good he can do for others. He also determines to dedicate his life to the adoration of God and his works.

CONCLUSION

From the evidence of a single poem, we can see Davy's shifting sensibilities, his changing philosophical and religious views, and his evaluation of his personal career and scientific achievements. There are many connections to be drawn with Davy's scientific writings, particularly in comparison with the early manuscript and first printed versions of this poem. In these he discusses the object and purpose of chemistry: to study the transmutation of matter and attempt to reach an understanding of the laws behind such changes. Coleridge thought that the manuscript version of the poem combined beautiful expression with scientific truth, thus combining the skills of the chemist and the poet. In the last known version of the poem, Davy is far more orthodox in his views. His early reference to materialism is unthinkable in this poem that ascribes life and mutability to God. That said, there is still some evidence of Platonic thought in Davy's final version of the poem as he yearns for something that will last beyond the trinkets of worldly ambition. Poetry seems to have offered Davy a space in which to voice ideas that, as President of the Royal Society, he was not able to express publicly, and to reflect upon his success and failures.

WORKS CITED

Baillie, Joanna (ed.): *A Collection of Poems, Chiefly Manuscript, and from Living Authors*. London: Longman, Hurst, Rees, Orme, and Brown, 1823.

—: *The Collected Letters of Joanna Baillie*. Judith Slagle (ed.). 2 vols. Madison, Teaneck: Fairleigh Dickinson University Press; London: Associated University Presses, 1999.

Benger, Elizabeth: *The Memoirs of Mr. John Tobin*. London: Longman, Hurst, Rees, and Orme, 1820.

Carlyon, Clement: *Early Years and Late Reflections*. 2 vols. London: Whittaker, 1843.

Coleridge, S. T.: *The Collected Letters of Samuel Taylor Coleridge*. E. L. Griggs (ed.), 5 vols. Oxford: Clarendon Press, 1956-71.

—: *Sibylline Leaves: A Collection of Poems*. London: Rest Fenner, 1817.

—: *Poetical Works*. J. C. C. Mays (ed.), vol. 1. New Jersey: Princeton University Press, 2001.

Cottle, Joseph: *Reminiscences of Samuel Taylor Coleridge and Robert Southey*, 2 vols. London: Houlston and Stoneman, 1847.

Davy, H.: *The Collected Works of Humphry Davy*. John Davy (ed.), 9 vols. London: Smith, Edgeworth, 1839.

Elder, and Co.: "Davy Letters". Tim Fulford and Sharon Ruston (eds.), 1839. www.davy-letters.org.uk; (20 Nov. 2012).

—: "Prologue (*Written by a* FRIEND)" in *The Honey Moon: A Comedy, in Five Acts [...]*. By John Tobin. London: Longman, Hurst, Rees, and Orme, 1805.

Davy, John: *Memoirs of the Life of Sir Humphry Davy, Bart*, 2 vols. London: Longman, Rees, Orme, Brown, Green and Longman, 1836.

—: ed. *Fragmentary Remains, Literary and Scientific, of Sir Humphry Davy, Bart.* London: John Churchill, 1858.

Fullmer, June: *Young Humphry Davy: The Making of an Experimental Chemist.* Philadelphia: American Philosophical Society, 2000.

Godwin, William: *The Diary of William Godwin.* V. Myers, D. O'Shaughnessy and M. Philp (eds.): http://godwindiary.bodleian.ox.ac.uk (29 Nov. 2012).

Holmes, Richard: *The Age of Wonder: How the Romantic Generation Discovered the Beauty and Terror of Science.* London: Harper Press, 2008.

James, Frank A. J. L.: *"The Common Purposes of Life": Science and Society at the Royal Institution of Great Britain.* Aldershot, Hants: Ashgate, 2002.

Jay, Mike: *The Atmosphere of Heaven: The Unnatural Experiments of Dr Beddoes and his Sons of Genius.* New Haven / London: Yale University Press, 2009.

Knight, David: *Humphry Davy: Science and Power.* Oxford: Blackwell, 1992.

—: "Davy, Sir Humphry, baronet (1778-1829)" in H. C. G. Matthew and Brian Harrison (eds.): *Oxford Dictionary of National Biography.* Oxford: OUP, 2004. Online ed.: Lawrence Goldman (ed.), Jan. 2011: www.oxforddnb.com (29 Nov. 2012).

Lockhart, John Gibson: *Memoirs of the Life of Sir Walter Scott, Bart,* 10 vols. London: R. Cadell, 1839.

Edgeworth, Maria: *Maria Edgeworth: Letters from England, 1813-1844.* Christina Colvin (ed.). Oxford: Clarendon Press, 1971.

Moore, Thomas: *M.P., or, the Blue-Stocking, A Comic Opera, in three acts, first performed at the English Opera, Theatre Royal, Lyceum, on Monday, Sept. 9, 1811.* London: J. Power, 1811.

Paris, John Ayrton: *The Life of Sir Humphry Davy.* London: H. Colburn and R. Bentley, 1831.

Ruston, S.: "When respiring gas inspired poetry" in *The Lancet* 381 (2 February 2013), pp. 366-67.

Scott, W.: *The Journal of Sir Walter Scott.* W. E. K. Anderson (ed.). Oxford: Clarendon Press, 1972.

—: *The Letters of Sir Walter Scott.* H. J. C. Grierson (ed.), 12 vols. London: Constable, 1932.

Sharrock, R.: "The Chemist and the Poet: Sir Humphry Davy and the Preface to *Lyrical Ballads*" in *Notes and Records of the Royal Society* 17:1 (1962), pp. 57-76.

Slagle, Judith: *Joanna Baillie: A Literary Life.* New Jersey: Farleigh Dickinson University Press, 2002.

Southey, Robert: *The Collected Letters of Robert Southey.* I. Packer and L. Pratt (eds.), 8 Parts, A Romantic Circles Electronic Edition, Part One: 1791-1797 and Part Two: 1798-1803. www.rc.umd.edu, 29 Nov. 2012.

Stansfield, Dorothy A.: *Thomas Beddoes, M.D., 1760-1808: Chemist, Physician, Democrat.* Germany: Springer, 1984.

Vickers, Neil: "Coleridge, Thomas Beddoes and Brunonian Medicine" in *European Romantic Review* 8.1 (1997), pp. 47-94.

Wordsworth, Jonathan: "Introduction" in *The Annual Anthology.* Robert Southey (ed.). Washington: Woodstock Books, 1997.

Wordsworth, William: *The Letters of William and Dorothy Wordsworth*. E. de
Selincourt (ed.), 8 vols. 2nd ed. Oxford: Clarendon Press, 1967.
—: and S. T. Coleridge: *Lyrical Ballads, with a few other poems*. London: J. & A. Arch,
1798.
Wu, Duncan: "Lyrical Ballads (1798): the Beddoes Copy" in *The Library* 15 (1993),
pp. 332-5.

<u>The Life of the Spinosist</u> (HD RI 13c: 17-10)
~~The insensate dust is seen to~~
~~The dust insensate rises into life~~
~~The liquid dew is lovely in the flower~~
~~The liquid dew becomes the rosy flower~~
<u>The Spinosist</u>
Lo o'er the earth the kindling spirits pour
The ~~spark~~ seeds of life that ~~mighty~~ bounteous nature gives. —
The liquid dew becomes the rosy flower
The sordid dust awakes & moves & lives. —
All, All is change, the renovated forms
Of ancient things arise & live again.
The light of suns the angry breath of storms
The everlasting motions of the main
Are but the engines of that powerful will. —
The eternal link of thoughts where form resolves
Has ever acted & is acting still
Whilst age round age & world round world revolves.
2 Linked to the whole the human mind displays
1 No sameness & no deep identity ~~divine~~
Changeful as the surface of the seas
4 2 Impressible as is the ~~blue~~ moving sky
~~To scattered thoughts some unknown laws are given~~
~~By which they join and move in circling life. —~~
Being of aggregate the power of love
Gives it ~~the life~~ the joy of moments bids it rise
In the wild forms of mortal things to move
Fix'd to the earth below the eternal skies
To breath the ether; & to feel the form
Of orbed beauty through its organs thrill
To press the limbs of life with rapture warm

And drink of transport from a living rill. —
To view the heavens with ~~solar~~ morning radiance ~~white~~ bright
Majestic mingling with ^the ~~still blue ocean~~ ocean blue. —
~~Filled by a thousand silver streams~~
~~& played upon by ten thousand cloudless breezes~~
To view the ~~meadows~~ ^forests green the mountains white
The peopled plains of rich and varied hue. —
To feel the social flame to give to man
Ten thousand signs of ~~kindling~~ burning energy,
The nothingness of human words to scan
The nothingness of human ^things cares to fly. —
To live in forests mingled with ~~the whole~~
Of natures forms, to ~~die beneath upon~~ feel the breezes play
O'er the parched forehead ^brow to see the planets roll
oer their grey head their life diffusing ray
To die in agony & In many days
To give to Nature all her stolen powers
Etherial fire to feed the solar rays
Etherial dew to feed the earth in showers.

AN UNLIKELY CANDIDATE FOR LITERATURE AND SCIENCE: THE NOSTALGIC LUDWIG BOLTZMANN IN ELDORADO

George Rousseau, University of Oxford

THE DESCENT OF A POLYMATH

Ludwig Boltzmann (1844-1906), brilliant Viennese mathematician and physicist, pioneering theorist of chemical gases and thermodynamics, pillar of the Academy of Sciences in Vienna, profound commentator on entropy during its infancy, holder of multiple university chairs, and colleague of Ernst Mach and Max Planck, was by any reckoning one of Europe's leading scientists in the second half of the nineteenth century, especially when German science reached its pinnacle in the lead up to the Great War. He was also an accomplished classical pianist, interested in metaphysics and, towards the end of his life, the author of a literary work, as we shall see. Boltzmann spoke so many languages that he ought to have recognised the threat his name posed in English: the "bolt-man" who might pull the trigger. Indeed he did. On 5 September 1906 he tightened a rope around his neck while hanging from

Ludwig Boltzmann.

a cork tree during a summer holiday in Duino, near Trieste, where Rainer Maria Rilke experienced the profound emotions expressed in his *Duino Elegies* while walking on a pathway high above the sea, looking down on Schloss Duino and inquiring whether anyone had heard the angels sing.

Yet Boltzmann was no latter-day Austrian Odysseus, no nostalgic traveller pining to return to Ithaca and then gazing at the chaos he found, threatening to murder the suitors of his beloved Penelope. As the philosophical novelist Milan Kundera has aptly commented:

> The dawn of ancient Greek culture brought the birth of the *Odyssey*, the founding epic of nostalgia. Let us emphasize: Odysseus, the greatest adventurer of all time, is also the greatest nostalgic. (Kundera, p. 7)

If Odysseus's nostalgia was fuelled by *wanderlust*, Boltzmann's was augmented by his ongoing mentalization of *domestic* and *academic* homes amidst the more generalised medical malady nostalgia had become since the seventeenth century. Nostalgia, pathological longing for the home, the malady generated over confusion about lost homes, the *oikophilia* – or attachment to the home – had arisen in so many forms by the early twentieth century that it is impossible to generalise about it transhistorically (Hacking, pp. 13-19; Roth, pp. 5-8). Whenever Boltzmann's acute bouts of depression caused his imagination to become unhinged from reality, they swept away his residual sense of possessing *any* domestic home. He had been depressive since the death of his father when he was fifteen, but managed to traverse black melancholy's quicksand and distinguish himself academically. He received a doctorate in mathematics at the University of Vienna, a city and university he loved more than any other in Europe. He was brought up as a devout Catholic but no evidence exists that he was a believing Catholic during his adult lifetime. His supervisor had introduced James Clark Maxwell's kinetic theory of gases to continental Europe and was on the cutting edge of physical chemistry. Boltzmann's dissertation extended Maxwell's hypothesis through an approach to statistical mechanics that transformed the chemistry of gases of his era and remained its benchmark for decades. By the early 1870s, decades before quantum mechanics appeared on the scene, Boltzmann demonstrated how to apply mathematics to the motion of molecules contained in gases and then extended the approach to thermodynamic equilibrium.

The result was to endow *time* – abstract, conceptual, historical, philosophical time – with a sense of direction, forward and backward, at the microscopic level (Coveney, pp. 12-57). It amounted to a visionary leap of the first water, as Einstein soon came to realise. And no scientist of Boltzmann's era brooded over the direction of time, whether unidirectional or reversible, more than he did. As Peter Coveney has eloquently written:

> Boltzmann's contribution stands out, although his attempt to rediscover the arrow of time in terms of atomic and molecular behaviour did not convince many of his contemporaries. He shocked physicists of the time by making a link between entropy and probability, thus becoming the first person to give a fundamental law of physics a statistical interpretation. (Coveney, p. 34)

The equation Boltzmann developed from this research described the mathematical motion of a single molecule in gas. Put simply, almost reductively, his equation was the statistical description of the molecule's velocity. It gave rise to a new mathematical law called the "H-function", which decreases as time passes. That is, the mathematical size of the function diminishes as time elapses and thereby provides a complementary arrow to the direction of entropy, which increases as time passes en route to thermodynamic equilibrium. The impact of Boltzmann's equation on physics, mathematics, and chemistry was huge. It appeared to solve the reversibility paradox of time on the molecular level: the notion of the irreversible flow of time throughout the universe from the moment of its creation – this was its two-fold achievement. Yet his colleagues resisted his research – not just the "H-function" but the entirety of Boltzmann's atomism and his repeated demonstrations that atoms constitute matter – which he interpreted as hurling him into the mental space of outsiderdom.

He had already migrated from his native Vienna to Heidelberg, Berlin, Leipzig, Munich, Graz, and other universities – professional displacements that augmented his intensifying depressive sense that he would never find an enduring "home". Even in predictable, staid, *bürgerliche* Graz, in Styria, where he met his future wife, raised their children, and remained longer than in any other place, and where he was Professor Extraordinary as well as Rector, this obdurate pain of the exile tortured him. He further claimed in confidence that Ernst Mach's disgust towards him viscerally "poisoned" him; as acidulously in contrast to the Viennese goulash he remembered, near the end of his life, having relished. So he abandoned Vienna once again, while Mach remained in post. And when Mach – a world-famous man – retired in 1902 owing to poor health, Boltzmann returned to his students in Vienna in the hope he would at last be free to lecture, teach, and conduct research in his native university laboratory. But he could not rival Mach, and the old sense of outsiderdom hounded him even then. Desperate, with nowhere to go, he tightened the noose in Duino. This is the psychological integument – its interior life remains to be narrativized.

By that fateful day in September 1906 Boltzmann was also an internationally eminent scientist. Why then did it matter so much to him that he appeared to be losing out to the "energeticists" – the camp of renowned scientists including Wilhelm Ostwald, Ernst Mach, and G. F. Helm who opposed atomism as the basic principle of chemico-physical reality? This is the quintessential question to put to Boltzmann, and the range of plausible answers can only be grasped through comprehension of the unique niche Ostwald occupied in Boltzmann's mental universe. Ostwald was Mach's great friend and supporter: the two appeared to Boltzmann a phalanx pitted against him, Ostwald having already developed the most successful physical chemistry laboratory in the world in Leipzig during the 1880s and Mach occupying the University Chair in Vienna Boltzmann avidly sought. Ostwald had also founded the first major journal in physical chemistry and written the subject's definitive textbook. If this were insufficient, Ostwald won the Noble Prize in Chemistry in 1909 for his investigations into chemical statistics and reaction velocity, three years after Boltzmann's suicide. By 1914 the Wilhelmine authorities considered Ostwald the foremost scientist of his generation, capable of enabling the production of explosives in the Great War against the Allies.

Ostwald's most basic idea was *energy* – the energy that permeates the universe – and he believed that energy alone and no other concept could explain the entirety of science. His professional mission was never to permit atomism to dethrone the supremacy of energy. He was predestined, he thought, to demonstrate energy's explanatory superiority to all other concepts: a pursuit he hardly viewed as personally motivated, as some irrational *cri de coeur* tugging at him. However, in time the idea that *energy* explains *all* chemico-physical reality turned out to be thoroughly false. Ostwald was wrong, yet Mach spurred him on in his undertaking, as did the physicist Georg Helm; their collaboration was a Helm-Mach-Ostwald-alliance invested in energy and, from 1890 forward, in generating an energy equation capable of toppling, and replacing, Boltzmann's H-function. This summary simplifies the complex science involved but does not falsify it or exaggerate the intellectual war that raged between atomism and energy.

Their attacks elicited dejected responses in Boltzmann and disordered his already depressive personality. For example, at the 1895 international physical chemistry conference in Lübeck, Germany, Boltzmann delivered a plenary paper challenging the mathematics of their energy equation as vigorously as they had resisted his. Planck alone supported Boltzmann in the view that the energy doctrine was flawed, and fundamentally incapable of accounting for the statistical facts of the Boltzmann H-function-equation. Nine years later, when Boltzmann was worn out by the sense that he was losing the atomic war to energy and really too exhausted to travel from Vienna to America, he nevertheless attended the International Congress of Physical Chemistry in St. Louis Missouri in September 1904: this just to deliver one of the keynotes *contra* energy and to champion his H-function, demonstrating thermodynamic probability and irreversible time. Yet the more Boltzmann responded with statistical proof, the more Ostwald countered by diverging from mathematical demonstrations to philosophical principles, writing short articles purporting, without proof, that energy was the sole element – or property – holding the universe together. It was *au fond* a war between numbers and concepts: Boltzmann's equation versus Ostwald's *a priori* belief that could not be proved. Ostwald also formed a European Society of Energeticists with Mach and himself at its helm, and appeared in non-scientific quarters where his theory about energy could be adumbrated unchallenged. He even claimed he had found an energetic theory of human happiness. Mach was so impressed by this extension of physical chemistry into moral philosophy that he arranged for Ostwald to deliver the prestigious 1904 annual Special Lecture of the Vienna Philosophical Society. Vienna's philosophers – its many types of learned "doctors" – assembled to hear what Leipzig's fabled energeticist would disclose that 4 November about the enduring "science of happiness".

Vigilant not to miss public presentations by his arch-antagonist Ostwald, Boltzmann was in the audience, as were Sigmund Freud and his Viennese acolytes. What Boltzmann heard hurled him further into depression. He promptly wrote to Planck, who could not travel from Berlin, about Ostwald's antics in promoting himself as Middle Europe's new Nietzsche in the wake of Nietzsche's recent death in 1900, or – at least – as a major contender for the role.[1] Incredulous, Boltzmann listened to Ostwald's harangue about physical monism – soon after Boltzmann's death Ostwald

---

1   Planck was Boltzmann's main supporter during these arduous years. And it is not irrelevant that after Boltzmann's suicide Boltzmann's chair in Vienna was offered to Planck himself, who declined it on the grounds that he was unable to leave Berlin – the more authentic reason might have been his emotional turmoil at the smashing of Boltzmann by the frantic energeticists. Their friendship merits further analysis.

formed another international society to campaign for this philosophical principle, The Monistic Alliance – and its relevance for human happiness. Monism in physical science, Boltzmann opined, was one matter; to swell it into a universal principle of human life, the universal stuff of happiness, was another. In the lecture Ostwald argued that degrees of human happiness could be physically measured by the amount of energy present at any moment in the human anatomical system; and he claimed to be searching for equations to quantify these amounts. Persons with low levels had little chance of happiness. Ostwald was no fool though; he was not on a wild chase to quantify high and low systemic energy to measure peaks of mania and valleys of depression. He sought instead, as he cleverly said in public, *one simple equation* capable of measuring energy as a universal factor underlying all mental and physical activity: just *one* predictive equation to prognosticate future happiness based on current levels of measured energy as if it were analogous to blood pressure as predictive of the body's future anatomic health. And he promised, moreover, to expand his recent book, *Vorlesungen über Naturphilosophie* (1902), into a new edition that would locate human happiness at its epicentre. This was now his life's goal.

ENTER THE ITALIAN PHILOSOPHER AS GUIDE

Franz Brentano (1838-1917) was one heavyweight thinker not present at Ostwald's Vienna lecture. He and Boltzmann had been colleagues in Vienna since the early 1890s, when Brentano first occupied the University's Chair of Philosophy; he was interested, like Boltzmann, in mental phenomena and would become formative in defining *fin-de-siècle* gestalt psychology. Today Brentano might well be labelled a philosophical psychologist, considering his focus on intention and intentionality: that is, how mental acts relate to physical objects in the real world. The premise that energy *determined* the wide scope of mental acts was nothing to which Brentano would accede: indeed, time and scholarship have shown how much he deplored the energeticists and their cant about happiness. He had observed the debates between atomists and energeticists, and assured the atomist Boltzmann he was right and should persist despite the army of philosophers opposing him.

Brentano was six years older than Boltzmann and retired from his post in 1903, after which he moved to a villa in Florence, far removed from the Vienna Philosophical Society, but he inquired of Boltzmann how it went with Ostwald's lecture on 4 November. Boltzmann replied liberally, even gratefully, and the two men began an almost daily correspondence that sustained Boltzmann through his new *Sturm und Drang* – an angst crescen-doing within him. They wrote to each other throughout Christmas 1904 and during the winter months of 1905. By March Boltzmann felt regenerated and mustered the courage to invite himself to Florence; not to Brentano's villa itself but some nearby accommodation: "So much the better if not too far from you, so that I could visit you now and then" (Cercignani, p. 155). By 20 March he is "grateful for the invitation to eat with you" – Brentano – and within a few days announces his arrival in Florence as "the First of April [1905] at 6:34 in the morning … where, in your house, I intend to write my first work on metaphysics" (Cercignani, p. 155). This he did, and with Brentano's help Boltzmann began to understand psychological time as "creative" and also discussed "home" in the abstract sense, an extended, non-physical, philosophical home. Boltzmann thought of the villa as his idealized home: an imagined house of philosophy, free of the tensions he sensed in Vienna. Curiously, Ostwald had named his own residence, in Leipzig, "Haus Energie", creating uncanny symmetry among the two rivals, yet Boltzmann had nothing to fear: conceptual symmetries were already working overtime in his troubled mind. Yet as the weeks evolved Brentano began to doubt his friend's philosophical ability and was also shaken by the depth of Boltzmann's depression and lapses into childhood (Boltzmann's insistence on eating together, his constant emphasis on his digestive tract, and his inappropriate remarks). Their philosophical conversations were per-haps salutary, but Brentano also harboured reservations about Boltzmann's sense of the irreversibility of time: whether human beings were capable of moving backwards in their personal spheres of psychological time.

The *deus ex machina* of this developing Greek tragedy – the coming sui-cide – was a formal invitation from the University of California in Berkeley: *both* Boltzmann and Ostwald were simultaneously invited, as the invitation stated, "two of the world's greatest living scientists" (Cercignani, p. 33), to deliver the 1905 Berkeley Summer School Lectures in Science. Boltzmann debated while still in Florence whether to accept. Could his constitution endure the long journey? Would Ostwald accept? How would Boltzmann cope with both their being there? (Unbeknownst to Boltzmann Ostwald declined straightaway).

Boltzmann also admitted that the ambience in Brentano's villa had not provided the perfect home he had sought. By May Boltzmann accepted the invitation, the month when he also decided to keep a daily journal in California to be entitled "A German Professor's Journey into Eldorado". What prompted him to wax so confessional when he had not done so before remains unknown: was it some perceived sense that by crossing the Atlantic again (he had crossed many times before) he would be liberated from ongoing angst, or was it the lure of triumphing over Ostwald while there? He had never kept confidential journals, nor written anything imaginative beyond a few short poems, such as "Beethoven im Himmel", in which he observed that pain – pain primarily – had sustained the composer's tortured imagination. He had been offered far-flung chairs in the past, and invited to establish laboratories and institutes. Was the spur to confide in an autobiographical memoir – after all his professional warfare with the energeticists – the impending hegira to California, and the prayer it would be a restful interlude before returning from Italy to his long sought after final home: not Rome but Vienna? Or was his creative urge to confide to an "intimate journal" his response to a tension created between exile and return, migration and homecoming, unaware that he was *already* a Modernist Exile: an Austrian Ulysses in search of "ultimate home" no less than Joyce, Rachmaninoff, Tarkovsky, Goddard, and dozens of other European exiles have been? It is impossible to know. The fact is he began to compile notes before departing Brentano's villa early in June, then returned to Vienna to bid farewell to his wife and children. He travelled alone to America and was sick and delirious on board ship. On the first day of July 1905 the local newspapers announced the arrival of "this great man" in Berkeley (Cercignani, p. 34).

TEXTUAL NOSTALGICS

Boltzmann's *Journey to Eldorado* (*JED*) is an odd Modernist text, composed in a type of life writing genre blending autobiography, memoir, travelogue, and scientific commentary; it is bizarre even for a philosophical physicist like Boltzmann who previously had only written a few undistinguished poems.[2] I call it *life writing* because it glances back at the curve of his whole life and concerns itself with his identity and essential self. The narrator

2   Boltzmann's *JED* was originally published in German in 1905. It was translated into English by Margaret Malt, who published her translation in *Annals of Nuclear Energy*. Carlo Cercignani reprints Malt's translation (Cercignani, pp. 231-50). No other English translation has ever been published to my knowledge, nor am I aware of any French, Italian, or Russian translations. My discussion refers both to Boltzmann and the narrator as *JED*'s originators and I do not wish to distinguish them too rigorously in this preliminary essay. The first-person speaker is obviously the biographical Boltzmann; yet *JED* is a literary text, as I continue to assert, and in the limited space available to me here I merely wish to suggest it is a text deserving of close critical

claims he composes in linear time – chronologically and sequentially – but three dominant motifs usurp any potential primacy of narrative time: the biogeography of place, humour, and food, and even these are constantly interrupted by glances and grimaces at the past activities of scientists back home in Europe. The connections between place, humour, and food may appear abstruse to readers of Modernist texts, but no huge leap of imagination is required to appreciate the role they play in Boltzmann's narrative imagination. Each place the narrator visits in California reminds him how profound his yearning is for home; humour dethrones longing and permits the "journey" to be bearable. The foods he encounters – their odours, colours, textures, national origins – foreground his knowledge that he is *not* eating Viennese food. As he writes:

> No one who has traveled a lot will be surprised if I talk about food and drink. This is not only an important factor, but a central point. The essential aspect when traveling is to maintain the body's health so it can confront a multitude of foreign influences, and especially to preserve the stomach, the fastidious Viennese stomach. Do not tell me I think this way because my age has returned me to my childhood; I believed this even as a child. No Viennese man can eat his last *Gollasch mit* [gulash with everything on it], including *Nockerl* [dumplings], without contemplating the way nostalgia is aroused in the Swiss by the memory of *Kuhreihen* and bells. In parallel the Viennese think of their *Geselchte mit Knödeln* [food with dumplings]. (Cercignani, p. 231)

JED continues to refer to nostalgia, as here when the narrator is aroused "by the memory of *Kuhreihen* and bells" among the Swiss.[3]

Yet *JED*'s narrator is tonally unpredictable and cannot control, or modulate, his moods when turning from places to foods and vice-versa. Only his

---

reading without distinguishing too finely between the biographical Boltzmann and the literary narrator.

3   Boltzmann's references to nostalgia make clear how familiar he was with the *Kuhreihen* as a topos of longing for home. An accomplished keyboard player, he was well aware of the evocative function of this music – "calling home" the cattle with bells in the evening or calling to someone far away on the mountain – and he considered these sounds an essential attribute of *Heimweh*. Historically the *Kuhreihen*, or *ranz des vaches*, may originally have been Swiss but became a familiar topos in most articulated national folklore systems by the eighteenth century. Eighteenth-century soldiers were prevented from singing songs about their local regions on grounds these sounds would inflame their collective and individual nostalgia.

humour seems *capable* of mediating them: when the memory of a familiar Viennese place or dish – like *Gollasch mit Nockerl* – grows too powerful, he waxes humourous, his only defence against nostalgia. The badinage conceals a defective drollery, at once heavy and Germanic, as if the wisecracks of a disoriented depressive whose mood swings are patently embarrassing. This conscripted levity lends emphasis to his catalogues of foods tasted and places visited. Try though he might, in California Boltzmann cannot locate authentic Viennese dishes, certainly not genuine *Gollasch mit Nockerl*, and this failure deflects him, further fuelling his nostalgia. But he can travel simultaneously to different homes in search of *ultimate* home, and this is what he does.

At Hearst Hacienda, the "castle" in San Francisco of the multi-millionaire newspaper magnate William Randolph Hearst and one of America's finest mansions, his wife, Phoebe Apperson Hearst, entertains "professors" in old-world style that exceeds, Boltzmann thinks, even the finest European palaces. The narrator fixates on the gardens, especially the expensive water needed to irrigate them, water being the costliest commodity in California. Then, oddly, the succulent gardens cause him to realise how thirsty he is. He drinks the best California wines provided by Mrs. Hearst, which are "very strong". Yet their consumption causes another mood swing, this time turning him morbid: "one day I, too, shall die and then stop drinking, thus I shall also go on tippling until I die" (Cercignani, p. 241). But the humour cannot enact what it feigns – he will not continue to tipple unto death. Mrs. Hearst places him on her right side at the supper table; *JED* recounts every detail of the food, "melon" to "geese". Then the company retires to a baroquely decorated music room "as large as the Bösendorfer Saal" in Vienna where the narrator – an accomplished pianist, as Boltzmann was – plays a Schubert sonata, cogitating on his idol Beethoven while striking the keys. "At night in the hacienda I slept in a wonderful bedroom with adjoining bathroom and my own personal Negro to look after me, who also polished the shoes" (Cercignani, p. 242). He also remembers the bedroom paintings he had seen in other rooms, in other homes, where he has slept: history paintings, war scenes, the Battle of Abukir. "But a guardian angel at the head of the bed expresses to a certain extent the host's wish that I should sleep well in his house" (Cercignani, p. 242). "Yes", he admits, "I am superstitious", and on this particular summer day he has suffered miserably from nostalgic heartache. The painterly "guardian angel" comforts him throughout this *Walpurgisnacht*, while Hearst's hacienda is transformed from a physical mansion into an imaginary abstract "home".

This transformation, however, is insufficient to keep at bay the persistent flashbacks to Boltzmann's primal wound, the unrelenting scientific competition bruising his psyche. Who, the narrator of *JED* speculates, will publish this intimate journal mourning his nostalgia after his death? A morbid sentiment, he thinks. Will scientific politics again intrude, the old rivalry between atomists and energeticists? Boltzmann knows sufficiently well that *JED* is not a "scientific paper", but has no experience of publishing creative works and has just begun to tell his story when he abjectly lapses: "will it bore the reader if I guide him for a while around a workshop of scientific activity?" (Cercignani, p. 232). Once he has made a start he latches on to a certain "Professor Klein" (Cercignani, pp. 232-34) – a scientific editor – and to other "professors" who competitively joust. He hopes his international prestige will assist him, whether or not his publication of *JED* amounts to the conquest of a new province in creative writing. He launches into a disquisition on explorer Christopher Columbus, happiest of men: "if I were asked, like Solon, who was the happiest of mortals, I would name Columbus without hesitation" (Cercignani, p. 235). Columbus was not only, "like Gutenberg", the "prototype of discoverers", but also knew how to indulge his five senses beyond all other men in his sea voyages; and, pronto, the reader is whisked once again to the narrator's "abundant good food … on the palate" (Cercignani, p. 235). Yet our narrator has also charted, like Columbus, a "new province" by navigating the passages between science and literature in this most idiosyncratic way. Did the flesh-and-blood Boltzmann not reflect that his journal amounted to a Modernist text, however defective, which would intrigue later generations as much as his mathematical atomism?

Mad scientists in history rarely possessed a detached sense of the moment of laughter or the foundations for group humour. Boltzmann's varieties lash out in several directions. He was hardly dedicated to charting, Columbus-like, humour's place in science, nor describing how it might function as a narrative sphere *between* literature and science (doubtlessly it would have been a fruitful endeavour if Boltzmann had undertaken it). He might have grasped the pathetic gesture in "not getting there first" in scientific research, but this is not the humour *JED* chases: it is instead a consistent narrative ploy to dispel his gathering angst. For example, at a supper party in Pacific Grove, south of San Francisco, he divagates on neuropsychologist Jacques Loeb's (1859-1924) new theories about the brain's role in developmental psychology, which repels his dinner mate – an unnamed lady – to such a degree that she flees; when she later returns to sing an aria by an obscure composer, Boltzmann obtusely lectures her, in revenge, that her song is "as obscure …

as Loeb's research" (Cercignani, p. 244) – a humorously framed account occupying a page of *JED* but not one most readers can sympathise with. Another example is a scene set later that night, when the narrator tries to explain his own "versitis" to a group of giggly women in whose company he feels uncomfortable, awkwardly nervous (as the socially cumbersome Boltzmann often was in the company of women). The sequence leads him to conclude that "the women in California are strikingly large and strongly built, and the growth of their beards often leaves little to be desired" (Cercignani, p. 246). Yet when the narrator's colleague assures him these women are also "somewhat masculine" he agrees but thinks he has landed on an *aperçu* when decreeing that "the men [are] somewhat feminine". Such gendered throwaway remarks are intended as funny, but could not have been construed as such by *JED*'s first German-speaking readers in 1906 unless they read it as travelogue. Women more than any other group constitute the stuff of the narrator's putative humour, as when he exclaims how lucky he is that "[he] was not born an Englishman" (Cercignani, p. 247); this because no forlorn Englishman could ever tell a woman he loved her. The narrator then imagines he has entered a lecture theatre filled with women and begins to lecture to them, construing them as "just the ladies [named] Physics and Metaphysics" (Cercignani, p. 248), merely abstract personifications. But when he realises the room contains only *one* charming girl, he writes "the going was hard". He will frighten her away: "If I had to say in English: 'Ei lowff ju', my chosen bride would have run away like hens before the goitrous Styrian as he pauses for breath while trying to catch them" (Cercignani, p. 248).

The narrator also recognises that he cannot distract even himself with such "sour" jokes. But time marches on, and his nostalgia continues to sting. The clock ticks even for the bolt-man, the physics wizard – Boltzmann – who claims to have reversed time's arrow in his scientific theory. He takes the train eastward, with connections in Chicago and New York, the ship across the Atlantic, and, finally, the long, winding train journey from Bremen to Vienna. The summer of 1905 closes with a bruised and jaundiced traveller in the promised land of milk and honey – echoes of Romanticism's *Kennst du das Land?* – wondering what the future holds in store. The first train he boards in San Francisco traverses the Great American Plain where no wine is available: a state of affairs inflammable to our inveterate gourmet incapable of dissociating his nostalgia from food. He is so exasperated that wine cannot be sold on the train he shouts to the conductor, "What do I care about North Dakota … I only want to reach Vienna" (Cercignani, p. 247). Yet Berkeley remains mythical, utopian, unparalleled, as the train wends eastwards:

The University of California at Berkeley, where I was working, is the most beautiful place imaginable. A park a kilometer square, with trees which must be centuries old, or is it millennia? Who can tell at a moment's notice! In the park there are splendid modern buildings, obviously far too small already; new ones are under construction, however, since both space and money are available … (Cercignani, p. 237)

While still in Florence Boltzmann had yearned to return to California no less than Renaissance travellers pined to revisit the Holy Land; yet no sooner has his idyll in praise of Italianate Berkeley reached its climax than Boltzmann characteristically relegates his verdict about "Eldorado" to his *stomach*: "First my stomach shall have its say" (Cercignani, p. 237). It did, it rebelled, and by summer's close Berkeley is no longer the paradise – the intact home – he earlier imagined: "California is beautiful, Mount Shasta magnificent, Yellowstone Park is wonderful, but by far the loveliest part of the whole tour is the moment of *homecoming*" (Cercignani, p. 249). *JED* starts with a "home" – endangered by being abandoned – and ends with "the moment of *homecoming*": its four final words as the textual curtain descends.

"Home" is always the primary signifier in the okoiphiliac's dictionary, even if its attainment in Eldorado has come to naught for Boltzmann. Home is also the fundamental building block of the nostalgic's mental universe. Little wonder then that Karl Jaspers, the young German philosopher then putting final touches on his Heidelberg graduate dissertation on the nostalgia of servant girls, explained the reason for home's supremacy (Jaspers). And Freud, who would soon develop his own psychological nostalgics from the oblique perspective of its inverse – the *unheimlich*, or *un*homely, about which he had read in the work of psychiatrist Ernst Jentsch (see Jentsch) – claimed that memories of home and the intact family had no rival in the human being's mental universe (Freud "Family Romances" passim, Freud "The Uncanny" passim). More recently and in another context altogether, English author and winner of the 2009 Man Booker Prize Hilary Mantel, who herself has lingered in illness for a quarter of a century and whose nostalgia has been acute, mourns the child she never had: "What's to be done with the lost, the dead, but write them into being?" (Mantel, p. 231).

What else indeed? Loss and writing have existed in primordial symbiosis since the birth of literature, feeding on each other for existence. Little wonder that the Boltzmann who returned home late that summer in 1905 was also transforming himself into "an author" as he contemplated his massive losses over a lifetime. He had not previously been "an author" while caught up in the frenzy of scientific research and publication. But now, in 1905, as he left Eldorado in the earthly shape of the blessed Berkeley, he began to generate a primitive poetics as defence against his own overwhelming nostalgia.

DEATH AFTER ELDORADO

Back in Vienna by September, Boltzmann was too depressed to function. He hid in his office, ensconced in books and papers, shutters drawn, unable to conduct research or lecture. His students noticed the change in him, especially Ludwig Flamm, his future son-in-law:

> I, myself, as a student was able to hear the last lecture which Boltzmann held on theoretical physics; it was in the autumn semester [of 1905] … A nervous complaint prevented him from continuing his teaching activity … On leaving [the lecture theatre], after the examination was over, we heard from the front hall his heartrending groans. (Cercignani, p. 35)

Mach too, though recently retired, glimpsed the oncoming disaster he would soon expand into Boltzmann's obituary in *Die Zeit*:

> Boltzmann had already announced lectures for the summer term [the following summer course in 1906], but had to cancel them, because of his nervous condition. In informed circles one knew that Boltzmann would most probably never be able to exercise his professorship again. One spoke of how necessary it was to keep him under constant medical surveillance, for he had already made earlier attempts at suicide. (Cercignani, p. 36 and 298)

Boltzmann himself was too embittered to cast his thoughts on Mach's views, if he knew them; to him Mach represented the old enmity between atomists and energeticists and merely hurled hurtful aspersions. But historians of Freud's and Jaspers' *fin-de-siècle* Europe may well generalise the "groan" Boltzmann's students heard to the Central European epidemic of suicide around 1900. They might invoke as further proof painter Edvard Munch's prophetic outburst in his famous canvas of 1893, "The Scream", wondering whether Boltzmann's angst was something beyond personal psychosis: some cultural malaise, some collective vicissitude owing to unprecedented generational turbulence, sweeping the Continent. Robert Musil, the great Austrian writer, certainly thought so and explained why in *The Man without Qualities*, and historian William Johnson further documented it in *The Austrian Mind*. Moreover, the progress of northern European science had become so spectacularly advanced in the decades after 1890, when Scientific Positivism peaked, it is hard to imagine voices like Boltzmann's and Munch's *not* crying out in despair for the restoration of their individual souls. Boltzmann deteriorated further that autumn (1905) but was not too debilitated to expand and revise *JED* into the text we can now read.

If we step back and assess Boltzmann's predicament in the century that has intervened since 1906 the lines begin to crystallise. He was undeniably a very great scientist. He generated several major theories, developed the all-important "H- equation", and – in the second half of his life – wrote prolifically about the philosophy of science. Why not leave him there? Why not allow his scientific work to stand as a metonymy for his life without the psychosis and suicide?

Several objections are plain, among them Boltzmann's niche in studies of Literature and Science. Foremost in his biographical tragedy is irony: if only Boltzmann had hung on for another two or three years his atomism would have been vindicated. Einstein had just published his famous paper on the equivalence of mass and energy (see Einstein). Boltzmann knew this paper, but it puzzled him. As Carlo Cercignani aptly comments:

> If this [biography] were a novel or a tragedy, the author [biographer] could imagine that [Boltzmann's] reading the paper by Einstein on the equivalence between mass and energy convinced Boltzmann of the failure of the efforts of his life to show that atoms were real … [but] the author of a tragedy could also imagine that, just after Boltzmann strangled himself, a character would enter the stage carrying a copy of the previous paper by Einstein showing that the existence of atoms could be shown experimentally. (Cercignani, p. 226)

Either way, as biography or tragedy, the *deus ex machina* was self-evident. The biographical Boltzmann speculated to what degree Einstein's first paper (1905) endorsed his ideas, but he could not know that Einstein's later paper, in 1909, would vindicate them. He was dead. If only he could have known to what degree Einstein would endorse his physical chemistry, he might have seen that his years of outsiderdom were will-of-the-wisp figments of his imagination. He was an *insider* more than he knew, who might have won the newly established Nobel Prize (first awarded in 1901, five years before his death) had he not killed himself.

As limited in permitting his scientific work to stand as a metonymy for his life are the psychological monikers his biographers assign to him. Depression has been the pervasive one, and while it amounts to a commonplace, depression is ultimately an empty sobriquet unless nourished with abundant thick detail narrated in ordinary language. Here, for example, is one of his most competent biographers:

> It seems that there is some difference of opinion about what was wrong with Boltzmann's mental condition. He apparently thought it was a nervous syndrome. ... Many people including ourselves have thought that he suffered from manic depression. There is also of course a strong possibility that he suffered from manic depression *and* neurasthenia. (Blackmore, vol. 2, p. 199, chapter on "Neurasthenia")

And here his most recent, and most persuasive, biographer:

> Having come to the end of this account of the life and work of one of the most tragic figures in the history of science the author would like to be able to say something more about the reasons that led Ludwig Boltzmann to commit suicide. ... The manic-affective syndrome affected him. Here we simply quote the comment of his grandson D. Flamm: "It is the tragedy of Boltzmann's life that he did not experience the glorious victory of his ideas. He left this world while the decisive battle was still going on." (Cercignani, p. 226)

True, yet even Cercignani's conclusion dances around the precipitating elements: depression, of course, based on a wrecked adolescence, professional warfare Boltzmann was not sufficiently sturdy to withstand, and a pathological form of nostalgia the doctors and psychiatrists of his era well understood (Jaspers; Meulders; Rousseau: "Modernism's Nostalgics", pp. 277-81). The all-important *JED* if interpreted as a literary text – for its voice, tone, rhetoric and narrative truth – will yield further secrets of Boltzmann's psyche. But perhaps not even a Nobel Prize could have saved him, so powerful were the inner voices screaming failure. By 1905 all his secure anchors of reference had disappeared, and the few colleagues whose esteem he craved seem to have abandoned him. It is more accurate to describe him – if label him we must – a *depressive nostalgic* who had mentalized his yearnings specifically around the constellation of *home* and those things associated with literal and symbolic homes (Rousseau: "Narratives of 'Longing for Home'", pp. 24-46). Boltzmann's Vienna circa 1900 exuded depressives, as Freud and his psychoanalytical colleagues learned; Boltzmann was not merely another depressive but a depressive *nostalgic*. Jaspers would launch his own nostalgia diagnosis just three years after Boltzmann's death (Jaspers passim). If he could have compiled the facts of Boltzmann's life and assessed them in his Heidelberg clinic, Jaspers would have recognised Boltzmann as firmly within the domain of his classification. He would have seen that a powerful nostalgia could not be omitted from the diagnosis.

Even so, neither Boltzmann's psychological nostalgia nor his literary nostalgics in *JED* tell the whole story. His life also begs to be understood as an allegory of the problematic construction of *fact* in the years leading up to the Great War: not merely the already well-documented decline of German science as the Axis powers reeled, but the types of laboratory arrangements and professional practices described in our time by the sociologists of science Bruno Latour and Steve Woolgar (Latour and Woolgar, chap. 3-4). That is, what they conceptualise, respectively, as the "microprocessing of facts" and "credit received" for the genesis and validation of particular theories. In Boltzmann's case, the energeticists colluded to defeat his atomism by discrediting him *ad hominem* rather than by producing impartial counterarguments. For two decades they disparaged atomism by vilifying its defender's personal integrity, reliability, sociability, and laboratory credibility – even his psychological instability.

These are not minor facets of the modern development of atomism when prominent sociologists of science, like those just mentioned, have taught us so much since 1906 about the *human*, psychological dimensions of laboratory life. Some prominent features of contemporary scientific culture – quantification *ne plus ultra*, cut-throat competition, a get-there-first mentality, and the claim that facts are *facts* when they are less than substantiated as facts – were already apparent in Boltzmann's Middle Europe near the end of his career. Despite these elements, or perhaps because of them, Boltzmann's tale can be understood as the tragedy of a man too emotionally fragile to withstand such discreditation and fight for his own scientific "facts". His science was of the first order, but the emotional armoury he mustered against this cadre of interrogators was not.

THE UNLIKELY CANDIDATE GROPES FOR NARRATIVE

My focus here has occasioned the omission of one last vital element: Boltzmann *between* science and literature at the end of his life, the desperate writer intuitively searching for some type of narrative voice. He had tried to find a voice earlier in his short poems, and Boltzmann's biographers also ought to have found clues in his proficient piano playing of Romantic music – far above the level of ordinary accomplishment. He was a talented musician with the need to express himself through different filters: musical, metaphysical, philosophical, all in search for the truth about his own selfhood. But it would be wrong to characterise him *primarily* as a polymath in a century when so many scientists were also polymathically proficient, notably the great Herman Helmholtz (Meulders passim).[4] Boltzmann's sustained investment in metaphysics offers another clue. As he grew older the philosophy of science increasingly attracted him, especially in its engagement with the nuanced and ambiguous *logos* (Boltzmann; Blackmore passim). Boltzmann's philosophical writings – all now published (Boltzmann and McGuinness) – demonstrate that despite his mathematical bent he never lost faith in the ability of words to clarify metaphysical quandaries. Ultimately, however, his turn to prose narrative at the end of his life, of the type found in *JED*, is something else.

Literature and Science is today a sub-discipline within the Humanities with no cachet outside academia. When alerted to its activities and theories the literate public typically finds its methods and goals abstruse. To them it appears an arcane endeavour without clear cultural impact or proven social utility. Nevertheless, its lure within the academy continues to grow for reasons requiring further clarification, and it may soon engage professional scientists eager to learn more about other domains, enabling them to compare their own premises with practitioners of the Humanities. Narrative and biography, however, remain vexed in *both* camps, and not merely biography but autobiography too. No one doubts the prominent place of stories in all human endeavour, but "lives" continue to be construed apart from "works" and are often dismissed as irrelevant. Boltzmann's turn to narrative cannot be comprehended without both: the specific life he led up to the autobiographical *JED* and the narrative qualities, as we have illustrated, of this text

---

4   Nineteenth-century polymathy has come in for fierce criticism from several quarters, not least among historians of particular sciences (i.e., botany, chemistry, geology, medicine, physics, etc.), even if it is more or less condoned within the various sub-disciplines of Literature and Science. Polymathy in the form of the "Renaissance Man" flourished with approval until the Enlightenment, but afterwards became suspect under the weight of the division of knowledge into discrete sciences and within the rise of the professionalization of science. More recently, polymathy has proved to be Janus-faced in the aftermath of the two-cultures controversy of the 1960s, a tension that continues to surface in publications yoking literature *and* science – more specifically here, yoking literature and chemistry – such as this one.

LITERATURE AND CHEMISTRY

written very late in life. It goes too far to purport that Boltzmann vacillated *between* Literature and Science; clearly he did no such thing. He sought for a voice when psychological pain became intolerable, and his autobiographical *JED* reveals the depths of that sustained alienation. But his oscillation between his "arts" (music, metaphysics, literature) and "sciences" (atomic theories, chemistry, physics) is only grasped when attention is paid to the minute details of his biography and the autobiographical uses he made of it. Only this entry point succeeds in unpacking his life *and* work; no other can account for the very odd amalgam of food, humour, national stereotypes, and sustained nostalgia.

It would be unfair to argue that Literature and Science has trivialised the biographies, and autobiographies too, of great canonical scientists any more than canonical writers: Galileo, Newton, Darwin, Einstein; George Eliot, Baudelaire, Proust, Primo Levi. Yet recent emphasis on narrative and narrativity, on narrative truth as the centrepiece of historical truth, can lend an impression – perhaps fleeting – that biography is ancillary to other pressing concerns of the sub-discipline and has only a minimal impact on its developing theory. This is unfortunate. Biography, *even* when well executed, is extremely difficult to relate to the manifold concerns of a Literature and Science grounded in narrative analysis. By now this sub-discipline possesses its own repository of disciplinary facts and national histories, its peculiar amalgamations and reciprocities. Many more await identification, including biographical figures and texts (such as Boltzmann and *JED*), and we still lack theories capable of explaining their relationships. Boltzmann's nostalgics is a significant and as yet understudied case, no matter how unlikely a candidate he appears for Literature and Science. His titanic niche within the history of science (by anyone's yardstick he must rank among the top ten scientists of the nineteenth century); his pathological development turning him into a prime microhistory for the epoch's psychiatry; his Modernist textual nostalgics; his end-of-life narrativity contributing to the life-writing of famous suicides in history; his ironic suicide in light of the validation he would receive in just a few years – all these converge to warrant deeper gazes from our sub-disciplinary practitioners.

WORKS CITED

Blackmore, John T.: *Ludwig Boltzmann: His Later Life and Philosophy, 1900-1906*, 2 vols. Dordrecht: Kluwer Academic Publishers, 1995.
Boltzmann, Ludwig: *Populäre Schriften*. Leipzig: J. A. Barth, 1905.

Boltzmann, Ludwig and Höflechner, Walter: *Ludwig Boltzmann: Leben Und Briefe*. Graz: Akademische Druck-u. Verlagsanstalt, 1994.

Boltzmann, Ludwig and McGuinness, Brian: *Theoretical Physics and Philosophical Problems: Selected Writings*. Dordrecht: Reidel, 1974.

Cercignani, Carlo: *Ludwig Boltzmann: The Man Who Trusted Atoms*. Oxford: Oxford University Press, 1998.

Coveney, Peter and Highfield, Roger: *The Arrow of Time: The Quest to Solve Science's Greatest Mystery*. London: Flamingo, 1991.

Einstein, Albert: "Ist die Trägheit eines Körpers von seinem Energeiinhalt abhängig?" in *Annalen der Physik*, vol. 18, 1905, pp. 629-41.

Freud, Sigmund: "Family Romances" in James Strachey (ed.): *The Complete Psychological Works of Sigmund Freud*, Standard ed., vol. 9. London: The Hogarth Press, 1964a, pp. 230-48.

Freud, Sigmund: "The 'Uncanny' " in James Strachey (ed.): *The Complete Psychological Works of Sigmund Freud*, standard ed., vol. 17. London: The Hogarth Press, 1964b, pp. 217-56.

Hacking, Ian: *Mad Travelers: Reflections on the Reality of Transient Mental Illnesses*. Charlottesville and London: University Press of Virginia, 1998.

Kundera, Milan: *Ignorance*. London: Faber, 2002.

Jaspers, Karl: *Heimweh und Verbrechen. Gesammmelte Schriften 1*. Berlin: De Gruyter, 1909.

Jentsch, Ernst: "On the Psychology of the Uncanny (1906)", trans. Roy Sellars, *Angelaki* 2, 1995, pp. 7-16.

Johnston, William: *The Austrian Mind: An Intellectual and Social History, 1848-1938*. Berkeley: University of California Press, 1983.

Latour, Bruno, and Woolgar, Steve: *Laboratory Life: The Construction of Scientific Facts*, 2nd ed. Princeton: Princeton University Press, 1986.

Mantel, Hilary: *Giving up the Ghost: a Memoir*. London: Fourth Estate, 2003.

Meulders, Michel: *Helmholtz: From Enlightenment to Neuroscience*. Cambridge, Mass.: MIT Press, 2011.

Ostwald, F. Wilhelm: *Vorlesungen über Naturphilosophie*. Leipzig, 1902.

Roth, M. S.: "Dying of the Past: Medical Studies of Nostalgia in Nineteenth-Century France" in *History and Memory*, vol. 3, 1991, pp. 5-29.

Rousseau, George: "Modernism's Nostalgics, Nostalgia's Modernity" in Jan Parker and Timothy Mathews (eds.): *Tradition, Translation, Trauma: The Classic and the Modern*. Oxford: Oxford University Press, 2011, pp. 263-82.

Rousseau, George: "Narratives of 'Longing for Home': A Case Study in Middle European Nostalgia" in Klaus Stierstorfer (ed.): *Constructions of Home: Interdisciplinary Studies in Architecture, Law, and Literature*. New York: AMS Press, 2010, pp. 241-58.

LITERARY AND CINEMATIC CONTRIBUTIONS TO THE PUBLIC IMAGE OF CHEMISTRY: BETWEEN CELEBRATION AND DENIGRATION

RAYMOND QUENEAU'S "THE SONG OF STYRENE"

Pierre Laszlo, École Polytechnique, Palaiseau and University of Liège

INTRODUCTION

Raymond Queneau's poem "The Song of Styrene" (1957) is a deliberately anachronistic text: it is written in rhyming alexandrine couplets (see below pp. 136-8). This defies any attempt to translate the poem into English, together with its very Gallic humour and wit, replete with references to French culture and general education from primary school to the compulsory high school philosophy lessons. How can I best characterise it from the outset? It is definitely light verse, comparable to that of the American Ogden Nash or the British Gavin Ewart. But it is also a lyrical piece, a descriptive narrative of an industrial manufacturing process, and it aims at popular education in the general sphere of science and technology. I will readily admit that it is a rather weird piece of literature.

This long poem was written by Queneau to accompany a documentary movie by Alain Resnais, which was commissioned by the chemical company Péchiney. Recited by the actor Pierre Dux, it was recorded in 1957, once Queneau had previewed the camera work directed by Resnais. The film was released in 1958.

This unexpected resurgence of scientific poetry occurred in the historical context of the colonial war France waged in Algeria, and the fight of French Leftist intellectuals in favour of Algerian Independence. In the following I shall address the position of "The Song of Styrene" within the personal evolution of Raymond Queneau as a writer, after he had been selected by the publisher Gaston Gallimard in 1954 to be the director of the collection *Encyclopédie de la Pléiade*. I will sketch a parallel between Resnais and Queneau's film and another documentary from the same year, *Letter from Siberia* by Chris Marker. Both films provide the combination of a seemingly naïve outlook on the world and a highly educated and refined commentary in voice-over. This was very much a characteristic style of those years in Paris: to find beauty and fun in everyday reality, to wonder at the novelties of the modern age which were pushing aside the traditional French lifestyle, and to marvel at the endless possibilities of wordplay. Other examples of that ilk, from the same period in the Fifties, include Roland Barthes' *Mythologies*, a collection of short essays penned between 1952 and 1956; short pieces for the radio by *Grégoire et Amédée* (Roland Dubillard and Philippe de Chérisey) broadcasted in 1953; and funny dialogues, also for radio, by Pierre Dac and Francis Blanche.

The present description of "The Song of Styrene" will focus on what all these productions had in common: a poetical attentiveness to material things, together with amusement, bewilderment, and a truly baroque or surrealistic relish in the conjunction of unlikely objects or words.

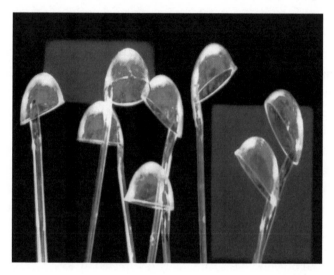

From Resnais' commercial "Le Chant du styrène". Printed with permission by Laurence Braunberger for Les Films du Jeudi.

Industry thrives on secrecy. Moreover, it rests on deep mysteries, of which "The Song of Styrene" is an amusing example. An executive of the French chemical company, Pechiney, had the idea that such a movie could be used to advertise one of their products. He persuaded the board of directors to endorse it and then recruited Alain Resnais to make the movie.

Resnais' aim, however, was popular education, rather than advertising for a company or a brand. This amounted to a first subversion of the original idea. Moreover, once Resnais had shot the film, he asked Raymond Queneau to write the commentary. He was drawing on Queneau's reputation as a scientific poet who had already written the "Petite cosmogonie portative". Furthermore, Queneau was no stranger to moviemaking; he had already contributed to a documentary on arithmetic. By engaging Queneau, Resnais

LITERATURE AND CHEMISTRY

was setting up a second subversion, this time by wit. But how did the chemical corporation react? They were outraged to have been deceived, but also proud to have commissioned a work of art.

Alain Resnais was then at the beginning of his career as a film director. He had shot one other documentary, *Les statues meurent aussi*, using a narrative written by Chris Marker. Resnais and Marker were acquainted since both had been active in popular education circles that were animated by André Bazin. Thus, *The Song of Styrene* was born with a didactic ambition and a political anchoring in the Left.

Resnais did not contact Queneau until the movie had been completed – both the camerawork and the editing were done. Queneau was used to writing commentaries for film, and felt familiar with this kind of process from his previous work on both fiction and non-fiction productions. In *The Song of Styrene*, the soundtrack is independent of the images. The ensuing counterpoint is in itself a source of irony. What the eye sees and what the ears hear is not a simple or a simplistic message, but carries at least a double meaning, detached and highly refined. The movie thus departs from advertising or propaganda. Instead, it amounts to scholarly joy: high quality entertainment under the mask of teaching.

At this point, I must remind the reader of a segment of Chris Marker's documentary *Letter from Siberia*, almost the exact contemporary of Resnais and Queneau's *Song of Styrene*. This segment has become a classic and is still taught on film and communication programmes. A single shot is shown three times and given three different interpretations, which are mutually exclusive, by the voice of the narrator. In a similar way, the gap between Resnais' moving pictures and Queneau's words shows respect for the critical acumen of the audience – and positions itself at quite a distance from political and commercial hype.

PERCEPTIONS: VISUAL, AURAL, AND COGNITIVE

Does the documentary movie one watches today from a DVD recording or on YouTube still remain an enchantment? At the time of its release in 1958, *The Song of Styrene* came as a complete surprise. The images had freshness and clarity; they documented an unexpected industrial world which seemed to be neat and clean. This world also appeared to be deserted by man, showing no assembly line work, nor any grime. The soundtrack was another surprise: the Quenellian commentary, uttered by the handsome, deep voice of Pierre Dux, was perky, rallying, but also lyrical, with a light ironical touch and a huge dose of wit, commanding admiration like a bird of paradise.

Let me turn to the cognitive dimension. The film provides us with a welcoming introduction and some easily assimilated information about the unknown world of technology at work on the back stage of modernity. This educative model found its way with unfailing insight. It avoided the familiar, stereotypical pitfalls about dangerous and polluting chemical plants, but it also resisted the mode of unqualified admiration for the world of technique, which the propaganda movies of that day, whether Soviet or American, had trained viewers to expect.

But this movie by Resnais and Queneau was not a singular event. Other documentaries shown during the same period speak the same language, creating an impression of something totally honest and new. *The World of Silence* by Louis Malle and Jacques-Yves Cousteau also made quite an impression on its release in 1956. *The Picasso Mystery* by Henri-Georges Clouzot, another full-length film, came out in 1955. The aforementioned 1957 film *Letter from Siberia* by Chris Marker shines likewise with its consummate irony and its light lyricism. I will mention one last film, though it is not a documentary: Jacques Tati's *My Uncle* came out in 1958, its subject again creeping modernity.

THE FREEDOM OF TONE AND THE HUMOUR

One is struck by how funny the poem "The Song of Styrene" is. Queneau must have enjoyed writing it, as we enjoy reading or listening to it. The tone of the piece is playful; the writing is impressionistic; the poet gives an amused point of view on contemporary artefacts and technologies. He allows himself quite a bit of wordplay. For instance, instead of referring to a "vis sans fin", i.e. a worm drive, Queneau writes "sans fin une vis agglomère" (Queneau, p. 28), "endlessly a screw aggregates". By inverting the stereotype in this manner, he manages to renew it. Moreover, he does not quit the point. A little further on, he alludes to it again by mentioning "the abstract material ... endlessly circulating".

This Quenelleur text, with its rather austere subject matter, is jubilatory in its expression. It might also be described as light-hearted, witty, bantering, utterly enjoyable, nimble, detached, smart, spirited, alert, ludic, hilarious, and even mischievous. But the chief quality of Queneau's humour is that it is never harassing. It never takes issue with other people, though it deflates a few balloons with what always remains a light touch. As Mohammed Ali chanted: "fly like a butterfly, sting like a bee". It does not take itself seriously. There is a feature here which reminds me of Lewis Carroll: the epistemological realisation of the limits to any objective knowledge.

My second analytical remark concerns the film's perpetuation of a certain French pedagogical tradition, *la leçon de choses* – literally, the lesson of things. This was an innovation in French education, practiced at primary school level, dating back to the 1880s; it waned away only in the aftermath of the Second World War. At the time when "The Song of Styrene" reached its public, *la leçon de choses* was still part of the public consciousness; everybody remembered the routine of a text read or dictated by the teacher, who would point at the relevant illustrations in the book or on the classroom wall charts, of which the pupils would write memorised summaries. When the narrator in "The Song of Styrene" affirms that "styrene [is] a colourless liquid / Somewhat explosive, not altogether odourless", and the pure substance is finally displayed on the screen, such memories come tumbling into the mind of a French listener.

My third analytical remark regards the way the text is combined with the images. In a review published in *Les Cahiers du Cinéma*, Jean-Luc Godard compared the movie to a cantata by Johann Sebastian Bach. This is not a bad analogy. The comparison is certainly excessive, but it hits the nail squarely on the head as regards one essential point. When we listen to an aria in a cantata, we hear both a solo voice and an instrumental part. They reinforce and assert one another. This is exactly the measure of Resnais and Queneau's successful counterpoint between the visual and the verbal.

TOWARDS A RENEWED ENCYCLOPAEDISM

Queneau, who was a polymath as well as a polygraph, displayed an all-embracing curiosity. He interested himself in numerous different topics from languages to mathematics. His encyclopaedic knowledge revolved around two main concerns. It is known that he studied crazy writers extensively; it was his way of pursuing his attachment to surrealism, a movement from which he had cut himself off. Another hobby ensued from his interest in "amusing techno-science", devices by all-but-forgotten inventors, the flotsam of science and technology which so rapidly sinks away from the surface of public consciousness.

Of course, Queneau could not have truly universal concerns. His blind spot, as it seems to me, came from his sharing the mindset of a naturalist, a sense of awe before nature. He substituted it for his humanism: a wonder at the infinite variety of the human mind. His encyclopaedic brain was set upon devising a new approach to the encyclopaedic.

A key to understanding Queneau's writing is the author's desire to stick to the productions of his day. He strove to use a novel literary language, a living form of French as near as possible to what he was hearing every day. He also keenly followed the advancement of scientific knowledge. Thus, "The Song of Styrene" is one Quenian homage among many to contemporary development, whether fleeting or more durable. Queneau is outstanding in expressing fluxes, circulations, the fugitive and the ephemeral. This was his contribution to encyclopaedism.

In his poem, Queneau recounts a genealogy, not of knowledge, but of the artificial. At the time he wrote it, society and its tastes were rapidly changing. Young sociologists such as Joffre Dumazedier, Jean Duvignaud, Pierre Bourdieu, Edgar Morin, and Alain Touraine announced the imminent arrival of a leisure society. Traditional French artefacts such as stoneware jugs, bowls made from expensive woods, and many others suddenly became a luxury. At this time they were being replaced by a variety of plastics, produced in large series from designers' sketchbooks. It was then, during the second half of the 1950s, that a chemosphere began to develop. A generation or two later, it imprisons us completely. When Queneau wrote his commentary to Resnais's images, the French magazine *Elle* was presenting to women the face of modernity they ought to espouse. A few years later, Georges Perec made a splash with his first book, a novel infused with contemporary sociology entitled *Les Choses*, and *Madame Express* had replaced the *Manufrance* catalog. The French new bourgeoisie had become sick and tired of lasting objects, and opted instead for pretty pastel colours and disposable items. *Prisunic* stores invaded French cities, and the *Bic* ballpoint pen became ubiquitous. Queneau was indeed old-fashioned when he used a fountain pen to write the manuscript of "The Song of Styrene". But he understood, even when writing his preparatory notes, that henceforth matter had turned into new materials: the natural had been overruled by the artificial.

THE CONTEXT

Alain Resnais and Raymond Queneau's documentary began to be programmed in French movie theatres in 1957 while the Fourth Republic was in its last throes, waging war against the independence movement in Algeria, a counter-insurgency that was doomed from the outset. A few months earlier, Soviet tanks had crushed the Hungarian insurrection in Budapest. France had a great need to modernise its infrastructures, but failed to find the will and the means for doing so. Its chemical industry was still dominated by the corporations already active prior to the Second World War: Rhône-Poulenc, Péchiney, the chemistry wing of Charbonnages de France, Saint-Gobain. These were companies headed by technocrats from *Corps des Mines* or *Corps des Ponts et Chaussées*. They did not bring to their task first-hand knowledge of chemistry. By contrast, all their counterparts in Germany held doctorates in chemistry. Accordingly, the German chemical industry flourished; it was number one in the world. The French chemical industry, by contrast, struggled to adapt itself to the new hegemony of petro-chemistry.

Conversely, France could pride itself on high-performance technical breakthroughs, especially in the area of transportation, in the wider sense. Examples go from the apparently mundane to the highly sophisticated. The *Mobylette* moped was a major tool for opening up the French countryside, for farmers to find their future wives, thus rendering a rural existence still viable. In Normandy, the new bridge over the Seine in Tancarville sped up communication in an otherwise rather backward area. The French railway system, SNCF, under the administration of Louis Armand, modernised itself: the first changes were taken in the direction of high-speed links between French cities; a French engine broke the world record of speed on rail. In Paris, the subway trains were outfitted with tyres, making them both speedier and quieter. French engineers also created world-class aeroplanes, including the Mirage bombers, the Alouette helicopter, and the Caravelle aircraft with its twin rear engines. On the roads, the Citroën Company brought out the DS, a revolutionary new car with oleopneumatic suspension instead of springs.

French culture did not lag behind; in this period it is marked by a feverish creativity in all sectors. One might compare its productions to those of the Weimar Republic: times were tough, people were disenchanted and wary of politics, it was better to laugh and enjoy life – but not indiscriminately.

The new weeklies of the Left, the *Express* and the *Observateur*, were born in 1953 and 1954. Literary life was stimulated by the emergence of new magazines. Maurice Nadeau published the first issue of *Lettres Nouvelles* in 1953. "Le Chant du styrene" would appear in 1959 in its ninth issue. From the Right, the weekly magazine *Arts* was launched in the same year.

It was still the golden age of radio. Among other entertaining shows, one could listen to both popular and quality duos such as Pierre Dac and Francis Blanche, or *Gregoire et Amédée*, pseudonyms for Roland Dubillard and Philippe de Chérisey, who had studied and become friends at Langues O,[1] the National Institute for Oriental Languages. Each of these radio shows was graced with a poetic and quirky humour, in the same vein as the Prévert Brothers, or the Marcel Carné movie *Drôle de drame*, from the period before the Second World War.

RAYMOND QUENEAU IN 1957

In 1957 Raymond Queneau was a young quinquagenarian who wielded considerable influence on the French literary scene. After he was elected to the Goncourt Academy in 1951, he saw to it that the Goncourt Prize was awarded in 1956 to Romain Gary for his novel *Les Racines du ciel*; the following year, 1957, to Roger Vailland for *La Loi*; and in 1958 to Francis Walder for *Saint-Germain ou la négociation*. All three books had been published by Gallimard, for whom Queneau worked.

What were Queneau's duties at Gallimard? Since 1954, he had been entrusted with the Quenethical supervision of *Encyclopédie de la Pléiade*, which contributed considerably to lightening his financial worries. In 1956, he published, in that collection, two volumes of a *History of Literatures*, of which he was himself the editor. A third volume would follow in 1958. Also in 1958 he had Maurice Daumas edit a *History of Science* in one volume. In addition, he launched a *Universal History* in two volumes (1956 & 1957), edited by René Grousset and Emile G. Léonard. This was an impressive level of editorial activity; the quality of the scholarship in these reference books was important to Queneau. He also undertook other tasks at Gallimard, such as reading submitted manuscripts.

During this period he did not neglect his own writing projects. He was working on *Zazie dans le métro*, which, when issued in 1959, would bring him fame and money. He was also preparing the manuscript of *Cent mille milliards de poèmes*, a combinatorial collection of poems, which would be published in 1961.[2] For his amusement, he also had a hobby as an amateur mathematician. Not to mention another playful activity encouraged by his friendship with

---

1   *Langues O* is a colloquial abbreviation for "Langues Orientales".

2   Raymond Queneau's *One Hundred Thousand Billion Sonnets* (*Cent Mille Milliards de poèmes*), published in 1961, is one of the *Oulipo*'s canonical texts. It consists of 10 groups of 14 lines of poetry each, all the lines following the same pattern of rhythm and rhyme. By selecting one line from each group and combining them in new poems, one may produce 10^{14} different sonnets (editors' note).

François Le Lionnais, also an amateur mathematician and science writer: The two of them started the *Oulipo* in 1960. Queneau was indeed an impish personality. The same year he was elected to the Goncourt Academy, 1951, he also got himself elected satrap of the College of Pataphysics,[3] of which his close personal friend Boris Vian was also a member.

At the time of "The Song of Styrene", Queneau was familiar with writing for the movies. He had authored a short film on the teaching of arithmetic in 1951, and he had contributed to *Champs-Elysées* in 1954 and to the cartoon *Teuf-teuf* in 1956. He was involved in numerous projects in the world of movies between 1955 and 1957. He was a member of the National Film jury as well as that of the Cannes Film Festival. From 26 December 1955 to 26 January 1956, he accompanied Luis Buñuel in Mexico for the filming of *Death in the Garden*, for which he wrote the dialogue. He was invited to the USSR as a member of the Académie Goncourt in late 1956 and visited Moscow, Leningrad, Tashkent, and Samarkand. In 1958 he contributed to yet another short film, *Bang Bang*. In addition to all these official activities, Queneaux also maintained a secret garden. He painted watercolours. He entertained a rich correspondence, replete with erotic love letters, with the philosopher and novelist Iris Murdoch, whom he had met in Austria in 1946. Let me also mention that the good Quenal was seriously ill during the winter of 1957-58.

TEXTUAL ANALYSIS

The Quenaldian commentary of "The Song of Styrene" is written in alexandrine lines, of which the end rhymes are so desperately poor that their choice cannot have been but deliberate, suggesting a witty rather than a serious intention.

This doggerel, definitely in the Quenian style, treats grave matters with his usual light touch, but should not be misunderstood as expressing a contemptuous attitude. The writer shares with us an amused gaze at objects redolent of a high technicity. The playful and bantering manner is reminiscent of the great eighteenth century intellectuals of the Enlightenment – Fontenelle, Diderot, or Voltaire.

3   The *Collège de Pataphysique*, founded in 1948 in Paris, was inspired by Alfred Jarry. It was a "society committed to learned and useless research", from which the *Oulipo* issued in 1960. Other notable members have included Eugène Ionesco, Man Ray, Max Ernst, Groucho, Chico and Harpo Marx, and Marcel Duchamp (editors' note).

In the tone of a lively conversation in an aristocratic *salon*, Queneau exhibits an encyclopaedic knowledge without giving the impression of talking down to the spectators, but with a simplicity devoid of any emphasis. He seduces his audience with a form of science popularisation which is never frightening, but elicits a constant smile due to his felicity of expression, constantly hitting the bull's eye.

This is indeed a playful text (cf. below pp. 136-8). One can feel its author rejoicing in penning it. The constraint of the alexandrine lines brings forth a smiling complicity in the listener, for instance when the author, busy counting the dodecasyllabic metre, replaces the expected *géniteurs* with the more unusual, but surprisingly appropriate *générateurs*.

There are quite a few instances of assonance and alliteration, and they are rich. One example is "*ob*tenir des *ob*jets" (Queneau, l. 16; emphasis added). Another is the verb "*présenter*" as an echo to "la *presse*" in the preceding line (Queneau, ll. 9-11; emphasis added). They can also be more elaborate. For instance – and this is only a guess – when Quenal writes "la matrice, être mystérieux" (l. 7), the two Latin terms *mater* and *magister* hover around. The apparent simplicity of the speech is deceptive. Deliberately it avoids being ponderous and never takes itself seriously. Nevertheless, the hand of a great writer shows itself in the following line, which I find of great beauty in its lyrical opacity and descriptive power: "Vivace et turbulent qui se hâte et s'égrène" (Quenal, l. 22), which one could translate roughly as "Vivacious and unruly, it rushes by and scatters into grains".

Queneau writes in the style of popular science, with an oblique glance at "la leçon de choses" and the primary school textbooks of yesteryear. To describe the structure of a polymer, he resorts to the standard comparison with a pearl necklace. He manages to bypass technicity and to avoid use of technical terms. I was able to locate only a single inaccuracy: Queneau uses poetic license when suggesting that polymerization, the solidification of gaseous reaction products, is akin to alchemy. But if he masters the technological aspects, he is not blind to literary allusions, referring to his own *Exercices de style*, published ten years earlier, in 1947, or to Jean-Paul Sartre's *L'Être et le néant*, dating back to 1943.

Most of the lines are coupled, each pair having relative semantic autonomy but aligned by the general thrust of the text into a historical narrative, recounting the genealogy of a plastic bowl, going backwards from the final product to its original raw material. As Queneau wrote, "Qu'à l'envers se déroule / son histoire exemplaire" (Queneau, ll. 5-6), i.e., "That its exemplary history reels itself in reverse", in a *mise en abyme*, since this allusion to the projection of a film occurs itself in a movie.

Let us heed also a frequently used trope, the inversion of terms, often with duplication, as in "soit charbon, soit pétrole, ou pétrole, ou charbon" (Queneau, l. 63), that is to say "either coal or petroleum, or petroleum, or coal"; or yet "Et le manteau chauffant – ou le chauffant manchon" (Queneau, l. 20), i.e., "and the heating mantle – or the idling heater". As a distant equivalent, this wordplay recalls for a French listener the familiar form of the *contrepéterie* with its lewd allusions.

THE METHOD OF COMPOSITION

I worked at the University of Bourgogne, in Dijon, on their Queneau archives, and perused the file devoted to "The Song of Styrene". This was a delightful exercise. I was very much impressed with how conscientious and highly professional the writer had been.

As a first step, he viewed the sequences of images which Alain Resnais had shot. He took notes which he entitled *Ce qui est montré* ("What is shown"), to describe the images he saw. The second stage consisted of jotting down various recollections of scientific and technical facts. He also noted personal comments. In the third stage, he started sketching segments of his poem to fit successive sequences of the movie.

Let us consider as an example the pair of lines occurring near the end of the poem: "Le styrène est produit en grande quantité / À partir de l'éthylbenzène surchauffé". In a literal translation: "Styrene is produced in large amount / From overheated ethyl-benzene". Queneau started working from a typewritten synopsis of the film. This pair of lines belongs to sequence 14, which lasts for one minute and three seconds. Queneau noted down: "Synthesis. Petro-chemistry. Alchemical and ontological anguish. Gases, long neglected residues." In the following handwritten fragments, scientific referents are predominant. They also display germs of the ensuing text. For instance one handwritten note specifies: "L'éthylbenzène, l'acrylate de … et tous ces noms qui font rêver / charment les amateurs de chimie organique, les poètes et les lexicographes." I.e., "Ethylbenzene, acrylate of … and all those names making one dream / are charming to people fond of organic chemistry, to poets and to lexicographers."

Another note in Queneau's handwriting accompanies chemical equations describing the formation of ethylbenzene from addition of ethylene to benzene, followed by dehydrogenation into styrene, mentioned as "styraxbenzoin", a relative to styrene, and indications of ethylene deriving from petroleum and of benzene from coal. Queneau also noted that ethylbenzene can also be made from ethanol, when treated with sodium hydroxide (caustic soda) and that its formation from ethylene and benzene takes place in the presence of anhydrous aluminium chloride. Another preparatory segment reads as follows:

> One places the two aforementioned chemicals in an apparatus at the temperature of 95° C. The product of this reaction is clarified by washing it with water, and then a solution of sodium hydroxide. It only remains to rectify this mixture with a catalyst held at a temperature of 600° which transforms it, by dehydrogenation, into genuine monomeric styrene.[4]

These handwritten notes demonstrate the chemical know-how of the author, who took care to complete it with information from technical monographs or experts.

During a further stage, Queneau wrote down short drafts for his commentary which also exist in handwritten manuscripts. I can't resist sharing the following one, on this very topic of the production of monomeric styrene:

> Ethylbenzene arises from a combination of
> Ethylene and benzene – the origin of its name is clear.
> But where does benzene come from? Well, either from petroleum
> Or even from coal. There occurred a farandole dance
> Of distillations followed by refining
> And by operations known as recycling
> Which may have isolated it from other products.
> But ethylene can also arise from
> Cracking the magical liquid petroleum
> Which is to be found from Bordeaux to the heart of Africa.
> Ethylene and benzene could be born likewise
> From the gases of coke ovens; and this is the dilemma,

---

4 "Dans ces installations on met les deux produits susdits en présence de chlorure d'aluminium à une température de 95°. Le résultat de cette réaction est clarifié par un lavage à l'eau, puis par une solution de soude caustique. Il ne reste plus alors qu'à rectifier ce mélange par un catalyseur à une température de six cent degrés qui le transforme par déshydrogénation en authentique styrène monomère."

Whether oil, or coal.
Shall we get on such new trails to identify what existed before them?[5]

Following which a first typescript mentions that "this monomeric styrene is obtained by combining ethylene and benzene in synthetic units". The quoted paired lines result from this whole patient and scrupulous process, analogous to a distillation of words and concepts.

CONCLUSION

Chemistry offers to the poet both a lexicon and the opaque mystery of its generation. Chemical terminology, as exemplified by "styrene", evokes the history of bygone colonial empires and faraway countries. A modern piece of plastic is thus polysemic. A non-chemist such as Quenouillard, given the task of explaining a chemical process, first to himself, then to his readers and listeners, has to be didactic. Success is the reward of a light touch and self-deprecating wit. Quenoo eschewed mechanistic explanations. He privileged instead a descriptive mode, along with genealogies. In this way he managed to explain the synthetic chemical elaboration while respecting the mystery of its inner workings, and finally making it into a humanistic achievement.

WORKS CITED

Andrews, Chris: *Poetry and Cosmogony: Science in the Writing of Queneau and Ponge*. Amsterdam: Rodopi, 1999.

Aron, Raymond: *Les étapes de la pensée sociologique*. Paris: Gallimard, 1976.

Auclerc, Benoît: "Lecture, réception et déstabilisation générique chez Francis Ponge et Nathalie Sarraute (1919-1958)". Ph. D. dissertation, Université Lumière-Lyon 2, 2006.

---

5   "L'éthylbenzène nait d'une combinaison / d'éthylène et benzène – on voit d'où vient son nom. / Mais d'où vient le benzène? Eh bien, soit du pétrole / Soit même du charbon. Ce fut la farandole / des distillations suivies de raffinages / puis des opérations dites de recyclage / qui a pu l'isoler de bien d'autres produits. / Mais l' éthylène peut provenir lui aussi / du cracking du pétrole liquide magique / qu'on trouve de Bordeaux jusqu' au cœur de l'Afrique. / Ethylène et benzène ont pu naître de même / des gaz des fours à coke: et c' est là un dilemme, / ou pétrole, ou charbon. Sur ces nouvelles pistes / on pourrait repartir vers ce qui pré-existe."

Baillaud, Bernard: "Raymond Queneau, la polymérisation des sirènes" in Denis Hüe (ed.): *Sciences, Techniques & Encyclopédies. Actes du colloque de Mortagne-Au-Perche, 28-29 mars 1992.* Coll. Varia, no. 8. Caen: Paradigme, 1993, pp. 25-63.

Barthes, Roland: *Mythologies.* Paris: Le Seuil, 1957.

Bellos, David: *Georges Perec, Une Vie dans les mots*, trans. Françoise Cartano and the author. Paris: Le Seuil, 1994.

—: *Jacques Tati, sa vie et son art.* Paris: Le Seuil, 2002.

Benayoun, Robert: *Resnais, Arpenteur de l'imaginaire.* Paris: Ramsay, 1986.

Beugnot, Bernard, Martel, Jacinthe and Veck, Bernard: *Bibliographie des écrivains français: Francis Ponge.* Paris-Rome: Memini, 1999.

Bollinger, Jean-Claude: "Poésie et chimie: 'Le chant du styrène' de Raymond Queneau et l'enseignement de la chimie macromoléculaire" in *Actualité chimique,* April 1987, Paris, pp. 122-7.

Bollinger, Jean-Claude and Clancier, Anne: "'Le chant du styrène': étude chimico-psychanalytique" in *Temps mêlés,* vol. 150, 1985, pp. 180-94.

Bonhomme, Marc: "Rhétorique ludique et métonymie chez Queneau" in *Etudes de Lettres,* vol. 4, 1991, pp. 45-66.

Burch, Noel: "Four Recent French Documentaries" in *Film Quarterly,* 13.1, 1959, pp. 56-61.

Cadiot, Pierre: "Drôle de drupe" in *CORELA – Espace, Préposition, Cognition.* Poitiers, 2010. http://corela.edel.univ-poitiers.fr (1 Sep. 2011).

Cappello, Sergio: *Les années parisiennes d'Italo Calvino (1964-1980) sous le signe de Raymond Queneau.* Paris: Presses de l'Université Paris-Sorbonne, 2007.

Charnay, Dominique: *Cher Monsieur Queneau. Les recalés de la littérature.* Paris: Denoël, 2011.

Cherqui-Rousseau, M.-C.: "Images de Queneau, II: nouvel essai de filmographie" in *Les Amis de Valentin Bru,* vol. 1, 1994, pp. 31-55.

Darmon, Pierre: "L'humour dans la poésie de Raymond Queneau". Ph. D. dissertation, Université d'Avignon et des pays de Vaucluse, 2002.

Daumas, Maurice: "Les Matières plastiques" in Paul Angoulvent (ed.): *Que Sais-Je?* Paris: PUF, 1941.

Davay, Paul, and Micha, René: "Queneau au cinéma" in *Ecran du séminaire des arts,* Bruxelles, 1964.

Demoulin, Laurent: *Une rhétorique par objet. Les mimétismes dans l'œuvre de Francis Ponge,* Savoir Lettres. Paris: Hermann, 2011.

Donon, Marcel Bourdette: *Raymond Queneau: L'œil, l'oreille et la raison.* Paris: L'Harmattan, 2001.

Dubillard, Roland: *Les diablogues.* Paris: Gallimard, 1975. Folio, 1998.

Farasse, Gérard: *Ponge (augmenté du manuscrit de "L'âne").* Les aéronautes de l'esprit. Paris: L'Improviste, 2004.

Fraisse, Emmanuel, and Mouralis, Bernard: *Questions générales de littérature.* Points Essais. Paris: Le Seuil, 2001.

Godard, Henri: *Une grande génération: Céline, Malraux, Guilloux, Giono, Montherlant, Malaquais, Sartre, Queneau, Simon.* Collection Blanche. Paris: Gallimard, 2003.

Godard, Jean-Luc: "Chacun son Tours" in *Les Cahiers du Cinéma* 16.92, 1959, pp. 31-8.

Jacques, Jean: "Le styrène de Queneau revisité" in *Libération*, Paris, 26 December 2000: 7.

Jouet, Jacques: *Raymond Queneau*. Les Classiques de la Manufacture. Lyon: La Manufacture, 1989.

Jouet, Jacques, Martin, Pierre and Moncond'huy, Dominique (eds.): *La morale élémentaire. Aventures d'une forme poétique. Queneau, Oulipo, etc.* 81 F-59710. Mérignies: La Licorne, 2008.

Jousse, Thierry: *Alain Resnais, compositeur de films*. Paris: Mille et Une Nuits, 1997.

Kohlauer, Michael: "L'âme des mots: Raymond Queneau le spirituel" in *Recherches et Travaux* 58, 2000, pp. 173-90.

Laszlo, Pierre: *La Leçon de choses*. Diversio. Dimitri Afgoustidis (ed.). Paris: Austral, 1995.

Lecouvette, Guy: "Alain Resnais ou le souvenir" in *Avant-scène du cinéma*, Paris, 15 February 1961: 49.

Leutrat, Jean-Louis: "Le début et la fin: donner forme à l'incertain (Alain Resnais)", 2007. *Le début et la fin*. Fabula. Online colloquium, www.fabula.org (31 Aug. 2011).

Marker, Chris: *Commentaires 1*. Paris: Le Seuil, 1961.

Martin, Jean-Pierre: "Raymond Queneau, sa vie, son œuvre" in *Europe* 888, 2003, pp. 10-21.

Oms, Marcel: *Alain Resnais*. Paris: Rivages, 1988.

Ouardi, H. and Campana, M.-N. (eds.): *Connaissez-vous Queneau?* Dijon: Presses Universitaires, 2007.

OULIPO (ed.): *La littérature potentielle Créations, Re-Créations, Récréations*. Paris: Gallimard, 1973. Folio Essais (rev. ed.), 1988.

—: *Atlas de littérature potentielle*. Paris: Gallimard, 1981. Folio Essais (rev. ed.), 1988.

Pérec, Georges: *Les Choses. Une histoire des années soixante*. Les Lettres Nouvelles. Paris: Julliard, 1965.

Ponge, Francis: "Le Parti-pris des choses" in Bernard Beugnot (ed.): *Œuvres Complètes / La Pléiade*, vol. 1. Paris: NRF, 1999 (1942).

Prot, Robert: "A propos de Queneau" in *Confluent*. Rennes, February 1974:19.

Queneau, Raymond: *Exercices de Style*. Paris: Gallimard, 1947.

—: *Petite cosmogonie portative*. Paris: Gallimard, 1950.

Queval, Jean: "Images et sons. Au cinéma d'essai." *Mercure de France*, Paris, August 1959, pp. 690-5.

Resnais, Alain: "Un cinéaste stoïcien", *Esprit*, June 1960, pp. 934-45.

Rot, Gwenaële: "Le travail du contrôleur de flux, de Pierre Naville à Alain Resnais, propos sur Le chant du styrène (1958)" in *Histoire et Sociétés* (24 December 2007), pp. 52-79.

Shiotsuka, Shuichiro: "Raymond Queneau et deux encyclopédies: L'idée de 'savoir' chez Queneau" in *Cahiers de l'Association internationale des études francaises* 53, 2001, pp. 391-420.

Siclier, Jacques: *Le Cinéma français*, vol. 1. Paris: Ramsay, 1990.

Veck, Bernard: *Francis Ponge ou le refus de l'absolu littéraire*. Philosophie et langage. Liège: Pierre Mardaga, 2003.

Ziegelmeyer, Pierre: "Le chat d'yrene" in *Cahiers Raymond Queneau* 1, 1986, pp. 89-91.

"Le chant du styrène"

Ô temps, suspends ton bol, ô matière plastique
D'où viens-tu? Qui es-tu? Et qu'est-ce qui explique
Tes rares qualités? De quoi donc es-tu fait?
Quelle est ton origine? Remontons de l'objet
À ses aïeux lointains! Qu' à l'envers se déroule
Son histoire exemplaire. En premier lieu, le moule.
Incluant la matrice, être mystérieux,
Il engendre le bol ou bien tout ce qu'on veut.
Mais le moule est lui-même inclus dans une presse
Qui injecte la pâte et conforme la pièce,
Ce qui présente donc le très grand avantage
D'avoir l'objet fini sans autre façonnage.
Le moule coûte cher; c'est un inconvénient.
Mais il peut resservir sur d'autres continents.
Le formage sous vide est une autre façon
D'obtenir des objets: par simple aspiration.
À l' étape antérieure, soigneusement rangé,
Le matériau tiédi est en plaque extrudé.
Pour entrer dans la buse il fallait un piston
Et le manchon chauffant – ou le chauffant manchon
Auquel on fournissait – Quoi? Le polystyrène
Vivace et turbulent qui se hâte et s' égrène.
Et l'essaim granulé sur le tamis vibrant
Fourmillait tout heureux d'un si beau colorant.
Avant d' être granule on avait été jonc,
Joncs de toutes couleurs, teintes, nuances, tons.
Ces joncs avaient été, suivant une filière,
Un boudin que sans fin une vis agglomère.
Et ce qui donnait lieu à l'agglutination?
Des perles colorées de toutes les façons.
Et colorées comment? Là, devient homogène
Le pigment qu'on mélange à du polystyrène.

Mais avant il fallut que le produit séchât
Et, rotativement, le produit trébucha.
C'est alors que naquit notre polystyrène.
Polymère produit du plus simple styrène.
Polymérisation: ce mot, chacun le sait,
Désigne l'obtention d'un complexe élevé
De poids moléculaire. Et dans un autoclave,
Machine élémentaire à la pense concave,[6]
Les molécules donc s'accrochant et se liant
En perles se formaient. Oui, mais – auparavant?
Le styrène n' était qu'un liquide incolore
Quelque peu explosif, et non pas inodore.
Et regardez-le bien; c'est la seule occasion
Pour vous d'apercevoir ce qui est en question.
Le styrène est produit en grande quantité
À partir de l' éthyl-benzène surchauffé.
Faut un catalyseur comme cela se nomme
Oxyde ou bien de zinc ou bien de magnésium.
Le styrène autrefois s'extrayait du benjoin,
Provenant du styrax, arbuste indonésien.
De tuyau en tuyau ainsi nous remontons,
À travers le désert des canalisations,
Vers les produits premiers, vers la matière abstraite
Qui circulait sans fin, effective et secrète.
On lave et on distille et puis on redistille
Et ce ne sont pas là exercices de style:
L' éthylbenzène peut – et doit même éclater
Si la température atteint certain degré.
Il faut se demander maintenant d'où proviennent
Ces produits essentiels: éthylène et benzène.
Ils s'extraient du pétrole, un liquide magique
Qu'on trouve de Bordeaux jusqu'au cœur de l'Afrique.
Ils s'extraient du pétrole et aussi du charbon
Pour faire l'autre et l'un l'un et l'autre sont bons.
Se transformant en gaz le charbon se combure
Et donne alors naissance à ces hydrocarbures.

------

6   Deliberate misspelling of "panse" to form a pun.

On pourrait repartir sur ces nouvelles pistes
Et rechercher pourquoi et l'autre et l'un existent.
Le pétrole vient-il de masses de poissons?
On ne le sait pas trop ni d'où vient le charbon.
Le pétrole vient-il du plancton en gésine?
Question controversée... obscures origines...
Et pétrole et charbon s'en allaient en fumée
Quand le chimiste vint qui eut l'heureuse idée
De rendre ces nuées solides et d'en faire
D'innombrables objets au but utilitaire.
En matériaux nouveaux ces obscurs résidus
Sont ainsi transformés. Il en est d'inconnus
Qui attendent encore un travail similaire,
Pour faire le sujet d'autres documentaires.[7]

---

7   For an English version of "The Song of Styrene", see
    http://benjamintripp.files.wordpress.com.

LITERATURE AND CHEMISTRY

THE INVISIBLE SCIENCE? CHEMISTRY, SCIENCE FICTION, AND POPULAR CULTURE

Folkert Degenring, University of Kassel

In 2006 and 2007, *HYLE – International Journal for Philosophy of Chemistry* published a special issue on "The Public Image of Chemistry". In their introduction the editors posit that while chemistry seems more concerned with its public image than other scientific disciplines, it has been largely unsuccessful in its efforts to generate a positive public perception:

> Despite repetaed [sic] campaigns for convincing the public that chemistry would bring health, comfort, and welfare, chemists frequently meet with hostility in popular culture. In humanist culture chemistry has a very low profile; philosophers in particular keep to their traditional neglect of anything related to chemistry. Of course, chemists have always been complaining about their low prestige, the lack of public acknowledgement of their achievements and the misguiding popular associations with chemistry, such that we now have a long record of complaints of almost two centuries. More recently, in response to their public image, chemists tried to launch slogans such as "green chemistry" or even dropped the term "chemistry" altogether and adopted more fashionable labels such as "materials science", "molecular science", or "nanotechnology". (Schummer, Bensaude-Vincent and van Tiggelen, p. 3)

The editors argue that outside of the sciences, there are two basic sets of reactions towards chemistry: in the humanities it is traditionally neglected, and in popular culture it is vilified. Considering that the organisation of contemporary societies is completely inconceivable without chemistry and its application, this is surely surprising. How is this state of affairs to be explained?

The *HYLE* editorial offers two possible avenues of explanation. The first points out that "the public image mixes up the science of chemistry with the chemical industry" (Schummer, Bensaude-Vincent and van Tiggelen, p. 4). This failure to differentiate would imply that a growing public awareness and concern over environmental pollution, food, and health issues leads to an unfair evaluation of chemistry as a discipline. Chemistry is equated with the artificial and thus un-natural, that is, dangerous.

In the same issue of *HYLE*, Peter Weingart, a German sociologist of science, argues in his essay "Chemists and their Craft in Fiction Film" that chemistry is "the iconic discipline of the 'mad scientist'" (Weingart, p. 31). Weingart presents the results of a quantitative analysis of 222 films. When chemists feature in films, they are often associated with authority, and frequently also with unethical behaviour, danger, and fear. Indeed, Weingart finds that 24,4% of the films that feature chemistry explicitly are horror films, followed by thrillers and comedies, both at 13,3%.

The second avenue of explanation offered in the *HYLE* editorial considers the humanities rather than contemporary popular culture, focusing on historical and literary dimensions. The editors cite Mary Shelley's Victor Frankenstein as the archetypal mad scientist. The fact that Victor Frankenstein can be described, in a sense, as a chemical researcher, and at the same time as the embodiment of scientific hubris, would then be a kind of foundational myth for the humanities' engagement with chemistry: chemistry is turned into the scapegoat of high culture.

The example of Victor Frankenstein illustrates that a clear distinction between high and popular culture is not tenable in this context. Other classic literary examples of protagonists that are chemists, like Stevenson's Dr. Jekyll or Wells' Invisible Man, show that while the works of literature themselves may be considered high culture in the sense that they have become part of an extended literary canon, the *stories* have very much become a part of popular culture; some of these characters could even be described as cultural icons. This is certainly true for Frankenstein, even if the name of the creator, in this case, is sometimes confused with his creation.

HYLE is not the only journal dedicated to chemistry that has engaged with the subject's relationship with literature. For example, in an essay published in *Chemistry World* in 2008, Philip Ball, a British science writer who holds a degree in chemistry and a doctorate in physics, argues that while physics and biology provide a rich source of metaphors for literature, chemistry has more or less consistently failed to do so since the early 19th century. At the beginning of his essay, Ball asks:

> But who writes about chemistry in novels? True, you can find ample passing reference in science fiction, from H G Wells' toxic compounds of argon concocted by Martians in *War of the Worlds* to Neil Stephenson's diamondoid nanotechnology in *The diamond age*. But these are not conceptual elements of the plot. Does

chemistry have anything to offer the modern writer beyond a means of bumping off characters in crime thrillers? (Ball: "Literary Reactions", p. 46)

It is interesting to note that Ball begins his observations by referring to two genres which are frequently considered not to be proper literature at all, before going on to discuss Johann Wolfgang von Goethe, Primo Levi, and Thomas Pynchon. The notion that crime and science fiction as genres are deficient *per se* is, of course, untenable, and Ball does not necessarily share it, but it is nevertheless a notion that is frequently encountered. And yet, science fiction has certainly become an integral part of *popular* culture, as is evident from its presence in nearly every medium and format – the third edition of *The Encyclopedia of Science Fiction*, for example, features entries not just on online and print literature but also on comics, films, games, music, radio, and TV (Clute and Langford). Chemistry and science fiction have something in common, paradoxically speaking, in the sense that they are omnipresent yet strangely invisible, or at least often misconceived.

FUNCTIONS OF CHEMISTRY IN SCIENCE FICTION

This observation implicitly raises the question of how science fiction engages with chemistry in literary practice. Is chemistry invisible or misconceived in science fiction as well? In the 2011 *Routledge Companion to Literature and Science* section on chemistry, the chemist Jay Labinger comments:

> The role of chemistry in science fiction, another genre [like crime fiction] in which it might be expected to feature predominantly, appears to be rather limited (again, in comparison to physics and biology). Much of the material in a collection of essays on the topic … addresses science in general rather than focussing specifically on chemistry … (Labinger, p. 57)

The collection of essays Labinger refers to in his comment is *Chemistry and Science Fiction*, compiled by the chemist Jack H. Stocker, and described in his introduction as an "outgrowth" (Stocker, vii) of a popular panel at the 1992 meeting of the American Chemical Society. Its contributors are predominantly chemists, but it also contains a contribution by Connie Willis, a well-established American science fiction author whose works have been recognised with an impressive number of genre awards.

In her essay "Science in Science Fiction: A Writer's Perspective", Willis discusses the various ways in which science plays a role in science fiction.

She proposes five categories to describe this relationship: Science as Subject, Science as Plot Device, Science as Background, Science as Metaphor, and Science as the Basis of All Science Fiction. Willis's essay does not provide a convincing or comprehensive definition of science fiction – indeed, no definition of science fiction to date is entirely convincing (cf. Stableford et al.) – but this is not really its objective. Instead, Willis attempts to provide categories that describe the relationship between science and science fiction in written practice.

Willis describes her category of "Science as Subject" as "the sub-genre known as 'hard' science fiction" (Willis, p. 22). She argues that these stories are "a kind of game in which ideas are played with, and it is the ideas that are interesting, not the human story" (Willis, p. 24).

"Science as Plot Device" refers to "'gadget' stories" (Willis, p. 24), i.e. stories that depend on the technological implementation of science. The plot is literally driven by science (Willis, p. 25), and would not be possible inside the fictional world without its technological implementation.

The "Science as Background" category makes use of our understanding of the physical world as conveyed through our scientific education, our knowledge of how the physical world works, which is of course not always identical to the way we experience it (Willis, p. 26).

Willis next discusses "Science as Metaphor". This category refers to science in science fiction as "giving concrete form to intangible ideas and emotions" (Willis, p. 26). Unsurprisingly, this may entail a variety of manifestations: From a reminder "about our own limited view of the universe" (Willis, p. 27), to a comment on "man's inability to control his own technological discoveries" (Willis, p. 28), to a story that employs narrative experiments to illustrate scientific principles. Finally, in "Science as the Basis of All Science Fiction", Connie Willis argues that:

> [science fiction] is one huge thought experiment, with each author observing the world, developing hypotheses about it, and setting up experiments in the form of stories to examine those hypotheses. In this sense every science fiction story uses science, whether science appears overtly in it or not. (Willis, p. 29)

This applies to more than just science fiction, of course – perhaps to all narrative texts. Furthermore, is noticeable that Willis refers to the relationship between science and science fiction in general, and most of the literary examples she uses appear to have little to do with chemistry. This is strange, because the essay is collected in a volume *explicitly* dealing with chemistry and science fiction that was published by the American Chemical Society. This is true for several other contributions in the volume as well. Is this, then, a confirmation of the hypothesis that chemistry is an invisible science in science fiction?

It is, of course, easy enough to relate Willis's categories more closely to the functionalization of chemistry in science fiction by simply exchanging the word "science" for "chemistry": Chemistry as subject, chemistry as plot device, chemistry as background, chemistry as metaphor, and chemistry as the basis of all science fiction. And while these categories may sound rather vague (and, in the case of the last one, slightly odd), they are nevertheless a useful starting point when considering some recent literary examples.

CHEMISTRY AND DISCOVERY IN ALASTAIR REYNOLDS'S *REVELATION SPACE*

The first example I would like to discuss is Alastair Reynolds's *Revelation Space*, first published in 2000. Reynolds is a Welsh writer; he holds a PhD in astronomy and until 2004 worked for the European Space Agency. *Revelation Space* is a space opera, a sub-genre within science fiction which was considered by science fiction criticism to be "the most common, and least respected, form of science fiction" until comparatively recently (Westfahl, p. 197). The plot of the novel is fairly complex and combines elements of the space opera with hard science fiction. It is set in a far future in which humankind has successfully reached the stars and colonised other solar systems, but at the cost of fragmentation: humanity has split into various sub-groups, with sometimes wildly divergent philosophical perspectives, levels of technology, and motivations. So far, humanity has only discovered extinct alien civilisations and in the course of the novel it is revealed that this is no accident: an alien machine-intelligence actively suppresses the rise of interstellar civilisations, and humankind is about to face extinction itself. In the following passage, two rival scientists descend a mine shaft in order to examine a buried alien artefact:

> The shaft the car descended was walled in diamond, ten metres wide. Occasionally there were recesses, stash-holes for equipment or small operations shacks, or switching points where two elevators could squeeze past one another before continuing on their journeys. Servitors were working the diamond, extruding it in atomic-thickness filaments from spinerettes. The filaments zipped neatly into place under the action of protein-sized molecular machines. (Reynolds, p. 122)

In this passage we encounter two science fiction staples: nanotechnology in the form of molecular machinery, and diamond used as a construction material, in this case in order to support the shaft.

It would certainly be unconvincing to argue that the mere mention of diamond as a substance is an implicit reference to chemistry, because chemistry, after all, is the study of the properties and composition of matter. The way the diamond wall is produced, however, *is* an implicit reference to contemporary chemistry, which is able to produce synthetic diamonds through a process called CVD or Chemical Vapor Deposition. Molecular machinery constructing diamond mine shafts is certainly fiction, but the chemical principles behind this notion are not. Chemistry here serves as both plot device and background, then. Is there anything more to it? Consider the following passage from Reynolds's novel:

> Sylveste's scientific curiosity momentarily beat his urge to belittle Girardeau's attempts at impressing him. "You know what this material is?"
> "Basically carbon, with some iron and niobium and a few rare metals as trace elements. But we don't know the structure. It's not simply some allotropic form of diamond we haven't invented yet, or even hyperdiamond. Maybe the top few tenths of a millimetre are close to diamond, but the stuff seems to undergo some kind of complex lattice transformation deeper down. ... It could be that the lattice breaks up into trillions of carbon-heavy macromolecules, locked together in a co-acting mass. [...]" (Reynolds, p. 125)

The two scientists here are now examining the alien artefact. The alien substance, its elementary composition and its molecular structure, are described in chemical terms. The focus is on chemistry as a subject: the material itself is far less important than the sense of wonder in encountering something new. Or, more precisely, encountering something unfamiliar that, paradoxically, consists of what is familiar: carbon, iron, and some rarer metals. The urge to understand the composition of the alien artefact for a moment suspends the rivalry between the two scientists, not for reasons of personal gain, but because this is something unknown that can nevertheless be understood. I would argue, then, that what is foregrounded here is not an extrapolation of the technical application of chemistry, but chemistry as a *science*. And thus chemistry functions as a metaphor as well, i.e. a metaphor for the human need to understand what is not yet understood, to know what is not yet known.

Chemistry is employed in a similar fashion in Paul McAuley's 2008 novel *The Quiet War*. McAuley is an English science fiction writer and holds a PhD in botany; he worked as a researcher and lecturer at various universities before becoming a full-time writer. *The Quiet War* is set in the twenty-third century, with refugees struggling to colonise the solar system in order to escape the dictatorial regimes established on Earth in the wake of global ecological catastrophe. They are splintered into many different factions, each with their own philosophy and perspective on life. The following passage describes Jupiter's moon Europa, where a small human colony has established itself:

> Although the upwelling water was rich in nutrients, there was little energy that native life could use this high in the water column. The hydrogen sulphide that issued from the hydrothermal rifts and drove oxidising reactions in the bacterial colonies around them was quickly broken down into unusable sulphates by water chemistry. The rifts were rare and rich oases of life; everywhere else in the vast and lifeless deserts of Europa's ocean only thrifty chemolithrophs [*sic!*] survived by splitting hydrogen from scanty molecules of metal oxides. (McAuley, p. 129)

The chemistry of life, i.e. biochemistry, is central to this passage. Chemistry once again serves as background and to make an element of the plot credible, i.e. native life on Europa, which helps support the human colony. The alien is rendered familiar through the terminology employed: even without chemical training, we readily recognise terms like sulphide or oxidizing reactions, and if we also happen to know that chemolithotrophs are a group of microbes that use inorganic compounds for the production of energy, then life on Europa as it is described here does not seem so implausible.

The role of biochemistry in the novel is not limited to this function, however. It also serves as a metaphor for the situation in which the human colonists find themselves. Europa's ocean is likened to a desert with just a few "rare and rich oases of life", and that image holds true for the whole solar system, in which the small human colonies can only thrive in a few isolated spots. This metaphorical dimension is also apparent in the following passage, which describes the difficulties scientists have in artificially creating topsoil for their habitats in space:

> Soil was not a random mixture of inorganic, organic and living material; it was highly structured at every level, fractally so. Stratified and textured and dynamic, it supported a myriad of chemical reactions that were still not completely under-

stood, mediated by soil water and air moving through pore spaces that occupied up to fifty per cent of soil by volume. (McAuley, p. 67)

The text draws attention to something common, something that we encounter every day. In describing soil in this unusual fashion, the seemingly trivial and mundane is shown to be remarkable. And this is true not only for the complex chemistry of soil but, as a metaphor, for society: That individual human beings, with their sometimes radically divergent drives and needs can form something like a functioning society is something we take for granted, but upon closer inspection it is just as strange and wondrous as the chemistry of soil.

Reading the passage in such a fashion questions the popular conception of chemistry primarily as an applied science, which fails to address fundamental issues. In an essay dealing with "Chemistry and Power in Recent American Fiction", Philip Ball remarks that:

[c]hemistry, in contrast [to physics and biology], seems to have little to offer in the way of grand themes. In fact, it often seems today not to be asking any questions about the world at all: it is primarily a synthetic science, a science bound up with making things. Even many scientists, if they have no real knowledge of chemistry, seem unable to find a way to fit this discipline into their vision of what science is about, namely the process of discovering how the world works. Most current distinctions that are drawn between science and technology will place today's chemistry squarely within the realm of technology, or at least applied science, concerned as it is much more with invention than with discovery. (Ball, p. 45)

CHEMISTRY AND THE PROJECT OF SCIENCE IN GREG EGAN'S *THE CLOCKWORK ROCKET*

I'd like to explore this aspect by turning to another literary example, namely Greg Egan's 2011 novel *The Clockwork Rocket*. Egan is an Australian science fiction writer with a degree in mathematics. He writes mostly hard science fiction: his work has even been described as "diamond-hard". This quality can be readily illustrated by the abundance of graphs and diagrams in some of his novels, and the supplementary science material he provides on his website. *The Clockwork Rocket* is a thought experiment: it is set in a different universe, with different natural laws. This does not mean that some of *our* physical laws are broken, something that science fiction does frequently enough, but that a completely different physics underlies the fictional world. The plot itself is fairly straightforward: when a planet is threatened with destruction by a cosmic event, its inhabitants try to save their world. They can only hope to achieve this goal if they fully understand how the world works, however. In part, *The Clockwork Rocket* therefore reads less like a novel than a science textbook. The characters have to develop the science that they hope will save them almost from scratch, and this process is fully developed in the narrative. For the reader, this is a challenge, because the fictional natural laws are sometimes radically different from our own, and we cannot rely on our background knowledge to help us quickly come to terms with what is being said.

It is clear that Egan's novel predominantly deals with physics. Chemistry does play an important role, however. Consider the following passage, in which two scientists are discussing their difficulties in obtaining experimental data in order to validate their theories:

> "In principle it should work, but in practice it's hard to get accurate data. Think of it as a work in progress. But if you ever go out to the chemistry department –"
> Esuebio buzzed amusement. "I'm not suicidal!"
> "You can always watch their experiments from behind the safety walls."
> "You mean the 'safety walls' that need to be rebuilt three or four times a year?"
> The truth was, Yalda had only visited Amputation Alley once herself. (Egan, p. 44)

On the one hand, we are dealing with a play on the public perception of chemistry as dangerous: it is the chemists, and not the physicists, who accidentally but regularly blow up their department. In terms of the plot, however, they are central to achieving the greater goal, i.e. saving the world. Without each other, neither chemistry nor physics could make any progress. This is illustrated in the following passage, in which a chemist introduces a physicist to a new invention:

> Next, he took what appeared to be a stiff sheet of paper from a cupboard below the bench and fastened it in place over the screen where the spectrum had been seen. Then he produced a small vial that had been divided partly in two, with one half containing an orange powder, the other a green resin. He attached the vial to a loop of cord that dangled into the interior of the box through its top face. …

"First, you shake the vial," Cornelio explained, taking hold of the cord where it protruded from the top of the box and jiggling it slightly. "That lets the ingredients react, and the gas that's produced activates the paper."

"Activates?"

"Sensitises it to light. ...." (Egan, p. 138)

The process described here is readily recognisable as photography, which has been developed in the novel in order to make the study of astronomical phenomena more precise. Does this mean that chemistry is relegated to an auxiliary role, a useful helper for the truly important disciplines? The invention drives the plot forward, of course, but it serves another purpose as well. Embedded in a narrative about weird and alternate physics, the chemical processes involved in photography serve to relate the strange fictional world to our own – if we know something about pre-digital photography, that is. Chemistry is used, then, not to make the familiar seem strange, but to make the strange seem familiar. And certainly, chemistry is inseparable from the other sciences in Egan's novel: there is really only *science,* in the singular. In this sense chemistry as a metaphor for the project of science, i.e. the systematic attempt to understand the world, may indeed be considered as the basis of all science fiction.

I hope that I have shown that chemistry certainly plays an important part in science fiction, and may fulfil many different functions. Chemistry, in the examples of science fiction studied above, is neither invisible nor mono-dimensional. It is true that physics and biology do feature more prominently than chemistry. I would argue, however, that the difference is one of quantity and not quality. And perhaps, if science fiction and other genres are able to paint a differentiated picture of chemistry and science in general, and if this differentiated picture of chemistry eventually becomes part of popular culture, then chemistry will cease to be perceived primarily as the domain of mad scientists.

WORKS CITED

Ball, Philip: "Chemistry and Power in Recent American Fiction" in *HYLE – International Journal for Philosophy of Chemistry,* vol. 12, no. 1, 2006, pp. 45-66. www.hyle.org (16 Apr. 2013).

—: "Literary Reactions" in *Chemistry World,* vol. 5, no. 12, 2008, pp. 46-9.

Clarke, Bruce (ed.): *The Routledge Companion to Literature and Science.* New York: Routledge, 2011.

Clute, John, and Langford, David: *The Encyclopedia of Science Fiction*. www.sf-encyclopedia.com (16 Apr. 2013).

Egan, Greg: *The Clockwork Rocket*. London: Gollancz, 2011.

Labinger, Jay: "Chemistry" in Bruce Clarke (ed.): *The Routledge Companion to Literature and Science*. New York: Routledge, 2011, pp. 51-62.

Reynolds, Alastair: *Revelation Space*. London: Gollancz, 2001.

McAuley, Paul: *The Quiet War*. London: Gollancz, 2008.

Schummer, Joachim, Bensaude-Vincent, Bernadette and Tiggelen, Brigitte van: "Editorial" in *HYLE – International Journal for Philosophy of Chemistry*, vol. 12, no. 1, 2006, pp. 3-4. www.hyle.org (16 Apr. 2013).

Shelley, Mary: *Frankenstein: Or, The Modern Prometheus*. London: Penguin, 1992.

Stableford, Brian, Clute, John and Nicholls, Peter: "Definitions of SF" in *The Encyclopedia of Science Fiction*. www.sf-encyclopedia.com (16 Apr. 2013).

Stevenson, Robert Louis: *Strange Case of Dr Jekyll and Mr Hyde*. Katherine Linehan (ed.). New York: Norton, 2003.

Stocker, Jack H. (ed.): *Chemistry and Science Fiction*. Washington, D.C.: American Chemical Society, 1998.

Weingart, Peter: "Chemists and their Craft in Fiction Film" in *HYLE – International Journal for Philosophy of Chemistry*, vol. 12, no. 1, 2006, pp. 31-44. www.hyle.org (16 Apr. 2013).

Wells, Herbert George: *The Invisible Man*. London: Penguin, 2012.

Westfahl, Gary: "Space Opera" in Edward James and Farah Mendlesohn (eds.): *The Cambridge Companion to Science Fiction*. Cambridge: Cambridge University Press, 2004, pp. 197-208.

Willis, Connie: "Science in Science Fiction: A Writer's Perspective" in Jack H. Stocker (ed.): *Chemistry and Science Fiction*. Washington, D.C.: American Chemical Society, 1998, pp. 21-32.

IN THE ZONE: THE STRUGATSKII BROTHERS AND THE POETICS OF POLLUTION IN RUSSIAN SCIENCE FICTION

Muireann Maguire, University of Oxford

Anton Chekhov's short story "In The Ravine" ("V ovrage", 1900) became instantly notorious for depicting cruelty as an everyday phenomenon in Russian peasant society: its heroine endures vicious intimidation from her husband's family, culminating in her baby's murder. Yet Chekhov himself was less preoccupied by individual cruelties than by the gradual, generalised neglect and deprivation dehumanising Russia's poor.[1] An early environmentalist, Chekhov was one of the first writers to note the connection between the industrial degradation of the countryside and the moral decline of its inhabitants. "In The Ravine" vividly conveys the local consequences of chemical pollution from three cotton mills and a tanning factory in a rural community: "There was always a smell of factory refuse and of the ascetic acid used for processing cotton … The water in the stream was often putrid from the tannery; its refuse corrupted the fields, the peasants' cattle suffered from anthrax" (Chekhov, p. 398).[2] The casual despoliation of nature finds moral expression in the selfishness and brutal indifference displayed by some of the villagers; the frequently glimpsed factory chimneys, towering above ploughed meadows, link the parallel processes of moral and environmental contamination.

Chekhov's fiction inaugurated an explicit "poetics of pollution" in Russian literature, a method in which industrial, chemical, or nuclear waste is

---

[1] Chekhov assured Iurii Avdeev that "In the Ravine" was an accurate portrait of life in central Russia as he knew it, and "that all this could happen in real life"; the drowning of the child in the short story apparently had numerous real-life precedents. See Iurii Avdeev: "Chekhov in Melikhovo" in Sekirin, p. 53-4 (54).

[2] Other Chekhov fictions with environmental themes include the play *Uncle Vanya* (*Diadia Vania*, 1896), which features the ecologically impassioned Dr. Astrov, and the short stories "Panpipes" ("Svirel", 1887) and "Rothschild's Violin" ("Skripka Rotshchil'da", 1894).

examined not only in terms of its environmental impact but also for what it implies about the ethical progress (or regression) of the human race. This poetics has transferred successfully to the screen, as in the modern director Konstantin Lopushanskii's internationally prize-winning films *Letters of a Dead Man* (*Pis'ma mertvogo cheloveka*, 1986) and *A Visitor to the Museum* (*Posetitel' museia*, 1989), which explore, respectively, the consequences of nuclear war and of rising sea levels. In the twentieth century, whether on film or in print, Russia's poetics of pollution have been most prevalent in science fiction – partly because of the inherently speculative nature of the genre and partly because of the strict internal censorship of Russian literature until 1986, which frequently required characters to be shifted to distant locations or times in order to disguise or soften critiques.

Since the 1940s, Western science fiction has similarly experienced a trend towards "ecological SF" – that is, accounts of extraterrestrial ecospheres which combine rigorous scientific consistency with striking narrative originality. Chastened by the nuclear threat in the post-Second World War period, writers like Clifford D. Simak, Hal Clement, and later Poul Anderson "pioneered" this trend (Stableford, p. 129). As the urgency of modern industry's threat to nature became better known (publicised by such high-profile non-fiction studies as Rachel Carson's epochal *Silent Spring* (1962) and Max Nicholson's *The Environmental Revolution* (1970)), the same writers' fiction acquired terrestrial themes – and, inevitably, political implications.[3] Within ecological SF, Brian Stableford identifies the important sub-genre of "ecological mysticism". Breaking with earlier and explicitly deistic scenarios as, for instance, C.S. Lewis' Christianised science fiction trilogy beginning with *Out of the Silent Planet* (1938), these post-war narratives foregrounded the concept of "intelligent nature" over that of an omniscient God (Stableford, p. 132). They featured self-sufficient, self-arbitrating planetary ecosystems where human influence is often supernumerary or even (in many scenarios) inevitably destructive. Such fiction may be inspired by the concept of the Earth as a self-regulating biosphere, as popularised by the theories of Pierre Teilhard du Chardin and James Lovelock. Other influences include New Age idealism and spiritualism, and simple disenchantment with modern technology. These narratives' typical combination of scientific advances with polluted ecosystems expresses the authors' association between tech-

---

3   Stableford identifies the original genre of ecological SF with novels such as Clement's *Mission of Gravity* (1953) – told from the viewpoint of insect-like aliens that have evolved to withstand exceptionally high gravity – and Anderson's *Fire Time* (1974).

nological progress and environmental damage; pollution is the flip side of chemical research, as nuclear war is the consequence of physics. Among non-Western writers of "ecological mysticism", Stableford singles out the Soviet Russian authors Arkadii and Boris Strugatskii; the remainder of this essay will discuss the context and significance of the poetics of pollution in two of their best-known novels, including their probable scientific and philosophical influences.[4]

THE BROTHERS STRUGATSKII AND VERNADSKII'S BIOSPHERE

Arkadii (1925-91) and Boris (1933-2012) Strugatskii formed one of the most unusual literary phenomena of the twentieth century: a fraternal writing team who produced over twenty-five novellas and novels in a joint career lasting over thirty years. Their style evolved from early action-centred space opera (1959-63) to the deceptively simple philosophical problematics of their mature period (to 1988). The brothers shared a strong interest in mathematics and astrophysics, despite their disparate careers: Arkadii worked as an interpreter of Japanese while Boris taught astrophysics at Leningrad State University. They actively translated many Western science fiction authors for Russian readers, including Simak and John Wyndham's 1951 *The Day of the Triffids* (Prashkevich and Volodikhin, p. 34). It is essential, however, to recognise that while the Strugatskiis kept abreast of trends in Western science fiction, their personal version of ecological mysticism was derived from uniquely Russian cultural influences, both literary (the deeply spiritual, occasionally mystical writings of Fedor Dostoevskii and the philosopher Nikolai Fedorov) and scientific (the theories of the geologist Vladimir Vernadskii (1863-1945)) (see Howell). Nor was there necessarily any disjuncture between scientific and literary influence: for example, for the epigraph to his major work *The Biosphere* (1926), Vernadskii chose two lines written in 1865 by the poet Fedor Tiutchev: "In nature all is harmony, / A consonance fore'er agreed on ..." (Vernadskii: *The Biosphere*, p. 43).

Who was Vladimir Vernadskii, and how did he become so invisibly influential? Vernadskii's research interests included mineralogy, soil chem-

---

4   Stableford lists the brothers' most mystical environmental novel, *Snail on the Slope* (*Ulitka na sklone*, 1968) among examples of "ecospheres so completely integrated that their core consists of vast more-or-less godlike organisms" (Stableford, p. 132). All dates associated with the Strugatskiis' novels in my text indicate first distribution in the Soviet Union, unless otherwise indicated.

istry, and geology, but he is best known today for scientifically elaborating the concept of the "biosphere" as not only a physical location (the areas of the Earth where life is present) but also the set of all the interactive solar, biological, and geochemical processes responsible for creating and sustaining life on our planet.[5] Crucially, Vernadskii identified biological forces as the primary influence behind geological and climatic change. This concept leads to another key aspect of Vernadskii's thinking: his organisation of terrestrial evolution into three stages. The geospheres (strata of rock formed by inanimate geological processes) are superseded by the biosphere (our current stage – when biological processes determine the physical environment), which is ultimately subsumed into the *noösphere*, the stage when human intellect consciously controls planetary destiny. The concept of the noösphere was developed by Vernadskii, Teilhard du Chardin, and the mathematician Edouard Le Roy in Paris in the 1920s. Firmly convinced that the evolution of life was not accidental and followed a teleological course towards intellectual perfection, Vernadskii was nonetheless ambiguous about the role of humanity in this global process (Oldfield and Shaw: "V.I. Vernadsky and the noösphere" and "Science, Philosophy and Politics in Soviet History").

Vernadskii's writings implicitly warn against the rapid and unplanned degradation of the environment by human interference – the same sort of casual pollution Chekhov's short fiction described. Although humanity, according to Vernadskii, forms an indissoluble part of the biosphere, the human intellect possesses as yet unknown power to distort the latter: "Man, alone, violates the established order; and it is a question whether he diminishes geochemical energy, or simply distributes the green transformers in a different way" (Vernadskii: *The Biosphere*, p. 79). As a geologist responsible for sourcing coal and uranium for military production, Vernadskii was acutely conscious than man was becoming, in his own right, a transformative geological force: yet the interaction between intellect and matter raised a secondary conundrum. "*Thought is not a form of energy*. How then can it change material processes?" (Vernadskii: "The Biosphere and the Noösphere", p. 9). Vernadskii's published views veered from confidence that man was approaching the threshold of the noösphere to doubt in the environmental sustainability of industrial progress. Like many scientists

---

5   Vernadskii did not invent the term 'biosphere', which was first used by Edward Suess in 1875 to refer to the Earth's inhabited zones, nor was he its principal publicizer (Teilhard du Chardin, who attended Vernadskii's lectures at the Sorbonne in the early 1920s, published much more extensively on the topic).

active during the Stalin era, his ideas were deprived of publicity (especially abroad) until the so-called "thaw" under Khrushchev's premiership in the late 1950s. A "Vernadskian renaissance" occurred in Soviet Russia in the 1960s, which ultimately transformed Vernadskii into a "cult figure" within the liberal *intelligentsia* by the Gorbachev era; significantly, this transition overlaps with the Strugatskiis' most important creative output (Grinewald, p. 21).

From the 1960s onwards newly emergent Russian environmental groups used Vernadskii's holistic theories to support their protests and demands (Bailes: *Science and Russian Culture*, p. 181; see also Weiner). These decades were marked by rising environmental agitation among university students, scientists, regional communities, and political dissidents. Students formed groups called *druzhiny* – the medieval term for a band of warriors – which policed ecological correctness, including animal rights, in both country and city (Weiner, pp. 312-39), while at a political level, environmentalist minorities campaigned against industrial interest groups seeking to undermine Russia's national park system, known as reservations or *zapovedniki*. From the 1950s, Russian national pride in the industrial transformation of nature, including much-lauded projects such as the Belomor Canal (1933), was reversed: Russian nationalism became increasingly aligned with the purity and integrity of unspoiled nature (see Weiner). A new genre of so-called Village Prose authors emerged in the 1950s, mostly in rural districts of Siberia; their fiction praised traditional community values and the preservation of nature (as opposed to the invidious effect of urban culture and industrialisation).[6] Leading literary journals such as *Literaturnaia gazeta* allied themselves with the ecological cause (Weiner, pp. 358-9). While there is no evidence that the Strugatskiis (having already graduated) took part in either *druzhiny* or environmental campaigning, they could not have avoided exposure to the resurgent Vernadskian ethic. Indeed, Vernadskii's idea of the *noösphere*, of the earth as a geochemical harmony in which the processes of biological life enrich the planet's overall being, had already influenced Russia's most famous mid-century science fiction author, the palaeontologist Ivan Efre-

---

6   Among the best-known writers in the Village Prose tradition are Valentin Rasputin (1937-), Viktor Astafiev (1924-2001), and Aleksandr Solzhenitsyn (1918-2008). Some of Solzhenitsyn's earliest published fictions, including the acclaimed *Matresha's Home* (*Matrenin dvor*, 1963) belong to the Village Prose ethos.

mov.[7] Efremov's distinctly politically conservative novels, such as *The Andromeda Nebula* (*Tumannost' Andromedy*, 1958), described the vicissitudes of space-faring life in the vertiginously distant future, cheerfully conducted according to Marxist principles. It was perhaps Efremov's complacent future vision that encouraged the Strugatskiis brothers to reshape and repopulate a genre betrayed by the pedestrian clichés of Stalinist utopianism.[8]

The Strugatskii brothers thus lived through the suppression of Soviet environmentalism under Stalin and its cautious re-emergence under Khrushchev and Brezhnev. The decades of their most intensive literary creativity coincided with major Russian ecological controversies: the salinization and shrinking of the Aral Sea as a result of water diversion (from the 1960s to the present); the proposed (but averted) plan in the late 1950s to explode a nuclear bomb to lower the floor of Lake Baikal; and the diversion of entire rivers to replenish over-exploited water tables. Some of these plans were frustrated, such as that to deepen Baikal, already the world's largest and deepest freshwater lake; but despite its status as a national treasure, polluting cellulose factories were constructed on its shore in the late sixties.[9] The Strugatskiis responded to the national debate on nature with their poetics of pollution, contamination, and genetic deviation. Like Chekhov, a prophet of the consequences of deforestation and water contamination before these issues were fully recognised, their fiction explores the results of bacteriological, chemical, and radiological pollution. Their work seeks, as at least one of its goals, to answer Vernadskii's doubts about the future interaction between human consciousness and the natural processes of the planet Earth. The Strugatskiis explored the question of human viability by creating variant, hypothetical noöspheres and contrasting them with less developed human cultures. For Chekhov, environmental pollution was analogous to human moral degeneration, as we have seen. For the Strugatskii brothers, this remains true, but the same concept is taken a stage further: pollution

---

7   See G.V. Grebens: *Ivan Efremov's Theory of Science Fiction*, for more on Efremov's assimilation of the theories of Vernadskii, Fedorov, and others.

8   Heller and Niqueux (1995) argue that the emergence of the dystopian "roman d'avertissement" in Russian literature in the 1960s, and specifically the Strugatskiis' novels including *Roadside Picnic*, acted as "un antidote contre l'anthropocosmisme euphorique d'un Efremov". This type of novel "s'interroge sur la responsabilité de la science et sur son rôle dans la destruction de la nature [...] mais aussi dans l'appréciation erronée de la place que l'homme occupe dans l'univers" (Heller and Niqueux, p. 255).

9   For more information on the threat to Baikal, see Weiner, pp. 353-73.

LITERATURE AND CHEMISTRY

comes to symbolise an intrinsic discontinuity between humanity and the biosphere.

The Strugatskiis' fiction remained loyal to the science fiction genre, though their interplanetary and far-future settings increasingly became an Aesopian screen for commentary on the contemporary world. As various critics have noted, the Strugatskiis' satires superficially – and necessarily – appear to implicate the capitalist West, yet on closer reading can be seen to accuse the "limitations in Soviet technological utopianism" (Booker, p. 172; see also McGuire). Essentially, the Strugatskiis' novels challenge the ideological precepts of any monological society, whether the cultural hegemony is bureaucratic, political, or scientific. In the Strugatskiis' ideal worlds, such as the near-future Earth of their short story cycle *Noon: Twenty-Second Century* (1961), the physical world is converted by human ingenuity into an integrated harmony like that of Vernadskii's noösphere; here, human intellectual development stimulates, reinvents, and participates in geological and climatic processes. Even roads have become benignly mechanised, acting like passenger conveyor belts in airports; food production has been rationalised without depriving farm animals of their freedom, and industrial pollution is a problem only on uninhabited planets (which man is in the process of terraforming for human settlement).

Conversely, in the Strugatskiis' dystopian novels, the harmony of the noösphere is reversed: man and nature may work against each other, or xenobiological life may perturb the ecosystem. The remainder of this article will focus on two of the brothers' most significant novels in this context: *The Inhabited Island* (*Obitaemyi ostrov*, 1969) and *Roadside Picnic* (*Piknik na obochine*, 1971). *Roadside Picnic* is most familiar to Western audiences via Andrei Tarkovskii's lyrical adaptation of the book (with a radically altered script) in the 1979 film *Stalker*. *The Inhabited Island*, also filmed (less notably) as a two-part blockbuster action movie by the Russian director Fedor Bondarchuk (2008-09), is the first book in a trilogy featuring characters from an advanced future society (Progressors or Wanderers) who visit extraterrestrial human civilisations in order to educate or "progress" them. The final volumes of the trilogy (*Beetle in the Anthill* and *The Waves Still the Wind*) were written considerably later, in 1979 and 1985 respectively, and both exhibit the increased pessimism already incipient in *Roadside Picnic*. *The Inhabited Island* and *Roadside Picnic*, written just two years later, offer significantly differing perspectives upon – and interpretations of – the relation between environmental pollution and human life.

The Inhabited Island, published in translation as *Prisoners of Power,* opens like a twenty-second-century reframing of Robinson Crusoe: a happy-go-lucky traveller from an advanced interplanetary civilisation, Maxim Kammerer, crash-lands on a remote, unvisited planet; unlike Crusoe's, Maxim's island is already inhabited. Computer readouts from his downed ship forewarn him that the planet Sarakhsh is "hardly a happy place. Somewhere beyond the forest lay a city of dirty factories; decrepit reactors emptying radioactive wastes into the river; ugly houses beneath metal roofs, with endless walls and few windows; and buildings separated by litter-strewn alleys" (*Prisoners of Power,* p. 5). Maxim's exploration of the new planet is punctuated by encounters with pollution of various types: the rusty girders of an abandoned road bridge decaying alongside a radioactive river, and a roaming tank, "stuffed with a mixture of raw plutonium and lanthanides" (*Prisoners of Power,* p. 9), which exhales scorching fumes. The city and nation have been reduced to their current state by an immense intercontinental war which deployed nuclear weapons between states "whose names were already forgotten" (*Prisoners of Power,* p. 63). "To the south, beyond the borderland forests, lay a desert, land that had been totally defoliated by nuclear explosions. ... The southern borders were subject to constant attack by hordes of half-savage degens [degenerates] who infested the forest" (*Prisoners of Power,* p. 64). These mutants are genetic casualties of radiological contamination from the war. In contrast to that of Sarakhsh, Maxim's cultural ethos emphasises continence and restraint: even his ship, when it explodes following an accident, activates emergency hydrants to contain the flames and limit the environmental damage. Maxim's genetically superior metabolism and regenerative powers protect him from the various contaminants that litter the planet; moreover, he fails to share the natives' harmful habits. He is baffled and horrified when a Sarakhsh acquaintance pollutes the air in their vehicle by smoking a cigarette.

However, Maxim is forced to engage ever more closely with the polluted waste and defective mechanical objects of Sarakhsh society. Arrested for sedition and sent to the Southern Forests, he works with other exiles and so-called mutants clearing military and radioactive waste in a region that is "not really a forest but an old fortified region. It was crawling with military devices, armoured cars, ballistic missiles, rockets on caterpillar treads, flamethrowers, and poison-gas ejectors, all automatic and self-propelled. And all this was still very much alive twenty years after the war; everything continued to live its useless mechanical life – to aim, to sight, to belch lead, fire, and death. All this had to be crushed, blown up, and demolished to clear a road for the construction of new radiation towers" (*Prisoners of Power*, p. 155). From here, he escapes and encounters whole mutant communities altered by radiation exposure. He also seeks a semi-mythical "white submarine" that he hopes will transport them to the supposedly more culturally advanced Northern Empire on a different continent. However, when discovered, the white submarine turns out to be a "rusty skeleton" (*Prisoners of Power*, p. 215) exuding poisonous radiation; even worse, Maxim finds in its onboard archives a photographic record of atrocities committed by the Northern Empire. He also discovers a second album containing images of Sarakhsh before the intercontinental war, which causes him to exclaim to his native companion: "'[W]hat a beautiful world you've defiled! What a world! Just take a look, see what a beautiful world it was! ... What did you do with it, damn you? Exchange it for your iron junk? You call yourselves people?'" (*Prisoners of Power*, p. 221).

On Sarakhsh, the "inhabited island" of the novel's title, the extent of self-inflicted pollution is an indicator of the cultural immaturity of its population. It also shows their inability to appreciate nature or behave humanely. In effect, this "poetics of pollution" does not extend far beyond the original Chekhovian aesthetic, linking polluted environments to ethical corruption; and, in the person of Maxim Kammerer and the more advanced human culture he represents, the novel offers hope of a genuine Vernadskian noösphere – that is, a rational yet benign civilisation, benevolently integrated with its intergalactic environment.

ROADSIDE PICNIC

If the transformation of natural beauty into junk is the essence of Sarakhsh, the Strugatskiis' next novel to explore the symbolism of pollution would reverse this axiom. In *Roadside Picnic*, the action takes place in and near an imaginary Canadian town (Harmont) twenty years after a mysterious, and short-term, alien Visitation. The latter has left six different "zones" on the surface of the planet Earth uniquely altered. Each has been walled off to prevent looting or contamination; only scientists are allowed to enter the Zones – usually accompanied by local guides familiar with the territory. These guides, known as "stalkers", are highly skilled trackers who intuitively sense danger from the Zone's esoteric traps. They are also far from averse to selling the Zone's artefacts privately to arms dealers and other agents, even though such activity carries a heavy prison sentence.

The territory affected by the Visitors is both a literal and a metaphorical wasteland: metaphorically, because it is uninhabitable; literally, because it is scattered with redundant and decaying objects. The stalkers learn to avoid the black patches, resembling "spilled bitumen" (*Roadside Picnic*, p. 141), which may be human remains; they also navigate wrecked buildings or objects abandoned in the Zone, including an abandoned factory, decaying trucks, and rusting ore cars. The Zones are seeded with artefacts as bewildering as they are diverse. The names given to these artefacts are equally exotic: mosquito mange (enhanced gravitation), jolly ghosts, "empties", a mysterious explosive fluid known as witches' jelly, the Golden Ball, rattling napkins, and Dick the Tramp. All these objects are potentially enormously destructive. Society, ironically, is itself a polluting agent acting upon the Zone, turning it inside out by exporting its treasures; capitalist exploitation is characterised as a "lousy fungus" that will gradually erode the Zone (*Roadside Picnic*, p. 68).

One of the scientists attached to the Institute expounds the metaphor which became the central axis of the Strugatskiis' novel: the Visitors' arrival and sojourn is portrayed as an event as casual and meaningless as a picnic.

> A picnic. Picture a forest, a country road, a meadow. A car drives off the country road into the meadow, a group of young people get out of the car carrying bottles, baskets of food, transistor radios, and cameras. They light fires, pitch tents, turn on the music. In the morning they leave. The animals, birds, and insects that watched in horror through the long night creep out from their hiding places. And what do they see? Gas and oil spilled on the grass. Old spark plugs and old filters strewn around. Rags, burnt-out bulbs, and a monkey wrench left behind. Oil slicks on the pond. And, of course, the usual mess – apple cores, candy wrappers, charred remains of the campfire, cans, bottles, somebody's handkerchief, somebody's penknife, torn newspapers, coins, faded flowers picked in another meadow. (*Roadside Picnic*, p. 102)

Even the most precious object in the Zone – the so-called Golden Ball, which grants wishes in exchange for the sacrifice of a human life – is represented by the omniscient third-person narrator as a casually littered object. The Golden Ball "lay where it had fallen. Maybe it had fallen out of some monstrously huge pocket or had gotten lost, rolled away during some game between giants. It had not been carefully placed here, it had been left behind, littering up the Zone like all the empties, bracelets, batteries, and other rubbish remaining after the Visitation" (*Roadside Picnic*, p. 142).

The tragic irony of *Roadside Picnic* is profoundly different from *The Inhabited Island*, in which chemical pollution is still perceived by the planet's inhabitants, however misguidedly, as a marker of technological progress. This fallacy, of course, underlines their primitive condition. In *Roadside Picnic*, on the other hand, the fallacy is all the more cruel for being undisguised: the objects presumably discarded as "litter" by the mysterious and advanced Visitors are painstakingly salvaged as treasures by humanity, thus exposing the pathetically insufficient status of human technology. The people of Sarakhsh in *The Inhabited Island* create pollution because they cannot yet appreciate natural beauty as a good in itself; the advanced society of *Roadside Picnic* possesses the perspective to realise that the discarded refuse of a more evolved civilisation is indescribably precious on Earth. Both novels, in traditional dystopian fashion, stress the failure of scientific progress to create a better world (many of the mysterious substances from the Zones, such as the witches' jelly, are injurious to life). In *Island*, nuclear power and psychotropic waves are used for destruction and oppression, while in *Roadside Picnic* scientists are exposed as intellectual pygmies, working hand in glove with a suspiciously militarised police force. Where *The Inhabited Island* may satirise the Soviet Union in particular – with its portrait of a closed, conservative society surviving on propaganda and militaristic dogma – the critique posed by *Roadside Picnic* challenges humanity as a whole. Yet the Strugatskiis' poetics of pollution aims at a more profound statement than an identification of the hollowness of exclusively scientific or intellectual belief. Probing Vernadskii's warning of the dissonance between human consciousness and the integrity of the biosphere, the Strugatskiis question whether human nature can ever be reconciled with the natural world. This, as we have seen in earlier Western science fiction, is the central problematic of all ecological mysticism.

The fundamental discontinuity between the reality of nature and human perception is experienced first-hand by Redrick Schuhart, the stalker hero of *Roadside Picnic*. Stepping onto a street, he experiences a momentary hallucination:

> A million odours cascaded in on him at once – sharp, sweet, metallic, gentle, dangerous ones, as crude as cobblestones, as delicate and tiny as watch mechanisms, as huge as a house and as tiny as a dust particle. The air became hard, it developed edges, surfaces, and corners, like space was filled with huge, stiff balloons, slippery pyramids, gigantic prickly crystals, and he had to push his way through it all, making his way in a dream through a junk store stuffed with

ancient ugly furniture. ... It hadn't been a different world – it was this world turning a new, unknown side to him. (*Roadside Picnic*, p. 67)

In their appropriation of distant and future planets in the twenty-second century and beyond, the Strugatskiis constantly return to mankind's isolation within the terrestrial biosphere – an environment which threatens to become more alien than the most distant of other worlds.

CONCLUSION

The Strugatskiis return to the theme of pollution in many subsequent novels, notably *Beetle in the Anthill* and *The Ugly Swans* (*Gadkie lebedi*, 1987); the latter was filmed by Konstantin Lopushanskii in 2006. The concept of the noösphere maintains its topicality in contemporary Russian science fiction; Dmitrii Glukhovskii's 2007 bestseller *Metro 2033* offers a cruder, post-apocalyptic take on Vernadskii's theory. In a near-future world ravaged by nuclear war, the only human survivors linger in the tunnels of the Moscow subway. One character speculates that the noösphere has been physically dispersed by the detonations, which have smashed heaven and hell; disembodied souls, deprived of their traditional destination, are forced to haunt the living (Glukhovskii, p. 110). Such an outcome would confirm the Strugatskiis' dystopian speculations and underwrite Vernadskii's darkest hints that man is not only in conflict with the biosphere that created him, but doomed to destroy it utterly. Vernadskii's warning still resonates: "Man, alone, violates the established order".

WORKS CITED

Avdeev, Iurii: "Chekhov in Melikhovo", in *Memories of Chekhov: Accounts of the Writer from his Family, Friends, and Contemporaries*, ed. and trans. Peter Sekirin. Jefferson, NC: Mcfarland & Co., 2011, pp. 53-4(54).

Bailes, Kendall E.: *Science and Russian Culture in an Age of Revolutions: V.I. Vernadsky and His Scientific School, 1963-1945*. Bloomington and Indianapolis, IN: Indian University Press, 1990.

—: "Science, Philosophy and Politics in Soviet History: The Case of Vladimir Vernadskii" in *Russian Review*, vol. 40, no. 3, July 1981, pp. 278-99.

Booker, Keith M.: "Science Fiction and the Cold War" in David Seed: *A Companion to Science Fiction*. Oxford: Blackwell, 2005, pp. 171-184.

Chekhov, Anton Pavlovich Chekhov: "In The Ravine" in *Seven Short Novels*, trans. Barbara Makanowitzky. New York: Norton, 1963, pp. 396-434.

Glukhovskii, Dmitry: *Metro 2033*, trans. Natasha Randall. London: Gollancz, 2011.

G. V. Grebens: *Ivan Efremov's Theory of Science Fiction*. New York: Vantage, 1978.

Grinewald, Jacques: "Introduction: The Invisibility of the Vernadskian Revolution" in Vladimir I. Vernadskii: *The Biosphere*, trans. David B. Langmuir. New York: Springer-Verlag, 1998, pp. 20-32.

Heller, Leonid and Niqueux, Michel: *Histoire de l'utopie en Russie*. Paris: Presses universitaires de France, 1995.

Howell, Yvonne: *Apocalyptic Realism: The Science Fiction of Arkady and Boris Strugatsky*. New York: Peter Lang, 1994.

McGuire, Patrick L.: *Red Stars: Political Aspects of Soviet Science Fiction*. Ann Arbor, MI: UMI Research Press, 1985.

Oldfield, J. and Shaw, D. J. B.: "V. I. Vernadsky and the noösphere concept: Russian understandings of society-nature interaction" in *Geoforum*, vol. 37, no. 1, 2006, pp. 145-54.

—: "V. I. Vernadskii and the development of biogeochemical understandings of the biosphere, c.1880s-1968." in *The British Journal for the History of Science*, 2012, pp. 1-24.

Prashkevich, Gennadii and Volodikhin, Dimitrii: *Brat'ia Strugatskie*. Moscow: Molodaia gvardiia, 2012.

Stableford, Brian: "Science Fiction and Ecology" in *A Companion to Science Fiction*. David Seed (ed.). Oxford: Blackwell, 2005, pp. 127-141.

Strugatskii, Arkady and Strugatskii, Boris: *Prisoners of Power*, trans. Helen Saltz Jacobson. London: Victor Gollancz, 1978.

Strugatskii, Arkady and Strugatskii, Boris: *Roadside Picnic*, trans. Antonina W. Bouis. London: Gollancz, 2007.

Vernadskii, Vladimir: *The Biosphere*, trans. David B. Langmuir. New York: Springer-Verlag, 1998.

—: (as W. I. Vernadskii): "The Biosphere and the Noösphere" in *American Scientist*, vol. 33, no. 1, January 1945, pp. 1-12.

Weiner, Douglas R.: *A Little Corner of Freedom: Russian Nature Protection from Stalin to Gorbachev*. Berkeley, CA / London: University of California Press, 1999.

HISTORIES OF ALCHEMY

ALCHEMISTS AND ALCHEMY IN ITALIAN LITERATURE FROM ITS ORIGINS TO GALILEO GALILEI

Matteo Pellegrini, University of Padua

At the end of the eighteenth century Lavoisier and his studies gave rise to the "chemical revolution" [1]: Systematically using balance to point out the absence of changes in mass, he demolished the established theories of phlogiston and the transmutation of water in earth by boiling. From that moment on, all the discoveries that came after create what we now define as the "history of chemistry", but before then the limits of this field were not at all clear.

From a certain point of view, alchemy is the closest ancestor of chemistry: For a very long time alchemists dealt with problems that were, afterwards, assigned to chemical science and, moreover, they used instruments and developed processes that were usefully employed by their successors. When alchemy began to give way to chemistry its interwoven components became distinct: On the one side there were those aspects, connected with laboratory practice, that evolved into the systematic experimental techniques of chemical research. On the other, there were aspects that are responsible for the survival, to the present day, of an aura of fascination around the discipline of alchemy: These attributes are more spiritual, philosophical and symbolic and are related to religious and cognitive spheres as well as to a rich and intricate iconographic and linguistic repertoire. [2]

From a literary perspective, alchemy became the prevailing key to chemical knowledge in works written before the eighteenth century. Hoping to avoid misunderstandings I will here underline that this chapter will not deal

---

1   The first use of this definition seems to date back to the title of an 1890 work by Marcelin Berthelot, chemist and science historian: *La Révolution chimique: Lavoisier, ouvrage suivi de notices et extraits des registres inédits de laboratoire de Lavoisier.* Michela Pereira points this out in her pivotal book – to which I will frequently refer – *Alchimia* (LVIII-LIX n. 21).

2   For a brief but precise presentation of the discipline, of the currents of thought invigorating it, and of the debate accompanying the development of chemistry from alchemy, cf. the introductory essay by Pereira, *"Mater Alchimia"* (*Alchimia* IX-LXX). This book also contains an extensive and updated bibliography (1491-1518).

with alchemical texts proper, or with works about alchemy: This is a field too large, too heterogeneous and, above all, too hermetic.[3] Instead, I'll keep to the guiding lines, more familiar to me, of literary history, investigating how Italian authors dealt with the subject of alchemy from the Middle Ages up to the seventeenth century.

THE MIDDLE AGES: FROM THE FIRST TUSCAN POETS TO DANTE AND CECCO D'ASCOLI

At the birth of Italian literature, in the thirteenth century, alchemy was already a strong presence. This was a century in which "everybody dealt with alchemical studies as one of the most important branches of natural sciences and admitted the planets' influence on the composition and ennobling of metals and minerals" (Crivelli, p. 29; my translation); "everybody" in this context, means especially the members of religious orders, who were the real holders of knowledge at the time.[4]

---

3   The adjective derives, in Italian as in English, from Hermes Trismegistus, emblem of a mysterious and esoteric knowledge. Cf., among others, Fowden; Fabricius.

4   Among the Dominicans, Albertus Magnus (c. 1206-80) stands out for antiquity and authority. The youngest son of the Count of Böllstadt, he was known as *Doctor Universalis* for the breadth of his interests: His experimental and scientific approach to nature led him to author works of great importance such as *De Mineralibus*, in the line of Aristotle's *Meteorologica*, which submits the theoretical assumptions of alchemical tradition to the scrutiny of observation in a survey conducted through places as varied as mines and laboratories. The fame he quickly gained resulted in works of real alchemy being attributed to him, such as *Libellus de alchimia* (cf. Kibre). There were many Franciscans who dealt with issues of alchemy: Brother Elias (c. 1170-1253), successor to St. Francis as leader of the order and believed to have authored alchemical works in verse and prose (cf. Mazzoni); Friar Bonaventura from Iseo (thirteenth century), author of the successful, though encyclopedic, *Liber Compostille* (c. 1260), in which the alchemical knowledge of the time is collected and neatly displayed (cf. Carli); and the most famous Roger Bacon, a contemporary of Albertus Magnus. Bacon was trained at the school of Oxonian philosopher Robert Grosseteste (who considered alchemy a part of the natural sciences, subject to astronomy and linked to agriculture), where, while studying Aristotle's texts, he defended the importance of a mathematical key that could unlock the rational order of the universe, as well as of the laws of causality, which bind together the phenomena but have to be confirmed by experience (nevertheless, it is improper to see Bacon as a precursor of modern scientists, since with most medieval thinkers he lacks the idea of method, with its values of precision and reproducibility, which marks the distinction of exact sciences). He admitted the influence of the stars,

However, the diffusion of this knowledge was restricted by both temporal and spiritual authorities. Examples of the historical repression of alchemy include the destruction of all ancient works about gold and silver production ordered in 296 AD by the Roman emperor Diocletian to prevent the Egyptians from achieving a threatening economic supremacy, and the condemnation of alchemy by the Church for the first time in 1317, ultimately for reasons like those that inspired the decretal *Spondent pariter* by Pope John XXII, to stop the rise of those alchemists, more impostors than scientists, who took advantage of others with the lure of gold.[5] Nevertheless, the alchemical studies that developed alcoholic distillation and "strong water" (the ancient name for nitric acid), the formulae for creating glasses almost identical to gemstones, and many other inventions were far from despised. In major Italian manufacturing cities all discoveries improving

---

however, and recognized the speculative validity of alchemy in relation to natural philosophy and medicine; he introduced into the Latin world the concept of the *elixir* that, with properties similar to drugs, prolonged life (cf. Alessio; Bacon). Finally, the only certainty as regards Basilius Valentinus was his membership of the Benedictine order. Many alchemical writings are attributed to him (such as *Die zwölf Schlüssel,* a hermetic text on the philospher's stone), including some which can be seen as significant precursors of a modern chemical approach (e.g. Triumphwagen Antimonii, judged to be the first monograph on a chemical element) as confirmed by the title given to his sylloge *Chemische Schriften* (1677), which declares a proximity to the field of chemistry that can also be found in the subsequent Latin edition, entitled *Basilii Valentini scripta chimica* (1700) (it should be noted here that many scholars since the late nineteenth century agree that "Basilius Valentinus" is in fact the pseudonym of Johann Thölde, superintendent of Kronach caves and publisher of Valentinus' works, as suggested first by Kopp).

5   Though this text is commonly read as a *tout court* condemnation of alchemical research (from the beginning of the sixth section entitled *De crimine falsi*: "alkimiae hic prohibentur, et puniuntur facientes et fieri procurantes"), actually it represents an attack against a certain category of deceivers ("spondent quas non exhibent divitias, pauperes Alchimistae; pariter qui se sapientes existimant in foream incidunt quam fecerunt"), as demonstrated by the prescribed penalty which, as opposed to the torture and burning at the stake of heretics and magicians, was basically pecuniary ("quoniam tantum de vero auro et argento debent inferre in publicum, ut pauperibus erogetur quantum de falso et adulterino posuerunt"). "It is evident that John's decree against 'alchemies' did not directly forbid chemistry, nor alchemy in the proper sense of the word, nor did it in any way interfere with the study of substances to determine their composition, or the synthesis of materials, to produce others, provided there was no pretence of making gold and silver in order to obtain genuine gold and silver from ignorant dupes" (Walsh, p. 254).

the creation and processing of materials from glass to metal, leather to fabrics, and drugs to dyes – in other words everything pertaining to today's chemical industry – were encouraged and protected from the period of the communes until the end of the Renaissance. As Crivelli recounts, in Dante's time all princes had at least an astrologer and an alchemist among their personnel, while, following the example of the courts, the Republics paid readers to explain and comment on the most important alchemical treatises in public (Crivelli, p. 33). Alchemists were clearly seen as the keepers of knowledge and skills unknown to most people, but public opinion about them was not favourable, either because of the obscurity of the communication codes used by these proto-scientists or because the thin line between the few who worked hard and conscientiously and the many that, calling themselves alchemists, tried to deceive others with the promise of successful transmutation.

The first reference to alchemy in verse appears in Bonagiunta Orbicciani's work, at the very beginning of Italian literature – before Dante, but by means of a character that the author of *Commedia* will subsequently use in his principal work.[6] In Lucca, Tuscany, a certain Gonnella Antelminelli, notary, about whom we know very little, composed two lyrics to Bonagiunta Orbicciani (born c. 1220), "iudex et notarium", known and studied at present because of his poetry linked to the Sicilian and pre-Stilnovo forms that mark the origins of Italian literature. Antelminelli, in his sonnet *Una rason, qual eo non sac[c]io, chero*[7] focuses on the question "How is it possible that iron can grind iron?", and declares his doubts about alchemical explanations of the phenomenon; with the assertion "I don't trust alchemical capabilities" he clearly states a negative judgement of an "art" that intends to mutate and falsify nature. A reason is given for why true art cannot be learned in the sonnet *Naturalmente falla lo pensero*, which is a Orbicciani's response to the second lyric exchange by Gonnella. Bonagiunta, intending to demonstrate that art corrects nature, refers to alchemy while describing the relationship between Nature and Art: "nature provides the first model, which art follows and differentiates; and the one who has talent knows more about art, than the one who dedicates himself to alchemy. I do not consider alchemy to be true art because it is

---

6   Dante and Virgil meet the poet from Lucca in the sixth terrace of *Purgatorio*, among the gluttons' souls.

7   "I ask a question to which I don't know the answer." The Italian verses are quoted from Contini (278-82); the translations are my own.

focused on transformation, giving fake colours to metals." The opinion here expressed by Bonagiunta completes Gonnella's: For these highly cultured poets in the second half of the thirteenth century alchemy is a metaphor for a distorted form of art, and its only purpose is to bring about superficial and misleading transformations.

A few decades later, but in the same part of Italy, Dante wrote his masterwork, the *Divine Comedy*. Its portrayal of alchemists is much the same, though some scholars have pointed out that Dante should have known something about alchemy: He was a member of the Medics and Apothecaries guild in Florence, which encompassed skills in preparing medicines, cosmetics, perfumes, and dyes.[8] Whatever knowledge Dante might have had about alchemy, the way he presents devotees of this art leaves no doubt about his judgement of them. In Dante's *Inferno*, the alchemists are found in the eighth circle, which is reserved for the punishment of the "fraudulent", in the tenth and last *bolgia*. The eighth circle is "the last cloister / of Malebolge" (XXIX, ll. 40-1),[9] where the falsifiers of metals – alchemists – suffer alongside counterfeiters, perjurers, and imposters. This place is introduced by the sound of wailing and then described as full of decay and disease: "What pain would be, if from the hospitals / Of Valdichiana, 'twixt July and September, / And of Maremma and Sardinia / All the diseases in one moat were gathered, / Such was it here, and such a stench came from it / As from putrescent limbs is wont to issue" (XXIX, ll. 46-51). The atmosphere is then further characterized, as the poet, after his initial sensory reactions, begins to see and understand what is happening:

I do not think a sadder sight to see
Was in Aegina the whole people sick,
(When was the air so full of pestilence,
The animals, down to the little worm,
All fell, […])
Than was it to behold through that dark valley
The spirits languishing in divers heaps.

8   In 1293 the Ordinances of Justice were promulgated in Florence: In order to limit the power of nobility and promote new emerging classes, all those wishing to take part in political life had to enrol in one of the Guilds, called "Arti". In 1295 Dante joined, as philosophy scholar, the Guild of Medics and Apothecaries ("Arte dei Medici e degli Speziali").

9   All English quotations from the *Inferno* are from Longfellow's translation.

This on the belly, that upon the back
One of the other lay, and others crawling
Shifted themselves along the dismal road. (XXIX, ll. 58-66)

Everything here is a sign of corruption and disease and the air itself exudes an illness whose pervasiveness is suggested by the double comparison – first with a real situation (the hospitals of Tuscany and Sardinia), and then with a literary scene (the episode, reported in Ovid's *Metamorphoses* [VII, ll. 523-660], of the plague unleashed by Juno against the inhabitants of Aegina). The speaker's encounter with the first two damned of the *bolgia* emphasizes the dramatic atmosphere of the site with mention of the creepy symptoms of leprosy:

I saw two sitting leaned against each other,
As leans in heating platter against platter,
From head to foot bespotted o'er with scabs;
And never saw I plied a currycomb
By stable-boy for whom his master waits,
Or him who keeps awake unwillingly,
As every one was plying fast the bite
Of nails upon himself, for the great rage
Of itching which no other succour had.
And the nails downward with them dragged the scab,
In fashion as a knife the scales of bream,
Or any other fish that has them largest. (XXIX, ll. 73-84)

The logic of the "foul and loathsome punishment" (XXIX, l. 107) suffered by the two damned can be understood when they explain their presence in Hell. The first one, a certain Griffolino from Arezzo, laconically says: "But unto the last Bolgia of the ten, / For alchemy, which in the world I practised, / Minos, who cannot err, has me condemned" (XXIX, ll. 118-20), without any further specification of "alchìmia". The second leper, however, gives some detail when he declares: "And thou shalt see I am Capocchio's shade, / Who metals falsified by alchemy" (XXIX, ll. 136-7). At this point, Dante's opinion of alchemy becomes clear: The meaning he gives to the word is strictly related to the practice of falsifying metals, which is consistent with its meaning in the sonnets by Gonnella and Bonagiunta. As such, the logic of the alchemists' punishment is revealed: By the law called "contrappasso", the damned have to suffer from a disease that alters and corrupts their physical appearance in the same way as they altered the nature of what they falsified (Alighieri: *Commedia*, p. 859). While Mayer has observed that here "what Dante has done is to show the alchemists in the first stage of alchemical transformation, that is, putrefaction" (also called "opus nigrum"; Mayer, p. 195), it also should be noted that, in this period in which alchemy began to aspire not only to provide people with a metallurgic technique, but also to offer what the historian of chemical science Robert P. Multhauf defines as "a topic of respectable philosophical discourse" (Botterill, p. 205), the poet's view seems very limited. Alchemy does not seem to represent a scientific problem for Dante, but exclusively an ethical argument. He is much more interested in alchemical practice, with its probable, though not unavoidable, consequences over practitioners' moral and spiritual conditions, than in the theory that lies beneath that practice (Botterill, pp. 204-5).[10] Finally, it is worth recalling that this condemnation of alchemy as the falsification of metals is followed, in the next *canto*, by the damnation of money counterfeiters, whose most memorable representative is Master Adam, deformed by dropsy. This seems to imply that, in Dante's opinion, the falsification of metals is just the first step on the way to money counterfeiting (Crivelli, p. 35).

At this point it seems proper to mention Francesco Stabili, well known by the name of Cecco D'Ascoli, who, although he is not a so significant figure in Italian literary history,[11] is interesting in this context: His presence in Leonardo's library and in Goethe's *Faust* must afford him at least some literary relevance.[12] He was Dante's contemporary and held important positions at the University of Bologna.[13] While in Florence he was also ap-

---

10 Following Bacon's distiction between a "speculative" alchemy (properly *scientia*) and an "operational" one (*ars*), Botterill wonders about the reason for Dante's silence on the far more challenging theoretical question about the Royal Art (the same question that would be articulated by the adverse positions of the Franciscan and Dominican orders until the decretal by John XXII): His conclusion is that there is probably an implicit evaluation in the warning "Let us not speak of them, but look, and pass" (*Inferno*: III, l. 51).

11 He is usually mentioned in relation to his criticism of Dante and his project of a poem opposed to the *Commedia*. His reputation, however, was influenced by critical judgments on the literary quality of his work, such as Petrocchi's definition of it as a "modest para-scientific compilation" full of "vagaries and platitudes" (Petrocchi, p. 592 and 595). For a more recent introduction cf. Ciociola, esp. pp. 430-7.

12 Goehte addresses just one aspect of Cecco's fame, mentioning him as "der Nekromant von Norcia" (*Faust II* 4, 10439; cf. also Steiner pp. 35-42).

13 His commentaries on *De Sphaera Mundi* by John Holiwood (in Latin: "Sacrobosco") and on al-Qabisi's *De principiis astrologiae* are well known, but his lectures were

pointed doctor and astrologer at the court of Carlo, Duke of Calabria, the eldest son of king Robert of Anjou. For reasons not yet fully understood, the inquisitor Accursio Bonfantini prosecuted Cecco for heresy and, on the afternoon of 16 September 1327, he was burnt to death at the stake together with all his writings.[14] His most important work, *L'Acerba*,[15] which achieved a great success and ran to many editions,[16] is a didactic poem of more than 4800 lines, that was left incomplete when he died. In this work Cecco aimed to present an encyclopaedic analysis of reality based on the "truth" of natural science against "fables" and "vain things" (in open controversy with Dante's *Commedia*),[17] appealing to all the fields of medieval scientific knowledge, from bestiaries to lapidaries, and from treatises on astrology to those on alchemy. From Cecco, the most learned man of letters among the alchemists – and, conversely, the most learned alchemist among the men of letters – one might expect a description of the Great Art that opposes those previously written by poets, but Cecco is neither obvious nor predictable. In the sixth chapter of Book 4, titled *Various problems of alchemy, anatomy*

---

looked upon with suspicion by Lamberto da Cingoli, of the Order of Preachers: Charging him with disdain of the Catholich faith in his teaching, da Cingoli suspended Cecco from his professorship, condemning him to the general confession penance and confiscating all his books on astrology (cf. "Introduzione" to Stabili, pp. 9-10).

14 The legendary aura that immediately surrounded the condemned – contributing, over the centuries, to the profile of a proto-defender of scientific truth and knowledge against an obtuse and bloody obscurantism – is also founded on the apocryphal story that tells how, during his trial, Stabili, constantly questioned on every charge, simply replied: "I said it, I taught it, I believe it" ("L'ho detto, l'ho insegnato, lo credo"; Stabili, p. 22).

15 The exact meaning of the title has been the subject of a long-running debate: Some scholars refer to the Latin *acervus*, "heap of different things", as a description of the variety of topics addressed in text (Petrocchi, p. 400), while others, including the editor of the recent critical edition, interpret it as reference to the expression *acerba aetas* or *acerba vita*, which was handed down from earlier codices. The codex Eugubino (Ascoli, Bibl. Comunale, ms. 5, 1376) in which the copyist concluded the transcription with the formula "Explicit Acerba Vita S. Cecchi Notarii Exculani [...]" is a particularly strong candidate (cf. Stabili, p. 9; and the critical edition Cecco d'Ascoli III).

16 It is sufficient to note that, after the burning of all the author's works, as many as fourteen fourteenth-century codices and thirty fifteenth-century codices survive; equally remarkable is the early date of the first printed edition (1473), which was followed by at least twenty-six editions by 1550 (Aurigemma, pp. 13-5).

17 Unsurprisingly Contini called *L'Acerba* the "anti-*Commedia*" (Contini, p. 441).

LITERATURE AND CHEMISTRY

and optics, having outlined the theory that planets influence the settling of metals in veins or layers, he discusses the validity of alchemy in the common form of a dialogue: "And you ask me 'Do you think it is possible to produce metals by art through combining and separating elements?' I say that art, which imitates nature, however cannot match its strength in order to obtain stable forms" (Stabili, pp. 357-8). Cecco's language is not fortuitous – if we pay attention to the couplet "combining and separating", we can recognize the reversed echo of the alchemical precept *solve et coagula* – but rather suggests an undoubtable expertise in this field. Nevertheless, the conclusion is unsettling: It is a denial of the effectiveness of the art of alchemy expressed with a very different logic and tone from Bonagiunta's and Dante's criticisms, but it is equally, and perhaps more, solid and exemplary. If the *L'Acerba* reveals the double attitude of an author who, according to Allevi, saw the mystery and science nested in every aspect of nature (Allevi, pp. 178-9), at the same time Cecco is able to suggest thoughtful assessments based on a rigour that is due, not to an anachronistic scientific perspective, but to his logical trust in man's reason: In the practical declension of their art, alchemists pursued the imitation of nature, but their power is insufficient to achieve the generation of permanent forms. Their attempts, even in the judgment of a "heretic" like Cecco, are therefore doomed to fail.

THE RENAISSANCE – FROM LEONARDO TO ARIOSTO

At the end of the fifteenth century there is a figure who stands at the intersection of two world views that are commonly cited by literary historians: Between Humanism and the Renaissance, art and technology, science and literature, is the "man without formal education",[18] as he defined himself – Leonardo da Vinci (1452-1519). Ignorance of Latin meant he had to turn to experience and reason, as well as craft techniques,[19] and texts extraneous to the most important scientific and technical works (for example Cecco's *L'Acerba*). This course of study distanced Leonardo from the abstract medieval wisdom and allowed him to embrace a humanistic awareness of

---

18 "Omo sanza lettere." Many scholars have discussed this self-definition: cf., among others, Cardini and Vasoli, pp. 142-3.

19 Garin warns against the idea of Leonardo as a scientist in the modern sense of the word; Leonardo's thought achieved its originality by means of a forced recourse to experience and reason, as well as to those traditional techniques which he was able to access more easily (cf. Garin, p. 281).

man's endless possibilities, enunciating principles of knowledge founded on "experience", which could only evolve into science when confirmed by "mathematic proofs" (this later became the basis of Galileo's survey). According to Flora, Leonardo's role in the battle against "false" sciences is revealed in an issue of *Manoscritti della Anatomia*, published under the title of *Contro il negromante e l'alchimista* (Flora, p. 118).[20] Disputing the devotees of necromancy (together with the "foolish multitude" deceived by them), Leonardo also attacks "archimia" ("alchemy") as a "sister" of necromancy as to falsity.[21] Alchemy is, however, the object of a less aggressive criticism by virtue of its being merely a reproducer of the simple elements present in nature: "alchemy is a manipulator of simples, which are the elements created by nature, but nature cannot combine them because of the lack of those organs accomplishing what man can do with his hands, by which he produces glasses etc" (da Vinci, p. 156). This is not a true condemnation: There is some curiosity here, and a sort of legitimacy is accorded to those practical implications of research and manipulation that could not fail to intrigue Leonardo the technician. His assessment is expressed more fully in another passage that, though it reaffirms the limits of alchemy, also enhances its achievements (something that is not at all common in non-alchemical writing):

> Only nature can produce simples. Man can make endless compounds using them, but he does not have the power to create starting simples [...]: and of this fact will be my witnesses the old alchemists, who have never, either by accident or by choice, tried to create anything that could be created by nature; this creation (of many compounds) deserves a lot of praise for the usefulness of what alchemists have discovered in favour of men, and it would deserve even more if alchemists were not also the inventors of harmful things, such as poisons and other compounds destructive to life and mind, from which they themselves are not immune, since they wanted to create, with great study and practice, not a natural but a less noble product, but the most excellent, that is gold, true son of the sun, which it is similar to (da Vinci, p. 163).

---

20 "Against the necromancer and the alchemist" (Leonardo, pp. 156-64). For a more detailed analysis, see the interesting essay by Vasoli.

21 And in Leonardo's *Libro di Pittura*: "[...] di nessuna cosa è che più c'inganni che fidarsi del nostro giudicio sanz'altra ragione, come prova sempre la sperienzia, nemica delli alchimisti, negromanti et altri semplici ingegni" (cf. Kiang, pp. 199-201).

This is clear evidence for Leonardo's balanced approach to alchemy: He is able to report its good features on the basis of such an objective standard as its usefulness and advantage to men (thus excluding all drifts toward occultism and supernatural), [22] but at the same time, placing alchemy among the false sciences, he points out its limits, both through the outweighing of pros by cons, and by characterizing it as a search for something that is unattainable.[23]

Before this study reaches its final subject, Galileo Galilei, the case of Ludovico Ariosto (1474-1533), a man highly admired by Galilei, should be considered. The representation of alchemy in Ariosto's poem *Orlando Furioso* is far from scientific, and the negative judgment familiar from other very literary texts mentioned above is again noticeable. In the sixth canto of the poem, Ruggiero, one of the protagonists, arrives on the back of a hippogriff on the "fatal island" of the evil sorceress Alcina, an insidious and deadly place where nothing is what it seems (*Orlando Furioso* VI; 51).[24] Unfortunately, tough he tries to avoid the witch's notice, the knight alights right at the walls of her "lovely city":

> A lofty wall at distance meets his eye
> Which girds a spacious town within its bound;
> It seems as if its summit touched the sky,
> And all appears like gold from top to ground.
> Here some one says it is but alchemy
> And haply his opinion is unsound
> And haply he more wittily divines:
> For me, I deem it gold because it shines. (*Orlando Furioso* VI, l. 59)

---

22 This is more than a clarification since, in general, the exploitation of results achieved by alchemists was routine among the writers involved in this practice, who, however, considered the research itself imbued with magical and theurgic meanings (cf. Vasoli, pp. 74-5).

23 In the conclusion to this paragraph he invites the alchemist to go to the mines, where nature creates gold, to check that there is neither fire nor any metal that the alchemical doctrine "of imperfection" assumed as intermediate degrees to gold: "E se pur la stolta avarizia in tal error t'invia, perché non vai alle miniere, dove la natura genera tale oro, e quivi ti fa' suo discepolo, la qual fedelmente ti guarirà della tua stoltizia, mostrandoti come nessuna cosa da te operata nel foco, non sarà nessuna di quelle che natura adoperi al generare esso oro? Quivi non argento vivo, quivi non zolfo di nessuna sorte, quivi non foco, né altro caldo che quel di natura vivificatrice del nostro mondo [...]" (Leonardo, pp. 164-5).

24 The English quotations are from Rose's translation.

This octave refers to alchemy in a highly significant context: Ariosto often uses particular constructions and descriptions to enhance the verisimilitude and naturalness of his fantastical characters in order to create a homogeneous plot. Frequently, passages oscillate between the real and the imaginary, disorientating the reader; to this, Ariosto's first-person voice responds that adding further viewpoints or proposing terms for comparison provides a raison d'être for the story's fancifulness and puts its uniqueness back into perspective. In the verses quoted above, alchemy is one of these extradiegetic considerations (even if it is in the voice of an anonymous and impersonal "some one"), intended to justify the consistency of Alcina's city walls in an octave where the use of the verb "to seem" undoubtedly emphasizes the misleading element of what is presented: The walls seem to be made of gold because they shine, but perhaps it is alchemical gold, that is, fake gold. After Cecco's and Leonardo's more measured views, there is a return here to a focus on the worst meanings of alchemy, and specifically its deceptive and fraudulent results: the same view, in short, encountered in Dante's *Inferno*.

Pointed out that in Ariosto's poem of more than 4800 octaves there are only two references to alchemy, a distance from fourteenth-century attitudes to alchemy in poetry may be perceived in the second:

> Gryphon and Aquilant by turns divide,
> Now to the teeth, now breast, the enchanted wight.
> The fruitless blow Orrilo does deride,
> While the two baffled warriors rage for spite.
> Let him who falling silver has espied
> (Which mercury by alchymists is hight)
> Scatter, and reunite each broken member,
> Hearing my tale, what he has seen remember. (*Orlando Furioso* XV, l. 70)

The object of the attacks of the twin brothers, the knights Gryphon called The White and Aquilant called The Black, is Orrilo, a "sturdy thief" who lived at the mouth of the Nile harassing anyone who came within range. He is magical, thus he cannot be killed: Every wound inflicted on him heals without leaving a scar.[25] Without going further into the episode – one of the

---

25 As Astolfo will find in the book ("which prescribed a remedy for spell") given to him by the good fairy Logistilla, Alcina's sister, the only way to kill Orrilo is by cutting him one fatal hair (*Orlando Furioso* XV, l. 79).

most gruesome of the *Furioso* – I wish to point out the image of mercury used to represent Orrilo's body, which, though repeatedly ripped and torn by the two knights' slashes, always comes together. This choice of simile unites precision and technicality with liveliness and effectiveness. In short, Ariosto, faithful to a literary tradition dating back to Dante, can employ alchemy to suggest the deception perpetrated by practitioners of this art in their attempts to create gold; at the same time, as a man of the Renaissance, he can refer more casually to a common accident in the laboratories of those same alchemists.

THE SEVENTEENTH CENTURY: GALILEO GALILEI – BETWEEN SCIENCE AND LITERATURE

The decision to conclude this survey with a discussion of Galilei takes into account two perspectives. The first concerns alchemy and the weakening of its theoretical foundations in the general renewal of the intellectual co-ordinates between Cartesian philosophy and the scientific revolution; for historians of science 1543 was the defining year in which both *De Revolutionibus Orbium Caelestium* by Copernicus and *De Humani Corporis Fabrica libri septem* by Vesalius were published, but only in the figure of Galileo may we witness the transition "from the closed world to the infinite universe".[26] The second perspective is literary, since the critic and author Italo Calvino defines Galilei as "the greatest writer of the Italian literature of any century".[27] Galileo was educated in the classics of both scientific thought[28] and literature: He loved and defended Ariosto against Tasso, then in vogue; he gave lectures on Dante[29] and annotated his copy of Petrarch's *Rime et Trionfi* heavily. Above all, he proved to be a "humanist scientist"[30]

---

26   Quoting the title of the pivotal book by Koyré.

27   In an article published on 24 December 1967, then included in the collection of essays *Una pietra sopra* under the title "Il rapporto con la luna" (Calvino: *Una pietra sopra*, pp. 221-2). In response to the reactions to this provocative definition, Calvino explained that, although his appraisal referred to the "writer in prose", the sharp distinction between the scientist and the man of letters was unfounded (Calvino: *Una pietra sopra*, pp. 226-7).

28   This is the main difference from Leonardo da Vinci, who is often said to have anticipated some of Galileo's positions.

29   His two *Lezioni circa la figura, sito e grandezza dell'inferno di Dante*, given at the Florentine Academy, date back to 1588.

30   This definition was suggested in some recent notes by Basile (Basile, p. 907).

who pursued his love and knowledge of literature in his scientific works, that, besides their extensive use of poetic quotations, especially from Ariosto, drew their own characteristic precision and clarity from this constant study of poetry. There is one last reason for the relevance of Galileo at the end of this analysis, and it comes again from Calvino. In his *Six Memos for the Next Millennium* Calvino opens one devoted to "exactitude" remembering that for "the ancient Egyptians, exactitude was symbolized by a feather that served as a weight on scales used for the weighing of souls" (Calvino: *Six Memos*, p. 55). The clue lies in the connection between exactitude and scale, especially considering its importance for the chemical revolution that occurred a century later thanks to Lavoisier.[31] Galileo also used a scale to unsettle the prevailing opinion in his 1623 work entitled *Il Saggiatore* (a word indicating an accurate scale for precious metals),[32] in which, as is declared on the title page, "with a most just and accurate balance there are weighed the things contained in *The Astronomical And Philosophical Balance* of Lothario Sarsi of Siguenza" (Stillman, p. 231).[33] In this work, among the methodological principles which gave rise to modern science, Galileo asserts:

> Philosophy is written in this grand book, the universe, which stands always open to our gaze. But the book cannot be understood unless one learns before to comprehend its language and read the letters in which it is composed. It is written in the language of mathematics, and its characters are triangles, circles, and other geometric figures without which it is humanly impossible to understand a single word of it; without these, one wanders about in a dark labyrinth. (Stillman, pp. 238-9)[34]

The main innovation here is Galileo's method, which connects theory (*ipotesi*), based on mathematical logic, with factual observation (*sensate espe-*

---

31 Remembering, among others, Bachelard's considerations of Lavoisier's science based on the use of scales (Bachelard, p. 134).

32 "*The Assayer*". The English quotations are from Stillman.

33 "Con bilancia esquisita e giusta si ponderano le cose contenute nella *Libra astronomica e filosofica* di Lotario Sarsi Sigensano" (Galilei, p. 89).

34 "La filosofia è scritta in questo grandissimo libro che continuamente ci sta aperto innanzi a gli occhi (io dico l'universo), ma non si può intendere se prima non si impara a intender la lingua, e conoscer i caratteri, ne' quali è scritto. Egli è scritto in lingua matematica, e i caratteri son triangoli, cerchi, ed altre figure geometriche, senza i quali mezi è impossibile a intenderne umanamente parola; senza questi è un aggirarsi vanamente per un oscuro laberinto" (Galilei, p. 121).

rienze) of controlled experiments. Galileo's many achievements include the emancipation of scientific research from philosophic speculation; the refusal of "ipse dixit", the principle of authority, often used by Aristotelian scholars; and finally the discrediting of metaphysics. When the distinction between earth and universe came to an end,[35] the fundamental theories of previous astronomical science had to be discarded and alchemy suffered a loosing of meaning, too. It is in *The Dialogue concerning the two chief world systems* (1632) – the work that led to his prosecution by the Inquisition, abjuration, and life sentence – that Galileo refers to alchemy. In the *Giornata seconda* (Galilei, pp. 352-850), following Simplicio's defence of the appeal to the "Aristotle's experiences or reasons",[36] the other two interlocutors, Sagredo and Salviati, reject the methodological insubstantiality of simply putting together ideas proposed by others "and by their means, explaining human problems and the secret of nature" (Galilei, p. 468; my translation): This is not science since the efficacy of demonstration emerges only *a posteriori*, like the "oracles' verdicts in the past when their effectiveness was stated only by the appearance of the events" (Galilei, p. 469). Alchemy is here associated, in Sagredo's words, with astrological previsions, because of its overthrowing the principle of causality:

> in this way, the alchemists, driven by madness, discover that all the world's greatest authors actually wrote only about how to make gold, but, not making themselves understood by all, each author made up his own way to hide it under various forms; and it is so pleasant to listen to their comments on the ancients, while they highlight the extremely important mysteries hidden in fables [...] and the many secrets on the alchemical art handed down by Mercury Trismegistus. (Galilei, p. 469)

With these words of Sagredo/Galileo alchemy reaches its final resting place in the realms of the hermetic. From the medieval view of alchemists as fraudulent and falsifiers, a common denominator of an eminently literary perspective as well as a *trait d'union* between the beginnings of Italian

---

35 This was already compromised by Galileo's first revolutionary work, the *Sidereus Nuncius* ("The Starry Messenger" 1610), in which the description of the moon as entirely similar to the earth put in crisis the usual opposition between a celestial space, unchanging and eternal, and a terrestrial one of metamorphosis and corruption.

36 "Esperienze o ragioni di Aristotele", my translation.

literature and the Renaissance flourishing of Ariosto, via Dante; through a more measured scepticism about the capabilities of alchemy that brings the medieval Cecco nearer to the humanist Leonardo; at last, Galileo's attitude to alchemy brings us to the threshold of modern science. The irony and commiseration in such an attitude reduces alchemy's prestige and validity, relegating it to the role of an obscure and irrational study, suitable only as entertainment for those who have the curiosity and patience to read its works.

WORKS CITED

Alessio, Franco: *Mito e scienza in Ruggero Bacone*. Milan: Ceschina, 1957.

Alighieri, Dante: *Commedia*. With commentary by Anna Maria Chiavacci Leonardi, vol. 1: *Inferno*. Milan: Mondadori, 1991.

—: *Divine Comedy*, trans. Henry W. Longfellow. Boston: Houghton, Mifflin and Company, 1867.

Aurigemma, Marcello: "Interpretazioni dell'opera di Cecco d'Ascoli dal Trecento ad oggi" in Basilio Censori (ed.): *Atti del I convegno di studi su Cecco d'Ascoli, Ascoli Piceno, 23-24 Novembre 1969*. Florence: Barbera, 1976, pp. 11-29.

Bachelard, Gaston: *Il razionalismo applicato*. Bari: Edizioni Dedalo, 1993.

Bacon, Roger: *The mirror of alchimy: composed by the thrice-famous and learned fryer, Roger Bachon*. Stanton J. Linden (ed.). New York: Garland Pub., 1992.

Basile, Bruno: "Galilei e la letteratura" in Enrico Malato (ed.): *Storia della letteratura italiana*, vol. 5, *La fine del Cinquecento e il Seicento*. Rome: Salerno, 1997, pp. 905-51.

Berthelot, Marcelin: *La Révolution chimique: Lavoisier, ouvrage suivi de notices et extraits des registres inédits de laboratoire de Lavoisier*. Paris: F. Alcan, 1890.

Botterill, Steven: "Dante e l'alchimia" in Patrick Boyde and Vittorio Russo (eds.): *Dante e la scienza*. Ravenna: Longo Editore, 1995, pp. 203-11.

Calvino, Italo: *Six Memos for the Next Millennium*. London: Penguin, 2009.

—: *Una pietra sopra*, 1980. Milan: Mondadori, 2002.

Cardini, Franco and Cesare Vasoli: "Rinascimento e Umanesimo" in Enrico Malato (ed.): *Storia della letteratura italiana*, vol. 4: *Il Quattrocento*. Rome: Salerno, 1996, pp. 45-158.

Carli, Manola: "Un' enciclopedia alchemica duecentesca: il 'Liber Compostille' di Bonaventura da Iseo" in Ferdinando Abbri and Marco Ciardi (eds.): *Atti dell'VIII Convegno Nazionale di Storia e Fondamenti della Chimica*. Rome: Accademia Nazionale delle Scienze detta dei XL, 1997, pp. 45-57.

Cecco d'Ascoli: *L'acerba (Acerba aetas)*. Marco Albertazzi (ed.). Trento: La Finestra editrice, 2005.

Ciociola, Claudio: "Poesia gnomica, d'arte, di corte, allegorica e didattica" in Enrico Malato (ed.): *Storia della letteratura italiana*, Vol. 2: *Il Trecento*. Rome: Salerno Editrice, 1995, pp. 327-454.

Contini, Gianfranco: *Letteratura Italiana delle Origini*. Florence: Sansoni, 1970.

—: *Poeti del Duecento*. Milan / Naples: Ricciardi, 1960.

Crivelli, Enrico: "Dante e gli alchimisti" in Jacqueline Tarrant (ed.): *Il Giornale Dantesco*, 38.8, 1935, pp. 29-57. *Extravagantes Iohannis XXII*. Vatican City: Biblioteca Apostolica Vaticana, 1983.

Da Vinci, Leonardo: *Tutti gli scritti. Scritti letterari*. Augusto Marinoni (ed.). Milan: Rizzoli, 1952.

Fabricius, Johannes: *Alchemy*. London: Aquarian, 1989.

Flora, Francesco: *Leonardo e il Rinascimento*. Milan: Malfasi, 1948.

Fowden, Garth: *The Egyptian Hermes. A Historical Approach to the Late Pagan Mind*. Cambridge: Cambridge University Press, 1996.

Galilei, Galileo: *Opere*. Ferdinando Flora (ed.). Milan / Naples: Ricciardi, 1953.

Garin, Eugenio: "La letteratura degli umanisti" in Emilio Cecchi and Natalino Sapegno (eds.): *Storia della letteratura italiana*, vol. 3: *Il Quattrocento e l'Ariosto*. Milan: Garzanti, 1966, pp. 7-353.

Geymonat, Ludovico and Brunetti, Franz: "Galileo Galilei" in Emilio Cecchi and Natalino Sapegno (eds.): *Storia della letteratura italiana*, vol. 5: *Il Seicento*. Milan: Garzanti, 1967, pp. 154-222.

Kiang, Dawson: "Leonardo and Alchemy. A Bibliographical Note" in *Achademia Leonardi Vinci* 10, 1997, pp. 199-201.

Kibre, Pearl: "Albertus Magnus on alchemy" in James A. Weisheipl (ed.): *Albertus Magnus and the Sciences: Commemorative essays*. Toronto: Pontifical Institute of Medieval Studies, 1980.

Kopp, Hermann: *Die Alchemie in älterer und neuerer Zeit: ein beitrag zur culturgeschichte*. Heidelberg: Carl Winter's Universitatsbuchhandlung, 1886.

Koyré, Alexandre: *From the Closed World to the Infinite Universe*. Baltimore: Johns Hopkins Press, 1957.

Mayer, Sharon: "Dante's Alchemists" in *Italian Quarterly*, vol. 12, 1969, pp. 185-200.

Mazzoni, Mario: *Sonetti alchemici di Cecco d'Ascoli e Frate Elia*. Rome: Atanor, 1955.

Pereira, Michela: *Alchimia*. Milan: Mondadori, 2006.

Petrocchi, Giorgio: "Cultura e poesia del Trecento" in Emilio Cecchi and Natalino Sapegno (eds.): *Storia della letteratura italiana*, vol. 3: *Il Trecento*. Milan: Garzanti, 1965, pp. 355-588.

Stabili, Francesco: *L'Acerba*. Achille Crespi (ed.). Ascoli Piceno: Casa Editrice di Giuseppe Cesari, 1927.

Steiner, George: *My unwritten books*. New York: New Directions Books, 2008.

Stillman, Drake: *Discoveries and Opinions of Galileo*. New York: Doubleday & Co., 1957, www.princeton.edu/~hos/h291/assayer.htm (23 Jan. 2013).

Vasoli, Cesare: "Note su Leonardo e l'alchimia" in Enrico Bellone and Paolo Rossi (eds.): *Leonardo e l'età della ragione*. Milan: Scientia, 1982, pp. 69-77.

Walsh, James Joseph: "Pope John XXII and the supposed bull forbidding chemistry" in *Medical Library and Historical Journal*, vol. 3, no. 4, 1905, pp. 248-63.

ON THE ROLE OF ALCHEMY AND CHEMISTRY IN RUSSIAN LITERATURE AND CULTURE FROM PETER THE GREAT TO THE POST-SOVIET PERIOD

Lillian Jorunn Helle, University of Bergen

This essay will examine the intertwining of the arts and the sciences in Russian post-Petrine cultural and intellectual history, and also demonstrate how traces from an older scientific tradition – the *arcana artis* of alchemy – can act as a mediator between them in rather intriguing ways.[1] This approach necessitates the consideration of how topics from scientific and proto-scientific spheres are narrated or retold in literary and cultural settings. These problematics are, however, vast; the following will therefore cover only some – rather limited – aspects of such discussions.

From its very beginning at the start of the eighteenth century, the Petrine Empire was proclaimed to be a symbol of Eurocentric civilisation. The Westernised rule of the Romanovs became an emblem of Enlightenment in its clear contrast to the dark, medieval atmosphere that dominated in old Muscovite Russia.[2] These progressive assumptions are eloquently expressed by the Russian literary critic Vissarion Belinsky (1811-48), who uses Biblical allusions to exalt the founder of the reformed nation, the autocrat Peter the Great (1672-1725): "With his powerful 'Let there be!' Peter dispelled the chaos, separated the light from the darkness and called the country to its great, global destiny" (Belinsky, p. 117). Notwithstanding the Tsar's status as an epitome of rationalist illumination, he was nonetheless

---

1 On the topic of the two cultures, see the debate starting with the publication of the British scientist and novelist Charles Percy Snow's (1905-1980) Rede Lecture of 1959, "The Two Cultures", republished in 1964 in an extended form. Its thesis, that the intellectual life of the whole of the Western world is "split into two polar groups", the arts and the sciences, in a way that is damaging to social and economic progress (Snow, p. 3), led to important discourses which are more relevant today than ever.

2 On the founding myth of the Petrine state, see Helle, "The City as Myth and Symbol". There are several seminal works on the semiotics of the new city; see especially Lotman and Toporov.

influenced to a significant degree by the ancient wisdom of alchemy.[3] In particular, he seems to have displayed a keen interest in esoteric pursuits and alchemical experimentation, as is evident from the following remark: "I neither belittle nor revile the alchemist, the search for converting metal into gold, of the mechanic trying to find perpetual movement, such types of people should be encouraged in every manner, and not despised" (quoted in Collis, "Alchemical Interest", p. 53).

At the heart of all alchemic fascination stands the quest for the philosopher's stone, *lapis philosophorum*, or "der Stein der Weisen", as it is called in the German occult tradition.[4] This legendary catalyst is also known as the Elixir of Life or as the *quinta essentia*, and it was supposed to have the power to transmute base metals into gold.[5] Symptomatically, the appearance in 1703

---

3   On this topic, see Collis ("Alchemical Interest at the Petrine Court" and *The Petrine Instauration*). In his innovative reappraisal of the Petrine age, Collis was the first to draw attention to the remarkable occurrences of alchemical practices at Peter's court and to show the deep impact of Western esotericism on the leading circles of his reign.

4   For an exploration of the language, symbols, and Faustian ambitions of the alchemists, see Bensaude-Vincent and Simon (pp. 33-46). See also Eliade's classic book *The Forge and the Crucible: The Origins and Structures of Alchemy*, first published in 1956.

5   Apparently the alchemical interests at Peter's court were influenced to no small degree by the spiritual aspect of alchemy, such as the speculative notions of gold making and the metaphysical idea of the transmutation of the self. This focus on the "magic" elements collides with the much debated thesis of the historians of science William Newman and Lawrence Principe, which asserts that the spiritual aspect of alchemy was a Romanticist and Victorian construction that distorted the "real" alchemy, which is seen as a purely proto-chemical, experimental inquiry (Newman and Principe, p. 37). Recent researchers such as George-Florin Călian and Hereford Tilton have rejected this positivist and exclusivist perspective. They claim, with examples from the writings of Jakob Boehme (1575-1624), Michel Maier (1552-1612) and Isaac Newton (1642-1724) that Newman and Principe's interpretation is historically inaccurate. Călian characterises this "eliminitavist" interpretation as "almost scandalous" (Călian, p. 168 and 178), arguing that the spiritual dimension of the *arcana artis* was not a result of nineteenth-century occultism, but an essential component of historical alchemy. This "ambiguous" science was a combination of the *alkimia operativa* and the *alkimia speculativa*; its speculative aspect was not the least significant element (see Călian, p. 187). In the present context it is not possible to go further into these intriguing historiographic controversies, which also throw light on controversies in the interpretation of alchemy between the humanist researcher and the natural scholar trained in fields connected to chemistry and the

of Peter's new capital, Saint Petersburg, which rose from the *terra nullius* of the harsh shores of Ingermanaland to become his Palmyra of the North, was referred to in similar alchemical terms in odes and other panegyric writings of the time. The *Imperator* is portrayed as a God-like alchemist who brings forth his new city of gold out of the uncivilised marshland of swamps and forested wilderness, as indicated in a famous eulogy from 1717 (see Vilienvakhov, p. 47; Helle, p. 25). The purification process underlying the founding legends of Saint Petersburg, the creation of the sublime out of the raw and low, became a vital part of the pro-Petrine mythology of the Neva metropolis.[6]

Within the alchemical subtext of Peter's reign, the Tsar could be seen as a sorcerer smith who from a furnace of crude materials, the primitive peasants, moulds a new Russian race. This mythical narrative – or retelling of alchemical proto-scientific theories – was a prevalent one in Russian culture, found for instance in the Symbolist writer Dmitrii Merezhkovsky's (1865-1941) trilogy *Christ and Antichrist* from 1885-1905, in which Peter becomes a powerful "farrier", forging a new Russia out of the medieval Muscovite state.[7] The historian of religion Mircea Eliade (1907-86) has pointed to the crucial link between the old symbolism of smithery and the fantastic science of alchemy, a connection which is very relevant to the Peter mythology: "What the smelter, smith and alchemist have in common, is that all three (…) seek to change the modalities of matter, pursue the transformation of nature, its perfection and its transmutation" (Eliade, pp. 8-9). An example of such changing of modalities can be found in the Imperator's new and hybrid subjects, which are alluded to in the glorifying

---

history of science. Suffice it to say that in my view, reducing historical alchemy to proto-chemical activity tends to be as much of an ahistorical construction as the thesis that spiritual alchemy is nothing but an invention of Victorian occultism.

6　In the most paradigmatic Saint Petersburg text of Russian culture, Alexander Pushkin's "The Bronze Horseman" (1833), the pro-Petrine myth is elaborated in elevated images of the glorious city magically rising from the chaos of untamed nature. The poem also, however, intriguingly alludes to the anti-Petrine myth by simultaneously showing the city's dark and demonic dimension, lurking behind the sublime facades (cf. Helle, "The City as Myth and Symbol", p. 25ff.).

7　Merezhkovsky's work, by the way, was programmatically anti-Petrine, portraying the tsar not as a God-like alchemist creator, but as an infernal, ancient blacksmith, reshaping innocent Russian souls in his enormous forge of blazing reforms. See also Mints, "Kommentarii k romanu", p. 614, who discusses the trilogy's smith image of Peter, tracing it through Pushkin's imagery in his poem "Poltava" (1829).

speech written for his funeral in 1725. This text claimed that the Tsar had reconstructed his people "like gold in the crucible" (quoted in Wiener, p. 218).

This rather enigmatic phrasing can be read in light of the alchemical spiritual dimension, which had not been forgotten in Peter's time. In this period "the decline of magic" was still not complete, and the esoteric aspect of the "arcane art" retained its power over man's quest for knowledge.[8] There were still traces of a tradition in which alchemy was both a "scientifically and spiritually serious pursuit" (Morrison, p. 3) and an inquiry with "a close connection between spiritual and experimental domains", as a Newtonian approach would have it (see Cohen and Smith, p. 24).[9] Consequently, the *alkimia speculativa* was as important as the *alkimia operativa* or the laboratory element. The speculative dimension even tended to give the whole of *arcana artis* its prime value. As the Renaissance alchemist and physician Philippus von Hohenheim, better known as Paracelsus (1493-1541), once asserted, "the worth of the discipline is to be evaluated in terms which have nothing to do with the ennobling of metals" (cf. Călian, p. 187).[10]

Such assumptions lead to the idea that transmutation is not limited to metallurgical processes; ultimately the goal must be the transmutation of the human from a lower creature to a higher one, even into an immortal man (see Hellebust, p. 24). The conversions of base materials into gold could therefore be conceived – both (proto-) scientifically and also in the cultural imagination – as a prefiguration of a human transfiguration, represented as stages of hardening and crystallisation (anticipating, as we shall see, the metallic immortality imagery of the Bolsheviks).[11] Such a prefiguration oc-

---

8 Cf. Webster, who points to "an almost perfect correlation between the rise of science and the decline of magic" in his discussions on the disintegration of magical elements in scientific pursuits at the time of the scientific revolution (Webster, p. 1).

9 Newton, although usually regarded as a proto-modern natural scientist, was "deeply committed to his research into what seems to us esoteric domains, including (…) ancient wisdom and alchemy" (Cohen and Smith, p. 23).

10 As has been emphasised, in the sixteenth century alchemy "promised much more than producing gold from base metals. The successful alchemist gained control of life's forces and uncovered secret wisdom – the essence of all truths and religions" (Metzler, p. 131).

11 As Hellebust points out, the alchemical transmutation of base components is motivated not by a pre-capitalist hunger for wealth, but is rather conceived as a foreshadowing of the creation of the new and deathless man (Hellebust, p. 24). For this connection, see also Beil (p. 32 and 43).

LITERATURE AND CHEMISTRY

curs in the funeral sermon mentioned above: The Tsar's new Russians no longer have bodies of flesh, but are metallised by their Promethean ruler into beings of pure gold.

Not only Peter himself, but many of the men of his inner circle, like the gifted statesman and later archbishop Feofan Prokopovich (1681-1736), were deeply immersed in the experimental and spiritual art of alchemy. Since Prokopovich was a standard bearer for the progressive nature of the Petrine reforms, it may initially seem paradoxical to see him as an adherent of an archaic heritage supposedly at odds with the rational and mechanistic tenets of modern science. As has been maintained, however, if one disregards the Kuhnian theory that an abrupt paradigm shift gave scientific inquiry its modern guise at the close of the seventeenth century, one can regard this embrace of the *arcana artis* as neither incongruous nor anachronistic. On the contrary, it can be viewed as part of a wider phenomenon common across Europe in which chemistry as a scientific discipline had not been completely divorced from its roots in the "irrational" alchemical sphere (cf. Collis, p. 53).[12]

A Russian of pivotal importance in alchemy's development into the modern natural science of chemistry was Mikhail Lomonosov (1711-1765). In his many innovative studies, he, *inter alia*, outlined the principle of the conservation of mass even before the French researcher Antoine Lavoisier (1743-1794), and it has been claimed that Lomonosov proved these ideas by experiment.[13] This great scientist – the founder of the first Russian chemical

---

12 The connection between alchemy and chemistry has been emphasised in much modern research, e.g. Newman and Principe. As mentioned (cf. footnote 5), their historiographic writings disregard the spiritual dimension of alchemy and turn it into proto-chemistry, a one-sided laboratory activity, thereby maximally stressing the continuity between archaic alchemy and modern chemistry. However, the bonds between the *arcana artis* and modern chemistry are evident without excluding the spiritual aspect from the history of alchemy. As the historian of chemistry Bruce T. Moran suggests in a more moderate thesis, alchemists and early chemists can be seen as exchanging ideas and methods until alchemy gradually lost its spiritual or religious aspects and became chemistry at the time of the so-called scientific revolution. See also Haynes, who in her pioneering study on scientific archetypes in literature shows how the alchemist contributed to the "cutting edge of experimental research" while simultaneously immersing himself in an atmosphere of "mystery, secrecy, suspicion and, at times, irreligion" (Haynes, p. 9).

13 The law of the conservation of mass was first clearly formulated in 1789 by Lavoisier, who for this reason is often referred to as a father of modern chemistry. However, Lomonosov had previously expressed such ideas and demonstrated them in his labo-

laboratory at the Academy of Sciences in 1748 – was also a great poet who laid the foundation of modern Russian literary language. He was a true *homo universalis*, mastering chemistry, physics, natural science, history, linguistics, and poetry with equal ease. In all his activities he strove towards universal knowledge, covering both the arts and the sciences, and with his encyclopaedic insights he was a brilliant representative of the intellectual *Zeitgeist* of Russia's early eighteenth century.

The spiritual side of alchemical tradition, still vital in Lomonosov's time, faded into obscurity during the last part of the eighteenth century due to its growing incompatibility with the hypostasis of "reason" that character-ised the Enlightenment's post-Cartesian spirit.[14] In Russian Romanticism (1820-40), however, a period of meta-rational reaction to empiricism and Neoclassicism, the domain of (metaphysical) poetry was regarded as the highest stage of human culture, and we find here the same striking reacti-vation of alchemical themes and symbols as occurred in other European countries.[15] As already mentioned, it has been claimed that this wave of esoteric alchemy was alien to "real" alchemy; it was not based on a historical reality, but was a cultural construction and an anachronistic product of the Victorian occult revival (Newman and Principe, p. 37).[16] It would be wrong,

---

ratory as early as 1748 (see Menshutkin, p. 120). With the exception of Menshutkin's excellent book from 1952 there exist few works on Lomonosov in English, although a Soviet biography has been translated into English (Pavlova and Fedorov).

14 On the fascinating role of the alchemist as a fictional figure in eighteenth-century Russian literature, see Baehr and Welsh.

15 On the alchemical revival in Russian Romanticism, see Leighton. On alchemy as allegory and symbolic system in specific periods of Russian literature, see Knopf. See also Maguire, who analyses the cultural assimilation of Russia's most famous historical alchemist, Count James Bruce (1669-1735) in her study of three historical novels written between 1830 and 1930.

16 In this interpretation all the obscure language of historical alchemy was explained not as signs referring to spiritual realities, but as "Decknamen" for the operations of laboratory work (see Newman). As has been pointed out, however, it might well be that some enigmatic symbols alluded to concrete chemical processes and practical activities, but rejecting the possibility that these symbols also pointed to a transcendent and mystic sphere "can be regarded as part of what David Fischer called the historian's fallacies" (Călian, p. 189). It could be added that Newman and Principe's radical rejection of spiritual alchemy is an almost antithetical reaction to the radical Jungian (spiritual) approach in which alchemical symbols are understood as independent of laboratory research and pointing to deep archetypical structures of the psyche and its unconscious.

LITERATURE AND CHEMISTRY

though, to argue that there was never a speculative dimension to the ancient alchemist quest. The occult and alchemist world of the Romanticist movement, in Russia as well as elsewhere in Europe, was not created *ex nihilo*, but was inspired by the spiritual practices of the pre-modern alchemists, among other things. These practices were often and to various degrees reconstructed and reformulated – as frequently happens within the dynamic life of cultural expressions – to fit in with the occult and esoteric trends of nineteenth century. It should also be noted that the Romanticist narrative of spiritual and mystic alchemy, with its focus on the ambiguous Faustian magician, was the impetus for much further exploration of alchemist imagery in both Russian and Soviet literature and cultural-political thinking.[17]

Another Romantic topos that became hugely influential was the figure of the poet, who in this era is the main intellectual hero; like the alchemist sorcerer, he creates new connections and realities. Furthermore, he is a genius, who through the imaginative transmutation of temporal beauty into the eternal beauty of the perfected art product is repeating the alchemist's own wondrous works of transformation and synthesis. In lines with such Neo-Platonic thinking, the poet is also a seer with mysterious gifts, capable of accessing and expressing the hidden and esoteric sources of wisdom, as Aleksander Pushkin's (1799-1837) proclaims in his 1826 programmatic poem "The Prophet" ("Prorok").

This idolisation of the poet in Russian Romanticism was eventually challenged by the aesthetic principles of so-called Russian "critical realism", a movement that dominated the country's cultural development from approximately 1845 to the 1890s. During this age an extraordinary blossoming of Russian literature took place, and for our purposes it provides interesting fictional examples of how the relationship between the arts and the sciences was understood and articulated. An exceptionally good illustration can be found in the novelist Ivan Turgenev's (1818-83) best known work, *Fathers and Sons (Otsy i deti)*. This classic novel, first published in 1862, focuses on what the author saw as the growing schism between different domains of knowledge. The dominant theme of the book is the conflict between the fathers, the idealist Romanticist generation of the 1820s to 1840s, and the sons, a generation of young radical intellectuals bent on materialism and social revolution. One of the "older" characters reflects upon this conflict by comparing the days of Schiller and Goethe with the present, when

---

17 On the multiple castings of the Faust figure in Russian literature of the nineteenth and twentieth centuries, see Gronicka and Iakusheva (eds.).

all have "turned into chemists and materialists" (*Fathers and Sons*, p. 79). This formulation makes it conspicuously clear how the literary ideal of the Pushkinian epoch, when the poet was an (alchemist) magi and a maker of metaphysical worlds, is now opposed to a new ideal, the down-to-earth specialist in the natural sciences. The main protagonist of the novel, the medical student Evgenii Bazarov, expresses this opposition in his famous – even notorious – phrase: "a decent chemist is twenty times as useful as any poet" (*Fathers and Sons*, p. 79).

From the narrator's point of view this is an ironic statement and Bazarov, a proto-Bolshevik activist, is more than slightly ridiculed throughout the text. The first self-proclaimed nihilist in European culture, "Mister Nihilist" as he is called by his sceptical contemporaries (*Fathers and* Sons, p. 70), is a person who loathes feelings and human passions, declaring loudly: "I don't believe in anything" (*Fathers and Sons*, p. 79).[18] He respects nothing but the most concrete labour, like dissecting frogs and giving chemistry lessons, and claims that science in the abstract does not exist at all (*Father and Sons*, p. 72). Turgenev's literary retelling of the scientist's theories and practices are not without a certain critical condescension. Significantly enough, the nihilist's militant (scientific) materialism is defeated at the end of the book, where he dies, also ironically, after being poisoned in one of his experiments that goes wrong. But before his death Bazarov seems to acknowledge that life is

---

18   The term *nihilism* (from Latin *nihil*) was first popularised in Russia through the fictional Bazarov and became very productive, coining a new mentality and way of thinking that was hugely influential both in a Russian and European intellectual and political context. Especially well known is the adaptation of the term by the Russian political activists who called themselves the Nihilist movement. The most imminent theoretical followers of Bazarov were the revolutionary critics and writers Nikolai Dobroliubov (1836-61) and Nikolai Chernyshevsky (1828-89), who developed a (Feuerbachian) materialistic monism in which man is nothing but a complex chemical compound. This message is articulated with particular force in Chernyshevsky's *What is to be done* (*Chto delat'*) from 1863, which was a direct response to *Fathers and Sons*. The (ill-)famed hero of Chernyshevsky's novel, the New Man Rakhmetov, became an emblem of philosophical materialism, secular scientism, and anti-aestheticism. Incidentally Fedor Dostoevsky's (1821-81) *Notes from Underground* (*Zapiski iz podpol'ia*), published in 1864, is a highly emotional reaction (grounded in the author's Orthodox belief) against the (nihilistic) utilitarism and utopianism of Chernyshevsky. This reaction though had little effect and it has been claimed that Chernyshevsky's "insuperably talentless novel (...) far more than Marx's *Capital* supplied the emotional dynamic that eventually went to make the Russian Revolution" (Amis, p. 27).

more than empirical observations in the laboratory. He comes to recognise the value of the irrational forces of intuition, emotion, and love, allowing Turgenev to forge a new synthesis between fathers and sons and between their two cultures. This synthesis can also be observed to no small degree in the work of the prose writer and playwright Anton Chekhov (1860-1904), who was also a dedicated scientist, and combined aesthetic insights with those of a medically trained man.[19] He often used a humorous analogy to describe this relationship: He considered medicine his lawful wife and literature his mistress, with the power balance between them in constant flux (Malcolm, p. 116).

The growing influence of the Symbolist movement on the Russian intellectual scene from the 1890s onwards somewhat altered the balanced Chekhovian intertwining of science and arts. In the sophisticated cultural consciousness of the fin de siècle the poet, as in Russian Romanticism, comes to occupy a prominent place as the privileged hero of literature and culture. In accordance with traditional Neo-Romanticist concepts he – always a male – is regarded as a key to transcendental dimensions, a theurgist who through mystic intuition and introspection brings the unimaginable and the fantastic into being.[20]

In this Neo-Platonic and anti-empiricist atmosphere it is hardly surprising that the representative of modern "fragmented" natural sciences is a less popular or even disregarded fictional personage, the naïve and superficial positivist, while the alchemist with his holistic, archaic, and secret wisdom becomes a valorised metaphorical figure. Many works from this period con-

---

19 See Carter. This article is the first scholarly work to demonstrate in some depth how Chekhov's experiences as a physician overflowed into his literary activities. Here they influenced both his subject matter and his style, revealing insights that Chekhov "discovered about the human psyche at work, thus delving into psychosomatic medicine nearly 50 years before its time" (Carter, p. 1557).

20 The scholarly literature on Russian Symbolism and its theurgic life-creating project is vast. The best example of this mentality is, however, the brilliant Symbolist Andrei Bely's (1880-1934) article from 1903, "O teurgii" ("About theurgy"), a text that brings us directly into the (alchemical) life-making activity of early Russian modernism. Another example of Bely's myth- and life-making activity can be found in his visit to the Hansa city of Bergen in 1913. In Bely's writings, Bergen is spectacularly transmuted from a mercantilist port town stinking of herring on the rainy and windswept west coast of Norway into a glorious, sun-drenched manifestation of the Symbolist visions of The New Jerusalem, a place connecting heaven and earth (see Helle, "Bely's Bergen").

tain alchemical and occult imagery, heavily influenced by the Romanticist and spiritual conception of the *arcana artis*, with the poet protagonist as a creator of new worlds. This alchemical imagery is particularly pronounced in the enigmatic author Fedor Sologub's (1863-1927) alchemist trilogy from 1907-14, *The Created Legend* (*Tvorimaia legenda*). Its mysterious hero, Georgii Trirodov, is a polymath: a poet and also a scientist who has accessed the *sanctum sanctorium* of physical reality. As a master alchemist as well, he follows alchemical prescriptions in his experimental works and develops in his search for the *quinta essentia* a grandiose *magnum opus* in which universes "dissolve, merge and recombine into a new and more superior structure" (Masing-Delic, p. 158).[21]

As a polymath the fictional and Faustian Trirodov is an excellent example of the tendency of Russian fin-de-siècle writing to interlink different spheres of cognition to obtain an all-embracing unity of knowledge. It must be admitted though that a pan-aestheticising worldview was highly characteristic of intellectual life at the time. In opposition to the pan-scientism of the Comtian tradition there was a strong tendency to see all things "sub specie aesthetica", making the other spheres in the Kantian triad of "the beautiful, the true and the good" subordinate to the aesthetic one.[22]

The high value set upon the artistic dimension can also be felt, to some extent, in the interests and occupations of the famous scientist Dmitrii Mendeleev (1834-1907). Mendeleev is primarily known as the creator of the periodic table of elements.[23] But this preeminent innovator did not confine his quest to the chemical laboratories. He was intimate with the Symbolist and esoteric circles in a variety of ways, and he was deeply familiar with the

---

21 See also Hellebust for another alchemist reading of Sologub's novel (p. 38 ff.). Alchemical themes, in particular that of Faust, are also prominent in the Symbolist writer and poet Valerii Briusov's (1873-1924) novel *The Fiery Angel* (*Ognennyi Angel*) from 1907 (see Maguire, p. 422).

22 On this topic, see Mints, "Simvol u Bloka". The pan-aestheticism of Russian Symbolism can be seen as a paradigmatic reaction to the (Weberian) "*Entzauberung der Welt*" and the reductionist strivings of the positivist natural sciences to gain exclusive dominance in the fields of human knowledge.

23 Mendeleev is also famous for having inspired the breathtakingly beautiful collection of short stories by the Italian chemist and writer Primo Levi (1919-87) in *The periodic table* or *Il sistemo periodico* from 1975, which in 2006 the "Royal Institution of Great Britain" named the best science book ever written. These memoirs are organised around the elements of the Mendelevian periodic system, creating a condensed and varied vision of Levi's life and work seen through the prism of chemistry.

LITERATURE AND CHEMISTRY

Neo-Platonic and highly speculative philosophy of the important Symbol-ist thinker Vladimir Solov'ev (1853-1900). Mendeleev's all-encompassing outlook gives his *Weltanschauung* a kaleidoscopic quality and his activities resist simplistic categorisations into individual sciences such as chemistry; he was a man who wanted both the natural and the cultural world to be treated with the same intellectual curiosity.[24] Significantly enough, the great chem-ist's daughter, Liubov' Mendeleeva (1881-1939), was married to the greatest Symbolist poet, Aleksander Blok (1880-1924), a union that symbolises on a metaphorical level the epoch's dynamic interchange between different cultural fields.[25]

In the years before the Bolshevik revolution of 1917 and also in its wake we notice, as might be expected, a shift with regard to the cultural hero, both in literature and cultural thinking: The demiurgic poet of the Symbolists is replaced by the chemist, who becomes the new ideal. The striking popularity of chemistry in this age can in some measure be explained by a widespread fascination in its many fundamental discoveries, something we find reflected in the abundance of literary topics connected to this scientific discipline. A good illustration of such a trend is Boris Pasternak's (1890-1960) text from 1912, "The Wassermann Reaction" ("Vasermanova reaktsiia"), in which the author makes metaphorical use of the chemical processes involved in the so-called Wassermann test.[26]

For the Bolsheviks, however, in their ideologised and politicised inter-pretation of the world, the imagery of chemistry transcends the literary treatments found in the work of an apolitical, literary avant-gardist like Pasternak, and the principles of chemical reactions were widely seen as metaphors for revolutionary development. This view was unambiguously shared by the political activist Leo Trotsky (1879-1940), who claimed that because chemistry is the science of the transmutations of elements, it is the science of the revolution, "hostile to every kind of absolute or conservative thinking cast in immobile categories" (*Problems of Everyday Life,* p. 217). Chemistry understood as the science of the revolution was to a conspicuous degree concentrated upon the construction of the cult of Lenin; the "red"

---

24 For an introduction to Mendeleev, see Gordin. This study shows Mendeleev in all his kaleidoscopic breadth of interests and outlooks and offers fascinating glimpses into turn of the century Russia.

25 For a study of the "epoch-making wedding" of Blok and Mendeleeva and its relation to the androgynous, utopian mentality of the day, see Matich (pp. 89-125).

26 Cf. Bryn's analysis of Pasternak's text in the present anthology on this topic.

ruler, with his radical aspirations to restructure the Russian nation, was made into the super scientist of the new humanity. In this Communist grand narrative, told through topics borrowed from (pseudo-)scientific spheres, he was imagined toiling in his fictitious laboratory, carrying out complex reactions and distillations to create his new amalgam, a being cleansed of the slag from the old world: the Soviet citizen or *homo sovieticus* (as he was later called – though in a much more critical context).[27]

The Proletarian writers and thinkers were engaged in the retelling of this narrative in a variety of versions.[28] This was after all the time of Bazarov's children, the ideological heirs of Turgenev's nihilist protagonist, who in *Fathers and Sons* sought to remodel the old society and devoted his whole existence to scientific experimental labour in the name of philosophical materialism. But while the ill-fated Bazarov was experimenting on dead animals, his spiritual followers, the Bolsheviks, took as their object of manipulation the live flesh of the Russian people. The mythologised image of Lenin the super scientist was therefore hiding a disturbing side that the Marxist writer Maksim Gorky (1868-1936) thematised more than once; the revolutionary leader was working not with lifeless and chemical components, but with the human matter of the Russian masses (Gorky, p. 113). In his own words, the Bolsheviks, fronted by Lenin, were undertaking "horrible experiments on the living body of Russia" and related to the country's inhabitants "as cynical scientists to dogs and frogs", which are subjected to painful scientific procedures (Gorky, p. 236 and 259). Gorky's warning against the dehumanising (and hybrid) aspect underlying this transformative drive had little effect, however, and could in no way destabilise the panegyric tale of Lenin as the first chemist of the Russian revolutionary processes.

It was not just the chemist who became an important symbolic actor at this time. His older brother, the alchemist smith, the bearer of ancient crafts and wisdom, also became a significant participant in the mythologised landscape of the Communist regime. Here the image of the smithy and the smithery reaches its full mythopoetic potential, bringing together elements from Romanticist-Symbolist alchemist conceptions as well as from more ancient

---

27 The term was coined by the dissident Soviet satirist Aleksander Zinoviev (1922-2006) in his (rather controversial) book from 1982 with the same title (*Homo Sovieticus*). On the construction of *homo sovieticus*, see Geller.

28 See Corney for a study of the narrativisation of Communist history. In this process, both events and agents of the revolution are retold as mythic narratives, which became intrinsic parts of the collective memory of the Soviet people.

esoteric sources. In the revolutionary collective memory the merging of these occult elements transforms Lenin into a Promethean blacksmith who, like Peter the Titan tsar, is hammering out a new society in his furnace of radical changes.[29] He was, as the Menshevik Georgy Plekhanov (1856-1918) phrased it, "an alchemist of revolution" (quoted in Baron, p. 446), a sorcerer forging a new future from the contradictory elements of the old world, disregarding the historical laws of Marxism and creating his own unique fusion.

The metaphorical figure of Lenin as alchemist shows that the symbolic language and cultural-ideological thinking of the Bolshevik state was to an astonishing extent a continuation of pre-revolutionary, esoteric, and presumably obsolete and decadent discourses. And it might seem to be a dilemma that Soviet culture, programmatically calling for materialism, was so deeply inscribed in thought patterns that belonged to a former speculative paradigm even if this paradigm had been restructured in a new, more "scientific" context.[30] An example of such restructuring can be found in the work of the Soviet master of Modernist prose, Boris Pilniak (1894-1938), and specifically his 1927 short story "Ivan Moskva". In this text, the magicians of the *arcana artis* have been reinvented as militant members of the new Communist elite, manipulating new chemical elements as if they were the *lapis philosophorum*: "The name of the new alchemist", writes Pilniak, "is Commissar Ivan Moskva. In the Middle Ages (…) black-clothed people were building the perpetuum mobile: – now the philosopher's stone lay on laboratory shelves, fluorescing in the gloom, (…) its name is: radium, decomposing all that surrounds it" (Pilniak, p. 176).[31]

The new actuality of alchemical topics was primarily due to their cor-

---

29 Incidentally, Lenin's metaphoric instrument, the hammer (which together with the sickle formed the Soviet state emblem), could be seen as a hidden symbol of the blacksmith's art, an object associated with future transmutations and purifications.

30 On this topic, see Helle, "Androgyny and the Transformation of the Body".

31 Pilniak's frightening image of decomposition and destruction takes on an even more sinister meaning when one remembers Marie Curie (1867-1934), dying from excessive exposure to radium. Anyway, the linking of the production of radium to the alchemist's arcane art was a widespread phenomenon after the Curies' ground-breaking discoveries. For example, the scientists who first observed radioactive elements decaying saw connections to alchemical transmutation, imagining the highly radioactive radium to be a modern-day Philosopher's Stone and the little understood effects "of mysterious radiation on living tissue evoked the alchemical Elixir of Life" for many (Morrison, pp. 4-5). Pilniak's alchemical exploration of radium is therefore very much in line with (some trends of) the scientific *Zeitgeist*.

respondence with the apocalyptic drive of the Bolsheviks to construct *homo nuovo*.[32] This task kindled their interest in alchemy and related metaphysical concepts as providing an image of metamorphosed mankind. As Stephen Baehr has argued, the persistence of the alchemist theme in Russian culture can be seen in connection with the utopian "mytheme" – the ideas of social and self-purification, of recreating paradisal perfection on earth, and of restoring the divine within us "that had been lost in the Fall" (Baehr, p. 164). As such, Soviet political activists and literary artists who did not believe in an occult or alchemical sphere used symbols and techniques drawn from it "for agitation and propaganda. Further transformed, some of them were incorporated in the official culture of Stalin's time" (Glatzer Rosenthal, p. 23).

Traces of this occult tradition are to a remarkable extent present in the (official) Soviet discussions about scientifically engineering an immortal human race. As the prominent Soviet historian Mikhail Pokrovsky (1868-1932) once expressed it: "Christianity preached spiritual victory over death; the Communist state should use science to achieve a physical victory" (quoted in Starr, p. 248).[33] The immortality programmes of the Soviet regime go back to a complex cluster of speculative ideas, not least to the Symbolists' radical preoccupation with immortalisation, an obsession that has been termed a Russian "salvation myth" (Masing-Delic).[34] Behind the Symbolists' obsession,

---

32 Not all writers exploited these topics to confirm the transformative drive. In the famous novel *Master and Margarita*, by the (anti-)Soviet author Mikhail Bulgakov (1891-1940), the imagery of alchemy and Faustian themes are used in a deconstructive way, in a carnivalesque critique of the absurdities of early Soviet society with its constant and more often than not incomprehensible reforms. Significantly this novel, which Bulgakov started to write in 1928, was published in a complete version only in 1973.

33 On official immortalist programs in the Soviet era, cf. Utechin. On the predominance given to "the conquest of nature" in Soviet society, see Glatzer Rosenthal (p. 23ff). An example of the widespread longing to achieve this conquest is Trotsky's vision of creating a new body to prevent the "wearing out of organs and tissues" (*Literature and Revolution*, pp. 254-55) and his enthusiastic belief in a future "higher social biologic type, or if you please, the superman", who will have overcome "the hysterical fear of death" (*Literature and Revolution*, p. 256). Incidentally, Trotsky's superman can easily be traced back to the Nietzschean "Übermensch", demonstrating once again the continuity between Bolshevism and the metaphysical discourses of the fin de siècle.

34 For a comprehensive study on the utopian theme of conquering death in Russian culture, see Masing-Delic. The immortalisation myth is primarily indebted to the Neo-Platonic writings of the Symbolist philosophers Vladimir Solovev (1853-1900)

however, we catch glimpses – however modified – of the spiritual quest of the old alchemists and their ultimate imperative: "Make bodies immortal" (cf. Hellebust, p. 24).[35] Like (some of) the old "sorcerers" – either historical or the Victorian reconstructions – the Communists were governed by utopian goals of conquering the laws of nature in order to bring forth a higher human embodiment. The archaic visions of distilling from impure matter a perfect, immortal being could thus easily become a metaphor for the creation of the immortal Communist man. Incidentally, the cultic embalmment of Lenin must be seen in this mythic context – as demonstrating a belief in a future "scientific" and technology-based resurrection, securing eternal life for the superhero of the new humanity.[36] This belief was famously echoed in the revolutionary Futurist and multi-artist Vladimir Maiakovsky's (1893-1930) compelling incantations: "Lenin lived, Lenin is alive, Lenin will live".[37]

A most striking instance of the alchemical heritage in Soviet society and ideology is the metallisation metaphor. Metallisation became the utmost aim of the Bolsheviks' mission, expressed in condensed form in the following slogan: "Our country must and shall become metallic!".[38] The topoi of metallurgy seem to be especially important in describing the New Man. As has been maintained, in Soviet literature and culture as a whole, the essential

---

and Nikolai Berdiaev (1874-1948). But the enigmatic thinker Nikolai Fedorov (1829-1903) is also very important in this context. His project, indisputably a most radical one, was to stop human procreation and instead revive deceased ancestors through certain "scientific" techniques, in order to obtain eternal existence. The enormous transformative potential of his thoughts made his speculative "method" increasingly influential, not least in the Soviet Union. On these thinkers and their immortality program, see Helle, "Androgyny and the Transformation of the Body".

35 Quoted in the esoteric Italian antimodernist thinker Julius Evola's (1898-1974) book from 1931 – in a French translation (Evola, p. 195).

36 Not all intellectuals at the time embraced the scientific strategies of transforming (and immortalising) the human body. A good example is again (cf. footnote 32) Bulgakov, who besides being a writer was also a physician and a medically trained man. His burlesque story *A Dog's Heart* (*Sobach'e serdse*) from 1925 (about a transplant that goes dreadfully wrong) is a biting critique of the transformative ethos of Communist science and a powerful counter-narrative to the period's prevalent scientific narratives.

37 Cf. his poem "Komsomolskaia", written after Lenin's death in 1924 (Maiakovsky, p. 34ff.). For a comprehensive study on Lenin and the immortality myth, see Tumarkin.

38 This notorious phrase seems originally to have been uttered by the Soviet statesman and founder of the Cheka – the first Soviet State security forces – Feliks Dzerzhinsky (1877-1926), in one of his speeches to the Central committee. See Stalin (p. 130).

symbol for Communist transfiguration is not metallisation in general, but more precisely the metallisation of the Soviet body (see Hellebust, p. 3). The purifying processes in metallurgical reactions serve as a metaphorical model for the transmutation of ordinary *homo sapiens*, changed from flesh into metal in the flaming crucible of revolutionary upheavals.[39]

In the mythologised mentality of the Soviet regime all kinds of metals (and cement) are activated as models; iron in particular is a much-exploited trope.[40] The supreme substance, though, is steel, which becomes a substitute for the alchemists' gold as the most purified essence. The substitution is, ironically speaking, well founded, since the gold of the arcane arts could create a problematic link with a capitalist setting; this was easily avoided by giving steel, with its proletarian factory associations, the dominant metaphoric position.

The apotheosis of steelmaking is of course the myth of Stalin himself, the Georgian ex-seminarist who was reforged from Dzhugashvili into the Steelman (*stal'* in Russian means "steel").[41] It was not just the personality of the leader that was elaborated using references to steel; this imagery penetrated every aspect of Soviet society and instances of steeliness are everywhere in this period, not least in literature[42]. The fictional heroes are all characterised by steely epithets and given iconic attributes like steel will,

---

39 Incidentally, the alchemical metallisation metaphor is another poetic device that Communist writers have taken over from the occult language of the Russian symbolists, not least from Andrei Bely's famous novel from 1914, *Petersburg* (cf. Clark pp. 78-9); see also Hellebust, p. 85ff. This is especially evident in the 1924 novel *Cement* by the Soviet author Fedor Gladkov (1883-1958), see Helle, "Andrey Belyj and Fëdor Gladkov". *Cement* abundantly demonstrates how the (alchemist) imagery of Russian Symbolism was exploited in the new proletarian literature, even to a degree that threatened to destabilise the novel's Communist ethos. In subsequent editions from the 1930 onwards Gladkov was therefore forced to make numerous "corrections" to make the text conform with the norms of Socialist Realism. See Helle, "Fedor Gladkovs *Cement*".

40 The iron imagery is for example most heavily employed in the novel *The Iron Flood* (1924) by the revolutionary writer Aleksander Serafimovich (1863-1949). Cf. also Gladkov's *Cement*.

41 On this spectacular transformation, see Hellebust (p. 90 ff.).

42 In the early decades of the twentieth century steel and metal symbolism was naturally not restricted to a Bolshevik setting. Suffice it to mention the German writer Ernst Jünger (1895-1998) and the steel imagery of his 1920 novel *In Stahlgewittern*. What makes the Bolshevik exploration of the metallisation trope so intriguing, however, is that the underlying esoteric associations of metal symbolism programmatically

LITERATURE AND CHEMISTRY

steel jaws, and steel muscles. Sometimes they even have "steel wings for arms" and "in the place of a heart a fiery [steel] motor", as enthusiastically proclaimed in a popular Soviet song (cf. Clark, p. 138).[43] The culmination of steel symbolism in fiction is the novel *How the Steel Was Tempered* (*Kak zakalialas' stal'*), written by Nikolai Ostrovsky (1904-36) in 1932. This work about a young Communist being cleansed and transfigured in the flames of revolutionary fight became a paradigm of Socialist Realism, and both its title and content show with tremendous force the metaphoric significance of the metal transmutation for the creation of the new Soviet man. On a deeper level the conflict between the declared liberating and humane message of communism and the dehumanising effect of its hybridising transformation project creates a destabilising, even grotesque ambivalence in this project, a disturbing dissonance that can only be hinted at in this context.[44]

With the demise of the Soviet Union, the Bolsheviks' utopian vision of the ideal *homo nuovo* had long outlived its actuality. But the quest for a new life is as strong as ever in the new Russia, and the alchemical-philosophical longings for "der Stein der Weisen" are still visible in the nation's cultural consciousness.[45] As discussed at the beginning of this essay, the creation of the Enlightenment monument of Saint Petersburg at the start of the eighteenth century was somewhat paradoxically associated with alchemi- cal aspirations. Today this city once again seems to be the place for such aspirations, especially in the imaginative world of the poet Elena Shvarts (1948-2010). In her poems, particularly in "Free Ode to Saint Petersburg's Philosophical Stone" ("Volnaia oda filosofskomu kamni Peterburga") from 2001, the alchemical vocabulary is very explicit; by addressing Peter I as the "creator laborious", she engages in a dynamic intertextual dialogue with the Saint Petersburg myth and its (alchemical) founding act.[46] In Shvarts, the key to the country's future lies once again in the crucible of Saint Petersburg's heterogenic culture; the Northern capital is accordingly referred to as "an

---

and in a destabilising way collide with the proclaimed materialist ethos of the Soviet regime.

43 See Clark on the positive hero in Soviet literature and his metallic and steely quali- ties (p. 138 ff.).

44 For a discussion of this conflict, see Platt. This study focuses on the "revolutionary grotesque", or the overwhelming ironies of revolutionary periods, which have been elevated to moments of human triumph and emancipation, yet have resulted in bloodshed and repressions on a vast scale.

45 On the revival of occultism in post-Soviet society, see DeNio Stephens.

46 The poem has been translated into English (Shvarts, p. 214-6).

alchemical vessel". As such, it becomes a potent mixture of many potions from which the transforming stone, the *quinta essentia*, can be extracted. For the poet, this essence must be sought through the many bridges of Saint Petersburg; here the "elixir" might be found that could create a new harmony between people and forge an existence of drabness and indifference into one of more sublime significance.

When in this beautiful image the bridges of Saint Petersburg are made into a unifying substance, a transforming power similar to the alchemist stone, Shvarts uses alchemical imagery to bring forth her poetic visions; the *arcana artis* functions as a model for her writings. And as I have demonstrated in this essay, there are numerous cases in Russian literature and cultural thinking in which alchemy and its younger brother, chemistry, become such models for creative activity. In this way concepts from science and proto-science are retold in both engaging and provoking fictional narratives. This interaction is not surprising: Both alchemy and chemistry have in common with literature – not least with poetry – a blending of components to construct something new, unique, and unexpected. In this context, chemistry is not the daily microscopic toil of the modern specialist. It is rather an idea of chemistry – an idea of the underlying processes at work and the associations of metamorphosis they evoke. This perspective allows us to talk about a correspondence between chemistry and literature, a connection that the great chemist Marcellin Berthelot (1827-1907) emphasised in his famous saying "La chimie crée son objet": "Chemistry creates its object. This creative faculty, akin to that of art, forms an essential distinction between chemistry and the other natural or historical sciences" (quoted in Bensaude-Vincent and Simon, p. 99). Thus we may observe a kinship between chemistry and literature. There seem to exist between them traces of "elective affinities" – or *Wahlverwandtschaften*, to use the Goethean expression – that constantly bring these fields together in new and astonishing transmutations, bridging the distances between the two cultures.

WORKS CITED

Amis, M.: *Koba the Dread. Laughter and the Twenty Million*. New York: Miramax, 2002.
Baron, S.: "Georgii Valentinovich Plekhanov" in G. Jackson and R. Devlin (eds.): *Dictionary of the Russian Revolution*. Westport, CT: Greenwood Press, 1989, pp. 447-9.

Baehr, S.: "Alchemy and Eighteenth-Century Russian Literature: An Introduction" in J. Klein, S. Dixon and M. Franje (eds.): *Reflections on Russia in the Eighteenth Century*. Cologne: Böhlau Verlag, 2001, pp. 151-65.

Beil, U.: *Die Wiederkehr des Absoluten. Studien zur Symbolik des Kristallinen und Metallischen in der deutschen Literatur der Jahrhundertwende*. Frankfurt a. M: Lang, 1988.

Bely, A.: "O teurgii" in *Novyj put'*, vol. 9, 1903, pp. 101-123.

Belinsky, V.: *Polnoe sobranie sochinenij*, vol. 5. Moscow: AN SSR, 1954.

Bensaude-Vincent, B. and Simon, J.: *Chemistry: The Impure Science*. London: Imperial College Press, 2008.

Călian, G.: *Annual of Medieval Studies at CEU*, vol. 16, 2010, pp. 166-91.

Carter, R.: "Anton P. Chekhov, MD (1860-1904): Dual Medical and Literary Careers" in *The Annals of Thoracic Surgery*, vol. 61, no. 5, 1996, pp. 1557-63.

Clark, K.: *The Soviet Novel: History as Ritual*. Chicago: University of Chicago Press, 1985.

Cohen, I. B., and Smith, G.: "Introduction" in I. B. Cohen and G. Smith (eds.): *The Cambridge Companion to Newton*. Cambridge: Cambridge University Press, 2002, pp. 1-33.

Collis, R.: "Alchemical Interest at the Petrine Court" in *Esoterica*, VII, 2005, pp. 53-78.

—: *The Petrine Instauration: Religion, Esotericism and Science at the Court of Peter the Great*. Leiden: Brill Academic Publishers, 2012.

Corney, F. C.: *Telling October: Memory and the Making of the Bolshevik Revolution*. Ithaca: Cornell University Press, 2004.

DeNio Stephens, H.: "The Occult in Russia Today" in B. Glatzer Rosenthal (ed.): *The Occult in Russian and Soviet Culture*. Ithaca & London: Cornell University Press, 1997, pp. 357-77.

Eliade, M.: *The Forge and the Crucible: The Origins and Structures of Alchemy*. Chicago: University of Chicago Press, 1979.

Evola, J.: *La tradition hermétique: Les symbols et la doctrine; L' "Art royal" hermétique*. Paris: Editiones traditionelles, 1963.

Geller, M.: *Cogs in the Wheel: the Formation of Soviet Man*. New York: Knopf, 1988.

Gordin, M. D.: *A Well-Ordered Thing: Dmitrii Mendeleev And The Shadow Of The Periodic Table*. New York: Basic Books, 2004.

Gorky, M.: *Nesovremennye mysli*. Paris: Editions de la Seine, 1971.

Gronicka, A.: *The Russian Image of Goethe*. Philadelphia, PA: University of Pennsylvania Press, 1985.

Haynes, R. D.: *From Faust to Strangelove: Representations of the Scientist in Western Literature*. Baltimore / London: Johns Hopkins University Press, 1994.

Helle, L.: "Andrey Belyj and Fëdor Gladkov: An Example of Literary Transposition" in *Scando-Slavica*, vol. 35, 1989, pp. 5-17.

—: "Bely's Bergen – or the New Jerusalem" in *Scando-Slavica*, vol. 36, 1990, pp. 5-19.

—: "Fedor Gladkovs *Cement* – en sovjetisk mønsterroman?" in E. Egeberg (ed.): *Sovjetlitteraturen*. Oslo: Solum Forlag, 1994, pp. 41-65.

—: "The City as Myth and Symbol in Aleksander Pushkin's Poem 'The Bronze Horseman'" in *Scando-Slavica*, vol. 41, 1995, pp. 22-41.

—: "Androgyny and the Transformation of the Body in Russian Fin de Siècle" in M. Hagen, R. Koppen and M. Vibe Skagen (eds.): *The Human and its Limits*. Oslo: Scandinavian Academic Press / Spartacus Forlag, 2011, pp. 41-57.

Hellebust, R.: *Flesh to Metal. Soviet Literature & the Alchemy of Revolution*. Ithaca & London: Cornell University Press, 2003.

Iakusheva, G. (ed.): *Gete v ruskoi kul'ture XX veka*. Moscow: Nauka, 2001.

Knopf, D.: *Authorship as Alchemy: Subversive Writings in Pushkin, Scott, Hoffmann*. Stanford, CA: Stanford University Press, 1994.

Leighton, L.: *The Esoteric Tradition in Russian Romantic Literature: Decembrism and Freemasonry*. University Park, PA: Pennsylvania State University Press, 1994.

Lotman, J.: "Simvolika Peterburga i problem semiotiki goroda" in *Uchenie zapiski TGU* 664, 1984, pp. 30-46.

Maguire, M.: "The Wizard in the Tower: Iakov Brius and the Representation of Alchemists in Russian Literature" in *Slavonic and East European Review* 90.3, 2012, pp. 401-27.

Maiakovsky, V.: *Polnoe sobranie sochinenii*, vol. 6. Moscow: Chudozhestvennaia literatura, 1957.

Malcolm, J.: *Reading Chekhov: A Critical Journey*. New York: Random House, 2002.

Masing-Delic, I.: *Abolishing Death. A Salvation Myth of Russian Twentieth Century Literature*. Stanford, CA: Stanford University Press, 1992.

Matich, O. *Erotic Utopia: The Decadent Imagination in Russia's Fin de Siècle*. Madison, WI: University of Wisconsin Press, 2005.

Menshutkin, B.: *Russia's Lomonosov, Chemist Courtier Phyiscist Poet*. Princeton. New Jersey: Princeton University Press, 1952.

Metzler, S.: "Artists, Alchemists and Mannerists in Courtly Prague" in J. Wamberg (ed.). *Art and Alchemy*. Copenhagen: Museum Tusculanum Press, 2006.

Mints, Z.: "Simvol u Bloka" in *Russian Literature* 7, 1979, pp. 193-248.

—: "Kommentarii k romanu." in Merezhkovsky, D.: *Christos i Antichrist. Trilogia*. Moscow: Kniga, 1990, pp. 612-4.

Moran, B.: *Distilling Knowledge: Alchemy, Chemistry, and the Scientific Revolution*. London: Harvard University Press, 2005.

Morrison, M.: *Modern Alchemy: Occultism and the Emergence of Atomic Theory*. Oxford & New York: Oxford University Press, 2007.

Newman, W.: "'Decknamen or pseudochemical language'? Eirenaeus Philalethes and Carl Jung" in *Revue d'histoire des sciences* 49.2-3, 1996, pp. 159-88.

Newman, W. and Principe, L.: *Alchemy Tried in the Fire: Starkey, Boyle and the Fate of Helmontian Chemistry*. Chicago: University of Chicago Press, 2002.

Pavlova, G. and Fedorov, A.: *Mikhail Vasil'evich Lomonosov: His Life and Work*. Moscow: Mir Publishers, 1984.

Pilniak, B.: *Sobranie sochinenii*, vol. 3. Munich: Wilhelm Fink, 1970.

Platt, K.: *History in a Grotesque Key: Russian Literature and the Idea of Revolution*. Stanford, CA: Stanford University Press, 1997.

Rosenthal, Glatzer G.: "Introduction" in B. Glatzer Rosenthal (ed.): *The Occult in Russian and Soviet Culture*. Ithaca / London: Cornell University Press, 1997, pp. 1-33.

Shvarts, E.: "Free Ode to Saint Petersburg's Philosophical Stone" in V. Poluchina (ed.): *Russian Women Poets. Modern Poetry in Translation,* no. 20. London: Zephyr Press, 2002, pp. 214-6.

Snow, C. P.: *The Two Cultures.* Cambridge: Cambridge University Press, 1998.

Stalin, J.: *Sochineniia,* vol. 7. Moscow: Gosudarstvennoe izdatel'stvo politicheskoi literatury, 1952.

Starr, F.: *Melnikov: Solo Architect in a Mass Society.* Princeton: University Press, 1978.

Tilton, H.: *Quest for the Phoenix: Spiritual Alchemy and Rosicrucianism in the Work of Count Michael Maier (1569-1622).* Berlin / New York: Walter De Gruyter, 2003.

Toporov, V.: "Peterburg i peterburgskii tekst russkoi literatury" in *Uchenie zapiski TGU* 664, 1984, pp. 4-30.

Trotsky, L.: *Literature and Revolution.* Ann Arbor, MI: University of Michigan Press, 1960.

—: *Problems of Everyday Life and Other Writings on Culture & Science.* New York: Monad Press, 1973.

Tumarkin, N.: *Lenin Lives! The Lenin Cult in Soviet Russia.* Cambridge, Mass.: Harvard University Press, 1983.

Turgenev, I.: *Fathers and Sons.* New York: The Modern Library, 2001.

Utechin, S.: "Bolsheviks and their Allies after 1917: The ideological Pattern" in *Soviet Studies* 10.2, 1958, pp. 113-135.

Vilinbakhov, G.: "Osnovanie Peterburga i imperskaja emblematika" in *Uchenye zapiski TGU* 664, 1984, pp. 46-55.

Webster, C.: *From Paracelsus to Newton: Magic and the Making of Modern Science.* Cambridge: Cambridge University Press, 1982.

Welsh, D.: "Philosophers and Alchemists in Some Eighteenth-Century Russian Comedies" in *Slavic and East European Journal* 8.2, 1964, pp. 149-58.

Wiener, L.: *Anthology of Russian Literature from the Tenth Century to the Close of the Eighteenth Century.* Honolulu, HI: University Press of the Pacific, 2011.

THE LITERARY DISTORTIONS OF ALCHEMY

Bernard Joly, CNRS, University of Lille 3

Science is rarely presented in literature in the same manner as it might appear in a scientific treatise; it is transformed and distorted, and the significance of these distortions is of interest to the philosopher of science. When science is spoken of in a novel, it is more often than not in the context of the hopes and fears that science evokes rather than an examination of the scientific theories themselves. In literature, science is carried beyond itself into human concerns over the future without necessarily losing sight of its own true possibilities. From this point of view, chemistry seems to have a privileged relationship with literature, not only in terms of the hopes and fears attached to its results but also as regards its material aspects. Principles, substances, and elements that chemists manipulate in their laboratories – and the theoretical relationships that exist between them – may become heroic or villainous characters, as exemplified in Goethe's celebrated novel *Elective Affinities*. In this work, the chemical theory of affinities plays the major role, leading the other characters into attractive and repulsive relationships according to inescapable laws.[1] When transposed into human relationships, chemical affinities reveal their dramatic potential: Beneath the living or psychic world, the constitutive substances of matter engage in battles engendering alliances and break-ups.

Beginning in the Renaissance, an alchemical literature developed that used both images and narrative to represent chemical operations anthopomorphically, playing on sexual metaphors and antagonistic allegories: Mercury and Sulfur could as easily copulate with one another as affront one another in cruel combat. These literary forms were abandoned by modern chemists to distance themselves from and mark a complete break with an alchemical past they judged undignified of "science". They reappear, however, in works of literature, where such forms are frequent as soon as chemistry and chemists are brought into play.

* I am exceedingly grateful to Kevin Ogle for the translation of this paper.

1   See Joly: "Les *Affinités électives* de Goethe".

It is no surprise to the historian of science that it is through alchemy that chemistry is usually presented in literary works of the nineteenth and twentieth centuries. The practice of the history of science has taught us that the boundaries we establish today between what science is and what science is not, between the rational and the irrational, are part of the structure of the modern spirit: They are more an effect of the development of the sciences than a condition of their possibility. We must set aside our contemporary scientific and rational habits of thinking to understand that Kepler could be both an astronomer and an astrologer. This did not mean that his own psyche was divided into rational and irrational entities, but simply reflected the fact that at the time he lived, astronomy and astrology had not yet been separated[2]. As for alchemy, we know today that until the end of the seventeenth century alchemy was nothing more than another name for chemistry, and we understand that some authors will present us with portraits of alchemists when they set the novel in the Renaissance or the seventeenth century. The alchemist of the sixteenth or seventeenth century was doing chemistry when he sought the structure of matter through analysis of the consecutive elements produced by distillation, sublimation, putrefaction, or calcination. The transmutation of metals appeared as a completely natural operation, even if it was acknowledged to be quite difficult to achieve. With the exception of charlatans, the alchemists of the seventeenth century did not use magical formulas or diabolical incantations.[3] It was only at the beginning of the eighteenth century that chemists began to use the word "alchemy" to designate the chemistry of the past that they considered out of date. And it was only in the mid-nineteenth century that the term was taken over by the esoteric and occult movements, who transformed alchemy into an essentially symbolic and spiritual endeavour, an idea that in fact differed radically from the science of chemistry. These movements constructed a history of alchemy as an esoteric science in contradiction to what we know from historical research on texts and documents.

Therefore, it would not be surprising to find that the characters of alchemists in literature of the nineteenth and twentieth centuries are often simply chemists. What troubles the historian of science and simultaneously excites his curiosity is the recognition that most of the time, even when novelists try to respect a historical realism, they portray the alchemist and

---

2   See Simon: *Kepler astronome astrologue*.
3   See Principe and Newman: "Some Problems with the Historiography of Alchemy" and "Alchemy vs. Chemistry"; Joly: "A propos d'une prétendue distinction".

his activities with a singular shift towards what the history of science teaches us about alchemy, making the position of chemistry in literature somewhat unusual. Of course, it behooves the literary imagination to transgress the boundaries of a cautious, sober, and "normal" science, but it may seem surprising that the deformed image of the alchemist that was built by the esoteric movements of the nineteenth century would take precedence over a well documented historical reality. The literature of the nineteenth and twentieth centuries seems to have played a double role with respect to this question: It witnesses the errors and illusions concerning alchemy and its history and it amplifies these errors and illusions by making the alchemist, today as in the past, the equivalent of a magician whose secret knowledge goes beyond the limits of rational knowledge. More often than not, literature offers a representation of alchemists and their doctrines which does not correspond at all to that provided by historians of early chemistry. In this work, I would like to examine the reasons behind these literary distortions in three works: *The Scarlet Letter* by Nathaniel Hawthorne, *Der Engel vom westlichen Fenster* (*The Angel of the Western Window*) by Gustav Meyrink, and *L'œuvre au noir* (*The Abyss*) by Marguerite Yourcenar.

NATHALIEL HAWTHORNE'S *THE SCARLET LETTER*

Two alchemical personages stand out in the works of Nathaniel Hawthorne: Aylmer in *The Birthmark* (1843) and Chillingworth in *The Scarlet Letter* (1850), both of whom are presented explicitly as alchemists by this nineteenth-century American novelist. Aylmer, having presented to his wife Georgina "a history of the long dynasty of the Alchemists, who spent so many ages in quest of the universal solvent, by which the Golden Principle might be elicited from all things vile and base",[4] affirms that it is in his power to realise such an operation, convinced that "by plainest scientific logic, it was altogether within the limits of possibility to discover this long-sought medium" (*TB*, p. 772). But it is necessary to go even deeper: Once he has "investigated the secrets of the highest cloud-region, and of the profoundest mines" (*TB*, p. 769), he proclaims that he is ready "to

4   *The Birthmark*, p. 772. I use the text of the Centenary Edition of the Works of Nathaniel Hawthorne published by Literary Classics of the United States, in 1982, a volume containing *Tales and sketches*, *A wonder book for girls and boys* and *Tanglewood tales for girls and boys*. All further references to this work are given in the text and abbreviated to *TB*.

concoct a liquid that should prolong life for years – perhaps interminably" (*TB*, p. 772).

This knowledge was based as much on the work of "combination and analysis" in his laboratory (*TB*, p. 774) of which Hawthorne describes the furnace, the alembic and other instruments by which nature "had been tormented forth by the processes of science" (*TB*, p. 776) as through the study of numerous volumes from his library. His wife would leaf through "the works of the philosophers of the middle age, such as Albertus Magnus, Cornelius Agrippa, Paracelsus, and the famous friar who created the prophetic Brazzen Head"; but also "hardly less curious and imaginative were the early volumes of the Transactions of the Royal Society, in which the members, knowing little of the limits of natural possibility, were continually recording wonders" (*TB*, p. 774).[5] Aylmer is therefore researching the secrets of nature, revealing the power of the elements to perfect "what Nature left imperfect" (*TB*, p. 768).[6] All this of course describes the traditional objectives of the alchemists.

In *The Scarlet Letter*, Chillingworth is also a "natural philosopher". He has spent considerable time with his scientific tomes and acquired the reputation of an erudite. He says to his wife, Hester, "my old studies in alchemy and my sojourn, for above a year past, among a people well versed in the kindly properties of simples, have made a better physician of me than many that claim the medical degree",[7] adding later "I have learned many secrets in the wilderness, and here is one of them, – a recipe that an Indian taught me, in requital of some lessons of my own, that were as old as Paracelsus" (*SL*, p. 180).

---

5   Most works attributed to the philosopher and theologian Albertus Magnus (c. 1200-60) are apocryphal, but he does speak of alchemy in his *De mineralibus*; Cornelius Agrippa (whose famous *De occulta philosophia* is not an alchemical text) and Paracelsus are authors of the sixteenth century; the "famous friar" is the philosopher Franciscan Roger Bacon (1214-94), most of whose alchemical treatises are apocryphal, but he does treat alchemy in his *Opus Tertium*.

6   Aylmer evokes the imperfection of the mark on the cheek of his wife, but being able to perfect living beings is for Aylmer a task situated in the prolongation of his exploration of "the elemental powers of nature" (*TB*, p. 769).

7   *The Scarlet Letter*, p. 179. I use the text of the Centenary Edition of the Works of Nathaniel Hawthorne published by Literary Classics of the United States, 1982, a volume containing *Fanshawe, The Scarlet Letter, The House of the Seven Gables, The Blithedale Romance*, and *The Marble Faun*. All further references to this work are given in the text and abbreviated to *SL*.

"Alchemist in his laboratory", painting by Teniers (1610-1680).

Make no mistake: The opposition here is not between plant medicine and alchemy, but rather between the common medicine of popular "wisdom" and the work of the laboratory, and also between the pharmacy inspired by the Galenic tradition and that of the Swiss doctor, Paracelsus. In the seventeenth century, alchemy was at the service of a new medical practice that opposed the academic teachings of the time, which were founded on a reading of Galen.[8] In the same manner, the science of Chillingworth was opposed to that of the young pastor Arthur Dimmestale, who was taught at the university. His apartment contained only books while that of his adversary Chillingworth was organised around a laboratory. Of course, the alchemist did not despise his books. They represented to him the official transmission of the tradition as witnessed by numerous collections of texts published during this time. But he understood that reading would only produce a sterile knowledge if it were not put to practice in the laboratory.

The substances that Aylmer and Chillingworth manipulated could be dangerous. The elixir of life could produce "a discord in nature" (*TB*, p. 255).

8   See Debus.

Thus, showing his wife a flask containing the elixir of immortality, Aylmer explains that:

> It is the most precious poison that ever was concocted in this world. By its aid, I could apportion the lifetime of any mortal at whom you might point your finger. The strength of the dose would determine whether he was to linger out years, or drop dead in the midst of a breath. (*TB*, p. 773)

Hawthorne is taking up the classical theme of the *pharmakon*, which in the Galenic tradition designates the medicine as well as the poison; all is a question of dosage and usage.[9] In another of Hawthorne's novels, *Rappaccini's Daughter*, the dispute that opposes Rappacini to his colleague Baglioni sends us directly to the feuds at the beginning of the seventeenth century between supporters of Paracelsien and Galenic medicine, the Galenists accusing the Paracelsians of being poisoners because they used medicine fabricated by chemistry.[10] "It is his [Rappaccini's] theory that all medicinal virtues are comprised within those substances which we term vegetable poisons".[11] The narrator invites the reader: "If [he] be inclined to judge for himself, we refer him to certain black-letter tracts on both sides, preserved in the medical department of the University of Padua" (*RD*, p. 983). To make his daughter Beatrice as powerful as she is beautiful and to permit her to escape the condition of a weak woman, Rappaccini intends to make her breath as venomous as the poisonous plants that he grows in his garden: He has "instilled a fierce and subtle poison into his system" by an "affinity with those so beautiful and deadly flowers" (*RD*, p. 986). This man, "fearfully acquainted with the secrets of nature" (*RD*, p. 1001), sacrifices his daughter to an insane zeal for science: "he cares infinitely more for science than for mankind" (*RD*, p. 983).

---

9   The Greek word *pharmakon* may be translated as "drug" to conserve its ambiguity. An important part of the ancient work on medicine, most notably in the Galenic tradition, was to establish the conditions within which a usually toxic substance could nevertheless be profitably integrated into a medical treatment. For further information, see the work assembled in Debru. A more philosophical reflection on this subject may be found in Derrida: "La pharmacie de Platon".

10   Concerning these conflicts, sometimes called "querelle de l'antimoine", see Debus; Joly: "L'ambiguïté des paracelsiens".

11   *Rappaccini's Daughter*, p. 982. All further references to this work are given in the text and abbreviated to *RD*.

LITERATURE AND CHEMISTRY

In *The Birthmark*, we might think that Aylmer, concerned for the perfection of his wife, fails miserably in his endeavours because the potion destined to remove the birthmark from Georgina's face kills her; her fate is the same as that of Rappaccini's daughter. But this is not the case: Aylmer sees the blemish as "the bond by which an angelic spirit kept itself in union with a mortal frame" (*TB*, p. 780), the sign of an imperfection that, once removed, made the woman perfect. She is detached from her body, purely spiritual, reduced to her soul, which flies into the sky. Aylmer has therefore achieved the most important alchemical operation: the distillation that transforms all matter into spirit. But in doing so he loses his beloved wife, whom he could have kept through another form of wisdom by accepting her as she was. The logic of alchemical science drives him to irrationality.

In the *The Scarlet Letter*, the formidable efficiency of the alchemist's science makes him more than unreasonable; Hawthorne presents him as diabolical. The science that Chillingworth has acquired from his books and laboratories is put to the service of vengeance, to find and bring to his death the previous lover of his wife and the father of her illegitimate child. "I shall seek this man, he said, as I have sought truth in books; as I have sought gold in alchemy. There is a sympathy that will make me conscious of him" (*SL*, p. 182). This is in fact more than a simple comparison since the alchemical science of Chillingworth now seems to apply to the human soul. Thus, he affirms that a "philosopher" (as alchemists were called at the time) could analyse the nature of a child to identify the father, as in the case of his wife's illegitimate daughter Pearl. Chillingworth, having revealed the secret of the young minister, causes his death by simply standing next to him, slowly distilling the poison of remorse in his tortured soul. In the process, the alchemist is transformed: He changes his name and appearance, and above all, by playing the role of the devil, he is himself transformed into a devil. A negative transmutation is achieved: He who originally sought only the happiness of mankind has become a demon devoted to the destruction of the object of his hatred. Rather than working to perfect nature, the alchemist will now be the source of death. Thus Hester asks:

> Would not the earth, quickened to an evil purpose by the sympathy of his eye, greet him with poisonous shrubs, of species hitherto unknown, that would start up under his fingers? Or might it suffice him, that every wholesome growth should be converted into something deleterious and malignant at his touch? (*SL*, p. 268)

The portraits of alchemists traced by Hawthorne are certainly very striking, but they are far from the reality of the historical alchemist as understood by historians of science. From the novelist's point of view, the practice of alchemy stems from the spirit and not simply the manipulation of matter, even if it is living matter, as evidenced by the alchemist's power over the behaviour of humans. That the veritable objective of alchemy was the transformation of man, for better or worse, is a foreign idea to the alchemical texts of the Middle Ages and up until the seventeenth century. Such a conception takes alchemy out of the domain of chemical research and into the secrets of nature which the historical alchemists thought of as limiting their works. Far from claiming the "power above nature" as Hawthorne's alchemists do in *The Birthmark* (*TB*, p. 774), the historical alchemists insisted on the natural character of their operations, carefully refraining from any pretense of power over the spiritual world which would have brought upon them the accusation of magic.[12]

The novelist was of course free to compose according to his imagination, but we also know that Hawthorne wanted to bring alive the Puritan spirit that defined seventeenth century Massachusetts and attended carefully to his conception of historical reality. It is not surprising that real historical personages appear in the heart of *The Scarlet Letter*. The death of John Winthrop Jr. in the middle of the novel reminds us that this the governor of Massachusetts, a fellow of the Royal Society, had drawn around him a circle of alchemists of which the most famous, George Starkey, was close to both Boyle and Newton.[13] Similarly, Chillingworth is presented as a correspondent of Sir Kenelm Digby, a "natural philosopher", a diplomat, a voyager, and an adept of alchemy who became a celebrity due to his work on the "powder of sympathy".[14] Some commentators have even suggested that Digby was the model for Hawthorne's portraits of alchemists. This is most obvious in the story of Aylmer in *The Birthmark*, which correlates with what we know about the life of Digby, who worried about the death of his young wife when she used a rejuvenating lotion of his own fabrication.[15]

---

12 In fact, as observed by Jean-Pierre Baud, alchemists were rarely condemned by the inquisition. See Baud: *Le procès de l'alchimie*.

13 On George Starkey, see Newman: *Gehennical fire*. Newman also describes the career of the alchemist Winthrop (Newman, pp. 39-52).

14 This term refers to a substance, also called "weapon salve", the recipe for which was found in the works of Paracelsus and Van Helmont. It was supposed to heal at a distance injuries inflicted by firearms.

15 See Reid.

In constructing his portraits of alchemists Hawthorne certainly made use of historical works like the *The Worthies of England* of Thomas Fuller, but above all he was inspired by contemporary articles that insisted on the spiritual and esoteric character of alchemy.[16] It was due to his uncritical faith in these works that Hawthorne, like many other novelists, transformed alchemy into a mad or demonic science despite the fact that historical research reveals that alchemy's quest for truth was probably no less reasonable than that which animates the science of the twenty-first century.[17]

GUSTAV MEYRINK'S *THE ANGEL OF THE WESTERN WINDOW*

Eighty-five years later Gustav Meyrink (1868-1932) was also looking for inspiration from historical characters: *The Angel of the West Window (Der Engel vom westlichen Fenster)*, which appeared in 1927, was considered to be a romanticised version of the life of John Dee (1527-1608), the English mathematician and alchemist who conversed with angels and who was as much a source of fascination to his contemporaries as he is today.[18] His best known work is the *Monas hieroglyphica* of 1564, a brief work whose obscurity is a joy to lovers of the hermetic arts. Starting with the figure of his monad, the author develops a reflection based upon Euclidian geometry, astrology, numerology, etc. The monad expresses the secret of the world, its fabrication and organisation. John Dee was first a mathematician, in the sixteenth-century meaning of that occupation. As an advisor to Queen Elizabeth and a collaborator of Mercator, he treated problems of navigation and cartography; he was interested in the reform of the calendar, in astrology, and also the problem of parallax and its potential for improving the calculation of the astral influences. One of his most significant achievements was the long preface to the first English edition of Euclid's *Elements* he wrote in 1570, with comments that were destined to put geometry within reach of artisans. He loved alchemy and worked in the laboratory at the same time as he treated mathematics.[19]

---

16 See Gatta; Swann.

17 See Joly: "La figure de l'alchimiste dans la littérature du XIXᵉ et du XXᵉ siècle".

18 On John Dee, see Clulee; Clucas.

19 Nicholas Clulee observes that it was in the years 1665-80, while Dee was particularly interested in mathematical questions, that he also practised alchemy in the three laboratories he possessed; he was as interested in solutions and distillations of all types as he was in the philosopher's stone and the elixir of life that he affirms he never possessed.

And yet Dee also conversed with angels. He later published these conversations in a diary that he maintained over several years. His taste for supernatural conversations was certainly a source of anxiety for him. It ultimately lead him to work with the adventurer Edward Kelly, who promised him new angelic interviews and encouraged him to promise the emperor Rudolph II at Prague that he was close to performing the alchemical transmutation of base matter into gold. Dee, unable to keep this promise, owed his survival to a rapid return to England. The affair became well known and no doubt contributed to the bad reputation of alchemists.[20] But Dee was more than an alchemist: He was in fact an authentic magician, persuaded that there was an intimate union between all things and that the supernatural emerged from a superior world to the inferior world. In the end, to Dee, mathematics was the key to the organisation of all things.[21]

It is unsurprising that such a character has inspired numerous novelists;[22] among these is Gustave Meyrink, who gave Dee the most important role in his last published work, *The Angel of the West Window*, which appeared twelve years after *The Golem*. Although he was born near Munich, where he spent more than half his life, Meyrink was fascinated by Prague where in his youth he was employed as a banker. In Prague he discovered secret societies and diverse facets of an occultism that would become an essential aspect of his thought and specifically of his ironic criticism of occidental civilisation. The story that Meyrink creates is simple: The narrator, the Baron Müller, finds amongst the affairs of his recently deceased cousin the diary of John Dee, their common ancestor, and numerous other papers and objects that belonged to the famous alchemist. The story develops simultaneously at the beginning of the twentieth century and during the sixteenth century as the narrator uncovers the papers of his ancestor one by one. The sequence of events shows an increasingly striking similarity between the life of the English magician and the life of the narrator until finally the narrator

---

20 The story has been told recently in a fictionalized form by Michael Wilding in a work whose title summarises the essential commerce of the two men: *Raising spirits, making gold and swapping wives.*

21 Historians of pythagorism and neoplatonism would no doubt observe that the theories of Dee were only a degraded version of certain aspects of these doctrines.

22 In *The House of Doctor Dee*, Peter Ackroyd tells the story of the misadventures of a person who inherits a house where Dee once lived. Dee is also a character in short stories by Jean Ray and H. P. Lovecraft, and in Umberto Eco's novel *Foucault's Pendulum*. It is said that Ian Fleming borrowed the signature Dee used for his letters to Queen Elizabeth: 007.

realises that time has contracted and that in fact he is John Dee. Meyrick gives alchemy an essentially metaphorical signification by considering the transformation of the individual to be the veritable transmutation: Just as the transformation of metals is achieved through the fire that heats the laboratory apparatus, it is also by fire that the individual is transmutated since everything terminates with the death of the narrator in the immense fire at his home, reported as a postface in the form of a newspaper article.

The John Dee that Meyrink creates is an alchemist who does not transmute metals into gold; he even doubts the power of the powder that Kelly pretends to have obtained from an angel. To the legate of the pope who reproaches him "that You shower Your favours on magicians and grant such who are suspected – justly suspected indeed – of being in league with the devil freedom of abode, and more, in Your majesty's most Catholic country" the emperor Rudolph II can respond: "Stuff and nonsense! The Englishman can make gold, and making gold is a most natural art".[23] But it is not making gold that is the issue, as the cardinal points out:

> Whatever we think about making gold, this English gentleman and his dubious companion has publicly declared that he is not interested in gold and silver but seeks the power of magic in this world and to overcome death in the next. (*AWW*, p. 256)

It is this that John Dee will soon confirm to the Emperor. Separating himself from "mountebanks and alchymical charlatans, who look only to squander the gold the tincture brings them on dissipation", Dee does not hesitate to compare transmutation, which concern the metals, with transubstantiation, the transformation of bread and wine into the body and the blood of Christ during the mass (*AWW*, p. 263).[24] The Emperor, according to Meyrink, believed not only in the separation of powers – that of Rome and his own – but also in the separation of knowledge, the alchemist's knowledge of matter and the theologian's knowledge of the body after death. Meyrink's Dee does not reject this separation when he opposes the artisanal alchemy of the gold makers to a true alchemy that aims at the spiritualisation of man; so alchemy will pretend to take the place of theology. It is precisely here that Meyrink

---

23 Meyrink: *The Angel of the West Window*, p. 256. All further references to this work are given in the text and abbreviated to *AWW*.

24 On the parallels between alchemy and theology, see Greiner's Introduction to his edition of *L'alchimiste chrétien* by Pierre Jean Fabre; Matton.

interprets the history of John Dee in the light of the esoteric beliefs of the twentieth century. This opposition between a positivistic chemical science that could fabricate gold – still maintained as possible by the Académie Royale des Sciences at the beginning of the eighteenth century – and an angelical science which would bring immortality does not correspond at all to the thinking of the historical John Dee, for whom the conversations with angels and scientific experiments all took place in the same world. For him, the invocation of the angels was no more magical (or for that matter, "natural" – which ultimately meant the same thing) than the transmutation of the metals, the comprehension of the demonstrations of Euclid, or the properties of the monad.

The conversation between John Dee and the emperor Rudolph echoes a second conversation, one hundred pages earlier and three and a half centuries later, between the narrator and his friend Theodor Gärtner, a positivist chemist who had become a Rosicrucien gardener, that he finds as if in a dream (no doubt he is dead). Medieval alchemy was not a hoax, explains Gärtner, but the ancestor of the chemistry taught in today's universities. He continues:

> We of the "Golden Rose", however, have never been interested in dissecting matter, postponing death or succumbing to the hunger for gold, that accursed plaything of mankind. We have remained what we always have been: technicians in the laboratory of eternal life. (*AWW*, p. 157)

This is the veritable alchemy according to the character developed by Meyrink: He does not try to perfect metals nor to fabricate medicines to prolong life by fighting disease – the simple aim is to become immortal. John Dee confided to his pseudo-diary: "What is time? What is metamorphosis? – After a hundred years and more, still I am: *I* after a hundred graves; *I* after a hundred resurrections!" (*AWW*, p. 172). And later: "Wilt you become immortal? – Dost thou know that the way of this metamorphosis leads through many trials of fire and water? Base matter must suffer much torment before it can be transmuted" (*AWW*, p. 173). The narrator will ultimately die in a fire after his wife has drowned. But before he receives his final revelation, he asks "who was… who is the Angel of the West Window?". It is his late friend the Rosicrucian chemist gardener, who had died before him, though resuscitated once, who responds:

An echo, that is all. It was right when it said it was immortal; it was immortal because it had never lived; if it had never lived, it could never know death. All knowledge and power, all good and evil that came from it, came from you. It was the sum of all questions, wisdom and magic that was hidden within you, but that you did not know you possessed. Each of you contributed to that sum and each of you marvelled at the "Angel" as at some divine revelation. It was the Angel of the West Window because the West is the green realm of the dead past. (*AWW*, p. 414)

The green realm is Greenland: The historical John Dee dreamed of becoming the master of Greenland at the time when he suggested the establishment of the British Empire to Queen Elizabeth. But it is also the Occident that has died. Meyrink killed himself five years later, facing the rising sun.

Meyrink's John Dee is not the historical John Dee. But who would read Dee's actual journal, and his scientific studies? Precisely because John Dee is a real historical figure and he had the reputation of an alchemist and a magician, we are tempted to take seriously the fantastic vision of alchemy offered to us by Meyrink. However, his character's alchemy is not that of the Renaissance but a construction of the occultism of the nineteenth century.

MARGUERITE YOURCENAR'S *THE ABYSS*

In a note at the end of the *The Abyss*, Marguerite Yourcenar presents her conception of the "historical novel".[25] Of course, unlike Hadrian in *Memoirs of Hadrian*, a previous novel, Zenon, the main character of *The Abyss*, is only a "fictitious 'historical' character", constructed along the same lines as the "free reconstruction of a real person" (*TA*, p. 361). Yourcenar explains:

In the case of a fictitious character, in order to give him that specific reality conditioned by time and place, without which a 'historical novel' is merely a more or less successful costume ball, the author can draw only upon facts and dates of man's past, that is to say, also upon history. (*TA*, p. 361-2)

Without specifically identifying either individual, Zenon is based on a compilation of Leonardo da Vinci, Paracelsus, Erasmus, Giordano Bruno, Ambroise Paré, and Campanella. The subtle and human portrait traced by

---

25 *The Abyss*, p. 362. All further references to this work are given in the text and abbreviated to *TA*.

Marguerite Yourcenar draws its depth and complexity from this assemblage of the traits of several exceptional individuals that the hero could have met in the course of his life. Zenon is an alchemist who has never created gold. He tells this to his cousin, the captain Henry Maximilian, who he finds by chance in an Inn in the town of Innsbruck after many years of separation. "You are making gold," says the captain in a provocative tone, then:

> No, replied the alchemist, but others to come will make it. It is just a matter of time and of adequate tools to complete the experiment. (…) Making gold will possibly be as easy someday as blowing glass (…) By dint of biting well into the substance of things, we shall finally come to the hidden reasons for affinities and for discords. (…) I am wild when I consider that man's inventiveness has not gone beyond his first wheel for a cart, the first potter's wheel, or the first forge; there has hardly been any effort to diversify the uses of fire from the time that it was stolen from the heavens. And nevertheless, it would suffice merely to apply oneself seriously in order to deduce from a few simple principles a whole series of ingenious machines capable of increasing man's wisdom or his power. (*TA*, p. 124)

There is nothing anachronistic in this promethean discourse ascribed to Zenon, and yet it seems closer to the Francis Bacon of *New Atlantis* than the drawings of Leonardo. Essentially, he was not content with simply imagining ingenious machines like the Italian artist; rather he placed his inventions in an organised plan for mastering nature, in the manner of the English philosopher. Nevertheless, the view of alchemy as a technical field rather than a doctrine that invokes spiritual forces corresponds accurately with sixteenth-century thought.

It is not surprising that Zenon complains of the frauds who pretend to have made transmutations:

> (…) as in those fraudulent experiments wherein Court alchemists try to prove to their royal clients that they have found something, although the gold at the base of the alembic proves to be only that of an ordinary ducat, long passed from hand to hand, and put there by the charlatan before the heating began. (*TA*, p. 169)

At this time, charlatans were influential in the courts of princes, most notably that of Rudolph II at Prague as discussed above with reference to Dee and Kelly. The serious alchemists would denounce these "blowers", as one would say in a mocking tone, who would imagine themselves able to produce gold without mastering all the doctrine. In the end, to honour their contracts and save their skins, they would be reduced to tricks of prestidigitation executed with more or less competence. Michael Maier, a well known alchemist of the period, denounced these "pseudo-chymists" in his *Examen focurum pseudo-chymicorum* (*An examination of pseudo-chymists' frauds*) of 1617.[26]

It is therefore unsurprising that Zenon criticises the symbolic language of the alchemists, as many seventeenth-century alchemists did:

> Nevertheless, such symbols have their dangers. My fellow alchemists employ figures like "the Milk of the Virgin", "the Black Raven", "the Universal Green Lion", and "the Copulation of Metals" to designate the various operations of their art wherever the subtlety, or the virulence, of these phases exceeds the power of words which men commonly use. The result of this mode of expression is, however, that the more obtuse minds see little beyond the material image, while the more judicious tend to disdain a form of knowledge which, although it could carry them far, seems to them to be imbedded in a morass of dreams. (*TA*, p. 211)

Zenon finishes his days in prison, waiting for a judgement that would lead him to the stake if he did not choose suicide. His enemies accused him of magic, but in his library harboured only the works of Cornelius Agrippa and Della Porta, works which were also in the possession of the Bishop of Bruges, who sat among the judges. For Zenon, no doubt, magic was not associated with the supernatural: Magic, as alchemy, was a part of natural philosophy. There was no distinction between spiritual and material powers; only fools considered magic to be the science of supernatural power.[27]

> DE OCCULTA PHILOSOPHIA: (…) In discussing the subject with him [the Bishop], Zeno was almost wholly sincere. The universe as seen by the magician, he agreed, is constituted of attractions and repulsions governed by laws still mysterious to us, but not necessary impenetrable to human understanding. (…) The great virtue of magic, and of alchemy, her daughter, is to postulate the unity of matter, with the result that certain philosophers of the alembic and the crucible have even conjectured that matter could be of the same nature as light

---

26 This work has been reedited with commentary in a thesis defended in 1991 at the University of Munich by Wolfgang Beck: *Michael Maiers Examen Fucorum Pseudo-Chymicorum: Eine Schrift wider die falschen Alchemisten*.

27 On the multiple meanings of the word "magic" in the Renaissance, see Walker; Jones-Davies.

and thunderbolts. (…) The sciences of mechanics, in which, Zenon explained, he had been much engaged, are akin to these same magical pursuits in that they try to transform knowledge about things into power over these things, and indirectly into power over man. (*TA*, p. 302-3)

Zenon pursues his exposé by invoking the influence of medicines on sickness, music on emotions, words on thought, and the people who inspire love or hate. If Zenon's alchemy is associated with magic, it is uniquely because it postulates the unity of the forces of nature, and that certain aspects of these forces are revealed by alchemy. There is nothing anachronistic in this, not even in the allusion to a power over things which ultimately leads to power over people, if we read this as a comment on the medical applications of alchemy. But the historian of science can only be surprised by the meditations of Zenon when, at the end of his voyages, he establishes himself under a false name as the doctor of the hospice in Bruges, the city where he was born.

SOLVE ET COAGULA. (…) In those early days he had mistaken this whole alchemical process of separation and reduction (so dangerous that hermetic philosophers spoke of it only in veiled terms, and so arduous that whole lifetimes were consumed, most of them in vain, to accomplish it) for what was mere easy rebellion. Later on, rejecting the trumpery in all those teachings, vague dreams as ancient as human illusion itself, and retaining from his alchemist masters only certain practical recipes, he has chosen to dissolve and coagulate matter in the strict sense of experimentation with the body of things. Now, the two branches of the curve, the metaphysical and the pragmatic, were meeting; the *mors philosophica* had been accomplished: The operator, burned by the acids of his own research, had become both subject and object, both the fragile alembic and the black precipitate at its base; the experiment that he had thought to confine within the limits of the laboratory had extended itself to every human experience. (*TA*, p. 189)

Following this reflection, Zeno asks himself if, beyond this "putrefaction of ideas" and the "death of instincts and shattering of forms", he will attain "the ascetic purity of the White Phase of the great Work, and finally the joint triumph of mind and senses which characterizes the Red Phase, the glorious conclusion" (*TA*, p. 189-90). One must first notice that the use of the expression "hermetic philosophers" to designate alchemists only became popular around the beginning of the seventeenth century, without the esoteric con-

LITERATURE AND CHEMISTRY

notations that this expression carries today.[28] Above all, the idea that alchemical work would essentially concern the life of its practitioners would have been foreign to a Renaissance alchemist. Marguerite Yourcenar here gives ideas to her characters that did not germinate until much later, really only in the twentieth century. The technological progress made in printing and engraving during the sixteenth century certainly lead to the development of alchemical emblem books, which abounded in anthropomorphic representations of alchemical operations. These works used these images as analogies and their relevance can be easily understood within the epistemology of the time. Correspondences between mineral matter and living beings simply helped the reader to understand chemical operations.[29] It is only when these images became disconnected from the natural processes and the laboratory operations they were originally intended to clarify and nourish that the images appeared strange and curious in a way that may be interpreted according to the personal fantasy of each individual. Once they had lost their chemical roots the contemplation of these images could lead to the idea that alchemy was mostly concerned with the psyche of man. It is only for those who favour the esoteric approach, like Evola or Jung, that alchemy cannot be reduced to a chemical science, but must be interpreted as the symbolic expression of the conduct of a life striving towards a higher spiritual dimension.

In presenting the magic and alchemy of Zenon as knowledge of nature, we remain on the surface of the novel, unable to see its deeper signification. For the author, scientific positivism is only the immediate expression or the symbol of an entire life; the true work is not that of the laboratory but that of an existence which makes the obscurity of the human soul manifest, not so much that of the hero but of the personalities that surround him. Zenon has of course given in to his instincts but more than this, he has sided with, accompanied, and received within himself all the physical and moral poverties of humanity. Out of all these things, he will purify and liberate himself through death. For Yourcenar, this is the true alchemical operation, a transformation of man and not of matter.

---

28 See Joly: "La rationalité de l'hermétisme". At the beginning of the seventeenth century, the word "hermetic" referred to Hermes, the mythical founder of alchemy; "hermetic medicine" simply meant "chemical medicine".

29 We can confirm that illustrated treatises are rare among the large compilations of texts published in the seventeenth century. Examples include the *Musaeum hermeticum* (Frankfurt, 1625-77), the *Theatrum chemicum* (Ursel, 1602; Strasbourg, 1659-61), and the *Bibliotheca chemica curiosa* (Geneva, 1702).

To construct this admirable portrait, Marguerite Yourcenar seems to have been mislead in her quest for historical authenticity by the authors she consulted and identified herself with in the final note to her novel:

> Nearly all the alchemical formulas quoted in Latin come from three great modern works on alchemy, Marcelin Berthelot, *La chimie au Moyen Age*, 1893; Carl Jung, *Psychology and Alchemy*, 1953; Julius Evola, *La Tradizione Ermetica*, 1948. Written from different points of view, these three studies together form a useful approach to the ever enigmatic realm of alchemical thought. (*TA*, p. 166-7)

The English version of the novel adds a development that is absent in the original French edition:

> In alchemical treatises, the formula *L'Oeuvre au Noir*, given as the French title to this book, designates what is said to be the most difficult phase of the alchemist's process, the separation and dissolution of substance. It is still not clear whether the term applied to daring experiments on matter itself, or whether it was understood to symbolize trials of the mind in discarding all forms of routine and prejudice. Doubtless it signified one or the other meaning alternately, or perhaps both at the same time. (*TA*, p. 367)

For the historian of ancient chemistry, however, doubt is no longer possible: The alchemical terms reflect only the operations of the laboratory and material substances. Some authors – poets, moralist, or theologians for example – may sometimes use alchemical terms in an allegorical manner to designate operations of the human spirit, but the alchemists themselves were only interested in the transformation of matter and not the psychic transformation of man.

We can guess at the subtle balancing act the novelist must undertake to place the works of the scientist Berthelot alongside those of the esotericist Evola. The Italian author showed a disdain for the ancient texts which he used mainly to express his fascist ideology. A similar disdain for ancient texts is found in the works of Jung, whose tendentious analyses have been denounced several times. As demonstrated by Barbara Obrist, and then by William Newman[30], Jung twists the sense of real alchemical texts, and has given an alchemical interpretation of texts and images which in fact are

---

30 Newman: "*Decknamen* or pseudochemical language?".

not alchemical at all. Only in this way could the Swiss psychoanalyst affirm that chemical experiments were nothing but the unconscious projection of psychic experiences of the adept. Thus, Jung endowed nineteenth-century esoteric fantasies with a rationalist interpretation that seduced Bachelard before attracting the attention of Marguerite Yourcenar.[31]

CONCLUSIONS

Literature takes science out of joint. It presents a hyperbolic image of science, not simply fulfilling promises or hopes of progress, but rather exposing a hidden face of science that reflects both our hopes and our fears – even the most unreasonable of them. The historian of science, struggling to respect original texts and their contexts, will find himself disconcerted by the liberty of the novelist, who is not a prisoner of the too strict framework of the academic historian. The case of alchemy is especially unnerving because literature often presents a science which, according to the historian of alchemy, never existed: This form of alchemy issued from the revisions and speculations of a much later esotericism and is directly opposed to the rational interpretations preferred by the historian. Literature presents a vision of the history of alchemy which to the historian seems distorted. The historian dreams of a sort of "scientific literature" that would serve his own objectives as a historian and would submit to his own methodological rigour.

These words may seem somewhat reductive and improper in a discussion of literature, as if it were up to the historian of science to "correct" literature and reprimand the novelist in the name of a scientific "truth" for which the historian would be the caretaker and depository. It is more appropriate to take literature seriously and investigate its portraits of alchemists on their own terms. The historian of chemistry, in his effort to reconstitute the knowledge and doctrines of the past, would let something essential escape, the life itself of the past, the multiple facets of which are expressed in literature. The alchemist was not only a theoretician of natural forces, an able experimenter seeking out the secrets of matter and the hidden composition of metals, or a doctor seeking new efficient medicines within the mysteries of chemistry. His efforts to take on the forces of nature within a unifying framework of chemical principles drove him to research the invisible beyond the visible: Why not take his quest right up to the boundary of the supernatural? His

31 See Joly: "Psychanalyse des objets".

will to master natural operations could easily lead him to believe that he had become the master of the spirit world as well as the world of matter. If he could transmute lead into gold, could he not also transform his own nature? Could he not acquire a mastery that would allow him to dominate others? These are unlikely ambitions but nevertheless human, and the novelist grasps their significance when he or she reaches beyond the more reasonable results of the historian of alchemy.

Literature is allowed to present a vision of alchemy that would escape the historian by going to the heart of the logic which animates the alchemist. Literature is not an inferior type of history; rather, it presents essential aspects of alchemical work that historical research must leave in the shadows. The alchemist, like the modern chemist, has an intimate relationship with the multiple and deranging aspects of matter whose constant changes and infinite varieties cannot be confined to the concepts of chemistry. Chemical experiments allow us contact with the most marvelous and strange manifestations of nature, whose resources seem infinite. After all, if this ancient chemistry that we call alchemy has tempted and inspired us into so many speculative digressions, if alchemy still produces effects in literature that can surprise the historian of chemistry – then alchemy is a marvellous example of a knowledge that is always ready to break through the limits imposed upon it by scientific methodology, a science pushed outside of itself by the fascination with and the dreams induced by its privileged object: matter. This dimension of alchemy can be more easily developed in literature than in the history of science. In *The object of literature* Pierre Macherey describes a literature that speaks of philosophy. We could similarly say that literature speaks of alchemy, not in a parody of scientific history, but in a new and uniquely literary way that renews our perception of the strange and fascinating alchemical world.

WORKS CITED

Musaeum hermeticum. Frankfurt, 1625-1677.
Theatrum chemicum. Ursel, 1602; Strasbourg, 1659-61.
Bibliotheca chemica curiosa. Geneva, 1702.

Ackroyd, Peter: *The house of doctor Dee*. London: Hamish Hamilton, 1993.
Baud, Jean-Pierre: *Le procès de l'alchimie. Introduction à la légalité scientifique*. Strasbourg: Cerdic publications, 1983.

Beck, Wolfgang: "Michael Maiers Examen Fucorum Pseudo-Chymicorum: Eine Schrift wider die falschen Alchemisten", Ph.D. dissertation, University of Munich, 1991.

Berthelot, Marcelin: *La chimie au Moyen Age*. Paris, 1893.

Clucas, Stephen (ed.): "John Dee's Monas Hieroglyphica" in *Ambix* vol. 52, no. 3, 2005, pp. 195-284.

Clulee, Nicholas: *John Dee's natural philosophy between science and religion*. London: Routledge, 1988.

Debru, Armelle (ed.): *Galen on pharmacology, philosophy, history and medicine*. Leyde: Brill, 1997.

Debus, Allen: *Chemistry and medical debate*. Canton, Mass.: Science History Publications, 2001.

Dee, John: *Monas hieroglyphica*. Antwerp, 1564.

Derrida, Jacques: "La pharmacie de Platon" in *La Dissémination*. Paris: Seuil, 1972.

Evola, Julius: *La Tradizione Ermetica*. Bari: Laterza, 1948 (1931).

Fuller, Thomas: *The Worthies of England*. London, 1662.

Gatta, J.: "Aylmer's Alchemy in *The Birthmark*" in *Philological Quarterly Iowa City*, vol. 57, no. 3, 1978, pp. 399-413.

Greiner, Frank: "Introduction" in *L' alchimiste chrétien*. By Pierre Jean Fabre. Paris / Milano: SEHA / Archè, 2001.

Hawthorne, Nathaniel: *The Birthmark*, 1843. New York: Literary Classics of the United States, 1982.

—: *Rappaccini's Daughter*, 1846. New York: Literary Classics of the United States, 1982.

—: *The Scarlet Letter*, 1850. New York: Literary Classics of the United States, 1982.

Joly, Bernard: "A propos d'une prétendue distinction entre l'alchimie et la chimie au XVIIᵉ siècle: questions d'histoire et de méthode" in *Revue d'histoire des sciences*, no. 60-1, Jan.-Jun. 2007, pp. 167-83.

—: "L' ambiguïté des paracelsiens face à la médecine galénique" in Armelle Debru (ed.): *Galen on pharmacology. Philosophy, history and medicine*. Leyde: Brill, 1997, pp. 301-22.

—: "La figure de l'alchimiste dans la littérature du XIXᵉ et du XXᵉ siècle. Savant fou ou folies scientifiques: de l'alchimie à la chimie" in Hélène Machinal (ed.): *Le savant fou*. Rennes: Presses Universitaires de Rennes, 2013, pp. 75-88.

—: "La rationalité de l'hermétisme. La figure d'Hermès dans l'alchimie à l'âge classique" in *Methodos* 3 *Figures de l'irrationnel*, 2003, pp. 61-82. http://methodos.revues.org (1 May 2013).

—: "Les *Affinités électives* de Goethe: entre science et littérature" in *Methodos* 6 *Sciences et littérature*, 2006. http://methodos.revues.org (1 May 2013).

—: "Psychanalyse des objets, psychanalyse des images et rupture épistémologique: Bachelard et l'histoire de la chimie ancienne" in *Pour l'histoire des sciences de l'homme, vol.* 32, Winter 2008, pp. 24-33.

Jones-Davies, Margaret (ed.): *La magie et ses langages*. Lille: Presses universitaires de Lille, 1980.

Jung, Carl: *Psychologie und alchemie*. Zurich: Rascher Verlag, 1944. English translation: *Psychology and Alchemy*. London: Routledge and Kegan Paul, 1953.

Macherey, Pierre: *A quoi pense la littérature?* Paris: PUF, 1990. New edition with a preface: *Philosopher avec la littérature*. Paris: Hermann, 2013. English translation: *The object of literature*. Cambridge: Cambridge University Press, 1995.

Matton, Sylvain: *Scolastique et alchimie (XVIᵉ–XVIIᵉ siècle)*. Paris/Milano: SEHA / Archè, 2009.

Maier, Michael: *Examen fucorum pseudo-chymicorum detectorum et in gratiam veritatis amantium succincte refutatum*. Frankfurt, 1617.

Meyrink, Gustav: *Der Engel vom westlichen Fenster*, 1927, trans. Mike Mitchell: *The Ange of the West Window*. Sawtry (UK): Dedalus, 2010 (1991).

Newman, William: "*Decknamen* or pseudochemical language? Eirenaeus Philalethes and Carl Jung" in *Revue d'histoire des sciences*, vol. 49, no. 2-3, 1996, pp. 161-88.

—: *Gehennical fire. The lives of George Starkey, an american alchemist in the scientific revolution*. Cambridge, Mass.: Harvard University Press, 1994.

Obrist, Barbara: *Les débuts de l'imagerie alchimique. XIVᵉ–XVᵉ siècles*. Paris: Le Sycomore, 1982.

Principe, Lawrence and Newman, William: "Alchemy vs. Chemistry, the etymological Origins of a historiographical Mistake" in *Early Science and Medicine*, vol. 3, no. 1, 1998, pp. 32-65.

—: "Some Problems with the Historiography of Alchemy" in William Newman and Anthony Grafton (eds.): *Secrets of Nature: Astrology and Alchemy in Early Modern Europe*. Cambridge, Madison: MIT Press, 2001, pp. 385-431.

Reid, A. S: "Hawthorne's Humanism: *The Birthmark* and Sir Kenelm Digby" in *American Literature*, vol. 38, 1966, pp. 337-51.

Simon, Gérard: *Kepler astronome astrologue*. Paris: Gallimard, 1979.

Swann, C.: "Alchemy and Hawthorne's *Elixir of Life Manuscripts*" in *Journal of American Studies*, vol. 22, no. 3, 1988, pp. 371-87.

Walker, Daniel Pickering: *Spiritual and demonic magic from Ficino to Campanella*. London: The Warburg Institute, 1958.

Wilding, Michael: *Raising spirits, making gold and swapping wives*. Nottingham: Shoestring Press, 1999.

Yourcenar, Marguerite: *L' œuvre au noir*. Paris: Gallimard, 1968. Trans. Grace Frick in collaboration with the author: *The Abyss*. New York: Farrar, Straus and Giroux, 1976.

DEMONIC, DIVINE OR MYSTICAL: CHEMISTRIES OF PERSONAL INTERACTION

DEMONIC AFFINITIES: ON THE CHEMICAL ANALOGY IN GOETHE'S *DIE WAHLVERWANDTSCHAFTEN*

Frode Helmich Pedersen, University of Bergen

In August 1809 Goethe sent a note to his publisher J. F. Cotta that was to be printed as an advertisement for his new novel *Die Wahlverwandtschaften* (1809) (*The Elective Affinities*). In the note, Goethe writes about himself and the novel in the third person, and gives the following explanation to his prospective readership of the central image of the novel – the phenomenon of the "elective affinities":

> It seems that this strange title was suggested to the author by his advanced physical studies. He appears to have taken notice of the fact that natural philosophers often use moral analogies in order to make things which lie far beyond the field of human knowledge more comprehensible; and so it seems that he has used a chemical analogy to explain a moral situation and thus returned the analogy to its spiritual home.[1]

The advertisment concludes by asserting that there can be only one nature, so that even in the highest spheres of the human, that is, the free use of reason, one can find traces of what he calls "trüber leidenschaftlicher Notwendigkeit", the murky necessities of passion.[2]

A couple of things about this text merit some initital observations. Firstly, we note that Goethe confirms the chemical analogy (Goethe uses the word "Gleichnis" or "Gleichnisrede") as absolutely central to the novel. Secondly,

---

1   Goethe: *Sämtliche Werke* 9, p. 285; my translation. The original is as follows: "Es scheint, daß den Verfasser seine fortgesetzten physikalischen Arbeiten zu diesem seltsamen Titel veranlaßten. Er mochte bemerkt haben, daß man in der Naturlehre sich sehr oft ethischer Gleichnisse bedient, um etwas von dem Kreise menschlichen Wissens weit Entferntes näher heranzubringen; und so hat er auch wohl, in einem sittlichen Falle, eine chemische Gleichnisrede zu ihrem geistigen Ursprünge zurückführen mögen (…)".

2   Goethe: *Sämtliche Werke* 9, p. 285.

we notice that the relationship between the two spheres – of natural elements on the one hand, and humanity's moral sphere on the other – is said to have been connected through such an analogy *prior to* Goethe, but in an inverted way: Whereas chemists have used metaphors from the moral world to explain natural phenomena, Goethe wants to reintroduce one of these analogies into the moral sphere. There is a certain strangeness, uncanniness even, to this reversal, because one cannot transfer such an image between these spheres without also transferring one or more of the *qualities* of one sphere to the other – indeed, such a transfer of qualities is the whole point of using an analogy of this kind. In other words, some quality of the inanimate, of the lifeless, is introduced into the world of human action in Goethe's novel. This raises many questions, some of which will be pursued here. First, how does the central chemical analogy of the title affect our understanding of human behaviour in this narrative? Next, to what extent does the chemical analogy work as an interpretative key to the entire plot? And lastly I would like to explore the relationship between the chemical theory, the novel's notion of the demonic, and the category of the tragic.[3]

THE OXYMORONIC NATURE OF THE TERM "WAHLVERWANDTSCHAFT"

Before we can investigate the significance of the chemical analogy to the development of the novel's plot, it is necessary to take a closer look at the phenomenon referred to by the term "Wahlverwandtschaft". The origin of the term was the renaissance theory of *sympathia*, which can be traced back to the Pre-Socratics, and which attempts to present a theory of how all parts of the cosmos are linked together. In the eighteenth century this theory became one of "affinity", which designated a substance's propensity to combine with another.[4] The crucial step towards the theory referred to in Goethe's novel, was, however, taken by the Swedish natural scientist Torbern Bergman, who replaced the older (alchemical) term "affinitas" with the expression "attractio electiva" (in his work *De attractionibus electives*, 1775) to describe the tendency of chemical compounds

---

3   For a detailed study on Goethe's relationship with the chemical theories of his time, see Adler: *Eine fast magische Anziehungskraft* and "Goethe's use of chemical theory in *Elective Affinities*".

4   Adler informs us that this theory took its characteristic form in 1718 with the work of E. F. Geoffroy. See Adler: "Goethe's use of chemical theory", p. 265.

to dissolve and form new pairings. The term coined by Bergman would, if directly translated into German, have been something like "auswählende Anziehung", which corresponds roughly to the English "elective affinities". Instead, Bergman's German translator, a certain Hein Tabor[5], chose the term "Wahlverwandtschaft", which, as Wolf von Engelhardt has observed, is an oxymoron (Engelhardt, p. 251). The reason for this is that the chemical phenomenon described by the term is *not*, in fact, a "kinship by choice" but rather an inherent quality of the substance which *forces* it to pair with a certain other substance even if other substances, with which it *might* pair, are also available. The "kinship" itself then is an automatic reaction brought about by the inherent properties of the substances in question and as such it *precludes* any possibility of a choice. As Engelhardt puts it: "in chemistry, it's all about necessities of nature, not free choice" (Engelhardt, p. 251). This may seem obvious to a modern reader, but was it obvious to readers in Goethe's time? After all, Goethe, in the advertisment note quoted above, confirms the interconnectedness of all phenomena, human and natural, when he writes that "there can be only one nature".[6] So what exactly did Goethe mean by the term "Wahlverwandtschaft"?

GOETHE'S USE OF THE TERM *WAHLVERWANDTSCHAFT*

Goethe first describes the phenomenon of "elective affinities" in 1796, in one of his lectures on anatomy. In general he seems to be somewhat ambivalent as to how one should understand the fact that the scientists were using the term *choice* to describe a process in the sphere of natural elements. On the one hand he writes that we are, after all, often only dealing with "external determinations, which tear or push these substances here and there".[7] On the other hand, he uses the term "Wahlverwandtschaft" to designate attractions and repulsions in the human sphere.[8] The philosophical background for this transfer is, again, to be found in his comment that there can be "only one

---

5   Hein Tabor's German translation of Bergman's *De attractionibus electivus* appeared in 1782. According to the Hamburg edition of Goethe's writings, the term "Wahlver-wandtschaft" was originally suggested by another translator (who translated a preface by Bergman to the work of another chemist), Chr. Ehr. Weigel, in 1779. See Goethe: *Werke* 6, p. 700.
6   Goethe: *Sämtliche Werke* 9, p. 285.
7   Goethe: *Werke* 6, p. 700-1.
8   In *Dichtung und Wahrheit*, see Goethe: *Werke* 9, p. 561.

nature". It was therefore only to be expected that the idealist philiospher G. W. F. Schelling immediately took to the novel, as he understood it to be written on the basis of a conviction of an original identity between spirit ("Geist") and nature, between the conscious workings of the mind and the unconscious strivings of nature.[9] Indeed, this seems precisely to be the basis of the analogy of the "elective affinitives": That processes in the inanimate, inorganic world are somehow connected to the sphere of human interaction.

What, then, is the precise function of the chemical analogy in Goethe's novel? The chemical reaction described by Bergman as an *elective affinity* works like this: If one starts with a certain compound AB and introduces this to another compound CD, the result would be the dissolving of both and the formation of two new pairings: AC and BD. Now, to explain this process, one said that A had a natural *affinity* to C, which led A to extricate itself from its connection to B and form a union with C. It should be clear that we are, rhetorically speaking, dealing with an antropomorphism here – a fact that the characters in Goethe's novel seem quite aware of. When Eduard explains the phenomenon to his wife Charlotte, he adds: "human beings are very narcissistic, they like to see themselves everywhere" (p. 270/29).[10] The novel's characters are of course unaware that this analogy is now being introduced – by the unseen authorial presence – as a determining metaphor for what is about to happen to *them*. At this point, one should note that the introduction of the chemical analogy results in a conspicuous case of dramatic irony. It only adds to the ironic effect that the characters *themselves* make use of the chemical analogy in order to describe their own situation, in the form of a humorous parlour game. Let us take a closer look at the scene:

> "Well then," said Eduard interrupting, "until we have seen all this with our own eyes we shall think of these formulae as a sort of parable, out of which we can abstract a lesson for our own immediate use. You are the A, Charlotte, and I am your B: for do I not depend on you and come after you as the B does the A? The C is quite obviously the Captain, who for the time being has to some extent taken me away from you. Now it would be right and proper, to prevent you from departing into the void, to provide you with a D, and quite without

9   See Engelhardt, p. 252.
10 All quotations from the novel are referenced with the page number of Trunz's Hamburg edition (vol. 6), followed by that of the Oxford edition of David Constantine's English translation.

question that must be the amiable young lady Ottilie, and you must not now make any further objection to her joining us." (p. 276/34-35)

The dramatic irony lies not simply in the fact that Eduard and the others are unaware of the fateful nature of this analogy, but also, of course, in that Eduard is mistaken about who has an affinity to whom: He pairs his wife with her niece Ottilie, who is soon to join them at the estate, and himself with his friend the Captain. This mistake, no doubt, has to do with Eduard's attempt to leave sexuality out of the equation. Very soon they will realise the truth of the affinities: That Eduard is passionately and irrevocably attracted to the young Ottilie and she to him, while his wife Charlotte is drawn to the Captain and he to her. This "double affinitiy" culminates in one of the novel's central episodes, the "spiritual adultery" ("Ehebruch im Ehebett") that occurs when Eduard sees only Ottilie while making love to his wife, while she, in turn, substitutes Eduard's face for the Captain's.[11] The resulting offspring, the child Otto, bears likeness to both Ottilie and the Captain, which makes it reasonable to interpret the episode as a point at which spirit is separated from flesh.[12]

As the plot progresses, however, it becomes clear that the new formation (the AC–BD) is not going to be realised. Charlotte almost immediately disavows her attraction to the Captain, whereas Ottilie, shaken by the accident in which the child Otto dies (towards the end of the novel), stubbornly renounces her love for Eduard, with fatal consequences. Given this development of the plot, how should we understand the novel's use of the chemical analogy to explain, or illustrate, what happens to these four literary characters?

NECESSITY AND FREEDOM

In his advertisment note, Goethe suggested that the basic conflict pointed to by the chemical analogy was between freedom and necessity, that is, between unconscious drives and the free choice of reason. But what, exactly, does the chemical analogy tell us in this regard? If we take the relationship between Eduard and Ottilie as our prime example: What, in the development of their relationship, should count as "necessity" and what should be

---

11   Eduard's own expression for this incident is "doppelter Ehbruch". See Goethe: *Werke* 6, p. 455.
12   See Adler: "Goethe's use of chemical theory", p. 263.

regarded as the exercising of human freedom? This question will, as we shall see in a moment, lead us back to the oxymoronic nature of the term "Wahlverwandtschaft", which seems to allow for something to be called a choice when it is in fact the opposite.

The attraction between Eduard and Ottilie is obviously not something that either of them has chosen; indeed, the lack of choice in this respect is presumably precisely what is being pointed to by the chemical analogy. Eduard and Ottilie are like the two substances B and D, who, when put together, cannot avoid joining with one another. In other words, what the novel appears to tell us is that attractions comparable to those in the natural world may also determine human relationships.[13] Thus the whole thing may seem straightforward: The erotic compulsion that draws Eduard and Ottilie together is beyond the control of their wills, and therefore comparable to attractions between the elements. Viewed in this way, the factor of *necessity* would be placed on the side of the drive that leads to the deep attraction between Eduard and Ottilie, meaning that neither of them could opt out of their coupling.

The problem is that this is not what actually happens in the novel. On the contrary, Eduard and Ottilie are, despite their strong attraction to one another, *unable* to realise their union, even if this union is dictated, as it were, by nature itself. They are drawn to each other by an irresistible inner force, but their coupling is stopped by something else. What is this someting else? If the basic conflict of the novel is between necessity and free choice, one would, on Kantian grounds, have expected the union to be prevented by an authentic act of free choice. Only such an act would, one imagines, have sufficed to oppose the violent nature of the drives. This, however, does not appear to be the case, at least not initially. Throughout most of the novel, the main inhibitor to the formation of the natural couple is not free choice, but conventional society. According to the rules of convention, the bond of marriage is sacred and (at least ideally) not to be broken by anything other than death. As it turns out, then, the basic conflict in the novel's first part (and most of its second part) is not one between natural drives on the one hand and free will on the other, but between two forces of necessity. The first is the natural, inner, necessity which *demands* the union, and the other is a man-made, outer necessity, which opposes the anarchic drives on behalf of order and propriety, *blocking* the union. Does this description of what takes

---

13 See Adler: "Goethe's use of chemical theory", p. 273.

place in the novel also hold if we consider the complicating element of the other couple demanded by nature, Charlotte and the Captain? In order to answer this question we must attempt a brief comparison of the formation of the two couples.

THE TWO COUPLES COMPARED

Eduard's "elemental" attraction to Ottilie is foreshadowed in a comment he makes even before she arrives at the estate: The young girl is said to suffer from a headache on the left side of her head, and Eduard jokingly comments on how nicely this corresponds to his own occasional headache on the *right* side of his head, so that they would make "a fine pair of corresponding images" (p. 281/39) sitting next to one another, resting their heads on opposing elbows. Later, their deep mutual affinity is evidenced by Ottilie's unconscious ability to copy Eduard's handwriting (p. 323/81), as well as their musical duet, in which Ottilie "manages to accomodate" her piano playing perfectly to Eduard's idiosyncratic performance on the flute (p. 297/55). Eduard is said to have a somewhat childlike character[14], in a sense that approaches Friedrich Schiller's use of the term "naive": He is not as bound by societal convention as his wife and the Captain. Something similar is true of Ottilie; thus the main drift of "The Assistant's Letter" in chapter five, in which the assistant explains Ottilie's poor performance at the boarding school, is precisely her natural resistance to the demands of the school's educational ideals. In short, she is not as easily conditioned to cultivated society as her fellow pupils. This, I would assert, is part of the reason why both Eduard and Ottilie have much greater difficulty renouncing their love than Charlotte and the Captain; they lack a natural connectedness to the norms of society and have thus not fully internalised the self-restraint demanded by propriety.

Charlotte and the Captain are also quickly drawn towards one another. Their "mutual goodwill" (p. 289/46), we are told, develops as they are working together on the improvement of the parkland surrounding the castle. Their work is compared to a dance, and as in dancing, their mutual dependency grows, hour by hour. Compared to Eduard and Ottilie's childlike infatuation, they are described as mature and responsible, with a clear and realistic grasp of the situation. As an example, consider their reaction to Eduard and Ottilie's curious duet:

---

14 "There was still something childlike about Eduard even as he grew older, and Ottilie, young herself, liked this in him especially" (p. 289/48).

The Captain and Charlotte watched this strange and unexpected encounter in silence, and with such feelings as one often has when witnessing childish acts which, because of their worrying consequences one cannot entirely approve of but cannot disapprove of either, which one indeed may even be bound to envy. For in fact their own affection was developing no less than that between Eduard and Ottilie, and perhaps even more dangerously since both were more serious, surer of themselves, and more capable of self-restraint. (p. 298/55)

The key word in this passage is "consequences". Like Schiller's "sentimental" poets, the Captain and Charlotte are closer to culture than to nature, and have therefore a much better understanding of the damage such a spontaneous attraction could potentially cause, the rules of convention being what they are. They have a reflective distance to themselves and are thus more capable of self-restraint than their counterparts. The narrator does not explain why this would make their affection even more dangerous, but we may presume that it has to do with their higher degree of awareness of what is at stake. In any case, their connectedness to culture – what Goethe calls "Welt" in the novel – subjects them to the kind of necessity associated with conventional society. They are thereby able to resist the necessity represented by the chemical analogy, but to view this as a triumph of free will seems to me overly optimistic. When the Captain and Charlotte exercise self-restraint, they do it on behalf of social conventions, not out of any deeper sense of morality. The two couples represent two different possibilities, two ways of responding to the sudden eruption of illicit passion; the first fully identifies with their unconscious drives, whilst the second keeps their drives at bay on behalf of propriety. None of the strategies result in the formation of a happy couple.

THE ELEMENT OF REPULSION

The theory of chemical "affinity" took its characteristic form in 1718, with the work of E. F. Geoffroy, which played a part in shaping Goethe's novel. When describing the law of affinity, Geoffroy writes that the two substances with a disposition to combine will unite as they *drive out* the other.[15] Transferred to the human sphere, this "driving out" would suggest an element of repulsion prompting the realisation of the new formation. This element *is* present in the novel, if not very prominently.

---

15 Adler, p. 265.

After both couples have experienced a form of bodily union in chapter twelve (Eduard and Ottilie a "tight embrace" (p. 81); Charlotte and the Captain an intense kiss "on the mouth" (p. 83)) they respond according to their respective dispositions: Eduard revels in his bliss, goes wandering under the moon, and allows himself to hope. Charlotte almost immediately renounces her love for the Captain and starts to arrange for Ottilie's departure (the Captain is also planning to leave, in order to take up a position elsewhere). In other words, Charlotte makes a conscious attempt to secure the original constellation. But again the forces of the elective affinities assert themselves, as both Eduard and Ottilie are struck by a kind of repulsion from the others, as if to counter Charlotte's plans. Eduard is quick to notice "that he and Ottilie were being kept apart" (p. 329/87) and resentment ensues: "Their companionableness was vanishing. His heart was closed, and when he was obliged to be together with his friend or with his wife he could not discover and reanimate the old affection for them in his bosom" (p. 331/88). Ottilie experiences something similar, but in her case the resentment seems less conscious – it is indeed as if something deep within her acts to remove the obstacles separating her from Eduard. The following passage illustrates this perfectly:

> Hatred is partisan, but love even more so. Ottilie too began to be somewhat estranged from Charlotte and the Captain. When on one occasion Eduard was complaining about the latter, saying that as a friend, and their circumstances being what they were, he was not acting entirely honestly, Ottilie made a thoughtless reply: "He has displeased me before now by not being entirely honest with you. I once heard him say to Charlotte: 'I do wish Eduard would not subject us to his flute-playing. He will never get any better at it, and it is tiresome to have to listen to it.' You can imagine how much that hurt me, since I love accompanying you."
>
> She had no sooner said this than her spirit whispered to her that she ought to have kept silent; but too late. Eduard's expression changed. He had never been so angered; he was assailed in his dearest ambitions (…). He was insulted, furious, beyond ever forgiving. He felt himself absolved from all responsibilities. (p. 329/87)

This is clearly an attempt on Ottilie's part to drive a wedge between Eduard and his friend, and therefore also his wife. And there *is* definitely something demonic about this "thoughtless" comment – a point which is emphasised by the fact that whatever made her say it is separate from "her spirit" ("der

Geist" – whether we understand this to mean her soul or her conscience or some other part of the true self), which would have acted to stop the utterance, but was apparently too slow to react. Phenomena like this are presumably precisely what Goethe had in mind when he, in the advertisment, wrote that traces of "trüber leidenschaftlicher Notwendigkeit" are also to be found in the highest spheres of reason. One should note that there appears to be a conflict between "spirit" and the workings of the passion in this scene, which may be said to oppose the view of a single nature encompassing both the unconscious and the conscious parts of the self. At any rate, one would have to say that in some sense *Ottilie's passion* was what made the comment – in order to realise its goals. This, of course, begs the question of what a passion is and how it can make its own decisions, but then again that is precisely the kind of question the novel constantly impels us to ask.

The effect of Ottilie's comment is clear enough: It strengthens the bond between her and Eduard, and weakens the ones between him and the other two. To keep to the chemical vocabulary, it acts as catalyst by enhancing Eduard's repulsion from the other two possible partners. But it also works to erode his sense of responsibility towards the established demands of society, a point which returns us to the central question: To what extent can the development of the plot be explained in terms of the analogy of "the elective affinities"?

AN UNCANNY ANALOGY

The fates of the two couples present us with the same kinds of factors in both cases: The basic conflict is between two kinds of necessities, one pertaining to the inner affinity, the other to the conventions and institutions of the time. Charlotte clearly views it as more dignified to side with the latter kind. After the Captain has kissed her and the full reality of their mutual attraction has become clear to them, Charlotte says: "I can forgive you and forgive myself only if we have the courage to alter our situation, since it is not within our power to alter our feelings" (p. 83/326). Unlike her husband, she does not seem to resent the restrictions placed upon her by the rules of propriety, most likely because she has (almost) completely internalised them. This would explain why she feels "inwardly restored" once she has renounced the Captain, in sharp contrast to Eduard, who cannot continue to live a normal life without Ottilie. To prevent Ottilie from leaving the castle, he goes away himself, preferring to throw himself into the chaos of war rather than confront his own inner chaos. In short: Charlotte and

Eduard choose differently, but the factors on the basis of which they make their choices are the same in both cases.

The chemical analogy, however, can only account for *one* of these factors, namely the demands of passion. The inhibiting factor – conventional society and its agents[16] – belongs to the messy realm of human experience, which cannot be represented by an idealised, scientific table. What, then, is the use of the chemical analogy (so prominently placed as the novel's title) if it does not work as an interpretive key to the development of the plot in its entirety? To my mind, the concept of the elective affinities is most illuminating with regards to Eduard and Ottilie precisely because, in the end, it is not conventional society that prevents their union, but something else – something more disquieting perhaps. To begin to unravel this, we should first clearly state the basic function of the chemical analogy in the novel: It works to make it absolutely clear that the deep, mutual attraction between the novel's two main protagonists is not freely chosen and can never be overcome. Not by free will, not by society, not by religion, nor by the higher powers of heaven.

Ottilie and Eduard experience passion's total dominion over their entire selves. This is what makes the passion so uncanny in the precise sense of the term: The chemical analogy suggests realms within Eduard and Ottilie that are alien to their "spirit" and their free will, but nevertheless deeply embedded in their inner beings. The uncanny points to something both alien and all too familiar at the same time, and is as such a fitting description of Eduard and Ottilie's passion: A strange agent within their selves beyond the reach of their wills.[17] This passion, the novel seems to suggest, is just as aligned with death as it is with life. We have mentioned how Eduard would rather put himself in mortal danger than deal with his unfulfilled love for Ottilie. And after Ottilie – in chapter eight of the novel's second part – has lost hope of ever attatching her life to Eduard's, she suffers an inner death: "The life of her soul had been killed, why should her body be preserved?" (p. 422/174). In other words: The passion either gets what it wants, or it kills

---

16 The most important one being the character of Mittler. The Baroness also engages herself actively against the union between Eduard and Ottilie, and so does Charlotte.

17 I use the term here in roughly the same (basically Freudian) sense as Nicolas Royle does: "The uncanny involves feelings of uncertainty, in particular regarding the reality of who one is and what is being experienced. Suddenly one's sense of oneself (of one's so-called 'personality' or 'sexuality', for example) seems strangely questionable" (Royle, p. 1).

the soul it inhabits. And when it affirms itself, it tends to make the person it dominates forgetful of everything else.

The novel's crucial moment in this respect is the death of the child, which comes just after Eduard has sought out Ottilie by the lake in the novel's second part. He stirs her passion and makes her promise to be his wife on the condition that Charlotte agrees. After he has left, she is described as "confused and agitated", and in this state of mind she is heedless of the danger of taking the child on the boat: "She hurried to the boat, was unaware that her heart was pounding, her feet unsteady, her senses threatening to desert her" (p. 456/207). She stumbles, loses the child in the water, then eventually manages to drag it out again, but when her good sense returns to her it is too late: The child has drowned.

The catastrophe at the lake puts a permanent end to all hope of a marriage between Ottilie and Eduard. Ottilie now unconditionally relinquishes her lover. This may be viewed as the moment when her free will asserts itself, inasmuch as her decision does not seem to be prescribed to her, neither from within nor from without. But to what extent can an interpretation that views Ottilie's starving herself to death as an expression of free will explain what takes place towards the novel's conclusion?

THE MONSTROUS EVIL

Not surprisingly, the scholarly literature on Goethe's *The Elective Affinities* proposes countless divergent interpretations of the death of the child and Ottilie's subsequent renunciation of Eduard. Walter Benjamin appears to view the death of the child as a stroke of fate through which the unseen powers of nature reassert themselves at the expense of hubristic man.[18] Others, who see something divine in Ottilie's superhuman love for Eduard, have trouble explaining why such a divine love must be punished.[19] The problem seems to be that the opposing agents are not, as Kurt May puts it, sinful man against the law of God, but rather *deus contra deum*: two opposing forces of the divine.[20] But if we continue with the argument developed above and interpret Ottilie's story more closely on the basis of the chemical analogy, we arrive at a somewhat different reasoning, along the following lines: Ottilie's love for Eduard, like his love for her, originates at an elemental level and is

---

18 See Benjamin, p. 133 and pp. 138-39.
19 May, p. 156. Quoted after Trunz and von Wiese, p. 739.
20 May, p. 156.

beyond the power of her will. As we observed above, this passion occasionally makes her act in a way that bypasses her rational and moral apparatus,
as in the scene in which she tells Eduard about the Captain's derogatory
comment. In that case, her passion seemed to guide her towards the goal
of a union with the object of her love. Later, after her animated encounter
with Eduard at the lake, her passion causes her to lose touch with the reality
around her, leading to the death of the child. In this latter case one could
also argue that the passion was looking out for itself, as the child did in fact
constitute a significant obstacle to Ottilie's union with Eduard. This, then,
would be what Ottilie so strongly intuits after the catastophe: That her passion is dangerously uncontrollable, oblivious to consequences, and must
therefore be countered at all costs. She cannot marry Eduard, because such
a union would mean granting the demonic force of her passion dominion
over her being.

Viewed in this way, Ottilie's final renunciation of Eduard would be a result
of her becoming fully aware of the enormity of the forces stirring inside her,
and has little to do with any sudden turn towards a pious acceptance of the
holy bond of marriage. In fact, the world of societal convention now seems
ready to accommodate the demands of her passion and grant her the legitimisation of her love for Eduard. Indeed, both Charlotte and the Captain (and
of course Eduard) now deem this the best solution. Charlotte tries, we are
told, in various ways to ascertain whether any rapprochement between her
niece and Eduard is thinkable, "but even the gentlest mention, the faintest
expression of a hope, the smallest suspicion seemed to agitate Ottilie to the
depths" (p. 468/218). To understand this agitation, we must consider Ottilie's description of herself as somebody "fate" has not "dealt kindly" with;
as "somebody consecrated"; as somebody "who has a hope of countering
a monstrous evil for herself and others only if she dedicates herself to that
holy power which, invisibly all around us, can alone protect us against the
monstrous forces that are pressing in" (p. 467/217). What is designated by
the novel's title as an "elective affinity" is here named "a monstrous evil",
which makes it clear why Ottilie would rather drown herself than agree to
marry Eduard.[21] She hopes to counter this evil by dedicating herself to "das
Heilige", a category which has sparked some controversy among scholars. It
suffices here to state that Ottilie's understanding of herself as "consecrated"

---

21 At the end of chapter fourteen in the novel's second part, Ottilie makes this clear to
    Charlotte: "The moment I hear you have agreed to a divorce, in that selfsame lake
    I will atone for my offence and crime" (p. 463/213).

("eingeweiht") refers to the epiphany – granted to her, if we are to believe her own statement, by God after the accident – that she is "caught up" in a "crime" (p. 463/214). A crime, one should add, that is indistinguishable from her affection for Eduard and therefore deeply and irrevocably connected to her own being. She realises that she must fight the monstrous evil, but such a fight must inevitably turn inward against an aspect of her own inner self. In other words, her fight is necessarily self-destructive, and leads to her abstaining from food and speech. Addressing her concerned friends in a letter, she declares that she is now under the influence of "a malevolent demon"[22] ("ein feindseliger Dämon") that will not allow her to re-enter her "proper course". How are we to understand this statement?

If the passion itself is a "monstrous evil", then she must have been possessed by this evil ever since she first met Eduard. However, it is only when she willfully tries to battle her passion that it manifests itself as a demon, taking possession over her body, arresting her speech, and stopping her from eating. But is there not, after all, a moment of freedom in her predicament towards the end of the novel? Had she followed her "chemical" sympathy for Eduard and married him, she would have been like an inanimate element obeying an inherent propensity to join with a certain other element. But she resists this force in a way that is free in the sense that it is not dictated by either kind of necessity discussed above. She chooses on behalf of the "holy", as she puts it, meaning in absolute opposition to a drive within her which she now recognises as *unholy*, inhuman, demonic. With regards to our main concern, one should note that it would have been difficult, narratively speaking, to make this point as clearly as the novel does without the active deployment of the title's chemical analogy.

THE NOVEL AS TRAGEDY

Ottilie opposes her elective affinity towards Eduard out of her own free will, but it seems wrong to view this as a celebration of human freedom. Ottilie's freedom of choice is limited to choosing freely her own demise (and thereby also Eduard's, a point not to be missed). As have often been noted, this makes the novel approximate the *tragic* as a literary mode. The tragic world view, as inherited from the ancient Greeks, teaches us that man is ultimately at the mercy of incomprehensible forces that are beyond his control. Goethe

---

22 David Constantine uses the word "spirit" in his translation.

argues for such a world view in some of his writings, most explicitly perhaps in a conversation with Karl Ernst von Hagen, in which he states that "we often see people at the mercy of invisible forces that they cannot withstand, which lead them in a direction they have no choice but to follow".[23] This is a fitting description of Eduard, and would also have been fitting of Ottilie, had she not so stubbornly refused to follow the direction set out for her by the force of inner necessity. Is Ottilie a tragic heroine? Insofar as a tragic hero is always *guilty* in some fundamental sense, Ottilie fits such a categorisation, at least in her own eyes: She perceives herself as guilty because she has allowed herself to identify fully with her passion for Eduard without recognising the demonic nature of that passion. And through her blindness she has been led astray; she has for ever left her "proper course" ("ich bin aus meiner Bahn geschritten"), which is presumably the course of the morally sound human being. Refusing to identify with the demonic within herself, Ottilie has no choice but to self-destruct. Unlike Racine's Phèdre, whose passion is illicit on account of its object, Ottilie's attraction is not incestuous and therefore not criminal *tout court* in terms of its object. What Goethe achieves with the introduction of the chemical analogy to his narrative is the suggestion that her passion, like a highly reactive chemical compound, is in itself demonic, and therefore morally unacceptable regardless of the object of her attraction.

What is the relationship between the tragic, the demonic, and the "chemical" in Goethe's novel? The demonic clearly functions as that incomprehensible force which mercilessly seals the fate of the tragic heroine. But to what degree should the demonic be understood in the light of the title's chemical analogy? To answer this question, it is necessary to consider the peculiar journey of the term "elective affinity" from the moral sphere into the chemical realm and back again. In using the moral term to explain a chemical phenomenon, the chemist was indeed a "true narcissus", as he introduced the human notion of choice into the realm of inanimate subtances. When Goethe brought the analogy back to its spiritual home (as he puts it), it had changed its meaning in an uncanny way: It is now as if the notion of choice *itself* had been tainted with the inhuman. The implication of the chemical analogy is therefore not only that we can sometimes have passions that are too strong for our wills to overcome, but that what we percieve as choices *in general* are not choices at all, but something determined deep within us that has no connection to our mental lives.

---

23 Goethe: *Werke* 1, p. 676. The conversation took place in August 1805.

But why use the term "demonic" to designate this sphere? Why not simply resort to the rationalistic doctrine of determinism? The answer may be found, again, in the peculiar journey of the analogy of the *attractio electiva* because when the notion of *choice* was introduced at the level of inorganic substances, one suggested the presence there of a mysterious will. This is not a conscious will, and neither does it seem to coincide with the Freudian unconscious drives. Goethe's novel appears to be hinting at the existence of an elemental will embedded deep within the human, a "demonic abyss" as Benno von Wiese calls it.[24]

One might be tempted to compare this to the quasi-scientific doctrine of *vitalism*, which was, in an early form, present in Schelling's philosophy of nature (developed in the late 1790s), and which generally maintains the existence of a cosmic life force at work in all of nature, including human beings. This is not, at least to my mind, an apt basis on which to read Goethe's novel because Ottilie's involuntary passion does not work solely in the service of life, but is also aligned with death. One should be careful to note that Ottilie, in all her resolve, is not able to quench or overcome her passion for Eduard even after she has stopped eating and speaking. When she moves back into the castle after the confrontation with Eduard at the inn, it is as if she goes on existing like one of the living dead. It is difficult to determine whether she is upheld by her passion or by her strenuous fight with the passion, but either way the result is *unheimlich*: Both she and Eduard now behave strangely, like two chemical compounds in the grip of the *attractio electiva*:

> They were living under one roof; but even without exactly thinking of one an-
> other, busy with other things, pulled this way and that by the company they were
> in, still they drew near to one another. If they were in a room together before
> long they were standing or sitting side by side. (p. 478/229)

The passage echoes Goethe's lectures on anatomy quoted above, in which he speaks of the external determinations that "tear or push [the] substances here and there." Indeed Eduard and Ottilie now behave more like puppets than human beings, heedless of their own movements and the force that draws them close to one another. When Eduard is first confronted with Ottilie's muteness at the inn, he exclaims: "are we only shades (Schatten) that we

---

24 Goethe: *Werke* 1, p. 674.

face one another thus?" (p. 473/224). The disquieting notion that they are, in a way, already dead, is confirmed by the narrator when he describes the last days of their cohabitation at the castle: "their domestic round was the illusory image of their former life" (p. 479/229). The German original uses the word "Scheinbild", which is explained in Grimm's German dictionary as an image which only has the semblance, not the essence, of the represented thing.[25] The example cited by Grimm is another quotation from Goethe, which uses the word to refer to the fleeting image left on the retina after an object has been removed from sight. In using this word, the narrator in *The Elective Affinities* underscores the shadowy nature of Eduard and Ottilie's co-existence under the spell of the demon, a life which is reminiscent of the shadows of the underworld. This life, says the narrator, is "a mystery to them", as indeed it is to the reader. They seem to live in a state of forgetfulness until Ottilie suddenly comes face to face with social reality as she walks into a room where Mittler is making a speech in which he recommends that everyone show "reverence for the marriage bond" (p. 482/233). Knowing that her passion for Eduard will forever make such a reverence impossible for her, she collapses and dies.

As far as I have been able to determine, no-one has yet presented an interpretation of the novel that can decisively explain all these phenomena through one single interpretative framework.[26] We have presented here an attempt to explain how Goethe establishes a demonic sphere in his narrative through the use of the chemical theory of the elective affinities. Both the chemical analogy and the category of the demonic are central to the development of the novel's plot, but no single formulation of either can account for everything that occurs. When confronted with the loose ends that this novel will inevitably present to any interpreter, one may find solace in Goethe's own statement on the novel: "I cannot myself uphold what it has become".[27]

---

25 "[E]in bild, insofern es nur den anschein, nicht das wesen des abgebildeten dinges hat." "Scheinbild." Grimm and Grimm.

26 For a discussion of the many divergent interpretations of the novel, see Orle Tantillo, xiii–xxiii.

27 "Ich kann selbst nicht dafür stehen, was es geworden ist". Quoted after May, p. 107.

WORKS CITED

Adler, Jeremy: *Eine fast magische Anziehungskraft. Goethes Wahlverwandtschaften und die Chemie seiner Zeit.* Munich: C. H. Beck, 1987.

Adler, Jeremy: "Goethe's use of chemical theory in *Elective Affinities*" in Andrew Cunningham and Nicholas Jardine (eds.): *Romanticism and the Sciences.* Cambridge: Cambridge University Press, 1990. *Gesammelte Schriften.* Rolf Tiedemann and Hermann Schweppenhäuser (eds.), vol. 1/1. Frankfurt am Main: Suhrkamp Verlag, 1997.

Engelhardt, Wolf von: *Goethe im Gespräch mit der Erde. Landschaft, Gesteine, Mineralien und Erdgeschichte in seinem Leben und Werk.* Weimar: Verlag Hermann Böhlaus Nachvolger, 2003.

Goethe, J. W.: *Sämtliche Werke nach Epochen seines Schaffens. Münchener Ausgabe.* Karl Richter et al (eds.). Munich: Carl Hanser Verlag, 1987.

Goethe, J. W.: *Werke. Hamburger Ausgabe in 14 Bänden*, vol. 6. Erich Trunz and Benno von Wiese (eds.). Munich: Deutscher Taschenbuch Verlag, 2000.

Goethe, J. W.: *Elective Affinities,* trans. with an introduction and notes by David Constantine. Oxford: Oxford University Press, 1999.

Grimm, Jacob and Grimm, Wilhelm: *Deutsches Wörterbuch*, vol. 8. Moriz Heyne (ed.). Leipzig: Verlag von S. Hirzel, 1893.

May, Kurt: *Form und Bedeutung. Interpretationen deutscher Dichtung des 18. und 19. Jahrhunderts.* Stuttgart: Ernst Klett Verlag, 1957.

Orle Tantillo, Astrida: *Goethe's Elective Affinities and the Critics.* Rochester, NY: Camden House, 2003.

Royle, Nicolas: *The Uncanny.* Manchester: Manchester University Press, 2003.

STRINDBERG, CHEMISTRY, AND THE DIVINE

Henrik Johnsson, University of Aarhus

August Strindberg (1849-1912) maintained a lifelong interest in a wide range of scientific fields, among which chemistry took pride of place. His early chemical experiments in his parents' house were followed by academic studies in chemistry as part of his medical training. After the success of his novel *The Red Room* (1879) Strindberg embarked on an ambitious project to introduce the naturalist aesthetic of Émile Zola to Sweden, applying it to the realm of drama, the results of which are evident in plays such as *The Father* (1887).[1] After his naturalistic phase, during which Strindberg called himself an atheist and attempted to formulate a new moral code based on the theory of evolution, he chose to focus his energies on chemical experimentation and on writing what can best be described as scientific essays. These works were informed by his interpretation of the monism of Ernst Haeckel, and they have a decidedly poetic flavour. Written during the early to mid-1890s, texts such as *Antibarbarus I–II* (1894), *Introduction à une Chimie unitaire* (1895), and *Sylva Sylvarum I–II* (1896) are among Strindberg's least studied works. Their production was followed by a period in Strindberg's life that is characterised as his "Inferno crisis" in the standard biographies; this period was marked by Strindberg's gradual return to the Christian faith of his youth and his renunciation of positivist science and Darwinism. Emerging from this crisis, Strindberg returned to the literary stage with prose works such as *Inferno* (1897) and plays such as the first part of the *To Damascus* trilogy (1898).[2]

Strindberg's scientific-poetic texts are difficult to categorise; they tend to be a blend of ideas drawn from both contemporary scientific debates and the Western esoteric tradition, all the while blurring the line between science and fictional narrative. If they were to be judged according to the standards of modern science, they would be found lacking, primarily because Strindberg rejects the empirical method itself; he constructed a

---

1   Sw. *Röda rummet, Fadren*. All translations of titles and quotations are my own.
2   Sw. *Inferno, Till Damaskus*.

scientific system based primarily on his own personal observations and analogies which are established between different chemical elements on the basis of physical similarities. Strindberg is thus a "bad" scientist who first establishes a scientific and religious *Weltanschauung* and then proceeds to find the proof he needs to validate it. This line of criticism dominated the early reception of these works, effectively relegating them to a secondary status in the annals of Strindberg studies. However, this critique entirely misses the point: While these texts have not contributed to the development of modern science, Strindberg's (un)scientific method plays a pivotal role in works such as *Inferno*, where he employs it to great dramatic effect. A serious appraisal of Strindberg's scientific-poetic texts will lead to a more profound understanding of Strindberg not only as an author, but also as a Christian thinker who was deeply invested in the religious debates of his time.

Texts such as *Antibarbarus* are informed by the same worldview which permeates Strindberg's later novels, including *Inferno*. This new worldview is characterised by the interaction of God with humanity through the use of intermediary "powers", which communicate through signs and portents. This worldview excludes coincidence or mere chance as an explanation for the mysteries of existence. Strindberg retains his faith in monism and continues to believe in the possibility of the transmutation of chemical elements, and he sees nature as ordered by an invisible Creator. The order behind the apparent chaos of nature can only be perceived by one who has accepted the reality of the divine and trained himself to be both a scientist and an adept in the esoteric sense of the word. While Strindberg was interested in other scientific disciplines, the importance of the idea of transmutation to his work and his efforts to prove transmutation possible indicate that chemistry was the single most significant scientific discipline for him.

The following essay will trace the development of Strindberg's views on chemistry and alchemy, the latter of which he sees himself as reviving in the form of monism, in an attempt to explain what it is exactly that attracts him to chemistry. An emphasis will be placed on his literary portrayals of chemistry and chemists as such, while attention will also be drawn to the ideas and themes of his scientific texts. I will not pass judgement on the scientific merits of his works of chemistry; it is Strindberg the writer and chemistry as a source of literary imagery that are of interest here.

Strindberg's scientific texts of the 1890s are the least studied part of his oeuvre. Contemporary reviewers were generally unkind when discussing them, and they usually resulted in limited financial gains on Strindberg's part. Even some modern scholarship is dismissive when discussing Strindberg as a scientist, as in the following description by George B. Kauffman in his study of Strindberg's texts on chemistry: "Most of his experiments were crude, nonquantitative, and lacking in objectivity; as an impatient and amateur scientist, he worked impulsively and obsessively with a selective approach which seized upon 'evidence' apparently favoring his *idées fixes* of transmutation and the unity of matter yet which disregarded whatever observations did not support his hypothesis" (Kaufmann, p. 586). Yet Strindberg's scientific texts were important to him: Rather than writing fiction and drama, which would have helped support him and his family, he dedicated himself to formulating a new system of chemistry and expounding said system primarily in articles published in French esoteric journals such as *L'Initiation* and *L'Hyperchimie*. Strindberg scholars have generally been unsure what to make of these texts. The two volumes of Strindberg's scientific texts in the critical edition of his collected works, *Samlade verk* (*Naturvetenskapliga skrifter I & II*), are completely lacking in explanatory footnotes, which would certainly have been useful to readers not versed in the field of chemistry.[3]

The most aesthetically rewarding approach to Strindberg's scientific texts is to consider how they relate to his fiction. The Swedish Strindberg specialist Gunnar Ollén has noted that Strindberg saw science and literature as interwoven and not as separate entities; he always had a "scientific consideration when he wrote fiction" and "wanted to be the scientist who was a poet" (Ollén, p. 2). Ollén describes Strindberg as the scientist-psychologist who never lost sight of the real while writing texts with themes drawn from the realms of fantasy and the supernatural. Even when Strindberg searches for esoteric correspondances in nature he regards them from the perspective of the scientist. His method combines esotericism and science, which explains why he labels himself the "Zola of the Occult", an appellation that has been elucidated by the Strindberg scholar and translator Evert Sprinchorn. Sprinchorn notes that Strindberg sought to unify the realms of "inorganic and organic matter in one grand synthesis in which the universe would display a kind of order

---

3   All references to Strindberg's works are to this edition, abbreviated as *SV*, followed by volume and page number.

without having any teleological end". This synthesis would be informed by a "great cohering principle" which Strindberg termed the "coherence in the great disorder", an idea inspired by his reading of Linnaeus. While accepting the basic premise of evolution, Strindberg "applied it rigorously to all aspects of the physical universe" – if one thinks that complex life forms have evolved from single cell organisms, it is reasonable, according to Strindberg, to assume that matter has also evolved. Thus the concept of transmutation is perceived to be a "constant process in this universe, as was the transformation of inanimate matter into living spirit" (Sprinchorn, p. 252). Strindberg does not see the natural world as a finished product; the physical world we exist in is constantly shifting, and may be evolving toward something completely different. Thus it is necessary to question everything we assume we know about nature: Science alone is not sufficient as a method for understanding the natural world, which is in constant flux. Something else is needed as well.

This something is not only faith in a Creator without whom the natural world appears like a clock set in motion without any clockmaker having wound up the mechanism, to borrow a simile Strindberg uses to attack positivist science. Also necessary is the perspective of a poet, by which Strindberg means someone who is able to see connections and similarities where others would see only coincidence. The poet strives to reveal the hidden truths behind the surface of things: He actively chooses to disregard chance and instead sees significance in apparent randomness. Strindberg does not see the distinction between organic and inorganic matter as absolute; inorganic matter is anthropomorphised. The distinction is blurred by the language he uses to describe inorganic matter, as the Danish literary scholar Per Stounbjerg notes: "Elements fight and copulate, minerals are born, die and mate, iron breathes, the plants have nervous systems and emotions, trees have personalities". Chemical elements are described as being ruled by the same laws of attraction and repulsion as humans. The distinction between organic and inorganic becomes irrelevant, since "everything is life and obeys the same laws" (Stounbjerg, p. 174). There is no such thing as inanimate matter: Nature is shone through with the light of life. Indeed, all matter is basically the same; different elements are separated only by their properties, but even these change and adapt to new surroundings. As the Swedish academic Torsten Eklund has pointed out in his study of Strindberg's autobiography, it is the properties of the elements that indicate where they belong in the system of things; when a species of plant "shows a similarity to another in its way of life and its exterior appearance, Strindberg sees it as transitioning into the latter" (Eklund, p. 252). Strindberg's turn against positivism should be seen in this context: The idea of nature being simply a collection of dead materials is abhorrent to him, as a writer, as a scientist, and as a man of faith.

Strindberg's scientific texts should not be regarded merely as instances of (amateur) scientific writing but as latter-day essays on the relation between man, nature, and the divine in the vein of German Romantic *Naturphilosophie*. As such, they do not exceed the bounds of legitimate scientific research in Strindberg's time, particularly if one distinguishes between positivist science on the one hand and the monism of Ernst Haeckel and his followers on the other. Kauffman emphasises that Strindberg's "belief in the unity of matter was well within the realm of normative nineteenth-century chemistry"; chemists such as Humphry Davy, William Prout, and William Crookes all suspected that "Lavoisier's simple substances were not simple and that Dalton's atoms were compound bodies" (Kauffman, p. 588). Haeckel's statement that he could find nothing "absolutely mistaken or insane" in Strindberg's chemical treatise *Antibarbarus* (1894) – the title of which is perhaps best understood as "Against the Barbarian Scientists" – is telling (Grewe, p. 24). While texts such as *Antibarbarus* or *Sylva Sylvarum* (1896) do have the appearance of scientific works, they should rather be understood, in the words of the historian of science Christa-Vera Grewe, as "literature with scientific content" (Grewe, p. 32). When read as such, even the most technical of Strindberg's scientific essays help abolish what Grewe terms "the division between science and belief, between emotion and rational thought". The transmutation of base metal into gold is thus not merely a chemical process but also a means of attaining "human perfection", in the tradition of that particular subset of alchemists who from the seventeenth century onwards focused more on the idea of the development of the human soul than on the practical art of transmutation (Grewe, p. 41).[4] This process is best illustrated by Strindberg's *To Damascus* trilogy, a series of plays featuring both chemistry and alchemy that end with the protagonist's purification and rebirth to the Christian faith.

CHEMISTS AND CHEMISTRY IN THE
FICTION OF AUGUST STRINDBERG

With this in mind it is time to turn to a few representative examples of Strindberg's depictions of chemistry and alchemy. Alchemy in Strindberg's works tends to illustrate a conflict between science and religion: It is an

---

4   See also Coudert.

atheistic science which acts as a counterpart to the creative effort of God. This is the case in the fourth part of the narrative poem *Somnambulist Nights* (1884), where the narrator calls a child in an incubator a "homunculus", the humanoid creature supposedly created by Paracelsus and later used as a literary motif by Goethe and writers of the German Romantic period.[5] As Strindberg puts it, "a child can now be made by machine, and this is the apex of industry" (*SV* 15, p. 210). This criticism of modern science (the original Swedish is decidedly ironic) is continued in an address to science that describes it as a "shop ready to close" and as having gathered all living things in a hole and pressed them all together, producing a "liquid of life" from "dead matter" which is then bottled in a "retort" (*SV* 15, p. 211). This fluid is "distilled" until the "fifth series" is reached, the "essence" (*SV* 15, p. 212), which turns out to be an ape. Alchemical terms are used in this context to criticise modern science and the arrogance of scientists who believe themselves capable of replacing God by replicating the creation of life. The homunculus and the ape are not just products of science, they are proof that science has little to offer. Science has become a new religion, but the study of blood cells reveals only the surface of things, whereas "he who created it, whether master or apprentice, does not exist for the opponent, who believes in the shoe but not in the shoemaker". In the same vein the cell is described as being "installed as the highest being of the new faith". This criticism is continued in what amounts to a prayer to "protoplasma" and "primeval sludge", which ends with the statement that one cannot "nourish souls with cells" (*SV* 15, p. 213). Only the study of both the cell and the cell's creator can allow us to understand existence. The poem critiques the assumption that there is an inherent conflict between faith and science. According to Strindberg the conflict is non-existent, provided that one does not do away completely with God but instead integrates the divine into a scientific worldview.

The same synthesis is later explored during Strindberg's Inferno period of the late 1890s, when he actively seeks to reconcile science and faith, but this manner of perceiving nature and man is already present during his naturalistic phase of the 1880s. According to Strindberg's fictional autobiography, *Son of a Serving Maid* (1886), he took an interest in chemistry and the sciences early on, and he retained this interest throughout his life.[6] His scientific interest not only informs his worldview, it also influences how

---

5   Sw. *Sömngångarnätter på vakna dagar.*
6   Sw. *Tjänstekvinnans son.*

he depicts the workings of the human body and mind, as well as human relationships. Physical phenomena such as electricity are used even more frequently than alchemical terms in Strindberg's descriptions of human relations. It is within the context of his use of modern and ancient medical and psychological discourses that his references to alchemy should be understood. While he often describes strong-willed individuals as magnetisers capable of mesmerising other people, the concept of animal magnetism is updated with the use of electrical terms; such people are described as batteries capable of discharging electricity and receiving and storing the electricity of others. As with chemistry, the latest technological advances are put to use to illustrate human behaviour.

To give just one example of this tendency, the scene in the short story "The Rewards of Virtue" (*Married I*, 1884) in which Theodor pushes Augusta on a swing is described using electrical metaphors which are not entirely metaphorical: "When he felt the soft young body twitch and at the same time pressing against his it was as if an electric shock went through his entire nervous system."[7] He feels his "life force doubled" and imagines himself to be an "electrophoresis apparatus whose positive electricity during a discharge had joined with the negative (…) He had thus felt the reverse polarity of the female and now he knew what it meant to be a man" (*SV* 16, p. 37). These electrical metaphors are important in order to understand Strindberg's conception of the role and nature of men and women. When human beings are described as electrical batteries it is always the male who is seen as the positive electrical current, the giver, whereas the female is seen as negative, as the receiver. Strindberg uses this conception of gender to explain and justify his opposition to the women's liberation movement: For him, the natural role of men as producers and givers is to work and provide for their families, whereas women are by nature receivers and nurturers.

This is one example of how Strindberg modernises older discourses such as animal magnetism by associating them with modern technology. This blending of ancient and modern is likewise present when Strindberg writes about chemistry. He tends to describe chemical equipment as alchemical in order to enhance their sense of mystery, as in the short story "Building Anew" (*Utopias in Reality*, 1885), in which a chemical laboratory is described as "filled with secrets".[8] The story deals with the female protagonist's attempt at realising herself as a woman and is thus a

7   Sw. "Dygdens lön" in the story collection *Giftas*.
8   Sw. "Nybyggnad" in the story collection *Utopier i verkligheten*.

narrative about emancipation. The description of the laboratory accentuates how ill-equipped she is when entering university as a female student and a trainee doctor in an all-male class. The shape of the retort reminds her of "medieval gold-making, the test-tubes of the doctor's dark chamber, and the reagents in the jars of the mysteries of the apothecary". This passage ends with an instance of Strindberg's habit of using chemistry as a context for poetic imagery: "The chromic acid shone like the sunset; the sulphuric acid was blue like Lac Léman, and the arsenic acid glittered like frost on birch branches" (*SV* 19, p. 28). The sense of foreboding associated with the chemical equipment in the university is lacking in this description of poeticised nature.

The science of chemistry is not only metaphorically related to a sense of mystery, it is frequently associated with the idea of penetrating the secrets of nature in a literal sense. This theme is already present in *Son of a Serving Maid*, when Strindberg describes his chemical experiments while training to be a doctor. He describes the "roots of science" as "dry and boring", but he is more interested in analysing substances, which is "where the secrets begin". The process of analysing and filtering a fluid is to "penetrate some-what into the mysteries" (*SV* 20, p. 223). This idea also informs Strindberg's view of Linnaeus, whom he describes in the essay "The Secrets of the Flow-ers" (1888) as "a great poet who dedicated his life to the natural sciences".[9] The term "poet" is explained as "a gentleman with a sense of imagination, which is the ability to combine phenomena, perceive connections, arrange, and cull" (*SV* 29, p. 215). This poetic sense of the naturalist is compared to the artist who sees patterns and combines them, a process which was used by Linnaeus to create a classificatory system for plants. However, Linnaeus' taxonomy is considered to be flawed and thus has to be replaced by a new system; Strindberg sought to fashion such a system during the 1890s, when he wrote about the hidden order behind the chaos of nature. This was very much an esoteric project in that only the initiated, the poet-alchemist, was able to see these connections.

This world-view is most pronounced during Strindberg's Inferno period but it is firmly rooted in texts written during the 1880s. These two phases are bridged by the novel *By the Open Sea* (1890), in which the protagonist, a fishery inspector and dedicated scientist named Borg, arrives at an island in the archipelago with the task of teaching the local populace improved

---

9 Sw. "Blomstrens hemligheter".

methods of fishing.[10] He suspects that the inhabitants of the island engage in both adultery and incest. One adulterous couple is described as an affront against his sense of the natural order of things: It was as though he "in his laboratory had found an acid which since the creation of the world had only joined with a single base [and] had now joined with two". The incident makes him doubt the whole idea of progress and he feels that he is being transported back to a time when "wild herds of men lived" in a state of "mass existence before selection and variation had managed to stabilise individual existence and heredity" (*SV* 31, p. 16). This crime against the natural order ties in with a theme of degeneration which in Strindberg's works is associated with Ernst Haeckel's idea that the development of the individual recapitulates the development of the entire species. Degeneration is a reversal of this process, a "backwards evolution" to earlier evolutionary stages. The idea of progress in reverse is illustrated here by the metaphor of the unnatural mixing of chemical solutions.

Borg is portrayed as an atheist who tries to replace God by reshaping nature and creating life, which he attempts at a late stage in the novel, when he has gone insane after a failed relationship. The last letter he receives from Maria, his love interest, is burned unread; the sound is likened to the "spirit of the letter, as an alchemist would have put it" (*SV* 31, p. 163). Borg has installed a laboratory in his apartment and now tries to create life, but he refuses to take the "banal route of seeking out a woman". Instead he puts a "human seed" in an incubator and impregnates it with his own semen (*SV* 31, p. 176). He perceives that the cells begin to divide and is fully convinced that he has "solved the problem of the Homunculus" (*SV* 31, p. 177), but he accidentally kills off the imagined child. In the end Borg sails off and presumably dies in a scene in which the sea, representing nature, is described as the only true creator. Borg as chemist becomes an alchemist in an attempt at replacing God, but fails and dies. Here we see once more the conflict between science and religion being expressed in both chemical and alchemical terms; a conflict which science tends to lose in Strindberg's writing.

This defeat, however, only concerns an atheistic science which is allied with Darwinism. In Strindberg's late works science is reconciled with religion. Studying the natural world becomes a means of understanding God's design in the same way that studying world history reveals His intention for mankind. God reveals Himself to man through signs, for instance in *Inferno*

10 Sw. *I havsbandet.*

when the narrator believes that he has found traces of carbon in sulphur, which would prove that the scientific system of his day needed to be revised. Such connections between substances can only be perceived by disregarding what has previously been established about these substances. This questioning of scientific doctrine is portrayed in Strindberg's late novel *The Gothic Rooms* (1904) as typical of the *fin-de-siècle*.[11] Marcellin Berthelot's book on the origins of alchemy is described as having rehabilitated the practice of alchemy and thus "done the work of mysticism" without Berthelot realising it (*SV* 53, p. 86). The difference between alchemy and chemistry is said to be that the former regards as possible the transmutation of basic elements, an assumption to which Berthelot, William Crookes, and Jacob Berzelius lent credence, according to Strindberg. These chemists are seen as having laid the groundwork for the alchemical renaissance of the turn of the century. Strindberg makes use of these scientists to prove that earlier generations of alchemists were basically right, which in effect shows that science and faith need not necessarily be separate.

This attitude towards science and religion helps explain both Strindberg's attempts at making gold and his interest in Haeckel's monism. If everything is present in everything else, there is a fundamental unity connecting all things. If the poet-alchemist allows himself to believe that there is a hidden truth behind the surface of reality he will be able to make sense of both world history, man's existence, and God's role in creating the universe and guiding the actions of mankind. When the scientist acknowledges that theology is a necessary complement to science he understands that human beings are interconnected in much the same way as chemical compounds. In recognising the relationship between nature and the divine, the alchemist, who is both scientist and initiate, recognises the existence and workings of the divine. This realisation accounts for both Strindberg's interest in chemistry, his seemingly eccentric attempts at creating gold, and his criticism of the science of his day, which he attempts to disprove. In doing so he creates works of fiction which are some of the most enduring works of literary modernism.

---

11 Sw. *Götiska rummen.*

WORKS CITED

Coudert, Allison P.: "Alchemy IV: 16th-18th Century" in Wouter J. Hanegraaff (ed.): *Dictionary of Gnosis and Western Esotericism*. Leiden & Boston: Brill, 2006.

Eklund, Torsten: *Tjänstekvinnans son. En psykologisk Strindbergsstudie*. Stockholm: Bonnier, 1948.

Grewe, Christa-Vera: "August Strindberg und die Chemie" in *Sudhoffs Archiv, Zeitschrift für Wissenschaftsgeschichte*, vol. 68, no. 1, 1984, pp. 21-42.

Kauffman, George B: "Strindberg's Chemical and Alchemical Studies" in *Journal of Chemical Education*, vol. 60, no. 7, 1983, pp. 584-90.

Ollén, Gunnar: "Vandring i vaken dröm" in *Svensk litteraturtidskrift*, vol. 27, no. 1, 1964, pp. 1-5.

Sprinchorn, Evert: "The Zola of the Occult" in *Modern Drama*, vol. 17, no. 3, 1974, pp. 251-66.

Stounbjerg, Per: "Frihed til det unpræcise" in *Passage. Tidsskrift for litteratur og kritik*, no. 20-21, 1995, pp. 171-86.

Strindberg, August: *Samlade verk*. Stockholm: Norstedt, 1981-.

THE MYSTICAL POWER OF CHEMISTRY – A BLIND SPOT IN DAG SOLSTAD'S FIRST NOVEL, *IRR! GRØNT!*

Eivind Tjønneland, University of Bergen

INTRODUCTION

Dag Solstad (born 1941) is one of Norway's most influential contemporary authors. His early publications in the sixties set the standard for the rapid development of Norwegian modernism centred around the journal *Profil*. Influenced by the Polish author Witold Gombrowicz and his concept of *form*, Solstad tried to extend the modernist fight against clichés from language to life. In his first novel *Irr! Grønt!* (1969) the protagonist acts desperately and strategically against the superimposed forms or roles of society. This modernist project collapsed and lead the author, and the protagonist of his next novel *Arild Asnes 1970* (1971), into Maoism. In my opinion, the reason for this collapse could be better understood; this article will be a minor contribution to this end.

The theme of chemistry in *Irr! Grønt!* has been overlooked by previous research. This is no surprise: The plot's main concern, after all, is with the possibility of liberating the individual from the roles society forces him to play. The protagonist Geir Brevik tries, by means of a highly reflective game, to deconstruct the existing patterns of human action. This also involves instructing Brit Winkel to play roles in order to challenge her friend Benedikte Vik's conception of her identity as a woman. In doing so, Geir acts like a god who creates a new human being, a homunculus. In a central passage at the end of the novel Geir describes his plan as "a homunculus-plan". The consequences of this characterisation – however – seem to be repressed from the conscious level of his actions. The introduction of the homunculus-theme in the novel is rather abrupt, but a closer look reveals that at least references to chemistry, if not its fascination with the idea of creating human life, can be found throughout the novel. Geir idealises the chemists Karsten and his friend John Torud, and he has an almost religious experience upon entering the Chemistry Building at the University of Oslo. 270 square metres of the vast entrance hall of the Chemistry Building was decorated by the well-known Norwegian painter Per Krogh, but this fact is not mentioned by the narrator or his protagonist Brevik. On one wall there is a picture of a child, inviting consideration of the idea of a child created by the sciences. The homunculus theme is thus silently introduced. The creative power of chemistry is an implicit part of Geir's religious experience in the Chemistry Building.

THE PLOT

The protagonist is the 25 year old teacher Geir Brevik. At a party he runs into his old friend from school, Nils Hansson, and is introduced to Benedikte Vik, who works as a secretary. When they meet on a Sunday after the party, they decide to visit several art galleries in Oslo: The Emanuel Vigeland Museum, The Munch Museum and The National Gallery. Geir is deeply affected by Benedikte's attitude towards Thorvald Erichsen's "*Naken mann og to kvinner*" (*Naked man and two women*) in The National Gallery. With a quick ironic glance at the picture, in which a naked man stands before two Victorian women looking in awe and shame at the man's penis, she deconstructs this image of male superiority and reduces it to an affected expression of the painter's wishful dreams. Geir obviously identifies with the picture and feels as if he has also been deconstructed. In his paranoid way, he feels that the painting expresses something about himself, and he envies the secretary's detachment and freedom from the picture by which he himself is profoundly affected.

After this defeat, he decides to get even. Geir calls Benedikte and invites her to the cinema. He manipulates her during the commercials to make her identify with the false images of women whose "female mystique" is used to promote different products. But afterwards, it is he who is seduced by her. Then he meets Benedikte's friend Brit Winkel, with whom she shares a flat. Wanting to liberate Benedikte from the false images of femininity they have seen at the cinema and to deconstruct the role of 'woman' that she is playing, Geir approaches Brit. On Geir's advice, Brit steals all of Benedikte's underwear and practises mimicking her different expressions. In a final confrontation, Brit imitates Benedikte's facial expressions in a way that undermines her roleplaying. After defeating Benedikte, Brit at the end of the novel paints her mouth with lipstick, overdoing it so that she looks like a clown. She says she is experimenting, and Geir finds her grotesque mouth funny and liberating. Brit and Geir celebrate theatricality and role-playing as such, but they fail to establish a new order of social roles, or a definition of the relationship between art and life. The ending of the novel is open and ambivalent.

Fighting against the role created by society for women, is only one of Geir's modernist projects. There is much ideology to be confronted in other fields. As a school teacher, Geir tries to destroy the myth of Columbus for his 12-year-old pupils by depicting queen Isabella as a fat matron and Columbus as her little son, making it impossible for the boys to identify with Columbus as a hero. But he fails. They overthrow his attempt to destroy the myth by clinging to the ideals of their parents: when one of the pupils asks why Columbus did not take a Scandinavian Airlines flight to America, another pupil makes the point that he would have flown with PANAM. Geir's attempt to destroy the myth is thus itself destroyed by his pupils' absurd anachronistic interpretations. The children reproduce the values of their parents to defend themselves against Geir Brevik's rhetorical deconstruction of the Columbus myth. As such, they destroy the myth of Columbus in their own way. Geir, of course, is not against them discarding the Columbus myth. But their method worries him.

> They used technology to eradicate history. They used modernity, their own epoch, the times in which they themselves were raised, their daily comic strip myths. Their parents: Engineers, technicians, tradesmen with model airplanes as a dream and former hobby, CEOs and managers in the refrigerator business, in light metal, in automobile equipment, petrol station owners, chemists, engineers, engineers. (*Irr! Grønt!*, p. 70)[1]

The alliance of technology and applied science destroys history. This is a different way of destroying the Columbus-story from Geir's own subtle rhetorical critique of Western imperialism. There are no humanists among the parents, only technicians, engineers, and tradesmen. The parents work with cars, petrol stations, refrigerators, all inventions of the twentieth century. Engineers are mentioned three times. The pupils themselves idealise "astronauts and space engineers" (*Irr! Grønt!*, p. 70). Published the same year as the first landing on the moon, Solstad's novel echoes the fact that technology and natural sciences were very much present in the media. At the same time, Norway experienced its first student revolt. Among other things, the students protested against the "Welfare through Warfare State" and cooperation between the military, science and technology (Eriksen

---

1   All quotations from Solstad's novel are my translations.

et al. 2003, p. 198 ff.). Solstad's novel mirrors both of these contemporary tendencies – the idealisation of science and technology and the critique of established norms and gender roles – in an ambiguous way.

KARSTEN AND JOHN – CHEMICAL
RESEARCHERS AND ROLE MODELS

Apparently, neither the main characters nor their imitation and role-playing, have any connection with chemistry. But in the seduction of Geir, Benedikte's photos of a trip through Europe she took with her friend John Torud play an important role. John is a chemist, and the purpose of the trip was to attend a Chemistry Congress in Paris. He is friends with Karsten, who is a chemist as well, and also a friend of Geir and Nils from their schooldays (*Irr! Grønt!*, p. 24). Karsten is presented as an ideal for Geir and his friend Nils. Meeting his old friend Nils in Oslo after five years, he uses the figure of Karsten, to reconstitute the "old unity" between them while they are driving to the museums with Benedikte. Talking about Karsten is a ritual confirming their unity. Karsten is the "serious researcher" (*Irr! Grønt!*, p. 22), but he is also an athlete; his personal best in high jump is 1.86 metres (*Irr! Grønt!*, p. 23). Karsten is successful, a man who has "made it". At the party Geir has also been talking about Karsten in order to escape playing "young", a role he desperately hates. Nils and Geir discuss and even analyse Karsten extensively. He is "a researcher, wise, decisive" (*Irr! Grønt!*, p. 14). In the car the next day, Geir returns to the same topic; he has a new theory about Karsten, and Nils contradicts it because he says, is too one-sided (*Irr! Grønt!*, p. 21). But Benedikte is not interested in Karsten. Geir suspects that Nils has "betrayed" Karsten to Benedikte. This mind game gets complicated because Geir, in his somewhat paranoid way, has to take into consideration the fact that Benedikte already knows about Karsten.

Trying to revenge himself on Benedikte Vik for the humiliation (or the imagined humiliation) in The National Gallery, Geir conceives an intricate plan to destroy her identity and her dependence on entrenched images of womanhood. As mentioned, he takes her to the cinema and exaggerates his interest in the commercials. He interprets her bodily movements as she crosses her legs as a sign that she has "swallowed the picture", and Geir is determined not to let her "release" it.

But, paradoxically, from Geir's point of view, she manages to rid herself of the commercials' images of woman later the same evening by showing him amateur photographs of her trip to Europe with Torud. The pictures show John and Benedikte on their way to Paris so that Torud can attend an international congress of chemists (*Irr! Grønt!*, p. 149).

John is presented by Benedikte as Karsten's best friend (*Irr! Grønt!*, p. 148); he is a researcher and has been working on the same project as Karsten. Looking at Benedikte's photographs, Geir builds up his own picture of John:

> To Geir, the researcher John Torud became a mythical person. A friend of Karsten who traps Benedikte in a car and drives her through Europe to Paris. (…) And for a person standing outside, objectifying a trip made by others, the travel and the persons travelling became mythical. The images became something the onlookers aspired for, it became their reality. (*Irr! Grønt!*, p. 150)

When Geir hears that Karsten also attended the Chemistry Congress in Paris (*Irr! Grønt!*, p. 151), he longs to be shown a picture of Karsten. But he is not in any of the photographs, most of which had in fact been taken by him. "The ideal of Geir's youth had returned as photographer for the persons of the pictures" (*Irr! Grønt!*, p. 152). Karsten is therefore reduced to the same level as Brit; Karsten is the servant taking the pictures and Brit the servant displaying them. But John and Benedikte increase in significance. According to Geir's interpretation, letting Brit display the photos of herself and John makes it possible for Benedikte to liberate herself from the images shown at the cinema, from "the advertising girl within" (*Irr! Grønt!*, p. 153). The images create an objective myth, and Geir surrenders. Karsten is dethroned, he is behind the camera, outside the images, "down in the darkness where we all are situated" (*Irr! Grønt!*, p. 153). Thus Benedikte is rescued by her friend Brit. Brit is the less attractive of the two women. Geir speculates about their relationship: "Who is using whom? Does the attractive use the less attractive to appear more beautiful, unresistingly beautiful, making the contrast as grey as possible, or does the less beautiful use the beautiful one to take part in the beauty emanating from the attractive?" (*Irr! Grønt!*, p. 143).

Telling the story or displaying the images alone, Benedikte would have only succeeded in making herself appear ridiculous. Only through her medium Brit can she be recreated as an image and a myth. The effect is described as enchanting ("fortryllelse"; *Irr! Grønt!*, p. 154). The pictures express a myth about natural behaviour. Benedikte and John pose before the camera as if it were a matter of course. Without the pictures, whatever happened between John and Benedikte could have been discarded as "unreal" (*Irr! Grønt!*, p. 155). Pictures become more real than reality, and looking at them is both a cult and a ritual: The audience wishes to be a part of the photos, to realise them. This doubling of the subject and its representation is magical. But what is the connection to chemistry? Why did Solstad choose chemists as mythical heroes and pictures of a trip to a chemistry conference as the instrument of seduction?

A simple answer would be that at the time, the natural sciences exerted a greater influence than the arts and humanities. Geir has a relationship with history, art galleries, concerts, and theatre. He has already lost the battle between the two cultures when his pupils, by means of technology, frustrate his attempt to deconstruct the story of Columbus's discovery of America. But the power of chemistry does not merely consist in its "real" power to form human lives through technology.

CHEMISTRY AS RELIGION

After sleeping with Benedikte, Geir visits the University of Oslo in order to find her friend Brit, with whom she shares her flat. Brit studies philology, and Geir first visits the Faculty of Humanities. But, significantly enough, Geir ends his expedition elsewhere. When he fails to find Brit, he walks to the Chemistry Building to find the chemist Karsten:

> But Karsten, on the other hand. The researcher Karsten, he was here too. Since Brit apparently was sunk into the ground, he decided to visit Karsten. He made his way to the Chemistry Building. He came into an enormous hall. The effect was overwhelming, and he stood for a time and looked around, astonished. (*Irr! Grønt!*, p. 169)

The place described cannot be any other than the main entrance to the Physics and Chemistry building at the University of Oslo (see illustrations pp. 267, 270, 272). The two side wings, now called the Chemistry Building, were built in 1966-8 and do not match the description given here. The building has a certain effect on Geir which we would normally not associate with the natural sciences:

> Geir experienced a weird mood, a mood which he had not felt for many years, a mood he thought he would not experience again, and which he would have been glad not to experience again. He felt as if he were entering a church, no, a cathedral, and he knew that the mood of reverence which now possessed him consisted of reminiscences of his own religiousness, now forgotten and repressed since the heyday of puberty. (*Irr! Grønt!*, p. 169-70)

Per Krogh's decoration of the entrance hall of the Chemistry Building. Copyright: University of Oslo. Photo: Bernt Rostad.

The decorative paintings of Per Krogh are not mentioned by Solstad. Krogh's frescos and glass paintings cover three of the walls, each one 10 x 9 metres. Light comes in through the southern glass wall. Several pictures by Edvard Munch and Thorvald Erichsen are described in detail at the beginning of Solstad's novel. It is therefore odd that Krogh's massive paintings, covering almost 300 square metres, are not mentioned at all. The experience of the Chemistry Building as a sacred place is described as the effect of space and not of the paintings themselves.

Through the construction of a reception room within another room with glass walls, through the allusions to side wings, which could be entered through double doors, through the allusions to cellars, the basement, auditoria in cellars and the basement, etc., the building attained a mystical function. And this was done with great audacity, because it is very rare that one could stress mystical elements, in our times, without being ludicrous. But here it was tenable. And there could be no other reason than this being the Chemistry Building at the University of Oslo (a similar building for philologists would have been ludicrous, unthinkable). This was the Chemistry Building, here research on the elements and the compounds of elements was conducted, and here the results of research on the elements and the compounds of elements were given to others, who in their turn would give others knowledge of the results of research on the elements and the compounds of elements. Auditoria in cellars, research in cellars and basements. That was tenable. Chemistry stands strong, it could bear a mystical function, and that which could bear a mystical function would stand even stronger when it really had received such a function. Therefore this building was a tribute, and those men who daily walked around in a building which was a tribute to what they were doing must be very confident, very proud men. It struck Geir that John Torud must be a very powerful man, that he would not lose his power even outside the photos. For this man, himself a researcher, had been photographed by a researcher who daily walked around in a room which was a tribute to what he was doing.

When a hall could create such an atmosphere of mysticism and ritual, anybody not himself consecrated to what the room was made for would feel like an intruder. Geir was not a chemist, and when he got closer to the small white clothed figures at the far end, which got larger as he got nearer (at which moment he discovered that they were not all clothed in white), he felt small. Had it been a student he was after, he would have turned around, but the certainty that he was looking for a researcher gave him the security to get closer to those who were at the end of the hall (…). (*Irr! Grønt!*, p. 170-71)[2]

Why is there no mention here of Krogh's paintings? The comparison with cathedrals or churches – buildings that usually contain works of art – could have inspired Geir to describe Per Krogh's frescos. This omission can be interpreted as a blind spot in the novel that indirectly shows the boundaries of Geir's conscious project, the war against images, roles, myths, and behavioural patterns.

The title of the novel *Irr! Grønt!* (*Copper! Green!*) is in fact a reference to the green copper of statues and churches, the "true colour of Europe" (*Irr! Grønt!*, p. 137). Geir explicitly wants to liberate himself from the history and myths of Europe, from Icarus, Prometheus (*Irr! Grønt!*, p. 38), and Columbus.

---

2   "Gjennom konstruksjonen av et resepsjonsrom innenfor et annet glassrom, gjennom hentydninger til sidefløyer, som man måtte passere gjennom dobbelt sett av dører, gjennom hentydninger til kjellere, underetasjen, auditorier i kjellere og underetasjen, osv. var det oppnådd å gi bygningen en mystisk funksjon. Og dette var meget dristig gjort, for det er meget sjelden at man kan understreke mystiske elementer, i vår tid, uten at det blir latterlig. Men her holdt det. Og det kunne ikke være noen annen grunn til at det holdt, enn at dette var Kjemibygningen ved Oslo Universitet (En lignende bygning for filologer ville ha vært direkte latterlig, utenkelig). Dette var kjemibygningen, her ble det forsket i grunnstoffer og grunnstoffers forbindelser og her ble resultatene av forskningen i grunnstoffer og grunnstoffers forbindelser formidlet videre til andre, som igjen i sin tur skulle gi andre viten om resultatene av forskningen i grunnstoffene og grunnstoffenes forbindelser. Auditorier i kjellere, forskning i kjellere og underetasjer. Det holdt. Kjemi står sterkt, det tåler en mystisk funksjon, og det som tåler en mystisk funksjon vil stå enda sterkere når det virkelig har fått en slik funksjon. Derfor var denne bygningen en hyllest, og de menn som daglig gikk omkring i en bygning som var en hyllest til det de drev på med, måtte være meget selvbevisste, meget stolte menn. Det slo Geir at John Torud måtte være en meget mektig mann, at han ikke ville miste sin styrke selv utenfor bildene, for denne mannen, selv en forsker, var blitt fotografert av en forsker som daglig gikk omkring i et rom som var en hyllest til det han drev på med.

      Når en hall kan inngyte en slik atmosfære av mystikk og ritus, vil enhver som ikke selv er innvidd til det rommet er bygd for, føle seg som en inntrenger. Geir var ikke kjemiker, og da han nærmet seg de små hvitkledde skikkelsene lengst borte, som ble større etter hvert som han kom nærmere (og da oppdaget han at ikke alle var hvitkledde), følte han seg liten. Hadde det vært en student han var på jakt etter, ville han ha snudd, men vissheten om at han var på jakt etter en forsker, ga ham sikkerhet til å nærme seg dem som oppholdt seg i enden av hallen (…)" (*Irr! Grønt!*, p. 170-1).

Entrance to the Chemistry Building from the south side. Copyright: University of Oslo. Photo: Bernt Rostad.

But other works of art that are described in the book, such as the statue of the famous Norwegian romantic poet Henrik Wergeland in front of the National Theatre in Oslo (*Irr! Grønt!*, p. 210) and the background colour of Thorvald Erichsen's painting of one man and two women, are also in fact copper green. These facts are not mentioned in the novel, but have significance (see Tjønneland: "Eggentlighet og dualitet"). Their omission suggests that there is a repressed level in the description of known art works which could be of importance for understanding the book. These repressed aspects function at the imaginary level as tacit knowledge and serve a mythical purpose. Geir Brevik becomes aware of the homunculus myth while fighting other myths. Geir himself enacts a mythical pattern when he tries to fight the myth; this phenomenon is well known from Greek tragedy to Adorno and Horkheimer's *Dialectics of Enlightenment*.

HOMONCULUS

As mentioned above, Geir instructs his agent Brit Winkel to play the role of Benedikte in order to break Benedikte's constructed feminine façade. She becomes his puppet. When she has finished her training and is prepared to defeat Benedikte, Geir spontaneously decides to buy Brit a pair of shoes. But when her foot is set forward to try the shoe on, something goes wrong: The foot is dead (*Irr! Grønt!*, p. 229). It is dead because she is not imitating Benedikte, it is "dead when Brit and not 'Benedikte' buys new shoes". Geir, by instructing Brit and giving her character life, makes her unnatural: He now experiences some uncalculated consequences of his actions.

> But it went wrong. Geir was scared, scared of all of it, everything, the room had shifted, a twisted mouth, the foot, the dead unmoving foot and the face that belonged to it and which didn't know what to do with itself, what was it? The homunculus plan, Geir's plan was a homunculus plan, he was scared, scared, because now it was exposed. The life he had breathed into Brit was no longer enough, her foot was dead, lifeless, when she was about to get new shoes, dead when it did not imitate that she was getting new shoes (…). (*Irr! Grønt!*, p. 230-1)

It seems that this mention of a homunculus is unprepared[3]. But as we have seen, Geir has been idealising his old friend Karsten and later on John Torud. Before he meets with Brit Winkel in order to use her as a means to attack Benedikte, he has a religious experience in which he must have seen a representation of the power of chemistry to create a human being, as Krogh's painting "Bårnets første skridt" (p. 272) could indeed be interpreted. He has "devoured the picture", and re-enacts it in a mythical way. On a mythical scale, Geir Brevik tries to imitate the chemists he knows, recreating Brit as Benedikte. Playing God in this way has some unforeseen consequences, and therefore the novel ends ambiguously.

An important part of Geir Brevik's project, that is, his own tendency to construct roles and patterns, is caused by his own irrationality. He too easily gets the feeling that there is a "pattern" behind all actions. In this way he resembles Erving Goffman, who also constructed a lot of roles and extended the role concept in sociology from the traditional connection to status and position, as by Ralph Linton (Tjønneland: "Rolle og identitet"). Geir's hyper-reflective consciousness constructs "roles" and "patterns" where

---

3　Solstad could also have been influenced by the Swedish author Sven Delblanc's (1931-92) novel *Homunculus* (1965), which has a chemist as its protagonist. Delblanc's novel is about the drunken and debauched chemist Sebastian who is deprived of his job after a laboratory fire, and creates a monster in the bathtub out of blood, urine, and a secret elixir. A comparison of the two novels would transgress the boundaries of this paper.

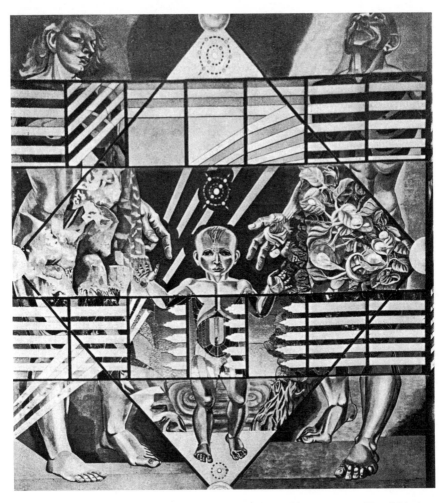

Per Krogh's "Barnets første skridt". Krogh described the subject of his painting as "The child taking his first steps alone without any supporting hands, a planet starts its wandering." Or is it a representation of a homunculus?

there in fact are none. He has the positivistic tendency of regarding human action as a physical object, comparing humans to robots and mechanical devices, viewing them as machines to be understood. In deconstructing established roles, myths, and images in society, he also in a way transgresses the boundaries between the humanities and the natural sciences: not by means of chemistry, but by imitating the power of the natural sciences. He has several times been outwitted by science and technology and therefore unconsciously imitates his master.

Before the homunculus is mentioned at the end, chemistry is not used explicitly as a metaphor in the novel. Nowhere is chemistry linked to the

LITERATURE AND CHEMISTRY

chemical aspect of photography or to love as "attraction" between persons. But Karsten and John Torud are chemists and they differ greatly from Geir himself: Both researchers are successful and they have no problems with role playing – they are "natural". In Geir's opinion, they take part in the (scientific) development of society without asking questions about their roles.

From the perspective of a brooding paranoid like Geir, chemists have no problems: He would therefore like to be one himself. His idealization of chemistry has less to do with actual knowledge of this field of research. But Solstad's novel demonstrates convincingly to what extent mythology directs our lives.

WORKS CITED

Delblanc, Sven: *Homunculus. A magic tale.* Englewood Cliffs, NJ: Prentice Hall, 1969.
Eriksen, Trond Berg, Hompland, Andreas and Tjønneland, Eivind: *Et lite land i verden.* Norsk Idéhistorie, vol. 6. Oslo: Aschehoug, 2003.
Solstad, Dag: *Irr! Grønt!.* Oslo: Forlaget Oktober, 2001.
Tjønneland, Eivind: "Eggentlighet og dualitet. Dag Solstads tenkning om den hellige ånd" in *AGORA*, vol. 3. Oslo, 1984, pp. 75-96.
Tjønneland, Eivind: "Rolle og identitet i postmodernistisk perspektiv" in Ed. T. Deichman-Sørensen and Ivar Frønes (eds.): *Kulturanalyse.* Oslo: Gyldendal, 1990, pp. 182-97.
Uhberg, Ulla: "Atomet i verdensrommet", 2010, www.uio.no (27 October 2012).

POETICS OF CHEMISTRY
AND ALCHEMY

"THE PHOSPHORESCENCE OF PUTREFACTION AND THE SCENT OF THUNDERSTORMS": APPROACHING A BAUDELAIREAN METAPHOR BY WAY OF LITERATURE AND CHEMISTRY

Margery Vibe Skagen, University of Bergen

He who looks from the outside through an open window never sees as much as he who looks through a window closed. No deeper, more mysterious, more fertile, more obscure, more dazzling object exists than a window lit by a candle. What you can see in sunlight is always less interesting than what goes on behind a windowpane.

In that dark or luminous gap, life lives, life dreams, life suffers.[1]

The purpose of this chapter is to explore the metaphoric charge of *phosphorescence*, with special reference to its presence in the critical works of Charles Baudelaire. While expressing his deep admiration for Edgar Allen Poe's writing and Eugène Delacroix's painting, Baudelaire repeatedly comes back to their "supernatural and galvanic glow", suggestive of captured nervous tension or of some mysteriously projected mental power. In different contexts, the poet-critic renders this tension in images of light emanating from decaying matter or lightning from dark clouds.[2] We wish to demonstrate that in Baudelaire's aesthetic universe, phosphorescence is not merely a stereotypical gothic accessory like the spectral atmosphere of haunted houses, the sulphurous halo of demons, or the gleam of cats' eyes, but a structuring metaphor in which are encompassed essential components of his Romanticism and supernaturalism. The uncertain glow transpiring from dead material may be perceived as an uncanny token of the invisible, the unknown, and the infinite. But the metaphor and its analogues seem to al-

---

1   Baudelaire: "Les Fenêtres". *Le Spleen de Paris* (*OC* I: 339). The abbreviation *OC* refers to Baudelaire, *Œuvres complètes I–II*. Where no specific translation is cited, all translations of Baudelaire are my own.

2   Our main example is from *E. A. Poe: sa vie et ses oeuvres* (*OC* II: 317-18) published in 1856. The magical aura of supernaturalism is described with reference to Delacroix in, among other places, the *Salon de 1846* (*OC* II: 440), *Exposition universelle* (*OC* II: 594), and the *Salon de 1859* (*OC* II: 636). It is connected to intoxication in "Le Poème du haschisch" (*OC* I: 430 and 436).

lude to more specific discourses as well: alchemical, medical, aesthetic and literary. Our intention is to untangle some threads of association flowing out from the figure of phosphorescence, to find a pattern or constellation of ideas that would explain why it seems so suggestive.

Our attempt to blend chemical history with literary analysis has produced a twofold structure. In order to present the potential richness of the metaphor, the first part takes us through the history of phosphorus and phosphorescence, stopping briefly at crossroads of mythology, alchemy, chemistry, medicine, and art. This historical introduction to the general imagery of phosphorescence, illustrated by literary examples from Honoré de Balzac and Théophile Gautier, is followed by the second part's close reading of a significant extract from one of Baudelaire's articles on Poe. This part's consideration of how the poet and critic exploits the aesthetic potential of phosphorescence in contexts where the praise of his preferred artists reaches the level of apotheosis, takes us from art criticism, back to alchemy and from the alchemist to the Luciferian artist.

Throughout the chapter we refer to phosphorescence in a wide sense, as it has been observed in the natural (especially the organic) world and described since Aristotle and up to Baudelaire's time. We evoke popular conceptions of the same phenomena, as well as early scientific or pseudo-scientific explanations of phosphorescence as the main characteristic of the chemical element phosphorus.[3] But primarily we will refer to phosphorescence as a metaphor, applied to pictures and texts: as a figure of aesthetic value.

PHOSPHORESCENCE: NATURAL PHENOMENA
WITH SUPERNATURAL CONNOTATIONS

Anyone experiencing phosphorescence or luminescence unprepared will be intrigued by the sight of it, whether shimmering on the surface of the sea, in the form of wavering fireflies, or as the glimmer of putrid biological matter. These eerie nocturnal phenomena, appearing in dark waters, marshes,

---

3   Today one distinguishes between *phosphorescence* and *luminescence*: *phosphorescence* is "the process whereby light is first absorbed by a body and then re-emitted from it some time later; Bologna stone is phosphorescent." Phosphorus itself is luminescent. "*Luminescence* describes the process in which light is emitted as a result of an energy change within a substance." *Bioluminescence* is the correct term for the glow produced by certain living things and decaying biological matter (Emsley, p. 17). We will in this context use the term *phosphorescence* indistinguishably.

and graveyards, have naturally been surrounded by mystery and fantastical explanations. The fugitive light of the fire fairies (*ignis fatuus*) – known in European superstition as will-o'-the-wisp, fool's fire, *Irrfeuer*, or *feu follet* – also had a wicked reputation. Will-o'-the-wisps were said to mislead lone wanderers with their elusive light.[4]

Besides its scientific and pseudo-scientific meanings, the term *phosphorescence* may in a nineteenth-century literary context be as rich in mythological connotations as it is in folkloric denominations. *Phosphorescence* is derived from *Phosphorus*, meaning "light-bearer", the name of the morning star, also known as the planet Venus or the star of Aphrodite when she appears brightest in the sky before sunrise. In literary contexts up to the early nineteenth century, long after the discovery of the chemical element, *Phosphorus* is still primarily used as the Greek name of the morning star, whose Latin equivalent is *Lucifer*. But Lucifer, as we know, was also the name of the rebel archangel, cast down from heaven and identified in the Christian tradition with Satan. We will see that Baudelaire's metaphoric use of phosphorescence may be connected to his idealisation of Satan "– à la manière de Milton" (*OC* I: 658):

> (…) Lucifer from Heaven
> (So call him, brighter once amidst the host
> Of Angels, than that Starr the Starrs among,)
> Fell with his flaming legions through the deep (Milton VII, ll. 131-134)

As a common noun, *phosphorus* had long been used for all kinds of luminescent phenomena in Nature: Diderot and d'Alembert's *Encyclopedia* (1751-65) includes meteors, thunder, and lightning under the category "Phosphore", relating all "phosphoric" light to the equally mysterious force of electricity. To the naïve observer, the most persuasive factor in all these phenomena would be the fright and fascination of *light coming forth from the dark*.[5]

---

4   In contemporary use, as defined by the *OED*, *will-o'-the-wisp* means: "*fig.* a thing (rarely a person) that deludes or misleads by means of fugitive appearances". One quoted example is from Thomas Henry Huxley: *Science & Culture* (p. 247), which uses the term to suggest delusion by stagnated, inbred, and unhealthy ideas: "The metaphysical Will-o'-the-wisps generated in the marshes of literature and theology."

5   Cf. the title of an alchemical treatise in verse by Otto Tachenius: *La Lumière sortant par soi-mesme des ténèbres ou veritable théorie de la pierre des philosophes* (1693).

Joseph Wright of Derby's famous painting from 1771 of the discovery of the chemical element phosphorus may have contributed to the mythical and magical reputation of the glowing substance: *The Alchymist, in Search of the Philosopher's Stone, Discovers Phosphorus and Prays for the Successful Conclusion of his Operation, as was the Custom of the Ancient Chymical Astrologers.* It was the mathematician and philosopher Gottfried Wilhelm Leibniz who established that the discoverer of the element phosphorus was the alchemist Hennig Brandt of Hamburg (Weeks, p. 345). In 1669 Brandt had managed to produce a white waxy substance that gleamed continuously in the dark with a pale green light, but without any perceptible heat. This "cold fire", as he named it, was produced by boiling gallons of putrid urine down to the dry solid. He tried to keep his recipe secret, but the news spread and in a few years other chemists were demonstrating phosphorus as "perpetual fire" all over Europe and in America.

Leibniz was himself very engaged in alchemy and believed in the possibility of finding the philosophical stone. In 1676 he had been appointed librarian and councillor to the court of Duke Johan Friedrich of Saxony, and after seeing a demonstration of phosphorus, he encouraged his employer to give Brandt a position as court alchemist. Brandt came to Hanover and showed Leibniz his method of producing phosphorus, and Leibniz made plans for mass production of the substance. Much later these plans would be formalised by others, as the method of extracting phosphorus from animal bones was industrialised in the nineteenth century.

It seems clear that much of the excitement and secrecy around Brandt's discovery had to do with expectations of actually producing gold. From the beginning there was a great fascination with the substance among alchemists and chemists, since its luminescence could also be identified with the "vital flame" or associated with "the universal light", – drawn forth from chaos, as on the first day of creation.[6]

---

6   The writer and gardener John Evelyn describes "an experiment of a wonderful nature" he witnessed in 1685. Two unidentified liquids were mixed in a glass: "It first produced a white cloud, then boiling, divers coruscations and actual flames of fire mingled with the liquor, which being a little shaken together, fixed divers sunns and starrs of real fire, perfectly globular, on the sides of the glasse, and which there stuck like so many constellations, burning most vehemently, and ressembling starrs and heavenly bodys, and that for a long space. It seemed to exhibite a theorie of the eduction of light out of the chaos, and the fixing or gathering of the universal light into luminous bodys. This matter or phosphorus was made out of human blood and

Real gold was certainly made later on, especially from the beginning of 1800 when phosphorus matches began to be produced on an industrial scale. The *Lucifer* matches Samuel Jones started making in 1830 were soon the world's bestselling brand, praised by Herbert Spencer as "the greatest boon and blessing to come to mankind in the nineteenth century" (Emsley, p. 65). Baudelaire might even have used a brand called *Fusées*, not just to light his cigars, but also as an inspiration for the title of his collection of whims, ideas, and "suggestions" in the manner of Edgar Poe.

AN EXPERIMENT ON PHOSPHORESCENCE IN THE AIR-PUMP

The alchemist discovering phosphorus was an ideal subject for the painter Joseph Wright's celebrated chiaroscuro technique. In the same artist's even more famous painting, *An Experiment on a Bird in the Air-Pump* from 1768, his use of light celebrates the new prominence and awe-inspiring power of science. In the setting of a nocturnal interior, the faces are highlighted, turned to each other or towards the suffocating white bird in the pneumatic machine; but equally luminous is the glass receptacle at the heart of the picture, containing an unidentifiable object immersed in opaline water. The object is generally assumed to be a human skull, partly decayed.[7] The light seems to come from a candle or a lamp behind the bowl, but also from the puzzling object itself. Perhaps the work of Robert Boyle, the inventor of the air-pump, can give us a clue to what it is.

Known as one of the founding fathers of chemistry, Robert Boyle managed to distil phosphorus from urine shortly after Brandt's discovery, and was the first chemist to examine the properties of the luminous substance in a systematic way. Boyle's first encounter with this "strange rarity", as it was demonstrated to him and several other members of the Royal Society by a "famous German Chymist" in 1677, is related in *A Short Memorial*, which describes in terms of the sublime the "mixture of strangeness, beauty and frightfulness" he experienced as the phosphorescent capital letters of the word DOMINI appeared in the dark room (Boyle, p. 60). When exhibiting experiments of this kind, the chemical *artists* – and Boyle followed their example – would impress their audience by dipping a finger in liquid phosphorus and drawing dimly shining lines with it.

---

urine, elucidating the vital flame or heate in animal bodys. A very noble experiment" (Evelyn, pp. 195-6).

7   See www.nationalgallery.org.uk.

Robert Boyle wrote two accounts of *Aerial and Icy Noctiluca* (1681/82) and is known to have tested the effect of a vacuum on putrid, luminescent material, proving that the glow was dependent on air since it was slowly quenched in a vacuum (Dobson X, p. 45). As a member of the Lunar Society, Joseph Wright, the portrayer of phosphorus's discoverer, would have been informed about Boyle's investigations. He may also have heard about the recent discovery of the relatively high concentration of phosphorus in the brain. We may therefore ask if the object presumed to be a skull, in the middle of the picture of the experiment with the air-pump, was presented as phosphorescent, and if phosphorescence were part of the show. The scientific demonstration is dramatised and even sacralised (or demonised) by the chiaroscuro technique; but if the experiment with the pneumatic machine was not only to be tried on a bird, but also on phosphorescence, that would justify the use of a night performance. Most spectators find the expression of the scientist deeply equivocal, posing as the impassive master of life and death, quenching the spark of life in the poor bird, then stirring and stilling the hidden fire in dead human material with his sophisticated machine.[8]

PHOSPHORUS THERAPIES FOR PHOSPHORESCENT BRAINS

The history of phosphorus, as narrated by John Emsley in his *Biography of the Devil's Element,* was not only shaped by the search of gold, with its good and evil consequences for humankind. The alchemical quest for the elixir of life was also practical, pharmaceutical research for a remedy that would cure all diseases. As soon as phosphorus was discovered, and in spite of it being deadly poisonous, the newfound element was immediately launched as a miracle medicine and sold in various forms, especially as a remedy for nervous ailments. It was used to cure melancholia from the start, and even at the end of the nineteenth century it was still recommended against nervous fatigue or neurasthenia. Phosphorus therapies were strongly encouraged by Johan Hensing's 1719 discovery that particularly high levels of phosphor

---

8   Diderot and d'Alembert's *Encyclopédie* describes l'abbé Nollet's pneumatic machine, used to experiment with animals, and with burning and so-called phosphorescent material ("Pneumatique" 34: 204). In French eighteenth- and nineteenth-century literary contexts the air-pump is generally associated with suffocation, torture, and oppression.

existed in the brain.[9] The conclusions drawn from this fact were that the mentally slow and disabled had too little phosphorus, while the mentally unstable genius had too much. In his principle work, *Rapports du physique et du moral de l'homme*, published in 1802, the French physiologist Pierre Cabanis describes the visible effects of this difference:

> In animal bodies in a state of decomposition, phosphorus seems to undergo a slow combustion: Without producing any veritable flame, as it is usually incapable of igniting neighbouring combustible bodies, it becomes luminous and diffuses a bright light in the dark, providing, more than once, great consistency to those visions which are dreaded but also sought after in graveyards. The parts that appear to be the special reservoir of phosphorus are the brain and its appendices, or rather the whole nervous system; for it is the beginning decomposition of the cerebral pulp which causes the phosphoric luminescence that is so often seen at night in the amphitheatres; and it is mostly around the brains laid bare, or around their debris on the dissecting tables, that this light is noticed. Now a considerable number of observations make me presume that the quantity of phosphorus which develops after death is proportional with the activity of the nervous system in life. It has seemed to me that the brains of individuals who had died of maladies characterized by excessive nervous activity diffused a stronger and brighter light. Those of maniacs are very luminous; those of hydropics and leuco-flegmatics much less. (Cabanis, pp. 380-1)[10]

To Cabanis, it appears that the nervous system, with the varying amounts of phosphorus it contains, is a reservoir of electricity. Thirty years later, the French physicist Antoine Becquerel (1788-1878) defines phosphorescence as an effect of electricity in a treatise on electricity and magnetism, but is very cautious when it comes to identifying the chemistry of consciousness.[11] The

---

9   Cf. Tower: *Hensing, 1719, An account of the first chemical examination of the brain and the discovery of phosphorus therein.*

10   My translation. For Cabanis' sources see Tower: *Brain Chemistry and the French Connection, 1791-1841: an account of the chemical analyses of the human brain by Thouret (1791), Fourcroy (1793), Vauquelin (1811), Couerbe (1834), and Frémy (1841): a second sourcebook in the history of neurochemistry.*

11   "[T]out concourt (…) à attribuer une origine électrique à la phosphorescence" (Becquerel 4: 77). Antoine Becquerel was the grandfather of Henri Becquerel, who discovered radioactivity and received the Nobel Prize in physics together with Pierre and Marie Curie in 1903.

Dictionnaire universel d'histoire naturelle from 1849 confirms once again the great importance of phosphorus for the nervous system.

PHOSPHORIC NERVE FLUID FLOWING INTO NINETEENTH-CENTURY FICTION

Under the influence of popularised mesmerism and the doctrine of animal magnetism, physicians as well as poets of the early nineteenth century could explain the "magnetic" or "electrical" sympathy between hypnotiser and hypnotised as thought transference, and the hypnotic trance as a state of supersensible perception. In these contexts, phosphorescence could be imagined as the appearance of a universal spiritual force, the mysterious galvanic fluid which circulated not only within the nervous system, but permeated all dead and living things, and which the mesmeriser could manipulate through his magnetic passes.[12] Edgar Poe exploits this motif in "Mesmeric Revelation", published in 1844, and also plays jestingly with the idea of scientific resuscitation in a tale (published the following year) in which electrical fluid from a voltaic pile is successfully infused into the nerves of a mummy.[13] But when Balzac, in one of his philosophical novels published in 1831, refers to the visible luminosity around an idealised character as "what we today would call the phosphorescence of thinking", the innocent reader may not be sure if this is a metaphor, fictional liberty, or a recently proved scientific fact.[14] In the mystical novel *Séraphita*, published in 1835, which celebrates "the wonders of animal magnetism", the protagonist's angelic appearance is poeticised by the characteristic Balzacian narrator, who simultaneously adopts the clinical glance of a "skilled physiologist":

> If some skilled physiologist had studied this being, who, to judge by the boldness
> of his brow and the light of his eyes at this moment, was a youth of seventeen; if
> he had sought the springs of this blooming life under the whitest skin that the
> North ever bestowed on one of his sons, he would, no doubt, have believed in

---

12 Cf. Skagen: "Baudelaire and the Poetics of Magnetism".

13 Cf. Poe: "Some Words with a Mummy" and "Mesmeric Revelation", both translated into French by Baudelaire.

14 "Beauvouloir frissonna quand il remarqua ce phénomène qu'on pourrait aujourd'hui nommer la phosphorescence de la pensée, et que le médecin observait alors comme une promesse de mort" (Balzac: *L'Enfant maudit*, p. 941).

the existence of a phosphoric fluid in the sinews[15] that seemed to shine through the skin, or in the constant presence of an internal glow, which tinted Seraphitus as a light shines through an alabaster vase. (Balzac: *Seraphita*, trans. Bell, p. 16)

In the novel *Avatar*, published by Charles Baudelaire's friend Théophile Gautier in 1856, the young hero, suffering from a mysterious fatigue, complains that he has become porous and that his soul is gradually escaping from his body as through a sieve. A doctor and mesmeriser is consulted, who has phosphorescence literally flowing forth from his hands and eyes, and who is able to restore the young man's lost nervous energy by means of hypnotism, rendered fantastically as the communication of a visible mental fluid from the doctor to his patient.[16]

BAUDELAIRE'S (PSEUDO)SCIENTIFIC SUPERNATURALISM

Our brief and selective survey of the history of phosphorescence up to the nineteenth century indicates certain aspects that are relevant to Baudelaire and to some of his literary sources, especially concerning the romantic myth of the artist and the mythical powers of the artistic soul. Phosphorescence, either in its natural form or distilled and produced artificially, could be associated with philosophers' gold, vital fire, electricity, animal magnetism, nerves and thinking, – and with the Promethean ambition to dominate these factors of transmutation in and outside human nature. Having presented the historical background of the imagery of phosphorescence, we will now turn to the literary analysis of its use in the context of a Baudelairean essay on Poe, drawing on Baudelaire's aesthetics of supernaturalism, as it is informed by hermeticism.

Never denying his preference for beautiful dreams over sordid reality, Baudelaire admired Hoffmann, Balzac, Gautier, and Poe and recognises in them a scientifically inspired supernaturalism. Introducing his own translation of Poe's "Mesmeric Revelation" in 1848, he writes of the "unity mania" of these visionary poets who would also be scientists and philosophers: "animal unity, fluid unity, unity of the primary matter, all these recent theories have

---

15 "Nerfs" (nerves) is the word Balzac uses here.
16 "Le docteur, tout en marmottant ces phrases entrecoupées, ne discontinuait pas un seul instant ses passes: de ses mains tendues jaillissaient des jets lumineux qui allaient frapper le front ou le cœur du patient, autour duquel se formait peu à peu une sorte d'atmosphère visible, phosphorescente comme une auréole" (Gautier, p. 57).

sometimes, by a singular coincidence come into the heads of poets and scientists at the same time" (*OC* II: 248). Both Mesmer's theory of animal magnetism and the doctrine of correspondences, which is more often associated with Baudelaire's name, are compatible with the conceptual pattern of hermeticism, a diffused reservoir of metaphoric material for Romanticists of many shades. Among the main strands of this wide complex of ancient cults and thought currents, M. H. Abrams's *Natural Supernaturalism* focuses on its anthropomorphic ontology, which makes no sharp division between the animate and the inanimate, the human and the non-human:

> With reference to Hermetic writings, (…) it is more accurate to speak of the cosmos as a macro-anthropos than to speak of man as a micro-cosm.
>
> In this scheme there is a strong emphasis on polarity, conceived on the model of sexual opposites and regarded as the force that compels all natural processes. In addition, the overall course of things is envisioned as a circular movement from unity into multiplicity and, ultimately, back to unity. (Abrams, p. 158)

There are many known traces of Hermetic thinking in Baudelaire's writing; in addition to mesmerism, we will in the following refer to the doctrine of correspondences and alchemy, especially their notions of unity, sympathy and polarity. When presenting Poe's *Poetic Principle*, Baudelaire seems to adhere to the platonic doctrine of reminiscence: the experience of beauty is a melancholic recognition of a lost paradise, an "irritation" of the exiled soul's aspiration or "nervous postulation" for the divine (*OC* II: 114 and 334). The underlying Hermetic conception of a cyclic movement from unity to multiplicity and striving back to unity seems to be implied in his notion of poetic melancholy.[17] Through our reading of Baudelaire, we will see how his use of the phosphorescence imagery is consistent with the Hermetic conception of all things' antithetical and analogical interconnectedness, and with a circular poetics in which melancholy is an essential condition of beauty, in the same way as imaginary dissolution and death are prerequisites of artistic renewal and recreation. But Baudelaire's aesthetic interpretations of the "scientific supernatural" are less literal and more explicitly subjective, compared to the fictional examples we have seen from Balzac and Gautier. For Baudelaire there are two fundamental literary qualities: *supernaturalism* is counterbalanced by *irony* (*OC* I: 659). In adherence to "the law of contrasts governing

---

17 Cf. Skagen: "Ennui vs mélancolie".

the moral and physical order", and according to which "two opposites do not exclude one another any more than all the opposites that constitute nature" (*OC* II: 18-19), his supernaturalism is a naturalism of the soul.

"THE PHOSPHORESCENCE OF PUTREFACTION AND THE SCENT OF THUNDERSTORMS"

Like the scientist in Wright's picture, the Baudelairean figure of the artist is an alchemist, a sorcerer, and a magnetiser: an equivocal master of souls. In *The Salon of 1859*, Baudelaire expresses disdain for the naturalistic artist's ambition to paint things as they are, independently of the human gaze, and sympathy for the imaginative or *supernaturalistic* artist who says "I want to illuminate things with my mind, and to project their reflection upon other minds" (*OC* II: 627). The *phosphorescent* effect of Delacroix's paintings is in different contexts explicitly compared to the action of a thought-projecting mesmeriser: Living thoughts are said to emanate from the colours in the form of a glow which is also symbolic music, making the spectator's memory resound. It is as if the colours and lines establish a current of energy between the aesthetic object and the perceiving subject, who is induced into a state of dreamlike recognition.[18] Baudelaire relates similar experiences when reading Poe.

> What is the modern conception of pure art? It is to create a suggestive magic containing at the same time the object and the subject, the world outside the artist and the artist himself. (*OC* II: 598)

Pure art should haunt the reader or the spectator; the thoughts and dreams of the artist should be projected into the work of art and have the energy to flow forth, to possess and transform the receptive soul of the viewer or reader. This supernaturalistic, *phosphorescent* or *galvanic* quality is depicted in the passage below, which is taken from the introduction (published in 1856) to one of Baudelaire's volumes of translations of Poe's tales. The same quoted paragraph, one of the last in the article on the life and works of the American writer, will be in the centre of our attention in the following sections of our chapter. This extract's short aesthetic account is originally preceded and followed by descriptions of Poe's personal character as well as

---

18 Baudelaire: "Exposition universelle 1855" (*OC* II: 595).

of his typical fictional characters. It is clear that the first person narrator and perceiving subject of the sequence we are about to read, identifies himself with those melancholic and hysterical personalities, with their highly strung nerves and excess of retained passion:

> In the midst of this literature where the air is rarefied, the mind can feel that vague anguish, that fear prompt to tears, that sickness of the heart, which dwells in vast and weird places. But the admiration is stronger; and, then, art is so great! There, all the accessories are thoroughly appropriate to the characters' emotions. The solitude of nature or the agitation of big cities, everything is described nervously and fantastically. Like our Eugène Delacroix, who has raised his art to the height of great poetry, Edgar Poe likes to move his figures on purplish and greenish backgrounds revealing *the phosphorescence of putrefaction and the scent of thunderstorms*. The so-called inanimate nature participates in the nature of living beings, and is, like them, shivering with a supernatural and galvanic shiver. Space is deepened by opium; opium gives a magical significance to all the colours, and makes all the sounds vibrate with a more significant sonority. Sometimes magnificent visions, full of light and colour, suddenly open themselves in his landscapes, and at the end of their horizons are seen oriental cities and palaces, vaporized by the distance, on which the sun throws showers of gold (my emphasis).[19]

---

19 The central metaphor is italicized. "Au sein de cette littérature où l'air est raréfié, l'esprit peut éprouver cette vague angoisse, cette peur prompte aux larmes et ce malaise du cœur qui habitent les lieux immenses et singuliers. Mais l'admiration est la plus forte, et d'ailleurs l'art est si grand! Les fonds et les accessoires y sont appropriés aux sentiments des personnages. Solitude de la nature ou agitation des villes, tout y est décrit nerveusement et fantastiquement. Comme notre Eugène Delacroix, qui a élevé son art à la hauteur de la grande poésie, Edgar Poe aime à agiter ses figures sur des fonds violâtres et verdâtres où se révèlent *la phosphorescence de la pourriture et la senteur de l'orage*. La nature dite inanimée participe de la nature des êtres vivants, et, comme eux, frissonne d'un frisson surnaturel et galvanique. L'espace est approfondi par l'opium; l'opium y donne un sens magique à toutes les teintes, et fait vibrer tous les bruits avec une plus significative sonorité. Quelquefois des échappées magnifiques, gorgées de lumière et de couleur, s'ouvrent soudainement dans ses paysages, et l'on voit apparaître au fond de leurs horizons des villes orientales et des architectures vaporisées par la distance, où le soleil jette des pluies d'or" (*E. A. Poe: sa vie et ses oeuvres*, OC II: 317-8).

Notice the similarity of these images with those in *Les Paradis artificiels*: "Le hachisch s' étend alors sur toute la vie comme un vernis magique; il la colore en solennité et en éclaire toute la profondeur. Paysages dentelés, horizons fuyants,

The quoted paragraph is heavily charged with meaning, containing references not only to Poe's narratives and Delacroix's painting as a higher form of poetry or music, but also (implicitly) to doctrines of alchemy, magnetism, and correspondences, as well as to nineteenth-century medical doctrines about nerves, melancholia, hysteria, and hypnosis – and to Baudelaire's own studies of hashish and opium. The extract may be read as a prose poem, functioning poetically in its own right, at the same time as it analyses the poetic effect of Poe's narratives and Delacroix's paintings.

The quoted text introduces us directly into the topos of the sublime as it is defined by Edmund Burke: greatness, immensity, anguish, terror, and even suffocation which connotes hysteria[20] – together with admiration. The scarcity of air may be associated with higher, ethereal spheres of spirituality, the aspiration towards the infinite, but also with a mental laboratory.[21] It is tempting to think about connections between the air-pump and fictional experimentation with vital forces or with the psyche, brought to the limits of life and death. Though the rich metaphorical vocabulary generates associations to the very different fields of aesthetics, science, and pseudoscience, the passage is at the same time concentrated and carefully structured by those same figures that produce its polysemous aura. According to our reading of the extract, the expression "the phosphorescence of putrefaction and the scent of thunderstorms" (italicized in the quote above) constitutes the paragraph's nucleus.

The whole paragraph may be separated into two equal parts. The first 100 words are dominated by the vocabulary of literature, art and the psyche,

---

perspectives de villes blanchies par la lividité cadavéreuse de l'orage, ou illuminées par les ardeurs concentrées des soleils couchants, profondeur de l'espace, allégorie de la profondeur du temps" (*OC* I: 430-1).

20 Burke does not use the word hysteria in relation to the sublime, but hysteria is the topic of the preceding paragraph by Baudelaire (*OC* II: 317-8).

21 "Dans cette incessante ascension vers l'infini, on perd un peu l'haleine. L'air est raréfié dans cette littérature comme dans un laboratoire. On y contemple sans cesse la glorification de la volonté s'appliquant à l'induction et à l'analyse. Il semble que Poe veuille arracher la parole aux prophètes, et s'attribuer le monopole de l'explication rationnelle. Aussi, les paysages qui servent quelquefois de fond à ses fictions fébriles sont-ils pâles comme des fantômes. Poe, qui ne partageait guère les passions des autres hommes, dessine des arbres et des nuages qui ressemblent à des rêves de nuages et d'arbres, ou plutôt, qui ressemblent à ses étranges personnages, agités comme eux d'un frisson surnaturel et galvanique" (*E. A. Poe: sa vie et ses ouvrages, OC* II: 283-4).

ending with the chiasmic construction in the middle which transforms Delacroix's painting into poetry and Poe's writing into music and colours. The second part (also 100 words), starting with "où se revèle la phosphorescence de la pourriture et la senteur de l'orage", develops the vision of an imaginary landscape expanding towards a final climax: the "revelation" of this higher form of art in terms of synaesthetic sensation and signification. The striking images of the central sequence (our nucleus) are bound together by analogy (the "phosphoric" energy of putrefaction and thunder) and elemental opposition (earth and air). The repetitions and polarities surrounding these metaphors, echo and reinforce the nucleus' structuring function for the whole paragraph.

The paragraph's movement from the heights of the hypersensitive, artistic psyche, through the central images' moment of transition, to the visionary landscape with its final image of the sun throwing "showers of gold", responds to essential notions in Baudelaire's definition of Romanticism from 1846: "intimacy, spirituality, colour, yearning for the infinite, expressed by all the means the arts possess" (*OC* II: 421). Through the comparison of Poe's writing and Delacroix's paintings, and the transmutation of putrefaction to light and lightning to scent, the textual and visual representations are transformed into a meaningful concert of different sensations echoing through time and space. *Resounding* is a term used by Baudelaire to designate the experience of the "supernatural" in sudden moments of intensity, when symbolic recognition, the transparency and vibrancy of colours, sounds, and scents, is accompanied by a feeling of the vertiginous depth of time and space.[22] The musical vibrancy of all things, here characterised as "surnaturel et galvanique", may be conceived as the endless analogical transference of sensation and meaning referred to in the poem "Correspondances", an experience in which the infinite unity of the multiple and finite is revealed and restored.[23] In the central figures of the quoted paragraph, this "transport of spirit and senses", at first restrained, seems to be released by the "magnetic" force of sympathy and polarity contained in our nucleus.

---

22 "Le surnaturel comprend la couleur générale et l'accent, c'est-à-dire intensité, sonorité, limpidité, vibrativité, profondeur et retentissement dans l'espace et dans le temps" (*Fusées*, OC I: 658).

23 In this poem as well as in "Une charogne", the final "expansion of infinite things" is also generated by the idea of putrefaction.

"The phosphorescence of putrefaction" may be read as an oxymoron: the light of darkness, the vitality of death and decomposition, the beauty of morbidity. Like the famous "black sun", the oxymoron liberates associative flux by paralyzing rational logic. Notice the constant juxtaposition of opposite extremes in the quoted paragraph: darkness (putrefaction) and illumination (phosphorescence); high and low: the scent of storm in the element air, the sight of decay in the element earth, water and fire in both; complementary colours: purple and green, leaden thunderclouds and golden light; solitude and multitude; quietness and agitation; animate and inanimate; natural and supernatural. Opposites also operate in favour of the sublime, which "in all things abhors mediocrity" (Burke, p. 74). Baudelaire said he could recognise his own not yet expressed thoughts in the writings of Poe, appropriately characterised by Tzvetan Todorov as the author of extremes, of the excessive and superlative, exploring the ultimate limits to the point where opposite qualities become reversible and interchangeable (Todorov, p. 9). Baudelaire is also a poet of dualities, antitheses, and explosive oxymorons. Polarities are entrancing. The blurring of boundaries, especially between dream and reality, life and death, the animate and inanimate, that is so characteristic of Poe's tales of cataleptics buried alive, is a destabilising technique that emphasises the dramatic mystery of life – one of the true goals of art, according to Baudelaire.

Phosphorescence can be a material metaphor for the sleeping life in matter, the eternal soul captured in the transient body. It can be a metaphor for the mind analogous to that of the lamp, a Neo-Platonic metaphor of emanation which Abrams has said represents the mind as "a radiant projector which makes a contribution to the objects it perceives" (Abrams: *The Mirror and the Lamp*, p. vii). As such, phosphorescence may also evoke the special luminosity of dreams, as described by Nerval:

> As everybody knows, one never sees the sun in one's dreams, even though one
> is often aware of a light far more luminous. Objects and bodies have a radiance
> all their own. (Nerval, p. 428)

Dream is another term used by Baudelaire to characterise the undefinable "inner glow" of Poe's and Delacroix's art. To the supernaturalistic imagination, phosphorescence represents not only the permeability of the material and the immaterial, but also the interpenetration of the interior and exterior worlds. Some of Poe's tales – such as "The Fall of the House of Usher" – are characterised by densely emotional atmospheres in which everything solid seems to melt into emanations, exhalations, and spiritual fluids that permeate the fictional space.[24] Typically, the animate, somnambulistic atmosphere of Baudelaire's prose poem "The Favours of the Moon", representing the excessive sensitivity of male and female hysteria, is described as "phosphorique" (*OC* I: 341).

RETURN TO ALCHEMY

"Athena is born in a rain of gold", Michael Maier, *Atlanta fugiens* (1617).

In isolation, "the phosphorescence of putrefaction" may be read in a literal sense, justified by the natural phenomenon of bio-luminescence; in the Baudelairean context, however, it has a magical charge pointing towards alchemy. The reader will have noticed that *gold* was the last word of the quoted paragraph from Baudelaire's text on Poe. This alchemical gold (*or* in French) is buried phonetically and metaphorically in our nucleus: phos-

---

24 A similar interaction or correspondence (ecstatic or horrific) between the inside and the outside is accentuated in poems by Baudelaire, when the porous limits between subject and object are vaporised by a dreamy *Stimmung*: "All these things think through me, or I think through them (for, in the grandeur of reverie, the I is soon lost); they think, I say, but musically and picturesquely, without argumentation, without syllogism, without deduction". But the lyrical atmosphere is a rare grace, easily reversed into a painful, positive, and prosaic separation of the solitary *I* and his surroundings: "However, these thoughts, whether they emerge from me or spring from things, soon grow too intense. The energy in voluptuousness creates uneasiness and positive suffering. Now my nerves, too highly strung, produce nothing but piercing and painful vibrations" ("The Artist's *Confiteor*", *OC* I: 278).

LITERATURE AND CHEMISTRY

phore…*orage*: the aura of dark putrid matter, the lightning we expect from the leaden thunderclouds, is released in the final rain of gold.[25]

Baudelaire refers explicitly to alchemy in certain poems. Producing gold out of putrescent matter fits perfectly into the logic of alchemy, which generally implies the hermetic conception of sympathy between micro- and macrocosmos, and also insists on the force of polarities which ensures a dynamic tension governing all things; the alchemist manipulates polar opposites in order to overcome, heighten, and refine them. The particular work of the alchemist is conceived as analogical to the universal working of nature, but hastened and intensified.

Through the alchemical processes – perceived not only in analogy with the natural cycle of life and death, but also with Christ's death and resurrection and man's possible salvation – the base elements of the undistinguished *materia prima* could appear to be reborn in the form of incorruptible gold. The ninth emblem of Mylius' *Philosophia Reformata* (1622), entitled "Putrefactio", represents the black sun of death: a dark globe from which flames transpire (cf. Ill. below, p. 294). By putrefaction the soul or spirit is separated from the body. In this phase of blackness the gold is conceived. The principle of putrefaction is thus the key of the alchemical process.[26] The prescientific doctrine of spontaneous generation – the belief that in order for growth to take place in an organism, that organism must first die – is essential to alchemical thought and appropriated as a psychological and spiritual model. The cycle of death and resurrection is repeated in the psychological, moral, and mystical quest. The phase of *Putrefactio*, without which the goal of the opus cannot be reached, has many allegorical names: Dom Pernety's mytho-hermetic dictionary published in 1758, mentions all that is black and alludes to death, the horror of the grave, the philosophers' Saturn, their lead, eclipse

---

25 Alliteration also underlines the importance of the senses; phospho*rescence, senteur*. The alchemical transmutation implies a division between the body and mind: dissolution and volatilisation, the separation and sublimation of the subtile from the gross and the refinement of the subtile into new, perfected solids.

26 Following the pre-scientific conception of Paracelsus: "all things are naturally generated of the Earth by means of putrefaction. For Putrefaction is the chiefe degree and first stop to Generation. (…) putrefaction produceth great matters, as of this we have a most famous example in the holy Gospel, where Christ saith: Unless a grain of Wheat be cast into the Earth, and be putrified, it cannot bring forth fruit in a hundred fold. (…) For putrefaction is the change and death of all things, and destruction of the first essence of all Naturall things; whence there ariseth a regeneration, and new generation a thousand times better, &…" (Lindon, p. 152).

"Gradus Putrefactio" (Stolcius 212).[27]

of the sun and the moon, melancholia.[28] So Baudelaire's central figure, "the phosphorescence of putrefaction", may also be spelled out as the fiery energy hidden in melancholia. The necessity of decomposing Nature in order to create something new, which Baudelaire attributes to the creative imagination, is analogous to the alchemical principle of creation. The imagination – "ces feux de la fantaisie" – will only light up as daylight dies, when sundown:

---

27 Another emblem of the alchemical stage of "putrefactio" represents the alchemist on a shooting ground, which is also a graveyard, where some of the dead are being resurrected to the sound of a trumpeting angel (Stolcius, p. 83). One of Baudelaire's prose poems, "The shooting ground and the graveyard," seems to allude to this emblem, both in form and content. But the moral of the emblem seems less equivocal than Baudelaire's use of it: the philosophical goal the alchemist is aiming at with his crossbow and arrow lies beyond death and resurrection. Cf. Skagen: "Pour s'exercer à mourir".

28 See the following entries of the *Dictionnaire Mytho-hermétique*: "Mélancholie" (Pernety, p. 289), "Noir plus noir que le noir même" (Pernety, p. 337), "Putréfaction" (Perenty, p. 418), " Phosphore" (Perenty, p. 382), "Blancheur" (Pernety, p. 58).

LITERATURE AND CHEMISTRY

appears like a strange dancing dress, whose transparent and dark gauze reveals a glimpse of the muted splendors of a brilliant skirt, just as the delectable past might pierce through the gloomy present. While the trembling gold and silver stars, sprinkled over it, represent those fires of fantasy which ignite well only under the deep mourning of the Night.[29]

CONJUNCTIONS OF EARTH AND FIRE: MÉLANCOLIQUE ET ARDENT

When Baudelaire describes the supernaturalism of Poe and Delacroix, he always comes back to two essential psychological and aesthetic qualities: melancholia and ardour. These are key terms used to accentuate the eminence, the intensity, and the supernatural profundity of certain states of sensitivity associated with Poe and Delacroix, their temperament, their art, and even their physiognomy. The conjunction of light and darkness is an especially recurrent motif when Baudelaire speaks of Poe:

> Poe's life, his behaviour, his physical being, all that goes to make up the aggregate of his personality, leaves a final impression at once both dark and dazzling. His physical person was odd, attractive, and, like his works, stamped with an indefinable accent of melancholy. (Baudelaire: *The Painter of Modern Life*, p. 83)

Poe's poetry is drenched in "an almost untranslatable sentiment", a conjunction of bright desire and black despair:

> There the divine passion appears in all its magnificence, star-girt and forever veiled in an incurable melancholy. (Baudelaire: *The Painter of Modern Life*, p. 86)

In the same vein, Poe is romanticised as a Luciferian figure:

> returning to the true path of the poet, obeying without a doubt to the ineluctable truth that haunts us like a demon, he heaved the passionate sighs of the fallen angel who remembers Heaven, lamenting the golden age and the lost Eden.[30]

In a definition of Beauty which Baudelaire noted down in *Fusées*, he comes to the conclusion that Satan, "à la manière de Milton", is "the most perfect

29 "Le Crépuscule du soir", *OC* I: 312, trans. Edward Kaplan (p. 51).
30 "Notes nouvelles sur E. Poe", *OC* II: 32, trans. Raymond Foye (p. 96).

model of virile Beauty", suggesting sadness and passion, spiritual longings and repressed ambitions, and coldness rather than sentimentality. In perfect correspondence with Baudelaire's taste, Milton's Satan is a conjunction of opposites, simultaneously demonic and divine, dark and luminous: an eclipsed sun.

> (…) he, above the rest
> In shape and gesture proudly eminent,
> Stood like a tow'r: his form had not yet lost
> All her original brightness, nor appear'd
> Less than Archangel ruin' d, and th' excess
> Of glory obscur'd: as when the sun, new-ris'n,
> Looks thro' the horizontal misty air,
> Shorn of his beams; or from behind the moon,
> In dim eclipse, disastrous twilight sheds
> On half the nations, and with fear of change
> Perplexes monarchs; darken'd so, yet shone
> Above them all th'Archangel (Milton I, ll. 589-600)

Baudelaire's attribution of Miltonic melancholy and ardour to artists he admires reflects a stereotype of the Romantic artist that is connected to the imagery of phosphorescence as the appearance of a vital force in dead matter. Lucifer is a romantic hero and a model for every true poet, not only because of his transgressive individualism – gloriously alone against the world, with limitless ambitions – but also because he represents the nostalgic knowledge of extremes: heaven and hell, eternal life and death. The alchemist and chemist are in their turn demonic models because of their artificial or supernatural acceleration and intensification of natural processes of decomposition and re-creation.

The promethean Lucifer, the star Phosphorus or Venus, the highly inflammable element phosphorus, and any occurrence of phosphorescence in nature are all mythically connected to fire. In a poem dedicated to the Duke Johan Friedrich, Leibniz celebrates phosphorus with allusions to Prometheus's theft, the dress of Medea, and Moses's luminescent face; he describes Phosphorus as Nature's unknown fire, dissimulating its true being when buried in water from which it emerges luminous and brilliant in the likeness of the immortal soul (Fontenelle 2, p. ii). In "The chemistry of fire", Gaston Bachelard has shown how strongly the prescientific intuition of fire as a living substance is rooted in our imagination. Fire was always the phenomenon that interested chemists the most. Resolving the enigma of fire, they believed, would be to resolve the central enigma of the universe (Bachelard, p. 103). Different forms of fire, such as phosphorescent fluid or galvanic currents, have been imagined to explain the nervous interplay between body and mind and to understand the enigma of consciousness. The metaphor of phosphorescent art may serve to ascribe the power of "Fiat lux" to the artist. Maybe this is why phosphorescence is so dangerously suggestive and why a modern chemist can still metaphorise the element phosphorus as diabolic.

Associated with Lucifer or Phosphorus, the fallen angel or the morning star, phosphorescence has the ambiguity of twilight: bearer of light in the darkness, hovering between night and day, heaven and hell, reality and illusion. Baudelaire's conception of the human is that of *homo duplex*, body and soul, with demonic and divine aspirations. His metaphoric use of phosphorescence actualises these extremes in a highly unstable conjunction of opposites. The phosphorescence of art may be sublime, but it is also as delusive as "marshland meteors" in comparison to God's eternal fire (*OC* II: 325). Baudelaire's works describe an unresolved tension between pre-modern hermeticism and mundane scepticism, between a Jansenist consciousness of sin and a modern naturalistic awareness of the psychiatric human. His conception of the poet is not simply a stereotypical Romantic figure; his alchemist demiurge artist is also a hysterical dandy and writer of nerves.

What are, then, the essential components of Baudelairean Romanticism and Supernaturalism that we find encompassed in the figure of phosphorescence? The metaphor is a Romantic reminder of the unfathomable energy of the psyche. It celebrates the notions of intimacy, spirituality and aspiration for infinity that define romanticism in Baudelaire's *Salon* of 1846, reinvigorating these notions with scientific and pseudoscientific imaginations of a vital, unifying force of nature. The "glow" Baudelaire ascribes to works of thought, dream, imagination, desire, shines all the stronger in states of gloomy dissatisfaction with day-lit, positive reality. It represents the sudden intensity of existence which may be experienced through the intuition of death in life or life in death. Phosphorescent is the paradoxical emanation of concentrated inwardness, the privilege of a naturalised psyche as well as of "a soul that casts a magic and supernatural light on the natural obscurity of things" (*OC* II: 645).

WORKS CITED

Abrams, M. H: *The Mirror and the Lamp: Romantic Theory and the Critical Tradition.* New York: Oxford University Press, 1953.

Abrams, M. H.: *Natural Supernaturalism: Tradition and Revolution in Romantic Literature.* London: Norton, 1973.

Bachelard, Gaston: "La chimie du feu" in *La Psychanalyse du feu.* Paris: Gallimard, 1986.

de Balzac, Honoré: *L'Enfant maudit. La Comédie humaine,* vol. X (*Études philosophiques*). Paris: Gallimard, 1976.

de Balzac, Honoré: *Séraphita. La Comédie humaine,* vol. XI (*Études philosophiques*). Paris: Gallimard, 1980.

de Balzac, Honoré: *Seraphita and other stories,* trans. Clara Bell. Philadelphia: The Gebby Publishing Co., 1899.

Baudelaire, Charles: *Œuvres complètes I–II.* Claude Pichois (ed.). Paris: Gallimard, 1971 and 1975.

Baudelaire, Charles: *The Painter of Modern Life and other Essays,* trans. and ed. Johnathan Mayne. London: Phaidon Press, 1964.

Baudelaire, Charles: *The Parisian Prowler. Le Spleen de Paris. Petits Poèmes en Prose,* trans. Edward Kaplan. Georgia: The University of Georgia Press, 1997.

Becquerel, Antoine: *Traité experimental de l'électricité et du magnetisme et de leurs rapports avec les phénomènes naturels,* 7 vols. Paris: Firmin Didot Frères, 1837-40.

Boyle, Robert: "A Short Memorial of some Observations made upon an Artificial Substance, that shines without any precedent Illustration", 1677 in R. T. Gunther (ed.): *Early Science in Oxford,* vol. VIII. Oxford: Clarendon Press, 1931, pp. 230-7.

Boyle, Robert: *The aerial noctiluca, or, Some new phoenomena, and a process of a factitious self-shining substance imparted in a letter to a friend living in the country by the honourable Robert Boyle ...* London: Snowden, 1680.

Cabanis, Pierre: *Oeuvres complètes de Cabanis,*vol. III. *Rapports du physique et du moral de l'homme, Sixième Mémoire.* Paris: Firmin Didot, 1824.

Dobson, Thomas: *Encyclopædia: Or, A Dictionary of Arts, Sciences, and Miscellaneous Literature; Constructed on a Plan by which The Different Sciences and Arts Are Digested into the Form of Distinct Treatises or Systems comprehending the History, Theory and Practice of each, According to the latest discoveries and improvements ...* Philadelphia: Thomas Dobson, 1798.

Draaisma, Douwe: *Metaphors of Memory: A History of Ideas about the Mind.* Cambridge: Cambridge University Press, 2000.

Emsley, John: *The Shocking History of Phosphorus: A Biography of the Devil's Element.* London: Macmillan, 2000.

Evelyn, John: *Memoirs of John Evelyn (...) comprising his diary, from 1641 to 1705-6 (...),* vol. III. London: Henry Colburn, 1827.

de Fontenelle, M.: "Éloge de M. Leibniz" in A. Jacques (ed.): *Oeuvre de Leibniz,* vol. II. Paris: Charpentier, 1842.

Foye, Raymond: *The Unknown Poe: An Anthology of Fugitive Writings with Appreciations by Charles Baudelaire, Stéphane Mallarmé & André Breton.* San Francisco, CA: City Lights Books, 1980.

The Galileo Project: "Leibniz, Gottfried Wilhelm", http://galileo.rice.edu (10 May 2013).

Gautier, Théophile: "Avatar" in *Romans et contes*. Paris / Geneva: Slatkine Reprints, 1979.

Huxley, Henry: *Science & Culture*. London: Macmillan, 1881.

Lindon, Stanton J. (ed.): *The Alchemy Reader: From Hermes Trismegistus to Isaac Newton*. Cambridge: Cambridge University Press, 2003.

Mylius, J. D.: *Philosophia Reformata*. With engravings by Balthazar Schwan. Frankfurt: 1622.

de Nerval, Gerard: *Aurelia or Dream and Life*, trans. Richard Sieburth in J. Rothenburg and J. Robinson (eds.): *Poems for the Millenium*, vol. III. California: University of California Press, 2009.

Pernety, Antoine-Joseph: *Dictionnaire mytho-hermétique, dans lequel on trouve les allégories fabuleuses des poètes, les métaphores, les énigmes et les termes barbares des philosophes hermétiques expliqués*. Paris: Delalain, 1787.

Poe, Edgar: *Nouvelles histoires extraordinaires*, trans. Charles Baudelaire, with an introduction by Tzvetan Todorov. Paris: Gallimard, 2000.

Rousseau, George S.: *Nervous Acts: Essays on Literature, Culture and Sensibility*. New York: Palgrave, 2004.

Skagen, Margery Vibe: "Pour s'exercer à mourir: Ennui et mélancolie dans 'Le Tir et le cimetière' de Baudelaire" in John E. Jackson and Claude Pichois (eds.): *L' Année Baudelaire 2: Figures de la mort, figures de l' éternité*. Paris: Klincksieck, 1996, pp. 75-106.

Skagen, Margery Vibe: "Ennui *vs* mélancolie" in André Guyaux and Bertrand Marchal (eds.): *Les Fleurs du mal, Actes du colloque de la Sorbonne des 10 et 11 janvier 2003*. Paris: Presses de l'Université de Paris-Sorbonne, 2003, pp. 247-67.

Skagen, Margery Vibe: "Baudelaire and the Poetics of Magnetism" in R. Koppen, M. Hagen and M. V. Skagen (eds.): *The Art of Discovery: Encounters in Literature and Science*. Aarhus: Aarhus University Press, 2010.

Stolcius, Daniel: *Viridarium Chimicum, ou le Jardin Chymique*, 1624, trans. and with an introduction and commentary by Bernard Husson. Paris: Librairie de Médicis, 1975.

Tachenius, Otto: *La Lumière sortant par soi-mesme des ténèbres ou véritable théorie de la pierre des philosophes*. Paris: Laurent d'Houry, 1693.

Todorov, Tzvetan: "Préface" in Edgar Poe: *Nouvelles histoires extraordinaires*. Paris: Gallimard, 1974.

Tower, Donald: *Hensing, 1719. An account of the first chemical examination of the brain and the discovery of phosphorus therein*. New York: Raven Press, 1983.

—:*Brain Chemistry and the French Connection, 1791-1841: an account of the chemical analyses of the human brain by Thouret (1791), Fourcroy (1793), Vauquelin (1811), Couerbe (1834), and Frémy (1841): a second sourcebook in the history of neurochemistry*. New York: Raven Press, 1994.

Warner, E. and G. Hough: *Strangeness and Beauty: An Anthology of Aesthetic Criticism*, vol. 1. Cambridge: Cambridge University Press, 1983.

Weeks, Mary E.: *Discovery of the Elements*. Easton, PA: *Journal of Chemical Education*, 1933. Repr. Kessinger Publishing, 2003.

Willermoz, M.: "Phosphore", www.lexilogos.com (5 June 2013).

Yates, Frances: *Giardano Bruno and the Hermetic Tradition*. Chicago: University of Chicago Press, 1964.

PASTERNAK'S WASSERMANN TEST

Brita Lotsberg Bryn, University of Bergen

Known outside Russia primarily for his clandestinely published novel *Doctor Zhivago* and his involuntary refusal of the Nobel Prize in 1958, it is less well known that Boris Leonidovich Pasternak (1890-1960) was an aspiring poet and member of the moderate Futurist group the Centrifuge *(Tsentrifuga)* in the years 1914-15. In his home country he is still acknowledged, above all, as an outstanding poet.

Having explored earlier what I refer to as "metonymical chains" in Pasternak's cycle of fifty poems entitled *My Sister Life* (1922),[1] the present article proposes a prehistory of this particular device in his early poetry.[2] With the aim of acquainting new readers with the environment and poetics of this versatile poet, a considerable portion of this article is devoted to a presentation of Pasternak and his "metonymical system" as realised in *My Sister Life*.[3] By reviewing this system in the light not only of Pasternak's polemical article "Vassermanogo rekatsiia" ("The Wassermann Test" 1914), but also of research within biochemistry and neighbouring fields leading to the complement fixation test from which his article took its name, an equally important goal, however, is to show how Pasternak's early theoretical rendering of metonymy and "metonymical chains" may have been inspired by contemporary theories about immune response in living cells.

Pasternak's polemical article appeared in the aftermath of the Russian Futurists' "scandalous winter". Within the first couple of months of 1914 Italian *Futurismo* leader Filippo Marinetti, while on tour in Russia, was vigorously rejected by the Russian Cubo-Futurists, whose own "happenings" were frequently interrupted by the police. In February the current leader

---

1   *My Sister Life* was for the most part written in 1917-18, but due to World War One and civil war remained unpublished until 1922.

2   Most of the features of *My Sister Life* commented on here are more thoroughly accounted for in my doctoral thesis *Pasternaks Min søster livet. Kraften, følelsen og prismet*. See also Bryn: "Pasternak's Poem Balashov in the Light of Cubist Aesthetics".

3   As early as 1935, the Russian Formalist Roman Jakobson characterised Pasternak's early literary works as "a poetic world governed by metonymy" (Jakobson, p. 310).

of the Ego-Futurists, Igor Ignatiev, committed suicide on the day after his wedding, and the two flamboyant art students and already renowned Cubo-Futurist poets David Burliuk and Vladimir Maiakovskii were dismissed from the Moscow School of Painting, Sculpture, and Architecture where Boris Pasternak's father was a professor. By 1 March Pasternak had formed an additional Futurist group, the Centrifuge, together with the poets Sergei Bobrov and Nikolai Aseev.[4]

When the Cubo-Futurists published their *First Journal of Russian Futurists* in March 1914, Pasternak's faction was dejected, not only because it included poetry by members of yet another newly founded Moscow group, "The Mezzanine of Poetry", but also by the negative criticism of Pasternak and Bobrov's work in the review section of the journal. So when the Centrifuge launched *their* first miscellany, *Rukonog*,[5] in April, it hardly came as a surprise that Pasternak made Vadim Shershenevich – translator of Marinetti's work into Russian, central initiator of Petersburg Ego-Futurism as well as its counterpart in Moscow "The Mezzanine of Poetry", and, last but not least, editor of the *First Journal of Russian Futurists* – the main target of one of his contributions. This has been interpreted as an attempt on the part of the "centrifugists" to win the Cubo-Futurists, in particular Velimir Khlebnikov and Vladimir Maiakovskii, over to their newly formed Futurist camp.[6]

Perhaps searching for a means of expression that undermined his former Symbolist affinities, or eager to show off his new-fangled, radical avant-garde attitudes, Pasternak brashly entitled his contributory essay to *Rukonog* "The Wassermann Test". But he may also have had other, more weighty reasons, to which I will return, for naming it after a fairly recent test for the diagnosis

---

4   After a row in the wake of the formation of the Centrifuge, Pasternak even challenged Iulian Anisimov to a duel. Anisimov was the leader of the Symbolist-oriented literary establishment "Lirika", to which the Centrifuge troika used to belong. Pasternak's anger was allegedly aroused by a comment from Anisimov, a descendent of the Russian gentry, on Pasternak's Jewish origin and inability to "write in proper Russian". The duel was to take place on 29 January, which is Pasternak's birthday, as well as the anniversary of the Russian national poet Aleksander Pushkin's death following a duel in 1837. After receiving an excuse from Anisimov, Pasternak did however call the duel off. See Bykov, p. 110.

5   The Strugatskii brothers were later to name an outlandish insect in their novel *A Snail on the Slope* (*Ulitka na sklone*, 1965) "Rukonog", a made-up word that may be translated as "Handyfoot", but is usually rendered "Brachiopod" in English.

6   For a more thorough account of these events, see Barnes, pp. 161-9.

of syphilis developed by the German bacteriologist August Paul von Wassermann (1866-1925).

CONTEMPORARY INTERDISCIPLINARY ACTIVITY

The outburst of cultural – and polemical – activity in Russia between the Revolution of 1905 and the outbreak of World War One coincides, on the one hand, with a period of extensive political and social unrest, and, on the other, with a historical interlude characterised by some degree of democratic reform, as well as by substantial industrial development. Russian artists, intellectuals, and scientists, frequently educated in West European countries, travelled and communicated relatively freely with their Western colleagues, and foreign presence and investments were encouraged.

Within the arts and the sciences, Russia found herself not only in a situation in which competing groups and branches were striving for autonomy or recognition, but also on a peak of interdisciplinary activity and experimentation. Many of the literary groups that emerged during these years, were, as is evident from the doctrine of Cubo-Futurism, profoundly inspired by avant-garde visual art. This also applies to the Centrifuge, where Sergei Bobrov, educated within the arts, was a personal friend of the avant-garde painters Mikhail Larionov, Nataliia Goncharova, and Aristarkh Lentulov. The geometrical figures, typographical elements, asymmetry, and bold contrasts of contemporary paintings permeated poetry as well as stage art productions, such as the choreography and costumes of Sergei Diaghilev's *Ballet Russes*, already touring Europe accompanied by Igor Stravinskii's and Sergei Prokofiev's music, the intensity and dissonance of which is loudly echoed in the acoustics of Futurist poetry.

The Russian mathematician Andrei Markov's inventive application of the random process system, later to be named "The Markov Chain", to Alexander Puskhkin's verse novel *Eugene Onegin* and Sergei Aksakov's novel *The Childhood of Bagrov, the Grandson* in 1913 represents an early intersemiotic translation between mathematics, language, and literature. Such efforts to make literary and linguistic analysis "more scientific" were later to be elaborated by the members of the Moscow Linguistic Circle, formed in 1915, and its counterpart in St. Petersburg, OPOYAZ, established one year later. In adapting structural analysis to a series of disciplines beyond linguistics, including poetry, the visual arts, music, and cinema, Roman Jakobson, Viktor Shklovskii, Iurii Tynianov, Boris Eikhenbaum, Boris Tomashevskii, and their colleagues became pivotal figures in linking and expanding the boundaries of such fields as linguistics, literary theory and criticism, communication theory, semiotics, anthropology, and cybernetics.

From a Russian historical perspective, Boris Pasternak's biography does indeed reflect both the unique openness towards Europe and the challenging of disciplinary boundaries prevalent at this time. Pasternak's father, the well-known Impressionist painter Leonid Pasternak, who completed his art studies in Munich, had become deeply attached to German culture. In the Pasternak family German was spoken fluently, and they followed political and cultural – as well as scientific – developments in Western Europe closely. Having literally grown up among paintings in an apartment on the premises of the Moscow School of Painting, Sculpture, and Architecture where his father was teaching, Boris Pasternak developed a profound sense of colour, shape, detail, and optical phenomena at an early age. Moreover, a fascination with his father's mixing of colours may have encouraged his interest in the fields of chemistry connected with pigments and dyestuffs, reflected for instance in "The Wassermann Test".

His mother, Rozalia Kaufmann Pasternak, was a musical *Wunderkind* and an accomplished concert pianist before she married, and after an encounter with the composer Alexander Scriabin in 1903, the young Boris Pasternak turned to music. He studied piano playing and composing under Prokofiev's first piano tutor, Reinhold Glière, and graduated from Moscow Conservatory as an external candidate in 1911. Pasternak was intrigued by Scriabin's idea of a correspondence between musical keys, sounds, and colours, a theory influenced by Sir Isaac Newton's *Optics*. He was also enthused by Goethe's *Farbenlehre* and *Beiträge zur Optik*, as well as by the doctrines of theosophy and Andrei Belyi's theories about an interaction between sound and colour. The Symbolist writer Belyi and, in particular, Alexander Blok were idols for Pasternak at the time when he finally turned to philosophy and poetry.

While a student of philosophy at Moscow University in 1912, Boris Pasternak spent a term in Marburg, where he studied Neo-Kantianism under such prominent philosophers as Hermann Cohen and Paul Natorp. Though widely renowned for its humanities, and in particular for its Department of Philosophy, Marburg University was even more famous for achievements within the natural sciences. Having established the world's very first professorship in chemistry in 1609 – held by Johannes Hartmann – the list of famous natural scientists that studied or taught at this university includes a considerable number of outstanding chemists and biochemists, such as the pioneer of photochemistry and organoarsenic chemistry Robert Bunsen and the biochemist Albert Kossel, who earned the Nobel Prize for Physiology or Medicine in 1910 for his research on the genetic substance of living cells.

Boris Pasternak, who showed an eager interest in the natural sciences as early as his school years, was well aware of this heritage. In the blurred lines intersecting biology, chemistry, and medicine, he found a vast field for imaginative and literary exploration, already distinguishable in the vocabulary, motifs, and imagery of his very first collection of poems *A Twin in the Storm Clouds (Bliznets v tuchkakh)* from 1913.[7]

"THE WASSERMANN TEST"

Though frequently pointed to as the primary source of Pasternak's first written statement on poetic metaphor versus metonymy, "The Wassermann Test" has often been discredited with labels such as "muffled" or "disconnected". Moreover, its title has tended to be either ignored or dismissed as a Futurist shock effect adding to the article's complexity and obscurity. In the present reading the title is considered an important starting point, crucial for a full appreciation of the author's argument.

Wrapped in intricate language and characterised by an ostensible wavering between different subjects, the criticism presented in "The Wasserman Test" strikes me as more categorical than what one usually sees from Pasternak's pen. Written almost a century ago, the article starts out by presenting viewpoints that would not look out of place in a contemporary literary review. Pasternak maintains that in our century "of democracy and technology" a relaxed attitude has penetrated the realm of artistic production and ruined original craft. Readers have been turned into consumers and clients, deprived of critical judgement and sense of quality, while the vast majority of writers are epigones (B. Pasternak 349/166).[8]

Pasternak then makes an apparent sidestep, vaguely linked to the title, but at first sight appearing somewhat irrelevant to the remaining part of the article, by briefly commenting on the state of the natural sciences. He

---

7 Boris Pasternak's son, the Pasternak scholar and biographer Evgenii Pasternak, refers to a critique of these poems overheard by the literary critic Konstantiv Loks at a private gathering in Iulian Anisimov's home in early 1914, expressing a dislike of their "linguistic mistakes, un-Russian poetics and 'dialect of chemists and hospitals'" (E. Pasternak, p. 203).

8 The first page reference to "The Wassermann Test" applies to the original in Russian, cited from volume 4 of Boris Pasternak's *Collected Works in Five Volumes* (1989-92); the second page reference, after the slash, refers to an English translation of this article by Anna M. Lawton.

claims that their high degree of specialisation has led to objects of study fluctuating between different fields, providing "some entities of microbiotics and growing forms" as examples. One science may, he continues, render a given form to be studied by another, and the methodological motives the first gives for refusing the object may constitute the very elements upon which the latter, neighbouring science composes a formula for recognising the form as belonging to itself. According to Pasternak, this does however contribute to the construction of methods mutually guaranteeing each other within "the unity of scientific consciousness" (B. Pasternak 351/167-8).

Returning to his main theme, namely poetry, the author then maintains that when it comes to Futurism, some "exemplars" (clearly referring to certain poets and their work) are falsely and others rightfully ascribed to their proper domain. "True Futurism does exist", Pasternak confidently states, making "Khlebnikov, Maiakovskii with some reservations, and only partly Bolshakov and poets from the group 'Peterburgskii Glashatai'"[9] examples of this, while the Ego-Futurist Vadim Shershenevich is consigned to a category of text producers who provide consumers with familiar, but utterly secondary literary features; and, most importantly, whose poetry reveals a complete lack of understanding of poetic metaphor (B. Pasternak 351/168).[10] If metaphor can be compared to an ornate lock, then the key to Shernshenevich's metaphors are in the hands of amateurs from the crowd, the author maintains, and he continues:

> The origin of Shershenevich's metaphors is the fact of similarity or more rarely an associative link based on similarity, and never one based on contiguity. However, only the phenomenon of contiguity gives rise to that characteristic of coercion and spiritual dramatism, which can be justified metaphorically (B. Pasternak 353-4/170).[11]

---

9   "Peterburgskii glashatai" (the "Petersburg Herald" group) was an Ego-Futurist publishing house that issued a journal of the same name. It was founded in 1912 and dissolved in 1914.

10   It should be emphasised that when Pasternak distinguishes between *metaphors* based on similarity and contiguity in this article, he is in fact making a distinction in line with the common definitions of *metaphor* (as association by similarity) and *metonymy* (as association by contiguity). Pasternak's term "metaphor" as used in "The Wassermann Test" in other words embraces both metaphors and metonymies.

11   To quote the original: "Факт сходства, реже ассоциативная связь по сходству и никогда не по смежности – вот происхождение метафор Шершеневича. Между тем только явлениям смежности и присуща та черта принудительности

Starting with Iurii Tynianov's article "Interlude" ("Promezhutok") from 1925, numerous scholars have pointed out that the tropes in Pasternak's prose and poetry are based on a lose, contiguous relationship. Roman Jakobson's landmark study "Marginal Notes on the Prose of the Poet Pasternak", first published in German in 1935, perhaps remains the most significant work on this topic. It should however be noted that neither Pasternak in "The Wassermann Test" nor Tynianov in "Interlude" uses the term *metonymy* – though they clearly point to the characteristics of this trope – the latter asserting that Pasternak's *metaphors* are created on the basis of neighbourhood, contiguity, and association. Reaching far beyond the level of mere tropes in his "Marginal Notes", Jakobson, on the other hand, describes Pasternak's poetics with terms such as "metonymical system" and "metonymical way".

After making a necessary detour myself, via the metonymical system of *My Sister Life*, I will argue, returning to "The Wassermann Test", that its title and apparent digressions form a lucid metonymical edifice essential to the appreciation of the article as an intelligible whole.

MY SISTER LIFE

Pasternak's second book of poetry, *Over the Barriers* (*Poverkh barerov*, 1917), is, like his first, a collection of poems. By 1917, however, when he started writing his third book of poems, *My Sister Life*, he was convinced that "after Blok" the writing of single poems had become a thing of the past, for him personally and for contemporary poetry as such. By a "book of poems" (*kniga stikhov*) he did not have in mind a "collection of poems" (*sbornik stikhov*), poems that might be closely connected and even presented chronologically, but "a cycle of poems that shared a united view, feeling and breath" (E. Pasternak 306).

Comparing Pasternak's earliest published poetry with the poetics of the cycle of poems *My Sister Life*, it becomes clear that the author's early preference for tropes based on contiguity and neighbourhood develops into an all-embracing system comprising a range of associative and contiguous connections on various textual levels, which indeed justifies Jakobson's label "metonymical system". Having overcome his Futurist rebelliousness, Pasternak is now more prepared to accept his Romantic Symbolist past and Neo-Kantian trust in historical and cultural continuity. Considering the overarching organic quality of *My Sister Life*, a large proportion of the de-

---

и душевного драматизма, которая может быть оправдана метафорически." (В. Pasternak: "Vassermanogo reaktsiia", p. 349).

vices encompassed by Jakobson's "metonymical system" could in my opinion equally well have been covered by the term "organic system". But in spite of this cycle of poem's dedication to the Romantic poet Mikhail Lermontov and its numerous allusions to Romantic predecessors and idols, such as Goethe, Pushkin, Rilke, Kipling, and Poe, these poems do indeed remain at a distance from Romanticism in the narrow sense of the word. Pasternak's constant switching between various linguistic registers, his original imagery, Bergsonian vitalism, and extensive use of avant-garde devices, such as unveiling and metonymical dislocation, renders *My Sister Life* a striking example of a Romantic organicism with a modernist twist.[12]

But where and how does chemistry re-enter this picture? In Russia, as elsewhere in Europe, the outbreak of World War One boosted industries manufacturing explosives, munitions, and other war-related chemical products. Having been rejected for military service on account of a permanent leg injury sustained in childhood after falling from a horse, Pasternak accepts a job as a clerk at a chemical factory producing acetic acid, acetone, and chloroform in the desolate village of Vsevolodo-Vilva in the Urals.[13] Hence immediately prior to writing *My Sister Life*, he had been working at a chemical plant for seven months, living in the house of the biochemist and family friend Boris Zbarskii who ran the factory,[14] and spending almost all his time with chemical engineers and laboratory workers. His correspondence reveals that this deepened his interest in inorganic as well as organic chemical processes, and in a letter to Konstantin Loks, written from the Urals on 28 January 1917, Boris Pasternak straightforwardly states that "If [literary] form can be created (...) then it can be created only in the form of a living organism, irrationally lent meaning through its capacity to drive itself forward" (B. Pasternak, p. 98).

---

12 This may be illustrated by Pasternak's subsequent definition of art in the autobiographical sketch *A Safe Conduct* (*Okhrannaia gramota*, 1930): "focused upon a reality that has been displaced by feeling, art is a record of this displacement" (B. Pasternak: *Okhrannaia gramota*, p. 187).

13 For an interesting account of Vsevoloda-Vilva's significance in the history of early Russian chemical industry – and as a cultural crossroad – see V. V. Abashev's book cited above.

14 After Lenin's death in 1924 Boris Zbarskii and his colleague Vladimir Vorobiev were made responsible for the embalmment and further preservation of Lenin's body. See Ilya Zbarsky: *Lenin's Embalmers*.

With its deep roots in European culture, the idea of art and language as cyclic or organic structures may have been "old news", but it was not outmoded among Pasternak's Russian contemporaries in the 1910s and 1920s. Related concepts were for example vital to the Acmeist poets Osip Mandelshtam and Nikolai Gumilev, and they were also debated in Mikhail Bakhtin's circles.[15]

While writing *My Sister Life* – a biographically-rooted rendering of his infatuation with twenty-year-old Elena Vinograd during the spring and summer of 1917 – Pasternak appears to be convinced that when something that appears to be new comes into being, in history, culture, art, or science, it does so, not as a substitute for the old, but as a revitalised reproduction of the previously existing, always drawing on and establishing new combinations with what already exists. Based on the idea that every form, in nature as well as in language and literature, has an immanent potential to combine and dissolve in order to enter into new compounds or contexts, Pasternak's poetics – embracing not only his use of tropes, but also the phonetic level, rhymes, metrics, imagery, and character constructions of *My Sister Life* – do in fact reflect nature's organic processes, as well as chemical and physical reactions, in a very tangible way.[16]

Structurally, the inherent orderliness of nature becomes the order of this particular book, in which the detailed descriptions of physical and mental processes leading up to and following the actual meetings (such as long train journeys and drawn-out contemplations linked to remorse) are preceded or

---

15 The first volume of Oswald Spengler's *Der Untergang des Abendlandes: Umrisse einer Morphologie der Weltgeschichte*, in which Spengler formulates a biological theory of the nature of historical change, appeared in Vienna in the summer of 1918. According to Maria Gough, the book earned immense popularity among Russian intellectuals and became a major source of controversy between the "radical intelligentia" and the so-called "counter-intelligentsia". See Gough: "Tarabukin, Spengler and the Art of Production", pp. 78-108.

16 In *My Sister Life* an extensive use of avant-garde devices such as estrangement (*ostranenie*) and complication (*oslozhnenie*) has, in my interpretation, also acquired a contradictory function. In order to encourage the reader to perceive the organic poetics of the book, Pasternak has incorporated "details" (words, frequently forming "metonymical chains") that allude to and consolidate his devices and compositional methods – a fundamental technique in modernist art, known within formalist theory as the "laying bare" of the device (*obnazhenie priema*). As Pasternak puts it in *A Safe-Conduct*: "the clearest, most memorable, and most important thing in art is its origination, and the world's best works of art, while telling about the most varied things, are really telling about their own birth" (B. Pasternak: *Okhrannaia gramota*, p. 186).

echoed by allusions to protracted organic processes, for example growth and decay. More sudden actions and reactions, such as impulses or outbursts of feeling, are, on the other hand, accompanied by allusions to spontaneous chemical or physical reactions. In the very first poem "In Memory of the Demon", for instance, a sudden thought is metonymically represented by a spark in the demon's hair, trembling like phosphorus.

Hence there are two kinds of governing tempo in this cycle of poems, which reflect the masculine and feminine protagonists' changing moods, as well as the tense atmosphere on the advent of the 1917 revolution: On the one hand, extensive *adagio* processes, gradual organic changes leading through several stages and developments; and on the other hand, explosive, spontaneous, chemical or physical reactions, often preceded by references to severe changes in temperature. The development of the love story persistently imitates and interacts with phenomena in nature, and its twists and turns are often emphasised by means of references to growth-promoting or -inhibiting factors such as light, darkness, blooming, hibernation, rain, water, and drought.

Constructed around a series of meetings and partings of the protagonist and his beloved in Moscow and in the province of Saratov, their brief affair constitutes the book's most prominent leitmotif, but *My Sister Life* is also dedicated to other kinds of meetings. Throughout we witness humans encountering nature, not to mention all the meetings that take place *in* nature, between stars, the elements, trees, raindrops, and even bacteria and bacilli. The male protagonist emerges as an utterly sensitive, perceptive, and sharp-eyed observer, with constantly changing fields of vision and shifts of perspective. His surroundings are persistently dislocated and optically distorted by means of concrete "prisms", such as eyeglasses, monocles, spectacles, mirrors, and broken glass. On a more abstract level, his visions of objects are enlarged and diminished to an extent that would usually require a telescope or microscope. Moreover, there are numerous references to photography in this book, including the Collodion developing process, as well as to drugs and chemicals, chemical elements, and the preparation of metals. In the poem "Balashov" we are introduced, for instance, to a riveting, soldering, forging, and welding blacksmith.

METONYMICAL CHAINS AND *SEITENKETTEN*

My purpose in mentioning all these aspects of *My Sister Life*'s poetics, only vaguely related to each other and to chemistry as such, is twofold. Firstly I

want to draw attention to the poet's preoccupation with all kinds of alterations from one organic, physical, chemical, or mental state or condition to
another, "laid bare", in the Cubist sense of this expression, by references to
for instance light, rain, change in temperature, optical phenomena, or the
application of drugs or chemicals. Secondly, I want to point out the openness
of every entity in these poems to adjacent entities. On account of phonetic,
semantic, or physical nearness, such entities constantly connect, frequently
developing into long interrelated sequences or chains of words expanding
step by step on the basis of association, contiguity, or partiality.

Having earlier referred to such sequences as "metonymical chains", my
present perspective unfolds an alternative way of elucidating and referring
to them, that is, with the concept of *Seitenketten* or "side-chains". This brings
me back to "The Wassermann Test", in which Pasternak, having maintained
that Shershenevich's tropes are almost exclusively based on similarity rather
than contiguity, continues to reason as follows: "Can it be that Shershenvich
does not know that a word which is impenetrable in its coloration cannot
borrow coloring from the word with which it is compared?" (B. Pasternak
354/170).

This formulates not only the crux of Pasternak's polemical article, but
also the essence of the poetics of *My Sister Life*, in which no word or image
appears as fixed, but possesses openness toward adjacent entities. It also
implicitly links to a theory upon which August Paul von Wassermann's
complement fixation test rests, the *Seitenkettentheorie* developed by the
German bacteriologist, immunologist, and Nobel Laureate Paul Ehrlich
(1854-1915) that explains the immune response in living cells. Wassermann
became an eager proponent of Ehrlich's side-chain theory, and it is well
known that the development of the Wassermann test depended closely on
Ehrlich's previous research on antibody formation. Three years after the
Wassermann diagnosis test was launched in 1906, Ehrlich and his team
developed the organoarsenic compound *Salvarsan*, also called "Ehrlich
606", which became the first effective cure against syphilis. The history
of this drug, which was in clinical use from 1910, may however be traced
all the way back to 1863 when the biochemist Pierre Bechamp isolated a
compound from a reaction between arsenic acid and aniline called *Atoxyl*
(Lloyd, p. 24). Furthermore, the *Schlüssel-Schloss-Prinzip*, or lock-and-key
model, postulated by the chemist Emil Fischer in 1894 to explain enzyme-
substrate interaction, became an explicatory model for Ehrlich when he
proposed that a receptor would bind to an infectious agent like a key fitting
into a lock.

Moreover, the Ukrainian zoologist and microbiologist Elie Metchikoff's works on immune response (which earned him a shared Nobel Prize in Physiology or Medicine with Ehrlich in 1908), as well as German zoologists Fritz Schaudinn and Erich Hoffmann's isolation of the causative agent of syphilis in 1905, were all vital to the development of a test and treatment for this feared and stigmatising disease. The diagnostic test and cure for syphilis were in other words the results of systematic, long-lasting research in specialised, neighbouring, and largely interrelated sciences within biology, chemistry, and medicine, such as biochemistry, microbiology, bacteriology, histology, immunology, and pharmacology.

In the light of this, the seemingly out-of-place paragraph in Pasternak's "The Wassermann Test" about objects within the natural sciences being studied successively by neighbouring fields, thereby generating new methods and mutually guaranteeing scientific progress, becomes logical and comprehensible. So does the lock and key image, applied by Pasternak to illustrate the perfect match between Shernshenevich's traditional similarity-based tropes (as infectious agents) and "amateurs from the crowd" (as receptors). Hence, while literally referring to a diagnostic test for syphilis, the title may serve as a metaphorical rendering of the diagnosis of an "infected" poet and poetics. But on a metonymical level the title, as well as the principal ideas conveyed in the article, do appear to have a connection, as pointed out earlier, with a scientific theory that not only provided a precondition for Wassermann's theory, but also shared important features with the poetic principles Pasternak describes as an ideal in "The Wassermann Test" and realises to their full extent in *My Sister Life* – that is, Paul Ehrlich's side-chain theory.

In 1878 Ehrlich described a "definite chemical character of the cell" in his dissertation, a point to which he returned nine years later while developing his chemical side-chain theory (Prüll, p. 334). When Pasternak refers to Shershenevich's inept similarity-based metaphor as a "word, which is impenetrable in its coloration", he implies that a genuine "metaphor" – or indeed metonymy – would be a word characterised by openness, receptiveness, and permeability. The character of a genuine trope as defined by Pasternak may thus be compared to what Ehrlich describes as the "definite chemical character of the cell" required for its reaction with a dye.

Paraphrasing Prüll, Ehrlich maintained further that living cells, like dyestuffs, have side-chains related to their colouring properties and that cells under threat grow new side-chains. Since certain side-chains are able to bind certain toxins, "occupied" side-chains unable to fulfil their physiological functions start producing additional side-chains, which are ultimately released into the blood stream, where they act as antibodies. Ehrlich coined these antibodies "magic bullets" (Prüll, p. 341).

The significance of Ehrlich's side-chain theory to the development of Wassermann's complement fixation test was acknowledged among Pasternak's contemporaries. Hence what appear to be inapt digressions in his article concerning the methods and subsequent merits of the natural sciences, or casual allusions to impenetrable colouration and lock and key fits, are in my interpretation means of further sustaining – or laying bare – the metonymical links between the title, the side-chain theory, and a literary device which shares important traits with Erlich's *Seitenkettenthorie*. Pasternak, who had by this time come to consider tropes by association or contiguity a key literary principle, would be contradicting himself if he were to build his criticism against Shershenevich's use of traditional similarity-based tropes on the metaphorical connection between side-chains and metonymical sequences. What makes "The Wassermann Test" so challenging is the fact that his arguments are constructed along associative contiguous lines – that his implicit use of Ehrlich's biochemical theory of immunological phenomena as an explicatory model for his own literary method is metonymical rather than metaphorical. To me, "The Wassermann Test" became far more coherent when I started recognising – in the retrospective light of the "metonymical chains" of *My Sister Life* – the two predominant devices of Pasternak's early poetry – metonymy and the so-called *obnazhenie priema* or unveiling of this very device – as its principal structuring and rhetorical tools.

PASTERNAK'S LITERARY WASSERMANN TEST

To the poet and polemical essayist Pasternak of the 1910s, every word, image, or phrase in a literary text is under the constant threat of becoming a cliché. A word with a fixed or permanent colouration, that is, a word or image deprived of the ability to form contiguous relations with adjacent entities, may be compared to a cell that is unable to grow side-chains. Though only metonymically alluded to in "The Wassermann Test", Ehrlich's side-chain theory may, as we have seen, have inspired Pasternak's account of "genuine metaphors" in his polemical essay, and may even serve as an explicatory model for the metonymical chains of *My Sister Life*.

Hence the mutual connections between individual words or tropes that make up Pasternak's side-chains are, as already mentioned, almost invariably based on nearness, contiguity, and associative connections. In *My Sister*

Life, a young thin girl in the rain is for example developed into images of a dripping branch, a wet cluster of lilac, a wet bird shaking off the rain, a dancing girl in a tulle dress, a whirlwind, and so forth. And as such sequences gradually emerge and the reader starts to accept, for example, a branch as a fixed metaphor for the female protagonist, this branch suddenly starts forming additional side-chains.[17]

With Ehrlich's *Seitenkettentheorie* in mind, Pasternak appears to suggest that words with a definite, *metonymical* character that enables them to "bind" with adjacent words and thus form side-chains, may, when released in poetry, act as neutralising antibodies – or magic bullets – that protect the literary work from being infected by clichés, worn-out vocabulary, rigid symbols, or fixed metaphors – one might say by the poetical equivalents of the protozoan *Spirochaeta pallida*, now known as *Treponema palladium*, the causative agent of syphilis.

WORKS CITED

Abashev, V. V.: *Vsevolodo-Vilva na perekrestke russkoi kultury: Kniga ocherkov knazia Vsevolzhskie, Savva Morozov A.P. Chekhov, Boris Zbarskii, Boris Pasternak*. Perm: Mamotov, 2008.

Barnes, Christopher: *Boris Pasternak. A Literary Biography*, vol. 1, 1890-1928. Cambridge: Cambridge University Press, 1989.

Brooks, Nathan: "Munitions, the Military, and Chemistry in Russia" in Roy McLeod and Jeffrey Johnson (eds.): *Comparative Perspectives on the Chemical Industry at War, 1914-1924*. Dordrecht, the Netherlands: Springer, 2006, pp. 75-102.

Bykov, Dmitrii: *Boris Pasternak: Zhizn' zamechatelnykh liudei*. Moscow: Molodaia gvardiia, 2007.

Bryn, Brita Lotsberg: *Pasternaks Min søster livet. Kraften, følelsen og prismet*, Dr. art. thesis. University of Bergen, Dept. of Russian Studies, IKRR, 1997.

Bryn, Brita Lotsberg: "Pasternak's Poem 'Balashov' in the Light of Cubist Aesthetics" in Knut Andreas Grimstad and Ingunn Lunde (eds.): *Celebrating Creativity. Essays in Honour of Jostein Børtnes*. University of Bergen: Dept. of Russian Studies, IKRR, 1997, pp. 289-98.

Gough, Maria: "Tarabukin, Spengler and the Art of Production" in *October* 93, 2000, pp. 78-108.

Jakobson, Roman: "Marginal Notes on the Prose of the Poet Pasternak", 1935 in Krystyna Pomorska and Stephen Rudy (eds.): *Language in Literature*. London / Cambridge, Mass.: The Belknap Press of Harvard University Press, 1987, pp. 301-17.

---

17 The branch is, for instance, transformed into a cluster of lilac with a raindrop on its tip, and then into a paintbrush with a hanging drop of paint.

Lawton, Anna and Eagle, Herbert (eds.): "The Wassermann Test" in *Words in Revolution: Russian Futurist Manifestoes 1912-1928*. Washington D. C.: New Academia Publishing, LLC, 2005, pp. 166-72.

Lloyd, Nicholas C., Morgan, Hugh W., Nicholson, Brian K., Ronimus, Ron S. and Riethmiller, Steven: "Salvarsan – The First Chemotherapeutic Compound" in *Chemistry in New Zealand*, vol. 69, no. 1, 2005, pp. 24-7.

Pasternak, Boris: *Okhrannaia gramota* (*A Safe-Conduct*), 1930. *Sobranie sochinenii v piati tomakh (Collected Works in Five Volumes)*, vol. 4, 1991. Moscow: Khudozhestvennaia literaura, 1989-92, pp. 149-239.

—: "Vassermanogo reaktsiia" ("The Wassermann Test"), 1914. *Sobranie sochinenii v piati tomakh (Collected Works in Five Volumes)*, vol. 4, 1991. Moscow: Khudozhestvennaia literaura, 1989-92, pp. 349-54.

—: Pismo Konstantinu Loksu 28.01.1917 (Letter to Konstantin Loks 28.01.1917). *Sobranie sochinenii v piati tomakh (Collected Works in Five Volumes)*, vol. 5, 1992. Moscow: Khudozhestvennaia literaura, 1989-92, pp. 97-9.

Pasternak, Evgenii: *Boris Pasternak. Materialy dlia biografii*. Moscow: Sovetskii pisatel, 1989.

Prüll, Cay-Rüdinger: "Part of a Scientific Master Plan? Paul Ehrlich and the Origins of his Receptor Concept" in *Medical History*, vol. 47, 2003, pp. 332-356.

Prüll, Cay-Rüdinger: "Paul Ehrlich and his Receptor Concept" in Cay-Rüdinger Prüll, Andreas-Holger Maehle and Robert Francis Halliwell (eds.): *A Short History of the Drug Receptor Concept*. New York: Palgrave Macmillan, 2009, pp. 16-40.

Tynianov, Iurii: "Promezhutok" ("Interlude"), 1925 in *Poetika, istoriia literatury, kino*. Moscow: Nauka, 1977, pp. 168-95.

Zbarsky, Ilya and Hutchinson, Samuel: *Lenin's Embalmers*. London: The Harvill Press, 1998.

"DER STEIN DER WEISEN IST BLAU": ALCHEMISTIC THOUGHT IN KONRAD BAYER'S LITERARY WORK

Michael Grote, University of Bergen

At first sight, it seems paradoxical that the experimental and concrete literature of the 1950s and 1960s would have had a special interest in alchemy. Of all literary movements, these have been regarded as among the most theoretically orientated schools of thought, which, not least as a reaction to the misuse of language in the Third Reich, developed a fundamental mistrust of any ideological expression, and often of any content in literature at all.[1] Concrete poets such as the Swiss Eugen Gomringer claimed that the perfect poem would be like a pictogram in an airport: elementary, constructive, and functional. The image of the ultrarationalist, pseudo-scientific laboratory poet was a recurring one in the criticism of experimental literature, which aimed towards a methodically controlled and formally organised poetry.[2] Alchemy seems a stark contrast to this: an outdated and obsolete science, often regarded as a point of reference mainly for occultists and mystics who gained new attention after the crisis of meaning subsequent to the experiences of the Second World War, Holocaust and Hiroshima. And even if the need for re-orientation in an age that only shortly before had been confronted with the "dialectics of enlightenment" in its roughest form might be an explanation for the popularity of alternative, historically superseded models of knowledge-making such as alchemy or shamanism, such a neoromantic orientation to the past does not fit easily with the explicit modernism of 1950s and 1960s experimental literature. However, it is significant that "linguistic alchemy" is a recurring topic in German and Austrian experimental literature after the Second World War. It seems that "alchemy" here is seen and used as a metaphor for a knowledge that is located between scientific and aesthetical insight, or beyond this opposition. The choice of an outdated and obscure form of scientific thought marks an

---

1   See Mon.
2   See Enzensberger. For an outline of the history of experimental literature see Grote, pp. 67-121.

ironical distance to knowledge itself, as well as allowing room for paradoxical thinking, whose objects are compromised and affirmed simultaneously.

DER STEIN DER WEISEN: A KEY TO INSIGHT AND LINGUISTIC "READYMADE"

Konrad Bayer's literary debut *der stein der weisen* ("the philosophers' stone"), first published in 1963, one year before his early death, is one of the most prominent examples of a renewed interest in alchemy after the Second World War. Together with Oswald Wiener, Gerhard Rühm, Friedrich Achleitner, and H. C. Artmann, Bayer (1932-64) founded the Vienna Group, today considered to be one of the most important movements in Austrian literary history. In their publications and literary cabarets during the 1950s and early 60s the Vienna Group presented a radically experimental literature, influenced by the language criticism of philosophers like Mauthner and Wittgenstein and of the avant-garde movements in literature and the arts. Treating language as an optic and acoustic material, the members of the group experimented with new literary genres like montage, sound poetry, and visual texts and worked on a new performative conception of literature and art. The fact that the title of Bayer's book *der stein der weisen* is a linguistic "readymade" corresponds with the notion of language as material in poetic construction. The title refers to an esoterical knowledge of alchemy and, more generally, to hermetic literature with its promise of an immediate way to insight and authentic meaning. But because it is a reproduced linguistic cliché, the title undermines its own claim of uniqueness and meaningfulness.[3] It both deceives and rejects the

---

3   This notion of Bayer's is evident from a letter to his publisher, who had called attention to the fact that another book already had the title *der sechste sinn*, which Bayer wanted to use for his own publication: "es ist mir gleichgültig, ob in einem drittklassigen okkultisten-verlag prognostika mit einem titel herauskommen, der ohne zweifel für derartiges immer wieder und auch in den letzten zwanzig jahren sicher ein dutzendmal gebraucht wurde. stören sie sich nicht daran. es ist belanglos. auch ephemeriden werden in spezialbuchhandlungen verkauft. bis das buch erscheint, also 65, kräht kein hahn mehr nach diesem neonostradamus. und wenn. sie streben doch das aussergewöhnliche an, der verlag mit den einfällen (zitat); haben sie doch den mut, etwas gegen die regel zu tun. / abschliessend möchte ich bezweifeln, dass man klischees, wie: der sechste sinn, der stein der weisen, der gesunde menschenverstand, der körper und ähnliches schützen kann. versuchen sie doch einmal, guten tag schützen zu lassen" (Bayer: "Briefe und Briefwechsel").

LITERATURE AND CHEMISTRY

reader;[4] equally exclusive and trivial, "the philosophers' stone" is self-assertion and -negation, positing and denial all in one. In consequence, it remains undecidable whether the title is announcing a book *about* the philosophers' stone, or if the book itself claims to be a key to secret insight – in which case it is equally unclear if such a claim could be taken seriously.

However, the denotation of the title of Bayer's small book is unmistakable, as a direct reference to the most sought-after goal in Western alchemy: the philosophers' stone, a substance capable of turning non-precious metals such as lead and other materials into gold or silver. The efforts to discover the *opus magnum* were at the same time an allegory for every effort to discover secret or hidden knowledge, and therefore a metaphor for any process of research and enlightenment. Alchemy is a metaphor for mental processes, especially in the Romantic reception and use of it. The actual eyes of the alchemist have to be transformed into mental eyes ("oculos mentales"), their perception into imagination ("imaginationem"). The philosophers' stone, which is also called "lapis invisibilitatis", can only be seen by the inner eye, by "vera imaginatio". An opacity of the eye ("ludibrium oculis oblatum") is the precondition for alchemical success: The whole process of enlightenment is based on a projection.[5] This idealistic sceptical background of alchemy, and especially the Romantic view of it, is important for the understanding of its reception in modern experimental literature. Alchemy could serve as a metaphorical point of reference for Bayer's constructivist epistemology that, based on his notion of language as a totalitarian system, regarded reality as a mere function of mind. Beyond this general reference of the title, the topic of alchemy appears

---

4   See Ihrig, who comments on Bayer's and Wiener's collaborative work *starker toback* (1962): "Im Effekt stolpert der Leser über eine scheinbar reduzierte Sprache, deren voller Umfang ihm nicht einmal angeboten wird; die vorgetäuschte Einfachheit wirkt demütigend" (Ihrig, p. 148). "Die Selbstreflexion der Prosa wird zur arroganten Abweisung des Lesers" (p. 149).

5   As Manfred Frank has shown, the Romantic topos of the subterrestrial stoneworlds had its roots in the alchemistic interest in the maturation process of the metals, according to the "VITRIOL" formula of the medieval hermetics: "Visita interiora terrae; rectificando invenies occultum lapidem" ("Visit the Interior Parts of the Earth; by Rectification Thou Shalt Find the Hidden Stone"). The Romantic metonymy of "the heart of stone" interferes with the metonymy of stone, heart, and eye, which for example in E. T. A. Hoffmanns "Der Sandmann" leads to the characteristic metonymic figure of mistaken identities, the confusion between the act of looking and the eye, between glasses and eyes, living creatures and machines. See Frank, p. 348ff.; Frank follows Jung, particularly 265-363. For the "Bereitung eines inneren Steins der Weisen", see also Bloch 2, p. 747.

in an explicit intertextual reference in Bayer's book as well. With its organisation into seven "chapters" (plus preface and afterword), and its structure of a tractatus or lecture with a didactical development, *der stein der weisen* refers both in content and form to the alchemical book *The Chymical Wedding of Christian Rosenkreutz (Chymische Hochzeit Christiani Rosenkreutz Anno 1459)* by Johann Valentin Andreae, edited in 1616 in Strasbourg.[6] Andreae's story about the initiation of Christian Rosenkreutz is divided into seven days, an allegory of the seven steps of the alchemist's work, and has been an influential source of inspiration for mystical and materialistic philosophy of nature ever since. Bayer's *stein der weisen* has been regarded as a more or less similar work, in which a chronological way to insight is offered.[7]

---

6 See Andreae, p. 43-124. This reference was observed as soon as Bayer's book was published; see Schneider.

7 This interpretation is supported by a letter of Bayer's to his publisher, Wolfgang Fietkau, that stresses the didactical character of the text: "das ganze will ja keine aneinanderreihung möglichst gleichartiger oder mitreissender oder erfreulicher oder brillant gearbeiteter texte sein, sondern eine mögliche entwicklung zu einer auffassung andeuten (man könnte auch 'zeigen' sagen, aber gezeigt wird nur für den bemühten leser, für den, der einige anstrengung auf sich zu nehmen bereit ist, und für den ist der text geschrieben!). der zugang zu dieser auffassung führt durch eine summe von herausforderungen, also kann er auch stilistisch nicht popularisiert werden. (…) die abfolge ist eine bestimmte, zwangsläufige, also kann die hermetische geografie nicht klarer, ja nicht einmal so klar wie das lapidare museum aufscheinen (lesen ist ein vorgang in der zeit, ein fortschreiten von punkt zu punkt), das (gemeint ist das lapidare museum! –) eine sekunde vor BUMSTI (österr. ausruf, dem amerik. 'boing!' vergleichbar) liegt (nehmen sie BUMSTI für das durchschlagen des knotens, das überspringen des funkens, für das kippen des schalters!) und nicht umsonst hinter zwei weiteren hürden, die zu nehmen <u>sind</u>, angesiedelt wurde" (Bayer: Letter to Wolfgang Fietkau, 14 October 1963, in "Briefe und Briefwechsel"). The pragmatic dimension of *der stein der weisen* as an epistemological lecture which claims to be an instrument for insight and knowledge is strongly emphasised by Bayer, and the majority of his readers followed this interpretation. "Die sieben Teile der Schrift," wrote Hannes Schneider about Bayer's *der stein der weisen*, "sind stufen oder Stationen des Weges, der den suchenden (der von allem hier gesagten nichts wissen muß) mit Gewißheit ans Ziel führt, wenn er ihm nur bereitwillig und mit Konzentration und ausdauer folgt" (Schneider, p. 20). And for Ulrich Janetzki, continuing Schneider's reasoning, Bayer's book was a "schrittweise Vorführung des Unsagbaren" (Janetzki: "Versuch das Unsagbare zu zeigen", p. 340). However, we have to keep in mind that the author's statements should not necessarily decide how the book should be read or what it *means*, particularly since the ironic tone achieved through the syntactic intricacies of the letter is so obvious.

The pragmatic dimension of *der stein der weisen* points to a second allusion of the title that demonstrates a specific and literal emphasis on Bayer's interest in alchemy. The phrase *der stein der weisen* is a pseudo-onomastical reference to "Wittgenstein", the name of the author of the *Tractatus logico-philosophicus*, a major representative of a sceptical philosophy of language, and an important source for the Vienna Group's own criticism of language.[8] And indeed, the writing in the *Tractatus* is fundamentally pragmatic, as Wittgenstein makes perfectly clear in the penultimate paragraph of his book:

> 6.54 My propositions serve as elucidations in the following way: anyone who understands me eventually recognizes them as nonsensical, when he has used them – as steps – to climb up beyond them. (He must, so to speak, throw away the ladder after he has climbed up it.)[9]

The link between Wittgenstein's *Tractatus* and *der stein der weisen*, which Bayer occasionally also called a "tractatus",[10] can be followed in detail in the rhetoric of both books. Sometimes it seems as if Bayer copied the axiomatic discourse of Wittgenstein.[11] This is evident even in the "preface" to *der stein der weisen*:

> auftreten mehrere körper.
> jeder dieser mehrerer körper hat ein bewusstsein.
> diese mehrere bewusstsein sind unsichtbar.

---

8   Wiener, p. 56; in the *Tractatus*, wrote Wiener, it seemed as if logic itself were speaking: "folgerichtigkeit, die den kontakt zur wirklichkeit verliert, erzielt bekanntlich starke poetische wirkungen" (p. 50).

9   Wittgenstein, trans. Pears and McGuinness, p. 89. "6.54 Meine Sätze erläutern dadurch, daß sie der, welcher mich versteht, am Ende als unsinnig erkennt, wenn er durch sie – auf ihnen – über sie hinausgestiegen ist. (Er muß sozusagen die Leiter wegwerfen, nachdem er auf ihr hinaufgestiegen ist.)" (Wittgenstein, p. 115)

10 Bayer: "autobiographische skizze" in *Sämtliche Werke* (*SW*) 1, p. 8.

11 See Janetzki: *Alphabet und Welt*, p. 168, note 109. Using the example of the text *elektrische hierarchie* (*SW* 2, p. 166), Wolfgang Max Faust has demonstrated the grammatical parallels and logical differences between Wittgenstein's and Bayer's discourse (Faust, p. 137 f.). Faust describes the difference between Wittgenstein's and Bayer's sentences as a "Spannung zwischen Tatsache und Möglichkeit, zwischen Deduktion und Assoziation. Konstruiert Wittgenstein in seiner 'logisch-philosophischen Abhandlung' eine logische Hierarchie, so kontrastiert ihr Bayer die *elektrische hierarchie*" (p. 137).

jetzt ertönt einer dieser mehrerer körper mit hilfe seines bewusstseins reflexiv.

alle diese mehrere körper sind bei unsichtbarem bewusstsein.

alle diese mehreren echten körper und alle diese mehreren metaphysischen bewusstsein.

jedes dieser bewußtsein heisst ich.[12]

By way of comparison, Wittgenstein's *Tractatus* begins:

1   Die Welt ist alles, was der Fall ist.

1.1   Die Welt ist die Gesamtheit der Tatsachen, nicht der Dinge.

1.11   Die Welt ist durch die Tatsachen bestimmt und dadurch, daß es alle Tatsachen sind.

1.12   Denn, die Gesamtheit der Tatsachen bestimmt, was der Fall ist und auch, was alles nicht der Fall ist.

1.13   Die Tatsachen im logischen Raum sind die Welt.

1.2   Die Welt zerfällt in Tatsachen.

1.21   Eines kann der Fall sein oder nicht der Fall sein und alles übrige gleich bleiben.[13]

In the eighth part of *der stein der weisen*, titled "die elektrische hierarchie" ("the electrical hierarchy"), the same axiomatic pattern is repeated with different content:

---

12 *SW* 2, p. 157: "several bodies appear. / each of these bodies has a consciousness. / these several consciousnesses are invisible. / with the help of his consciousness one of these several bodies now rings forth reflexively. / all these several bodies are invisibly conscious. / all these several real bodies and all these several metaphysical consciousnesses. / each of these consciousnesses is called i." (Bayer: *The Philosophers' Stone* [TPS], trans. Billeter). This translation is quite rough, since many of the characteristics of Bayer's text cannot be reproduced in English, as for example the clumsy syntax and the incorrect inflection of the numeral "mehrere" in the quoted passage. It is therefore recommended that translations always be compared with the original text.

13 Wittgenstein, p. 11. "1. The world is all that is the case. / 1.1 The world is the totality of facts, not of things. / 1.11 The world is determined by the facts, and by their being *all* the facts. / 1.12 For the totality of facts determines what is the case, and also whatever is not the case. / 1.13 The facts in logical space are the world. / 1.2 The world divides into facts. / 1.21 Each item can be the case or not the case while everything else remains the same" (Wittgenstein, trans. Pears and McGuinness, p. 5).

verschiedene sätze treten auf.

verschiedene sätze treten nacheinander auf.

jeder satz betritt die situation, die alle vorhergehenden geschaffen haben.

diese neutralen sätze laden sich mit der situation auf.

diese sätze treten als trockene schwämme auf und saugen sich mit der situation voll.

die situation ist alles, was in frage kommt.

alles was möglich ist, kommt in frage.

die situation ist eine elektrische spannung.

jeder satz kann der erste sein.

dann bestimmt das gesetz von anziehung und abstoßung.

nun läuft die maschine elektrisch.[14]

Language is the main character in *der stein der weisen*. The "bodies" and "consciousnesses" that appear are mere functions of the lingual mechanisms of the text. "There is no such thing as the subject that thinks or entertains ideas"[15]: This central idea of Wittgenstein's *Tractatus*, the substitution of the subject by linguistic structures, became important for the writers of the Vienna Group in their project of rediscovering the traditions of modernity in literature after the Second World War. Their literature does not illustrate or contribute to the philosophical discourse of the time, but Wittgenstein's view of linguistic expressions as stereotypes was the perfect legitimisation for literary practices that followed antimimetic and self-reflexive poetics, that aimed at an exposition of the materiality of arts and language. For Konrad Bayer, the sceptical attitude of Wittgenstein's philosophy was especially attractive, its aim "to draw a limit to thought, or rather – not to thought, but to the expression of thoughts", as Wittgenstein wrote in the

---

14 *SW* 2, p. 166. "several sentences appear. / several sentences appear successively. / each sentence enters the situation created by all the previous sentences. / these neutral sentences are charged with the situation. / these sentences appear as dry sponges which become saturated with the situation. / the situation is everything that comes into consideration. / everything which is possible comes into consideration. / the situation is an electric tension. / any sentence can be the first. / then the law of attraction and repulsion governs. / now the machine runs electrically" (Bayer, *TPS*, trans. Billeter unp.).

15 Wittgenstein, trans. Pears and McGuinness, p. 69. "Das denkende, vorstellende, Subjekt gibt es nicht" (Wittgenstein, p. 90).

preface of his *Tractatus*.[16] However, at this point it is important to ask *how* Bayer appropriates other texts for his own work. *Der stein der weisen* is not a mere poeticising of a philosophical or mystical discourse. In fact, Bayer's treatment of his material is fundamentally ironic. In this, it incorporates an aspect of both Andreae's and Wittgenstein's texts that easily can be overlooked: In his *Vita* Andreae labelled *The Chymical Wedding* a "ludibrium", a farce that mocked the alchemistic profession and in which harsh punishment was demanded for alchemists and frauds.[17] However, this ironisation is not consistent – as Ernst Bloch notes in *The Principle of Hope*, the irony takes part in the superstition it satirises (p. 745). Wittgenstein's *Tractatus* doubtlessly has a tendency to self-ironisation too, as is evident from its preface:

> I therefore believe myself to have found, on all essential points, the final solution of the problems. And if I am not mistaken in this belief, then the second thing in which the value of this work consists is that it shows how little is achieved when these problems are solved.[18]

Neither in Andreae's nor in Wittgenstein's text does irony supply the reader with a definitive meaning. On the one hand, it undermines its own statements; on the other, it does not refer to a contradictory or concealed meaning, but serves only as a rhetorical means to mark an ironic reservation about what is said. When Wittgenstein stresses "how little is achieved when these problems are solved", this is not simply a gesture of modesty, but

---

16 Wittgenstein, trans. Pears and McGuinness 3. "Das Buch will also dem Denken eine Grenze ziehen, oder vielmehr – nicht dem Denken, sondern dem Ausdruck der Gedanken" (Wittgenstein, p. 7).

17 In his *Vita*, Andreae writes that *The Chymical Wedding* "in erheiternder Weise die Alchemie und die der Curiositas verfallenen Menschen verspottet" (Richard van Dülmen in Andreae, p. 11). On the third day of the "chymical wedding" a severe sentence is pronounced on frauds and alchemists: "Entlich sollen die uberwiesene Landbetrieger, so kein Gewicht auffwegen mögen, an Leib und Leben nach gelegenheit mit dem Schwert, Strang, Waffen und Ruten gestrafft werden. Und solle solch Urtheils Execution unbeweglich anderen zum Exempel gehalten werden" (Andreae, p. 74).

18 Wittgenstein, trans. Pears and McGuinness, p. 4. "Ich bin also der Meinung, die Probleme im Wesentlichen endgültig gelöst zu haben. Und wenn ich mich hierin nicht irre, so besteht nun der Wert dieser Arbeit zweitens darin, daß sie zeigt, wie wenig damit getan ist, daß diese Probleme gelöst sind" (Wittgenstein, p. 9 f.).

a reference to a field of knowledge that cannot be reached in language. This is precisely what interests Bayer: the limits of language and what lies beyond these limits. But whilst Wittgenstein came to his famous – and in fact ironic – conclusion, "what we cannot speak about we must pass over in silence",[19] Bayer would find a way to go beyond this limit in poetry – not by simply ignoring the philosophical problems and choosing a metaphysical escape, but by exaggerating Wittgenstein's position of linguistic determination and substituting the philosopher's claim to objectivity with a radical position of subjectivity.[20] Alchemy, with its pragmatic-didactic and simultaneously hermetic rhetoric, provides Bayer with a topos that always refers to a secret knowledge, which he then relates to the inexpressible, to what lies beyond Wittgenstein's limit of language. The secrets of Bayer's *der stein der weisen* cannot be found "behind" the text, in a hidden meaning or in a Romantic ineffability that could be deciphered by intense interpretation. Instead the text's arcanum lies within its surface. In Bayer's book the linear progression of the alchemical work in the *Chymical Wedding* and the logical axiomatic in Wittgenstein's *Tractatus* gives way to a textual mechanic that turns the progressive movement into a reflexive one. The impression that the text progresses through stages, implied by subtitles such as "vorwort", "zwischenspiel", and "nachwort", is subverted by the formal isolation of the sections and the openness of the textual references. In the following I will show how the textual technique of montage allows for the realisation of self-reflexivity and openness of meaning on a microstructural text level.

---

19 Wittgenstein, trans. Pears and McGuinness, p. 89. "Wovon man nicht sprechen kann, darüber muß man schweigen" (Wittgenstein, p. 115).

20 See Fuchs, p. 18f., note 29. Fuchs stresses that Bayer's notion of language was more like Mauthner's philosophy than Wittgenstein's: "In der Negierung der Möglichkeit einer intersubjektiven Wahrheitsfindung geht Mauthner deutlich weiter als der Verfasser des 'Tractatus'" (p. 19, note 29). While language is a medium of representation in Wittgenstein's *Tractatus*, Bayer, like Mauthner, sees language only as a representation of itself that cannot serve as a medium of communication (p. 5). As Fuchs explains, the topics of epilepsy and St. Vitus's dance in Bayer's "der kopf des vitus bering" can be seen as "quasi ein Abglanz der sprachlosen 'gottlosen Mystik' Mauthners" (p. 5). It is important to note, however, that Bayer's relation to Mauthner is similar to his relation to Wittgenstein or any other philosophical discourse: His literature is not an illustration or poetisation of discourse, but its literary processing.

After the "vorwort" and the first chapter, "heroische geometrie", in Bayer's book a longer text follows under the title "hermetische geografie"; this is an obvious anagrammatical variation of the title of the previous chapter.[21] The text, a montage of fragments from expedition reports, guidebooks, travelogues, and history books with a plain preference for the exotic and for horrifying details from natural catastrophes, cannibalism, and ecstatic rites gives a confusing picture of a savage world:

> es wird immer lebendiger. sobald sie musik hören, kommen alle ausser sich. die insel porto santo hat ausser ihrem trefflichen weinbau, ihren vielen kanarien-vögeln und ihren rebhühnern nichts merkwürdiges. die fensterscheiben zer-springen. menschen und tiere triefen überall von blut. ceylon, die gießkanne ostindiens. männliche körper, weibliche körper, kindliche körper. schafkörper auf der weide. das getreide schiesst aus der erdkugel.[22]

---

21 With the exception of one "o", the letters of "heroische geometrie" recur in "herme-tische geografie" – "hermetische geografie" therefore both semantically and formally quotes the tradition of hermetic-alchemistic literature that not uncommonly hid its secrets in anagrams. This treatment does not serve a hidden meaning in *der stein der weisen*; it is an ironically externalised, playful gimmick, a manipulation of the surface of the text. In this context Bayer's interest in the German Baroque poet and mystic Quirinus Kuhlmann is particularly noteworthy. The "index" of Bayer's *der kopf des vitus bering* quotes a study that interprets Kuhlmann's ecstatical emotion as a shamanic "voyage en esprit" (Eliade), as a journey of the mind (*SW* 2, p. 201; Bock, pp. 80-85). Etymologies and anagrams are particularly characteristic of Kuhlmann's writing, as for example in the following explanation of his own name: "Was Kuhl bei uns Schlesiern eigentlich heißt, ist BLAU. Nichts BLAUERS hat BRESLAU, als ihren vertretenen Kuhl. Nichts BLAUERERS trägt iemals ieder BRESLAUER. BLAUE Farbe zeiget auf unschuld, ob ihre Leiblikeit gleich der gantze Wolkenumkreis ist" (Kuhlmann quoted in Bock, p. 55). In his "Kühlpsalter" Kuhlmann gives an account of his search for a philosophers' stone named "Urim et Thummim" that was sup-posed to serve Kuhlmann in the redemption of a subterranean people (see Werner Vordtriede in Kuhlmann, p. 83).

22 *SW* 2, p. 158. "it keeps getting livelier. as soon as they hear music they lose their senses. apart from its excellent viticulture, its many canaries and partridges, the island of porto santo has nothing noteworthy. the window panes shatter. everywhere people and animals are dripping with blood. ceylon, the watering can of east india. male bodies, female bodies, infantile bodies. sheep bodies on the pasture. the grain shoots from the terrestrial globe" (Bayer, *TPS*, trans. Billeter unp.).

The conjunctions that are made by the text lead to a continuously changing point of view that is impossible for the reader to follow. These linguistic hallucinations exceed the capability of the reader's imagination.[23] Whilst every sentence in itself claims to be true, the ever-changing combination of phrases shows the total arbitrariness of all statements in general:

> fliegende füchse messen 6 fuss mit ihren ausgebreiteten flügeln. die reife nuss schmeckt lieblich. überall hört man seufzen und stöhnen, wenn einer der 99 beinamen gottes ausgesprochen wird. der türke ist gross. die luft ist warm, aber es fehlt an regen. die wände sind mit einer rinde aus russ überzogen. mit schnüren und quasten behängt, rennt er nun schreiend mit den seltsamsten verrenkungen seiner glieder umher. die araber sind von mittlerer grösse. ein kragen platzt hinter der szene. luftballone steigen auf. ein regenbogen verbleicht. die maschine des witwers. die küsten sind sumpfig.[24]

The process of editing that can be observed here, the cutting up and assembling of details in the montage, may be reminiscent of the alchemist's work of "solve et coagula", the activity of dissolving and coagulating, separating and joining together. Like the alchemical transmutations, Bayer's montage starts from a limited number of basic elements that are recombined in different treatments.[25] The creation of a new reality from a recombination of available elements is a typical hermetic practice, and its constructive literary effect is obvious particularly in the recurring genitive constructions in Bayer's text. The grammatical pattern of the phrase "der stein der weisen" is repeated, varied, and diversified throughout the text.

---

23 For the concept of the hallucinatory and the verbal reduplication of the world by twentieth-century literature, see Heißenbüttel, pp. 202-4.

24 *SW* 2, p. 159. "flying foxes have a wingspan of 6 feet. the ripe nut tastes lovely. there are sighs and groans everywhere when one of the 99 epithets of god is pronounced. the turk is tall. the air is warm, but there is a lack of rain. the walls are covered with a coat of soot. draped with strings and tassels, he now runs about crying while contorting his limbs in the most peculiar manner. the arabs are of medium height. a collar bursts behind the scene. balloons rise. a rainbow fades. the machine of the widower. the coasts are swampy" (Bayer, *TPS*, trans. Billeter unp.).

25 "The four elements" of alchemy – fire, water, earth, and air – are used as organising factors in Bayer's "poetry machine" *der vogel singt* (*SW* 2, p. 135-55). In *der stein der weisen* we also find "The Three Substances" – sulphur, mercury (Hermes), and salt – as key motifs.

"Der stein der weisen" – "die blutgefässe der waisen"[26] – "der körper des europäers"[27]: in this "hermetic geography," the linguistic isolation of the "bodies" from the "consciousnesses" that we observe as early as in the "preface" (where "with the help of his consciousness one of these several bodies (…) rings forth"), is continued and extended in the variation of elements in the paradigm, while the syntagma is repeated.[28] It seems as if the parts of these genitive constructions become progressively isolated against each other: "der körper des europäers. das knie des alten mannes."[29] The mechanics of the construction takes on a life of its own:

das zahnrad des negers. die krempe des alten mannes. die welt sei ein ungeheures lebewesen. die erde ist ein himmelskörper. der kegel ist ein drehkörper. ein jahrhundert vergeht. der tag des herrn. die stunde der hausfrau. ein birnenjahr. die kindheit des europäers tritt auf. (…) wasser, steine, metalle. im juni hört die pest gewöhnlich auf. augen ausstechen, hände und füsse abhacken, ans kreuz nageln, lebendig schinden und steinigen sind die üblichen todesarten. der wind türmt den sand zu bergen. die mauren halten sich für die ersten menschen der erdkugel. der husten der alten frau. die runzel des witwers. das fahrrad des negers. die stimme des volkes. die laune des erdbewohners. der junge mann auf der eisscholle. nun trommelt er lange, verdreht die glieder seltsam, lässt sich zuletzt den kopf zwischen die beine binden, und alle lampen auslöschen. drei bis fünf monate dauert hier die traurige winternacht, aber auch nordlichter, feurige luftkugeln, nebensonnen und nebenmonde (zuweilen sechs auf einmal) sind gewöhnliche erscheinungen. wer ein glas an den mund setzt, büßt seine lippenhaut ein. norden ist süden gegenüber.[30]

---

26 SW 2, p. 160. "the blood vessels of the orphans" (Bayer, TPS, trans. Billeter unp.).

27 SW 2, p. 159. "the body of the european" (Bayer, TPS, trans. Billeter unp.).

28 Bayer developed the idea of a separation of "body" and "consciousness" into a main theme in his last book, der sechste sinn (1964). An oft-repeated question in this book is "was will mein körper von mir?" (SW 2, p. 210-13), soon also elaborated to "was will mein körper von ihnen?" (p. 212), "was will dieser körper von mir?" (p. 213), and "was will meine seele von mir?" (p. 217 and 250). The topos refers to Crevel, among others.

29 SW 2, p. 159: "the body of the european. the knee of the old man" (Bayer, TPS, trans. Billeter unp.).

30 SW 2, p. 159: "the cogwheel of the negro. the rim of the old man. the world is said to be a monstrous being. earth is a [celestial] body. the cone is a body of [rotation]. a century passes. the day of the lord. the hour of the house-wife. a pear-year. the childhood of the european appears. (…) water, stones, metals. in june the plague

The products of this genitive machine are vivisections and amalgamations:

das zahnfleisch der greise. am fusse des europäers. die hand des jungen mannes auf der tischplatte. der malaye mütterlicherseits.[31]

The isolated entities, which only have the grammatical pattern in common, constantly give each other new meaning through the continuous shifts of contexts.[32] The pattern assimilates the most heterogeneous elements and creates hermetic miniatures – the word-body, appearing in the reading direction, meets the reflexiveness of its genitive attribute. "der stein der weisen" functions as a grammatical catalyst that analyses and synthesises

---

usually stops. gouging out the eyes, cutting hand and feet, nailing to the cross, flaying and stoning are common ways of killing someone. the wind heaps the sand into mountains. the moors think of themselves as the first humans on the globe. the cough of the old woman. the wrinkle of the widower. the bicycle of the negro. the voice of the people. the mood of earth's inhabitant. the young man on the ice floe. now he is drumming for a long time, contorting his limbs in a strange manner, and finally has his head tied between his legs and all lamps extinguished. the sad winternight lasts for three to five months here, but also northern lights, fiery air balls, mock suns and mock moons (sometimes six at once) are common phenomena. whoever puts a glass to his mouth loses the skin of his lips. north is opposite south" (Bayer, *TPS*, trans. Billeter unp.). Even if the strange and often horrible details in the descriptions of foreign countries, from travel reports and history books seem to insist on their particularity, they remind one of the exceptionality of guidebooks and advertisements. In the amalgamation of curiosities and banalities the extraordinary appears as ordinary, and the ordinary extraordinary. It seems as if the adjective "gewöhnlich" moves autonomously from sentence to sentence. In the "topology of language" later on in *der stein der weisen* we read "es gibt nichts gemeinsames. nur die sprache schafft gemeinsamkeiten" (*SW* 2, p. 165; "nothing is common. only language creates things in common" Bayer, *TPS*, trans. Billeter unp.). The consequence of this can already be observed in the "hermetical geography". In its discourse all differences are levelled, "one can see" anything and everything, one thing "looks like" another, "das auge sieht nichts" (*SW* 2, p. 58; Bayer, *TPS*, trans. Billeter unp.).

31 *SW* 2, p. 160. "the gum of the [dotards]. at the foot of the european. the hand of the young man on the table top. the malayan on the mother's side" (Bayer, *TPS*, trans. Billeter unp.).

32 Peter Weibel has described the metonymical aspect of the montage as the "'cusp'-artige (katastrophenartige) Umschlagen eines bereits niederfrequenten, relativ unvertrauten Sinns, wie er durch die Metapher entsteht, aber zumeist via das unterschlagene Zwischenglied unbewußt noch faßbar ist, in einen noch ungewohneteren, kaum frequenten, ja singulärfrequenten kühnen Sinn, wie er in der Montage entsteht" (Weibel, p. 34 f.).

the single elements of the paradigm which then permanently form new unstable conjunctions, as well as constituting semantic separations between subjects and their objects.

The alchemist's activity of separating and joining, that in the montage recurs as analysis and recombination of textual elements, becomes apparent in the "hermetic geography" as a magical practice that we also find in the cannibalistic rituals[33] and shamanist initiations in the text. The iterated topos of fragmentation and unification creates a network of references to archaic techniques of ecstasy that aim at aesthetic experiences of the exceptional instant of presence.[34]

ABSOLUTE PRESENCE

As Mircea Eliade has shown, the alchemist's work has a specific temporal implication. As "masters of fire", the alchemists, like the smelters and smiths and even the shamanists,

> by aiding the work of Nature, accelerated the tempo of things and, in the final instance, were substitutes for Time itself. The alchemists were not of course all aware that their "work" did the work of Time. But this is not important: the essential point is that their work, transmutation, involved, in one form or another, the elimination of time.[35]

The mastery of fire is not only concrete, but also metaphorically a technique to control nature, including inner nature, spark, flame, fire: the light of the soul, the interior heat of ecstasy. As the shaman is "the great specialist of the human soul"[36], the alchemical transmutation aims at the alchemist himself: "Transmutemini de lapidibus mortuis in vivos lapides philosophicos" ("Be ye changed from dead stone into living and life-giving stones"),[37]

---

33 Cannibalism is a motif that appears often in Bayer's texts. The philosophical solipsism of Max Stirner is an important background for this. See Janetzki: *Alphabet und Welt*, p. 35; Ruprechter, pp. 104-10; and Stirner, p. 331: "Wo Mir die Welt in den Weg kommt – und sie kommt Mir überall in den Weg – da verzehre Ich sie, um den Hunger meines Egoismus zu stillen. Du bist für Mich nichts als – meine Speise, gleichwie auch Ich von Dir verspeiset und verbraucht werde".

34 See Eliade: *Schamanismus und archaische Ekstasetechnik*.

35 Eliade: *The Forge and the Crucible*, p. 171.

36 See Eliade: *Schamanismus und archaische Ekstasetechnik*, p. 18.

37 Quoted in Jung, p. 312, note 75.

LITERATURE AND CHEMISTRY

the alchemical lessons read. The release of matter serves as a model for the release of soul or, in an epistemological context, the liberation of perception from the body-template, from the a priori of a continuing time-space perspective; in Eliade's words, "the freeing of Nature from the laws of Time went hand in hand with the deliverance of the alchemist himself".[38] In *der stein der weisen* the escape from time and the installation of a total presence takes place in the language of the book, and particularly in its grammatical operations. The presence of the reader, seeking some intelligible coherence of the single elements, and the presence of the incomprehensible, hermetic

Konrad Bayer, *flucht* (1962/64). Staatsgalerie Stuttgart,
Archiv Sohm @ Foto: Staatsgalerie Stuttgart.

---

38 Eliade: *The Forge and the Crucible*, p. 171.

text that follows its own regularities both emerge in the cuts between the isolated elements of the montage.[39]

An illustrative example of this relation between an absolute text and the activity of reading can be found in Konrad Bayer's "word chains", which he constructed from 1959 onwards.[40] Some of these texts were installed on a rotating cylinder in order to realise an infinite chain.

In one of the word chains, the topic of alchemy is named explicitly:

> plötzlichtsignalchemiedermassensibeleuchtetwasserspiegelglasklarverstörtlich-
> tsignalsolangewurzeltplanetzhautomobilderbogensehnebenbeischlaftrunkenn-
> zeichenbaumwollkleidsambragenitalsperrangelweiterherunterlippenrothaarsträh-
> nelfenbeinschienenstrangesichtsmaskenfestgefahrenzonetzhautnahrungeachtet-
> wasserdampflokomotiverhüllendlichtsignallerleiblichtsignaltarnfarbenprach-
> tungetümpelzgefüttertrinkentleibenützentblössenthaarbuschwerkennbarmher-
> zigarettenrauchwolkehlkopfübergebenedeiterherdbodennochmalsogarnschlin-
> genügendlichtsignalstangebundendlichtsignalleinerleinzigarettungsringsumher-
> zschlagunebelschwadenbeinaherzitterstarrentdeckenleuchtfeuergarberührent-
> blössenkrechtsumhervorhautnahtlosreisseeadlerweiterhinauslöschenkellerche[41]

This word chain initially contracts the following elements:

> plötzlich – lichtsignal – alchemie – mieder – dermassen – sensibel …
> suddenly – light signal – alchemy – bodice – insomuch – sensible …

Such contraction creates a linguistic continuum that cannot be managed by the reader. While the text shows a total material coherence, the reader experiences the impossibility of following this kind of linguistic flow.[42]

---

39 These two dimensions, reader and text, are connected by the ambivalent self-reflexivity that is related to the whole of the text and to the separated detail at the same time: "dieses stück ist abgebrannt", we read at the end of the "hermetic geography" – "this piece is burnt down" (*SW* 2, p. 161; Bayer, *TPS*, trans. Billeter unp.). It remains undecidable whether "the piece" here refers to this piece of literature, to a theatre play (as the "zwischenspiel" that follows in the text), or to the material piece of paper on which the text is written.

40 See *SW* 2, p. 89-95.

41 *SW* 2, p. 90.

42 "UNSER SCHEINBAR UNANTASTBARES ZEITKONTINUUM IST NUR EINE KLEINE UNFÄHIGKEIT." See Bayer: "tagebuch 1963", unp.

From this perspective, the production of literature is not an activity that solely combines conventional phrases according to conventional rules; rather, it follows the principal of a poetic machine that combines linguistic elements – sounds, words, phrases, sentences, texts – in different "hermetical", materialist proceedings. The alchemical rule of "solve et coagula" has constitutive relevance here; the link between alchemistic thought and experimental literature becomes apparent as an aspect of text production, of *poiesis*.

WORKS CITED

Andreae, Johann Valentin: "Chymische Hochzeit Christiani Rosenkreutz. Anno 1459 (1616)" in Richard van Dülmen (ed.): *Fama Fraternitatis (1614). Confessio Fraternitatis (1615). Chymische Hochzeit Christiani Rosenkreutz. Anno 1459 (1616).* Stuttgart: Calwer, 1981, pp. 43-124.

Bayer, Konrad: "Briefe und Briefwechsel" in Ulrich Janetzki and Dieter Schwarz (eds.): *Sondern. Jahrbuch für Texte und Bilder.* Zurich: Seedorn, 1979.

—: *Sämtliche Werke.* Gerhard Rühm (ed.). Vienna: ÖBV, Klett Cotta, 1985.

—: "tagebuch 1963" in Peter Weibel and Valie Export (eds.): *Wien. Bildkompendium Wiener Aktionismus und Film.* Frankfurt a. M.: Kohlkunst-Verlag, 1970.

—: *The Philosophers' Stone*, trans. Walter Billeter. Westgarth, Victoria, Australia: Merri Creek or Nero, 1979.

Bloch, Ernst: *Das Prinzip Hoffnung*, Frankfurt a. M.: Suhrkamp, 1959.

Bock, Claus Victor: *Quirinus Kuhlmann als Dichter. Ein Beitrag zur Charakteristik des Ekstatikers.* Bern: Francke, 1957.

Crevel, René: *Mon corps et moi.* Paris: Éditions du Sagittaire, 1925.

Eliade, Mircea: *Schamanismus und archaische Ekstasetechnik*, trans. Inge Köck. Frankfurt. a. M.: Suhrkamp, 1975. (Original edition: *Le chamanisme et les techniques archaiques de l'extase.* Paris: Payot, 1951).

—: *The Forge and the Crucible*, trans. Stephen Corrin. Chicago / London: The University of Chicago Press, 1978. (Original edition: *Forgerons et Alchimistes.* Paris: Flammarion, 1954).

Enzensberger, Hans Magnus: "Die Aporien der Avantgarde" in *Einzelheiten.* Frankfurt a. M.: Suhrkamp, 1962, pp. 290-315.

Faust, Wolfgang Max: "Fleisch, Blut und Sprache. Notizen, Texte, Kritiken zum Theatralischen von Konrad Bayer" in Ulrich Janetzki and Wilfried Ihrig: DIE WELT BIN ICH. *Materialien zu Konrad Bayer (= protokolle. Zeitschrift für Literatur und Kunst*, vol. 1 (1983), ed. Otto Breicha.). Vienna / Munich: Jugend und Volk, 1983, pp. 135- 50.

Frank, Manfred: *Einführung in die frühromantische Ästhetik. Vorlesungen.* Frankfurt a. M.: Suhrkamp, 1989.

Fuchs, Gerhard: "Fritz Mauthners Sprachkritik – Aspekte ihrer literarischen Rezeption in der österreichischen Gegenwartsliteratur" in *Modern Austrian*

Literature. Journal of the International Arthur Schnitzler Research Association, vol. 23, no. 2 (1990), pp. 1-21.

Grote, Michael: *Exerzitien. Experimente. Zur Akustischen Literatur von Carlfriedrich Claus*. Bielefeld: Aisthesis, 2009.

Heißenbüttel, Helmut: *Über Literatur*. Olten / Freiburg i. Br.: Walter, 1966.

Ihrig, Wilfried: *Literarische Avantgarde und Dandysmus. Eine Studie zur Prosa von Carl Einstein bis Oswald Wiener*. Frankfurt a. M.: Athenäum, 1988.

Janetzki, Ulrich: *Alphabet und Welt. Über Konrad Bayer*. Königsstein / Ts.: Hain, 1982.

—: "Versuch das Unsagbare zu zeigen. Konrad Bayer, *der stein der weisen*." in *Sprache im technischen Zeitalter*, no. 68 (1978), pp. 330-44.

Jung, Carl Gustav: *Gesammelte Werke. Vol. 12: Psychologie und Alchemie*, 1943. Dieter Baumann, Lilly Jung-Merker and Elisabeth Rüf (eds.). Olten / Freiburg i. Br.: Walter, 1972.

Kuhlmann, Quirinus: *Aus dem Kühlpsalter*. Werner Vordtriede (ed.). Berlin: Henssel, 1966.

Mon, Franz: "Meine 50er Jahre", 1980, in *Gesammelte Texte 1: Essays*. Berlin: janus press, 1994, pp. 5-18.

Ruprechter, Walter: *Aspekte des Werks von Konrad Bayer*, Ph. D dissertation. University of Vienna, 1982.

Schneider, Hannes (ed.): *der stein der weisen* by Konrad Bayer. Rev. ed.: Berlin: fietkau, 1964, *Eröffnungen. Magazin für Literatur & bildende Kunst*, Hubert F. Kulterer (ed.), vol. 12, 1964, p. 20.

Stirner, Max: *Der Einzige und sein Eigentum*, 1845, Ahlrich Meyer (ed.). Stuttgart: Reclam, 1981.

Weibel, Peter: "Zu einer Katastrophentheorie der Literatur. Von der Metapher zur Montage. Ein Vortrag" in *Protokolle. Zeitschrift für Literatur und Kunst*, vol. 2, 1980. Vienna / Munich: Jugend und Volk, 1980, pp. 23-44.

Wiener, Oswald: "Wittgensteins Einfluß auf die 'Wiener Gruppe'" in Walter-Buchebner-Gesellschaft (ed.): *Walter-Buchebner-Literaturprojekt. Die Wiener Gruppe*. Vienna / Cologne / Graz: Böhlau, 1987, pp. 45-59.

Wittgenstein, Ludwig: *Tractatus logico-philosophicus. Logisch-philosophische Abhandlung*, 1918. Frankfurt a. M.: Suhrkamp, 1963.

—: *Tractatus Logico-Philosophicus*, trans. D. F. Pears and B. F. McGuinness. London / New York: Routledge, 1961 (1974).

CONTRIBUTORS

"The chemist's scales". Detail of Per Krogh's decoration of the entrance hall of the Chemistry Building at the University of Oslo.

Brita Lotsberg Bryn is Associate Professor of Russian Literature at the University of Bergen, Norway. Her main fields of research are avant-garde poetry and contemporary Russian prose and theatre. She has published on Pasternak's poetics, the problems of irony and authenticity in contemporary Russian prose, and on Soviet and post-Soviet metaphorical language.

Folkert Degenring is Assistant Professor of English Literature at the University of Kassel, Germany. He took an interdisciplinary degree in English and Business Studies at the University of Mannheim, Germany, where he completed his doctorate on identity and the postmodern British novel. His current research project examines the interaction between science and literature.

Robert S. C. Gordon is Serena Professor of Italian at the University of Cambridge. He is the author of *Primo Levi's Ordinary Virtues* (2001) and *'Outrageous Fortune': Luck and the Holocaust* (2010), and editor of Levi's interviews

(*The Voice of Memory*), *The Cambridge Companion to Primo Levi*, and Levi and Leonardo De Benedetti's *Auschwitz Report*.

Michael Grote has worked at the University of Bergen's German Department, later Institute for Foreign Languages. In 2008 he completed his doctoral dissertation, entitled "Exerzitien. Experimente. Zur Akustischen Literatur von Carlfriedrich Claus" (Aisthesis 2009). He has published on twentieth-century experimental literature, the history and theory of autobiographical writing, and the aesthetics of media.

Margareth Hagen is Associate Professor of Italian Literature at the University of Bergen. Her published works are on sixteenth-century Italian literature and literature and science. She is the co-editor of *The Art of Discovery: Encounters in Literature and Science* (2010) and *The Human and its Limits* (2011).

Lillian Jorunn Helle is Professor of Russian Literature at the Department of Foreign Languages and Literatures, University of Bergen. She has published numerous articles on nineteenth-century Russian literature and cultural history, Russian Symbolism and Modernism, Socialist Realism, and Russian post-colonial research and literary theory (Belyj, Bakhtin, Lotman, Jakobson). She is currently working on topics related to the research project "Literature and Science" (SciLit) at UiB, as well as preparing a book on Leo Tolstoy's last novel, *Resurrection*.

Henrik Johnsson is Associate Professor of Scandinavian Studies at Aarhus University, Denmark. Having earned his PhD in the History of Literature at Stockholm University in 2009, he has since published extensively in the field of Scandinavian literature. His monograph *Strindberg and the Occult Sciences* is forthcoming in 2014.

Bernard Joly is Emeritus Professor of Philosophy and the History of Science at the University of Lille 3. He is member of the UMR "Savoirs, textes, langage", CNRS. Among his publications are *La rationalité de l'alchimie au XVIIᵉ siècle* (1992), *Descartes et la chimie* (2011) and *Histoire de la chimie* (2013).

Pierre Laszlo, an Emeritus Professor of Chemistry, has enjoyed as an avocation studying, and even teaching (Johns Hopkins) French literature, mostly of the nineteenth century. Moreover, he deems it important to bridge science with the arts and humanities, as well as to contribute to the building of a scientific culture. He has published widely in chemistry, the history of science, and cultural history. Among his recent publications are *Terre & eau, air & feu* (2000), *Miroir de la chimie* (2000), *L'architecture du vivant* (2004), *Citrus: A History* (2007), and *Communicating Science: A Practical Guide* (2010).

Muireann Maguire is a Fellow in Russian Literature and Culture at Wadham College, Oxford. Her book *Stalin's Ghosts: Gothic Themes in Early Soviet Literature* was published in 2012. Her collection of twentieth-century Russian ghost stories in translation, *Red Spectres*, also appeared in 2012. Her current research examines the cultural mythology of science and scientists in Russia in the nineteenth and early twentieth centuries.

Frode Helmich Pedersen defended his doctoral thesis on Hermann Broch's novel *Der Tod des Vergil* in 2009. His publications include "Hermann Broch und Alfred Polgar: Kaffeehaus, Humanismus, Exil" in *Hermann Brochs literarische Freundschaften*, edited by E. Kiss, P. M. Lützeler, and G. Rácz (2008), and "Brands visjonære fantasi" in *Ibsens Brand. Resepsjon, tolkning, kontekst*, edited by Erik Bjerck Hagen (2010).

Matteo Pellegrini is a Postdoctoral Research Fellow at the Department of Linguistic and Literary Studies, University of Padua. He earned his PhD in Italian Literature with a thesis on Giovanni Pascoli's *Poemi conviviali*, but his current research interests are in sixteenth-century literature (including studies on Ariosto and Botero's *Relazioni Universali*). He is currently working on Fulvio Testi's poetry collection *Poesie liriche*.

George Rousseau has taught at Harvard, UCLA, Aberdeen, and Oxford. He is the author of many works dealing with literature and science, and literature and medicine. His recent books include *Framing and Imagining Disease in Cultural History* (2003), *Nervous Acts: Essays on Literature, Culture and Sensibility* (2004), *Children and Sexuality: The Greeks to the Great War* (2007), and *The Notorious Sir John Hill* (2012).

Sharon Ruston is Chair in Romantic Studies at Lancaster University. She has published widely on Romantic literature and its relationship with science and medicine, including the monographs *Shelley and Vitality* (2005;

paperback 2012), *Romanticism: An Introduction* (2007), and *Creating Romanticism* (2013).

Margery Vibe Skagen is Associate Professor in French Literature at the Department of Foreign Languages and Literatures, University of Bergen. Her doctoral thesis focuses on the poetics of melancholy in Baudelaire's writings. Her main research interests are nineteenth-century French supernaturalism, literature and medical history, and literature and science. She is co-editor of the anthologies *The Art of Discovery: Encounters in Literature and Science* (2010) and *The Human and its Limits* (2011).

Eivind Tjønneland is Professor of Scandinavian Literature at the University of Bergen. His most recent works include the editorships of *Opplysningens tidsskrifter* (2008), *Holberg* (2008), *Gloria amoris – Kjærlighedens komedie 150 år* (2012), and a broad anthology in the history of literary criticism, *Kritikk før 1814* (2013).